Books by
CLIFFORD DOWDEY

BUGLES BLOW NO MORE
EXPERIMENT IN REBELLION
THE LAND THEY FOUGHT FOR
DEATH OF A NATION
LEE'S LAST CAMPAIGN
THE SEVEN DAYS
LEE
THE VIRGINIA DYNASTIES
THE GOLDEN AGE

Editor with Louis H. Manarin

THE WARTIME PAPERS OF R. E. LEE

THE GOLDEN AGE

CLIFFORD DOWDEY

THE GOLDEN AGE

A Climate for Greatness, Virginia 1732–1775

Illustrated with photographs

LITTLE, BROWN AND COMPANY

Boston • Toronto

LIBRARY OF CONGRESS CATALOG CARD NO. 78–117034

FIRST EDITION

Published simultaneously in Canada by Little, Brown & Company (Canada) Limited

PRINTED IN THE UNITED STATES OF AMERICA

For Frances Wilson Dowdey
and my daughters,
Frances Blount Dowdey and Sarah Bowis Dowdey . . .

Contents

Illustrations

THE GOLDEN AGE

Overture

THE GENERATIONS OF THE GOLDEN AGE

THE "GOLDEN AGE" of colonial Virginia holds the contradictory images of the quality of a pastoral pageant, the figures fixed immutably in time, and the passions of revolutionary leaders. The tranquil lordliness of the plantation idyll became the "seedbed of the revolution." Families imperious in their baronial domains created a social upheaval on libertarian ideals. A people proud of developing an aristocratic order, and intensely aware of their aristocratic status, produced the spokesmen of democratic principles newly defined and acted upon.

The contradiction was more apparent than real. Libertarian ideals and democratic principles, essentially political, were more restricted in meaning than in later connotations. The revolutionary assertions developed first out of the very imperiousness of the colonial aristocrat, who, as an English visitor observed, "could scarcely bear the thought of the imposition of another's will."

Then, there were younger leaders, the products themselves of the grandees' assertiveness against outside authority, who later carried the implications of liberty and democracy beyond the fundamental grounds on which the old-line aristocrats made their stand. These younger leaders were also products of changing times, changing climates of attitudes, which had brought movement into the still pageants of plantation splendor.

Finally, the period of the tranquil idyll, where time seemed suspended in perpetuity, lasted only two decades at a midpoint in the seven-decade span of the golden age of the eighteenth century.

The impression of a static society, then, was not actually true of the whole golden age. It was only from the late 1720's to the late 1740's that life, momentarily holding the quality of a paradise, was indeed without change and could appear to be established in perpetuity. Before this static period the position had yet to be won; afterwards came the time of the struggle to maintain the idyll in changing circumstances. The assertiveness that led to the emergence of revolutionaries — and really only a few of those — was born of this struggle to maintain the established order against external pressures. The creation of a new order was a by-product, by many undesired, of the struggle to maintain the old order against the imposition of unbearable authority. Thus, the lordliness of the private domains — the imperiousness created in masters of the plantation communities — became "the seedbed of revolution" by circumstance, almost by accident, and certainly by the momentum of events set in motion by the aristocratic defense of the status quo.

2

The age which produced the aristocratic revolution was, in all truth, "golden" for only a few — or, rather, for *the* few. It was golden for those who comprised the aristocratic government, in the strict meaning of "government by a minority consisting, presumably, of those best qualified to govern." The distinction of Virginia's government in the golden age was that it *did* consist of those best qualified to govern. The men who gathered usually twice a year in the colonial capital of Williamsburg were the best educated as well as the richest and most influential in the Colony; habituated to authority, they were the most accustomed to making decisions which involved the lives of others and affected the events which shaped their society. Having the personal stake of property in a society in which land was the basis of wealth and the source of prestige, these men of families of the ruling order made government a personal responsibility. They had no concept of the "politician" as a professional sent to the capital to run their government for them. Politics to them meant the personal operation of the governing machinery. To this the men of the governing order brought the genius of their civilization.

The age was golden for a few because — with a few exceptions, of men themselves well connected — only those whose families had established them in positions of inherited wealth had the time and the means to devote the center of their interests and the direction of their energies into assuming the responsibilities of government. This meant quite literally "the responsibilities of government" as opposed to the partisan actions of party politics. Men maneuvered for position and rivalries caused personal enmities, but a political party as such was unknown. Since the holding of high office was, with rare exceptions, restricted to families of the ruling order, and in the Council, the upper house of the General Assembly, appointments were practically hereditary and held for life, the leaders could concentrate on governing the Colony without having their attention diverted by wooing constituents.

While the members of the General Assembly did not have to please the citizens, it was an aristocratic government by consent; the people had to be convinced that the men in government were acting for the common good. In acceptance of the hierarchical structure transplanted from England, the citizens generally believed their community leaders to be better qualified than they to make decisions at the capital which affected the total interests of the Colony.

The men in whom the citizens believed were by no means composed entirely of virtues. In assuming the time-consuming responsibilities which took them away from their sources of income, the men in Williamsburg certainly looked after one another when it came to parceling out posts of profit. In bids for power within the ruling class some were pretty tricky fellows. Fundamentally, however, by their comprehension of the implications of power, the leaders in government were scrupulous in legislating for the Colony as a whole.

Their comprehension of the implications of power also restricted to a few the privileges of the golden age. These few had been formed by growing up with the unique and absolute authority of the master of a slave-operated plantation community. Not only was their word law in their personal baronies: they held the power of life and death. Habituation to rule of a private community produced the side effects of pride and, in some, an overbearing arrogance; others inclined toward a Romanesque indulgence in pleasures. Yet because of this habituation to authority the rulers in government were not made heady by sudden power. Nor were they influenced by fears of themselves or their party going out of office. Governing was merely an aspect of the total leadership for which they had been trained from birth and to which they were accustomed.

Finally, since the Colony's economy was entirely bound up in the plantation system, with tobacco as the money crop, and since wealth was made and controlled by the planters (the few who acquired riches by other means married into the planter class), the leaders in government were not exposed to the importunities of pressure groups. Except for a small number of artisans and tradespeople, every freeholder (an enfranchised citizen by right of the ownership of land) was a planter, large or small. Hence, by acting for their own class, the men at Williamsburg acted for all citizens. This, of course, reduced their temptations enormously.

In acting for all planters, the rulers legislated within the commercial restrictions imposed by Great Britain, and these made volume production a requisite for material success. Since volume production required broad resourcefulness in a combination of acquisitiveness, agricultural competence and commercial enterprise, highly disciplined energy and the management of effort, along with the capital to invest in slaves for a labor force, few rose to the top. A large proportion of the population achieved a modest substance over a wide scale — ranging from just above the hard-pressed poor to just below the lower strata of the rich.

As in England, the actual poor were taken for granted. By the time-honored hierarchy of order and degree, the poor would always be among them. Parishes looked after those who, through age or infirmities, could not look after themselves. Those who would not look after themselves were not encouraged to tarry in Virginia. For those physically fit who tried hard at farming and simply could not make a go of it, the Colony assumed no responsibility, although measures were frequently taken to alleviate the lot of the honest poor.

Primarily, the body of legislation was directed toward protecting the planter population generally from the exploitive greed of the English merchant class which dominated the administration of colonial affairs. In doing this, the few who enjoyed the privileges did legislate for the many — the many here including those engaged in other work, for as the tobacco market went, so went Virginia. Tobacco was not only the Colony's gold: as tobacco was legal currency, it was also the Colony's money, its dollar.

Virginia's golden age was not golden for a few because those few enjoyed the power of governing the many; this power was the validation, the expression, of their total privilege — the magnificent style of living supported by inherited wealth and the deference of their fellows freely given to their position in the society. Leadership in government was, as in England, expected of those who, by wealth and social prestige and habituation to authority, were responsible leaders in their communities, and the two-story capitol at Williamsburg served as the meeting place for local leaders to combine in administration of the Colony's affairs. For the main part, since political government was the genius of their civilization, the plantation grandees were drawn to Williamsburg by an ideal combination of motivations — self-expression, duty, and the will to power. Having been born to riches and high status, the privileged minority could enhance their own egos only through authority and effectiveness in Virginia's government.

As their society was new and mobile, competitiveness for authority was intense and no position of real power could be maintained without effective performance in it. In the fluidity of a society recently emerged from the frontier (and still frontier on its borders) the members of the older families in the aristocracy could not afford to presume on their briefly established hereditary position. Just as their forebears, in making the adventure to Virginia, had participated in the upward thrust which characterized seventeenth-century England, so other families in the Colony, slower to gain the high places of big riches, were producing sons making their upward thrusts in Virginia — all aiming to cap their success with the power and glory at Williamsburg.

As Virginia had no financial center (like London), and eminence in the arts and entertainment was peripheral to the valued achievements in government, the mecca for every family seeking status was the small capital, where all talents and energies and consecration gathered to compete for the same prize. This singleness of values made Virginia's General Assembly the breeding ground for the very best that could be developed among the Colony's superior citizens.

3

From first to last, the golden age spanned three generations (allowing for cross-generations within the major categories) from the early part of the eighteenth century to the American Revolution. The early burgeoning of the golden age in the first years of the century came with the solidification in political power of a coagulation of rich, influential merchant-planters who formed a ruling order in a natively evolved hierarchal structure along the broader pattern of England's.

At the core of this newly sprung aristocracy were four powerful and determined men — Robert ("King") Carter, Benjamin Harrison II, and Harrison's sons-in-law, Philip Ludwell II and the Reverend James Blair. With William Byrd II and one or two others, these men formed the controlling bloc on the appointive Council of twelve. As the Advisory Council to the Governor and as the upper house of the General Assembly, as well as the General Court, the Council was in that period the place of highest honor and greatest influence in Virginia. Such was the power of this Council bloc, this nucleus of an oligarchy, that these men overthrew a royal governor, Francis Nicholson, and established the oligarchy's control of the Colony's internal affairs.

When, after an interim, Alexander Spotswood, a strong governor and a skillful battler, tried to break control of "the party" (as he called the power bloc), the home government removed him and advised his successor that it would be well not to ruffle the oligarchy. By 1730, through intermarriage and political loyalties and common interests, the aristocratic order had established a ruling class which, dominating the life of the Colony, gave its character to the golden age.

Except for James Blair, the Commissary (representative) of the Bishop of London, the leaders of the oligarchy were second-generation Virginians, born in the Colony, whose fathers had founded the family fortunes. Though all were men of some estate, they were highly acquisitive and used their initial advantages as bases from which to acquire vast riches. It was the period of the large importation of Negro slaves whose labor produced tobacco in the volume necessary to make profit against low prices in England and high charges.

Giving detailed attention to the money crop of tobacco, the big planters were also merchants: shipping the tobacco of small planters with their own cargoes, they imported goods for the "stores" that supplied the small planters. While nearly all the planters grew subsistence crops, the biggest grew in sufficient volume to trade in produce and beef. In their expansion, these early century merchant-planters brought to that precise time and place the precise methods that would produce great wealth under conditions which also created the private baronies of plantation centers.

The biggest of them all, King Carter, increased his inherited holdings from 8,000 acres to 300,000 — including forty-four separate plantations, in addition to the wharf and shipping center at the home-place of Corotoman, on the Rappahannock. He increased his slave-holdings to upwards of 1,000; he engaged in so many home manu-facturing operations, including the building of ships for his inland river traffic, that his home plantation resembled a thriving town; at his store he traded in everything under the sun; as a financier he discounted notes, lent money on Virginia mortgages (which often resulted in his claiming the property) and invested thousands of pounds more safely in interest-bearing bonds of the Bank of England. King Carter was the prototype of the generation, all born in the seventeenth century, of what might be called the Great Accumulators.

After the great accumulations and solidifications in power, with an English-type "web of kinship" uniting the ruling class, the golden age entered the second period — the 1720's and 1730's and into the 1740's — of the era truly described as "life in thrall." As those to whom the age was golden viewed the civilization developed on what Charles II called "the naked continent," they could only feel that man had achieved a oneness with his environment, an equilibrium with nature which left nothing to be desired. This was the idyll of the legend, when time seemed suspended, and the ladies and gentlemen in the great houses wanted only to hold this hour of life in perpetuity, "world without end."

This period of little more than two decades did not end abruptly. Nearly all the ruling class resisted change in the life-style and mental attitudes of the idyllic era, and many refused to admit that the perfected moment in time would not endure forever. But change came from the inside and from the outside, drawing the self-sufficient parochial Colony into entanglements that shattered its isolation and affected the absolute control of the oligarchy. It was in this third period, of Virginia's external involvements, that the practice of employing the society's genius in politics bore fruit in the quality of the products who went from the General Assembly at Williamsburg into world affairs.

In these two periods, the mid and the last, came the generations of the Inheritors. Their wealth and position secured for them by the Great Accumulators, the Inheritors cultivated the social graces of their aristocratic status, built manorial houses as dynastic seats for generations to come, and devoted their political energies to problems more complex than those which had confronted their fathers and grandfathers. Individuals and families continued to rise into the ruling class, ambitious men working as acquisitively as those of the Accumulators' generation. But the attitudes were determined by the majority in the ruling class who were essentially conservers and administrators of their inherited estates.

These two periods covered two generations of the Inheritors — those born in the early part of the eighteenth century and those toward the middle — and on the surface there was no difference between them. Fundamentally, however, they had been formed in different mental climates, and the effects of this were revealed when Virginia was drawn into the unwanted conflicts which threatened the perpetual tranquillity.

Because the leaders of the younger generation of the Inheritors belonged to the future, the leaders of the middle generation of the golden age have historically received short shrift. Yet they laid the groundwork for the generation which extended from theirs and they perfected the institutions of governing in which the younger generation was trained. It was what the older generation of Inheritors did with the advantages left by the great Accumulators that made possible the emergence of the younger generation as colonial leaders in the conflict with Great Britain. The older generation made the climate out of which the products of an aristocratic order grew to assume their places on the world stage.

By the comparative obscurity of the middle generation of the golden age (the first generation of the Inheritors), the young revolutionaries, the Thomas Jeffersons and Patrick Henrys, gave that impression of bursting full-blown out of a static society as stylized as a minuet. In point of fact they were the end of an evolutionary process, the result of all that had gone before. They were the final products, on whom the spotlight played, of the whole of the golden age.

• 1 •

Life in Thrall

Chapter One

THE DILETTANTE OF THE IDYLL

COLONEL WILLIAM BYRD II (1674–1744) was unique in the ruling class by virtue of being the last surviving man of prominence in the generation of the Great Accumulators and also a precursor of the generation of the Inheritors. The youngest of the seventeenth-century planters associated on the Council with the Carter-Harrison-Blair-Ludwell oligarchy, Byrd was atypical of his generation in that he was not basically an Accumulator. Inheriting more largely than the others, Byrd did little to increase his estate and devoted his life to cultivating those elegances of the great world which are commonly associated with the social habiliments of the aristocrat. He used the leisure earned him by his vastly acquisitive father to make of himself, in his own words, ''an ornament.''

As this ornament, who perfected the graces of the mind, of tastes, and of high style, in a colony still emerging from the wilderness, the second Colonel William Byrd most perfectly exemplified that idyllic era of the golden age when the tranquil and baronial life of the 1730's seemed impervious to the mutations of time. Byrd was a dilettante. As a full-blown, exquisite product, he was the first dilettante in Virginia.

While Colonel Byrd might have been a dilettante in any case, in his cosmopolitan tastes he was formed by his life in London from the age of seven until, with only one intervening year in Virginia, he was thirty-one. Again, from forty-one to fifty-two, except for one year in Virginia, he lived mostly in London. Byrd preferred life in the English capital and returned first to Virginia at thirty-one only when forced, by his father's death, to take personal supervision of the property left him.

Some of his older contemporaries, such as King Carter, and some of the generation following Byrd's, such as Carter's sons, had also been educated in London, but when their education was completed they returned (some sooner than they wished) to assume the responsibilities of operating a plantation. To King Carter (not among those reluctant to return — to "come in"), the proudest estate in the world was that of "a Virginia planter." But Byrd, an expatriate by preference, was proud of his London friends and of his English-formed tastes and interests. He was a custodian of an estate which included plantations, rather than a working planter.

Beginning with a larger inheritance than his contemporaries — 26,000 acres, an Indian trading post at the Falls (Richmond) on the James River, and several stores — Byrd through most of his life added little to this estate. The bulk of cultivated land he acquired, 9,710 acres, came through an unwise settlement of his father-in-law's estate, which saddled him with a lifelong debt. Then, late in life, as if seized with land hunger, he began acquiring cheaply large tracts of land, totaling more than 130,000 acres, in the distant, mostly unsettled regions along North Carolina's border. No profit accrued from these acquisitions, although the holdings contained some rich bottomland and Byrd vaguely planned a colonizing venture. Land to Byrd meant status. While land was a measure of status throughout Virginia, before Byrd's late-life purchase of the unsettled tracts, the idea of the income-producing "landed estate" appealed to him more as a duplication of the style of his admired English friends than as an extension of planting-mercantile operations. It was this vanity which lured him into the trap of his father-in-law's estate.

His first wife's father, Colonel Daniel Parke, had been a handsome and tumultuous gentleman who, like Byrd, was more at home in England than in the Colony. Coming into an inherited Virginia estate while still in his teens, Parke was overbearingly arrogant and cut about the gaudiest figure in the seventeenth century before leaving the Colony with a mistress. Through his friendship with the Duke of

William Byrd II
Portrait by an unknown artist, about 1715-1725
(Colonial Williamsburg Collection)

Marlborough, Parke was given the assignment of carrying the news of the victory at Blenheim to Queen Anne, who rewarded him with a miniature bearing her likeness and the governorship of the Leeward Islands. While his abandoned wife and two daughters were barely able to maintain appearances through the pride and scrimping of Jane Ludwell Parke and the charity of relatives, Colonel Parke lived with seignorial magnificence and encouraged his sons-in-law, Byrd and John Custis IV, to believe his daughters would come into estates of consequence.

When, after a spectacular amorous career in the Leeward Islands, Parke was murdered, he left his valuable properties to illegitimate daughters, his entangled estates to Frances Parke Custis, and to Lucy Parke Byrd only £1,000 — the exact amount of her unpaid dowry. Byrd's pride was hurt at his wife's being "fobbed off" with a cash settlement which, in any case, she was owed. In a complicated arrangement with John Custis, Byrd assumed Parke's debts in exchange for some property in England and the 9,710 acres in Virginia which were settled and seated with slaves and stock. While the English property proved to be worth less than estimated, Parke's debts never ceased turning up: the amount approximated £10,000 before interest, and Byrd was still settling the debts near the end of his life.

The burden of this debt to Perry, the London merchant-financiers, was the one shadow over Byrd's paradise, and it caused a wishfulness to warp his judgment. Since his early thirties Byrd had aspired to be governor of Virginia. Before his debt to Perry this ambition was more for honor and power of office than for its cash income, although Byrd was always among the foremost of those colonial Inheritors who expected lucrative plums by the right of position in the small society. Then, when he was over sixty, Byrd had unrealistically appealed to London friends to use their influence to have him supplant Governor Gooch. William Gooch was not only the most beloved governor in the Colony's history (the only governor of his day in the American colonies of whom the people never complained), but his administration brought Virginia to that peak of prosperity which yielded the idyllic era of "life in thrall."

When nothing came of that wan appeal, the following year (1737) Byrd asked another London friend to use his influence in obtaining for him the office of Surveyor (Collector) of Customs of the

Southern District of America. Here Byrd, finally relinquishing his aspiration for the highest honor in the Colony, was concerned only with the income of £500 a year. This would, he wrote, ''disentangle me from all my difficulties and make me perfectly easy.'' By that candid statement (which did not win him the post) Byrd revealed the extent to which the influence of his handsomely endowed English friends had convinced him — unlike the majority of his generation — that society should make life ''easy'' for him.

In his early forties Byrd had become outraged when then Governor Spotswood demanded that he do the work for which he received commissions as Receiver General. In the custom of the close-knit ruling order in the early part of the century, Byrd had ''inherited'' the post from his father, and when Spotswood refused to have this source of income operated as a sinecure, Byrd sold the post for £500 to make a payment on his debt to Perry.

Despite his failures to secure income from the public revenue, Byrd fancied himself ''a splendid economist.'' Although this self-image was another aspect of vanity, Byrd, except for the foolishly acquired debt, never lived beyond his means. He was a prudent manager of his own properties. Having no interest in commerce and little in the practical day-to-day details of operating a tobacco plantation and stores, he depended more on overseers than was usual among those Inheritors of his generation who were also acquisitors. For ten out of eleven years the operations went on profitably during his absence, in a time when upwards of six months was required for the sender of a letter from England to Virginia to receive a reply.

When Byrd was in residence, he knew generally what was going on in the fields and in the tobacco sheds, in the prizing of the leaves into hogsheads and in the loading for shipping, and he was familiar in some detail with the cargoes shipped out from and into the post at the Falls. But, while his father had taken intense interest in his stores, Byrd allowed the stores to be run by tradesmen and gave his personal attention to his garden of ''sweet flowers.'' He grew roses and iris and crocus, larkspur and jasmine, Indian honeysuckle around a summer-house where, according to his brother-in-law Robert Beverley, ''humming birds delight.''

The center of his interest was his library, for which a librarian was hired to arrange Byrd's four thousand volumes. This librarian, a

Scotsman named William Proctor (who later took orders and held a Virginia parish), also acted as tutor for Byrd's children and the children of some of his relatives. Proctor's work in the library was important, since Byrd was a book collector as well as an ardent reader. His tastes ranged from the classics (he read Hebrew and Greek the first thing every morning) through philosophy and history to "entertainment" — including plays, poetry, essays, and translations — and fourteen shelves of books written in French.

Other planters' sons of his generation, of the generation before theirs, and of the generation then growing into maturity, had habits of reading in the classics, of reading widely in history and philosophy and theology, and some enjoyed plays and poetry. Even the smallest libraries contained books on medicine and law, since planters doctored their own communities and usually themselves, and they needed legal background for their services as county justices or, as Councilors, judges of the General Court. Byrd's brother-in-law, the second Robert Beverley, was Virginia's first historian. But Byrd was the only one to whom the pleasures of literature — writing as well as reading — were a continuous avocation.

In his younger days in England, when an intimate of the Restoration dramatist William Congreve and of titled gentlemen who played at letters, Byrd wrote several bawdily satirical (sometimes scatological) sketches and verses in the attitudes of cynical worldliness fashionable in early eighteenth-century London. When older in Virginia, he wrote a full-length travel book, *History of the Dividing Line,* and two shorter works, *A Journey to the Land of Eden* and *A Progress to the Mines.* The full-length book was a reflective, observant account of his trip as one of the commissioners to determine the long-disputed border between Virginia and North Carolina. It was on this trip that he became interested in patenting land in that largely abandoned area, and *A Journey to the Land of Eden* was an engaging account of a surveying trip over some of the new property.

Byrd refused to publish these writings in his lifetime, giving as the reason that they were not sufficiently polished. It was possible that he feared that published work would not live up to the promise of his reputation for wit and learning. Byrd was, in fact, a good light writer. His prose was fresh and sprightly, reflecting his worldly turn of humor, and in his descriptions he had an eye for the telling detail and a gift of original phrase. While not writing for the ages, he left a sizable volume of highly readable work that remains unsurpassed for its evocation of the times and the mental temper of the era.

His most representative work, however, was not in the travel books but in his day-by-day secret diaries, which he wrote in a shorthand code, and in his mannered letters — especially those to English ladies whom he courted in vain.

2

In love and marriage Byrd's career was untypical of all generations of planter Inheritors. His first marriage was conventional enough according to the customs among the privileged families in Tidewater. Lucy Parke was one of two daughters of the highly placed Colonel Parke, whose father had been a Councilor, and of Jane Ludwell, the sister of Colonel Philip Ludwell II. Among the more favored Inheritors, Ludwell had come into Governor Sir William Berkeley's manorial Green Spring estate (the Colony's first manor house) through the marriage of his father to Berkeley's widow. Ludwell was also among the most acquisitive, using his political offices to acquire choice land and operating a mercantile store in Williamsburg in partnership with Commissary Blair's brother. Although affairs with the Parke family had not been as sound as they looked on the surface, neither Byrd nor John Custis IV, who married Lucy's sister Frances Parke, had any way of knowing that.

It was after the death of his temperamental wife in London in 1716 that Byrd, then in his forties, adopted the attitude of his London friends in seeking an English wife of position and fortune. It was this period as the rich colonial in London that, placing Byrd outside the main currents of the evolutionary growth in Virginia's golden age, made him the last of the English-oriented Virginians as well as the epitome of these untroubled times when the government and the estates seemed to run themselves. Although Byrd served conscientiously on the Council when in Virginia, nothing changed at Williamsburg when he was off aping the London gallants in chasing heiresses.

He seems to have fallen in love with the first heiress of his choice,

Mary Smith, daughter of the rich Commissioner of Excise. Lacking the favor of her father, despite Byrd's impressive cataloguing of his colonial properties and promise to live in London, he gained the support of Miss Smith's sister and brother-in-law, Lord and Lady Dunkellen. Conniving with them to carry on a clandestine correspondence with the lady whom he addressed as "Sabrina," Byrd used invisible ink in conducting his literary, though genuinely passionate, courtship.

Sabrina evidently encouraged the middle-aged colonial. The plot action with her father and Byrd's chief rival (with his seconds) ran like one of the dramatic comedies which Byrd loved to attend in London, and Byrd was both hurt and outraged when Mary Smith married the rival, Sir Edward Des Bouverie. Des Bouverie was wholly eligible: the son of a wealthy and eminent trader with Turkey, Sabrina's husband came into a large estate. Byrd, in trying to impress her father with his Virginia holdings, had said he had an annual income of between £1,500 and £1,800. As Lord Dunkellen revealed to Byrd that Mary Smith's father spent the then enormous sum of £1,500 on her wedding clothes alone, the colonial had obviously been aiming out of his financial class. But Byrd was very bitter about Sabrina and, for one of the few times in his life, held vindictive feelings long after his disappointment.

He was a sanguine man, however, and his natural ebullience was quickly restored. Within the year he was publicly courting a rich widow, who had no "dragon" (as Byrd had referred to Mary Smith's father in his Sabrina letters) to guard against his importunities. Although he saw her frequently, Byrd practiced his literary skills by writing her letters addressed to "Zenobia." Zenobia rejected him three times before he gave up. Much of his courtship had been conducted at the watering place Tunbridge Wells, and he included Zenobia in a group of verses to fashionable ladies, published under a pseudonym as *Tunbrigalia* in London in 1719.

While vainly courting the widow he solaced himself with a laundress who doubled as his mistress, and then took on her sister also. When the sister tried to borrow fifty pounds he broke with them both and returned to Virginia. where he suffered the humiliation of having an indentured maid refuse to become his mistress.

After little more than a year in Virginia, Byrd returned to his amorous sieges in London. First he courted the "blameless beauty"

Lady Elizabeth Lee, granddaughter of Charles II and his mistress Barbara Villiers, Countess of Castlemaine. She was a recent widow, and so ardent was Byrd's pursuit that his brother-in-law John Custis wrote him that they had heard in Virginia "that you have a keen appetite for a young widow morsel of about sixteen years old." Then pushing fifty, Byrd certainly had self-confidence. Addressing Lady Elizabeth as "Charmante," he resumed his literary lovemaking with mannered letters which evidently failed to awaken the desired response. Lady Elizabeth married Edward Young, a plain-featured poet without fortune and (as Byrd wrote in a spiteful post mortem) without chin.

As with the heiress he had first sought, Byrd felt that Charmante had led him on. He preserved copies of his letters to her, as to the other courted ladies, and on the package he wrote, "These passionate billets were sent to a lady who had more charm than honor, more wit than discretion. In the beginning she gave the writer of them the plainest marks of her favor. He did not hint his passion to her, but spoke it openly and confirmed it with many a tender squeeze of the hand which she suffered with the patience of a martyr; nay, that she might have no doubt of his intention, he put the question to her in the plainest terms, which she seemed to agree to by a modest silence . . . and fed his flame by the gentlest behavior in the world." Suddenly "she grew resty, and, in a moment, turned all her smiles into frowns, and all his hopes into despair."

Soon he was writing more "passionate billets" to a friend of Charmante's, whom he addressed as "Minionet" and whose identity was never established. Minionet's rejection of him seemed to leave fewer scars. While there was no doubt that he had loved Sabrina, if briefly, and experienced a middle-aged infatuation for Charmante, all the four ladies of fortune whom he was known to court served to kindle his literary spark, and he was sufficiently proud of his romantic compositions to preserve them for posterity.

Finally, at the age of fifty, Byrd found a receptive heiress in Maria Taylor. Twenty-six herself, she was getting a little long in the tooth for an unmarried lady of her time, and although her late father had been a gentleman of substance, she seems to have brought no fortune to Byrd. There were no rivals to compete with and, to avoid the possible disapproval of her mother, Byrd wed Miss Taylor and two weeks later informed her mother (privately "Medusa" to Byrd) of the marriage.

Winning Maria must have been serious business, for she inspired Byrd to none of his polished prose. He wrote her only one brief letter, in Greek, and this was trite and mechanical, unworthy of inclusion with the literary love letters which showed fervor and care and a craftsman's pride in the product. The translation of his note in Greek reads: "You thought you were in the good graces of Mistress Maria. When I thought you knew only your mother tongue, I was passionately in love with you; but when indeed I learned that you also spoke Greek, the tongue of the Muses, I went completely crazy about you. In beauty you surpassed Helen, in culture of mind and ready wit Sappho: It is not meet therefore to be astonished I was smitten by such grandeur of body and soul when I admitted the poison of love both through my eyes and ears."

The conclusion cannot be escaped that Mistress Maria, of Kensington, was naïve in comparison to the ladies of fashion, to whom he would scarcely have addressed such a clumsy compliment. The second Mrs. Byrd went willingly to the colonies, made him a good if unexciting wife, and provided Westover with a new family of four children.

In contrast to the widely known tempestuousness and careless inefficiency of the first Mrs. Byrd, almost nothing was known about Maria Byrd beyond the fact that she was a sensible woman who efficiently managed a household made complicated by the continual appearance of unexpected guests for meals and their occasional impromptu parties. The meals were extensive affairs and were the measure of a hostess, since visits constituted the whole of social life (except when the General Assembly convened during the Public Times in Williamsburg), and table hospitality was a source of pride to the planter families. The hostess was never threatened with a shortage of food, as the big plantations grew more than enough to support their communities in abundance, but quality had to be maintained in cooking and elegance in the service. No matter how many kept coming and how long they tarried, the lady of the house was never supposed to falter in her graciousness. There is no record that Maria Byrd ever did.

Beyond her house-managing efficiency, it was known that she did not get along well with Byrd's daughter by his first wife, Wilhelmina, or Mina. Byrd took no sides. His only comment was, "A great quarrel between my wife and Mina, which made me retire." Then, Byrd's nephew, William Beverley, the son of his sister Ursula and Robert Beverley, made an extremely bitter remark about Maria Byrd. His young son had died while at school under Byrd's librarian-tutor, and while this may only have reflected Beverley's inconsolable grief, he nevertheless blamed the neglect of "the inhuman Lady at Westover."

Despite these interfamily difficulties, Byrd appeared satisfied with the English "heiress" whom he had brought to share his declining years in the enforced exile in his native land.

3

At home, Byrd continued to practice self-expression in letters to (mostly high-placed) English friends, and he indulged his ribald turns in frivolous letters to Maria's sister. In all this late-life correspondence, Colonel Byrd reflected more the temper of London than of the Colony. While he was naturally good-humored, with a fanciful lightness in his turn of mind, in his letters he so carefully maintained the attitude fashionable in London as to suggest a self-aware pose: it was not so much that he posed as something he wasn't, as that he seemed to be always aware of making an unvarying impression. He was very conscious of *writing,* and very self-conscious about the picture he presented of Colonel William Byrd II.

With this self-centered self-awareness reflecting his attitude to life, Byrd the dilettante was something of a poseur. In a day when Virginia duplicated the sharp cleavage between the gentry and the people ("people of the meaner sort") that existed in England, no colonial was stricter than Byrd in keeping his inferiors at a distance or in adopting the airs of the "aristocrat."

The aristocracy in Virginia, into which Byrd was born, was — as all aristocracies have been originally — a newly sprung class. It was founded and grew entirely in the Colony; that is, none had come to Virginia as an English aristocrat. The majority of the early fortune-founders came to the Colony between 1640 and 1670, during a time of ferment and mobility in England's social hierarchy, when yeomen ascended into the gentry, gentry into the peerage, and families of all conditions dropped into obscurity. Those who made the Virginia adventure might have, with their ambition and energy and resourcefulness, increased their estates and advanced their positions at home. But the combination of gifts — including most especially some money, some education, some connections — which they brought to the frontier conditions of the unexplored wilderness, won them riches, political influence, and social prestige.

All of the founders of the dynasties had showed evidence of familiarity with polite social usage. At least, they had the manners and presence to be made intimates of Governor Sir William Berkeley, the old-line aristocrat and ex-London courtier in whose long administration the emigrants of consequence received political positions of power and profit. When the (at first) relatively few families of importance drifted into a natural coagulation, to form the nucleus of an aristocracy in its strictest meaning of a governing class, the individuals did not refer to themselves as "aristocrats." In transplanting the hierarchical English customs, however, they assumed the privileges of gentry, went to pains to authenticate a coat of arms, and were meticulous in using their titles of rank. Their military titles designated the rank held in their county's militia unit. Since the militia comprised the only force in the Colony for maintaining law and order, repelling invasion, and crushing Indian uprisings, the titles were far more than honorary. However, the "Colonel," the commander of the county's militia, was always a person of consequence, usually a Councilor, and this title designated the highest social rank in Virginia.

In the practical life of the Colony, the titles of the new aristocrats were most nearly the equivalent of the English "squire," as the aristocracy was similar to the English "squirearchy" — except there were no peers with their House of Lords above them in scale. The character of their lives on the isolated plantations was also similar to that of the English country squires. While many or perhaps most of them read seriously in order to fit themselves for their station, they were fundamentally practical, busy, hardworking men of enterprise. These were the first and second generations.

Byrd's father belonged to the second generation although, the son of a London goldsmith, he came to the Colony at the age of eighteen. He came in 1670 to the ready-made planting-mercantile operation of his uncle Thomas Stegg. At his uncle's death soon after his arrival

William Byrd I inherited the lands, the store at the Falls, the Indian trading caravans and Stegg's political position among the small governing class. This first William Byrd was all business, and a man of boundless acquisitiveness. His son never evinced any appreciation of his father's rise from the class of London craft workers into a place among the colonial powers. In fact, in the English custom, William Byrd II referred to his inheritance of an "ample fortune" as though it had existed always.

During the first fifty-two years of his life (1674–1726), which Byrd lived mostly in London, the men of his father's generation and the older men of his own generation did not as a generality devote much of their time and money to ostentatious living. With few exceptions their houses were built for comfort rather than style or permanence: there was no sense of the manorial seat as in the English model. Houses either rambled, with additions of wings, or, outgrown, were casually demolished and rebuilt.

Usually the rich merchant-planters imported furniture that was fine by colonial standards, even magnificent in comparison to the plain, serviceable pieces in the average settler's home. In these houses, which ranged from one room and "jump" (sleeping attic) to four rooms, meals were served "on the boards" — planks brought out from a corner to be laid across wooden horses to form a trestle. The big merchant-planters had dining rooms, and considerable stress was placed on tablecloths and napkins.

Silver was an early symbol of wealth. While all the new squires used or possessed some, only a few in the late seventeenth or early eighteenth centuries collected quantities of silverware for its obvious status value. Among the largest early silver collectors was William Fitzhugh, who, like Byrd's father, came to Virginia around 1670. One of the most successful of his generation, and one of the most inwardly insecure, Fitzhugh was also among the first to provide lavish hospitality. Byrd's father was not known for any such prodigality, and King Carter, the most successful of them all, abhorred ostentation and show of all kinds.

In their similarity to the English squire, these were largely outdoor men. Though each had his "chariot" (coach) and fours or sixes, they loved to ride horses. Carter was known to have been in the saddle from first daylight to dark riding over his home plantation, and, going by boat to one of his forty-four outlying plantations, he kept familiar with every detail of his operations by riding over these holdings. Next to social drinking, with its break in the loneliness of plantation life, their favorite entertainment was gathering at horse-races. These were informal affairs — without blooded stock — held on some planter's cleared field, where high officials in the government served as volunteer judges. Betting was lively.

The second William Byrd was never anything of this squire type. He was an indoor man. When he returned from London and friends gathered at a nearby race meet, he sent his wagers by a servant and spent the time in composing letters in which he complained of the lack of choice scandals in the Colony. In London, he wrote his wife's sister, "people play the fool in a well-bred way, and furnish their neighbors with discourse. . . . But alas what can we poor hermits do who know of no intrigues, but such as are carried on by the amorous turtles, or some such innocent lovers? Our vices and disorders want all that wit and refinement, which make them palatable to the fine world."

In the sedulous cultivation of these tastes for the "wit and refinement" of "the fine world," Byrd was not in any way representative of his time in Virginia — or of any time in Virginia. By using the privileges (particularly the leisure) of an Inheritor to become a stylist in life as in letters, Byrd's unvexed elegance and changeless pattern of days without time was a distillation of the brief era of the idyll which held eternity in the hours on the shores of the broad tidal rivers. Yet those coming after Byrd, who cultivated the graces befitting a landed aristocracy, were neither under Byrd's English urban influences nor consecrated to his dilettantism. Thus, although a precursor of the aristocrat in the full social meaning, Byrd served as the chief ornament of the era of "life in thrall" rather than as an influence. The last of the seventeenth-century men of prominence, he belonged precisely in his exact time.

4

When Byrd returned to Charles City County to stay in 1726, his younger contemporaries (third- and fourth-generation Virginians) were beginning to build baronial brick houses after the manner of

English manorial seats. The impetus had come in the magnificent Governor's Palace in Williamsburg designed by Alexander Spotswood. This was the first mansion in Virginia to combine architecture indigenous to the climate with a classic symmetry on a grand scale. Though built in Williamsburg, it was ideally adaptable to a plantation manor house, the center of an agricultural-shipping-mercantile community, with its quarters for field workers and small houses for skilled artisans. Most impressive to the planters, whose outbuildings sprawled helter-skelter in all directions, was the symmetrical design of the outbuildings in a formal forecourt stretching from either side of the main house, with other outbuildings partially concealed in the rear by shrubbery and gardens, of flowers and fruit and vegetables.

The first and most massive of the new manorial houses was Rosewell, on the York River, begun by King Carter's son-in-law Councilor Mann Page, who died before the expensive undertaking was completed. On the Rappahannock River, King Carter's son Landon began building at Sabine Hall a broad Georgian mansion overlooking terraces a mile back from his wharves. On the plantation adjoining Byrd's, in the year he came home, his friend Benjamin Harrison IV, another son-in-law of King Carter, built at Berkeley a handsome red-brick manor house. Harrison had indentured Rob Wilson, a young Scot, from an English debtors' prison and brought him to Virginia as the master builder of his mansion. Two full stories and basement, the main house rose on a knoll from which the ground sloped in terraces to the busy wharves on the James River a little more than a quarter of a mile away.

After Byrd had been home six years he began building, with unidentified artisans, a manor house at Westover which for purity of Georgian line, for grace and repose, surpassed them all. Since Byrd did no important shipping from Westover and there were no noisy wharves, he built his elegant house within fifty yards of the broad river. A shaded lawn rolled between the red-brick house and the high banks against which the tidal waves lapped. His outbuildings and distant quarters were on the land side, separated from the sanctuary by a brick wall, entered through a pair of beautifully designed wrought-iron gates. Imported from London, and believed to be the work of Thomas Robinson, the delicate gates at Westover were unlike anything seen in the colonies. Within those gates in the private barony on the river, the tranquil lordliness of life of the plantation master was captured as nowhere else for that precise hour of the idyll in the 1730's and early 1740's.

Byrd lavished the same care on the interior. Already possessing a fine collection of prints, he imported furniture, cut glass, and silver, and arranged a portrait gallery of paintings of titled ladies and gentlemen who had been his friends in London. He had three portraits of himself, looking dandified and haughty, but none of the acquisitive father who had made it all possible.

In these enchanted surroundings, the aging Byrd continued the pattern of his days in the leisured tempo designed to promote pleasure. He wrote to the friends of the portraits, read in the ancient languages and in French and English, sometimes with his linguistic wife, played billiards and a card game called piquet, tended his sweet-smelling garden, visited friends, and entertained: most of all, he entertained. Friends would drop in before the midday dinner, staying sometimes until night and occasionally for days.

He saw much of his neighbors, Benjamin and Anne (Carter) Harrison, whose parents had earlier been Byrd's friends: Harrison's mother, a Burwell, had been a cousin of Byrd's first wife. He often visited Lady Susannah (Beverley) Randolph, the niece of his brother-in-law Robert Beverley and widow of Byrd's late friend Sir John Randolph. Sir John's father, William Randolph I, one of the fortune-founders of the 1670 period, had been a friend and contemporary of Byrd's father. The younger Randolph, one of the few colonials to be knighted by the King, had served as Speaker of the House of Burgesses before the newly rising power, John Robinson.

Lady Randolph's was one of the few planter families who owned a house in Williamsburg. A large, broad frame house facing the public square, Lady Randolph's home *looked* hospitable, and its paneled rooms were never free of guests. She was famous as a hostess and her table for its elegance, and when Byrd was in Williamsburg during the Public Times he visited the Randolph house nearly every day. Byrd was an intimate of other Randolphs and other Harrisons, and indeed, his friends comprised a cross section of the ruling class.

As an ornament, Byrd was a delightful companion. Of cheerful disposition, he was urbane and witty, and communicated his pleasure in lively human companionship. Since social drinking (along with social eating) was the favorite pastime of families relieving the loneliness of their isolated plantations, when parties got rolling Byrd sometimes took on too much wine or brandy. But he was not normally a heavy drinker. He had the classic sense of moderation in all things, except that his sexual appetite was difficult to keep in control.

Although he wrote a friend that this was flagging, when he was sixty-five he wrote in his secret diary, "Folly with Caton, God forgive me." Caton was (supposedly) a daughter of a gentlewoman stranded in Virginia, whom Byrd befriended. The nature of the "folly" can only be deduced from the more explicit recordings of other seizures of lust, during which he smothered with kisses the wives of his friends and servant girls. At sixty-seven he recorded, "I played the fool with Sarah, God forgive me." Strangely for a man of his charm, he was continually rejected in his advances by all classes of women and usually found his gratification with paid mistresses and prostitutes.

With his second wife, Maria, his sexual relations were evidently more placid than with the tempestuous Lucy, for he did not record in his diary any of those sudden episodes that characterized life with his first wife. His English wife gave him three daughters and a son, a second family of his late years to replace the two daughters of his first marriage — of whom one had died and the other, married to Thomas Chamberlayne, had moved away. Then, in 1742, Byrd's two older daughters by Maria married younger sons of King Carter.

Both the Carters, who had recently lost their first wives, were intimates of Byrd's James River plantation neighborhood. Their older sister was mistress of Berkeley plantation, adjoining Westover on the east, and their older brother John lived at Shirley, the next plantation upriver and long the demesne of John Carter's wife's family, the Hills. John Carter, who also retained the family seat at Corotoman, was a Councilor and Secretary of the Colony. Although Byrd and "Secretary Carter" were neighbors, Byrd seems not to have been as intimate with him as with Carter's sister and brother-in-law, the Harrisons. John Carter died that year, leaving among other children an eleven-year-old daughter, Elizabeth Hill Carter, little younger than the Byrd girls when they married her uncles Landon and Charles.

Anne Byrd was seventeen when she married thirty-five-year-old Charles Carter of Cleve — upriver on the Rappahannock from Landon's Sabine Hall — and Maria was fifteen when she married thirty-two-year-old Landon. (King Carter had been the most successful of those big merchant-planters who, breaking with the English primogeniture system which left everything to the firstborn male child, provided working estates for all their sons. Carter also contributed substantially to his married daughters' families. Because of the repetition of family Christian names, the Carter sons — as those of some other families — were identified by their manor seats.)

Colonel Byrd was pleased at the marriage of his daughters to sons of his old friend, although Maria's marriage to Landon was sudden and unexpected. Byrd wrote of the surprise wedding (September 22, 1742) to Daniel Parke Custis, son of Byrd's eccentric brother-in-law, John Custis IV.

"Your kind present of Sorers [small birds] came in a good time when we had a vast deal of company. Amongst the rest was Colonel Harrison and his fair family. The reason of their coming was upon my invitation on account of a certain marriage, I hope made in Heaven, that was solemnized no longer ago than yesterday. If you will come before Sunday [four days later] you will be in time to wish the parties joy and eat a piece of the bride cake. Nothing ever fell out more suddenly than this affair. None of us thought anything about it at ten in the morning, and by three the Gordian knot was tied. When you come, you may hear more and see two happy persons."

When the daughters left for their new homes, as Byrd's son was off at school in England, his second family was reduced to fourteen-year-old Jane, but the marriages tightened the web of kinship in the ruling class, and deepened the illusion of perpetuity of order.

5

Although Byrd as dilettante was atypical of his older contemporaries, he was typical of his generation in the political and philosophical set of his mind. For their mental attitudes, like the unending minuet of life at Westover, were immutable. The Colony of Virginia was firmly fixed in the structure of the British Empire, whose hierarchical system was in turn planted eternally in the firmament ruled by God. With their sense of inner security in an ordered universe governed by a Divine Power, the planters varied in the nature and intensity of their individual devoutness. The worldly-minded Byrd was definitely not among those characterized by religious fervor.

In unreflective conformity to the doctrines practiced by the Church of England and good-mannered conformity to the rituals of the parish church, he could be most simply described as a "habit Anglican." He daily gave thanks to God for his good health and frequently asked forgiveness for acts that gave him momentarily a bad conscience. But, typical of his generation, he made no speculations on the nature of God or of man's relationship to eternity. In his earthly thoughts, of here and now, the most consistent line in his diary was of the food he ate at each meal.

In the late mellow years, Colonel Byrd seemed either uninterested in or unaffected by the two polar movements arising out of the era's lax religious sense and the deadening of spiritual values. At one extreme was the drift toward a new religion of the mind, embracing Deism, and at the other extreme was the Evangelical Revival, the Great Awakening of spiritual values, with emphasis upon the individual's personal and direct relationship with God.

The "rational religion" was part of the Enlightenment, with its political emphases on natural rights (in the deification of Nature) and on the influence of environment in relation to man's capacity to remold his institutions and his own destiny by reason. By the 1740's, the spread of this rationalism in the colonies was limited chiefly to liberal ministers in eastern urban centers, though by 1737 there was a Deist in Savannah and a "progressive" in Williamsburg. This new confidence in reason — reason superseding religious revelations and traditional institutions and, actually, the previously held views of mankind — was not in 1743 even beginning to become the mental climate of Virginia. Byrd was typical of his time in his indifference to these heralded changes in the familiar attitudes in which he had lived his life.

He had in his library, and presumably read, the advance guard philosophers of the new rationalism — Locke, Descartes, Hobbes, and Shaftesbury — who rejected the religious suppositions regarding ethical theories in favor of endowing man with a "moral sentiment." Byrd presumably read them, but it was late in his life and, like most Virginian merchant-planters of his generation, he was not drawn to philosophical speculation.

He was also typical of his class and generation in his indifference to the Evangelical Awakening brought directly to the colonies and to Virginia by George Whitefield. An Anglican priest, Whitefield first came under the Wesleyan (Methodist) influence, and then developed strong Calvinist convictions in personally acting as "an incarnation of the Christian conscience." His purpose and his gift was to arouse the individual conscience and reawaken a living faith in persons who were drifting into careless disregard of religious observances or drifting out of the church altogether. In England, where the body of unchurched persons was growing, Whitefield attracted enormous crowds by his dramatic preachings as a traveling evangelist. When he visited the colonies, in New England and South Carolina the clergy and the people opposed him as being disloyal to the church of which he was a minister. At Williamsburg in 1739 he was warmly welcomed by Governor Gooch and Commissary Blair, who invited him to preach in Bruton Church.

The *Gazette* in Williamsburg reported on December 21, 1739: "On Sunday last the Reverend Mr. Whitefield preached at our Church on the words, 'What think ye of Christ?' There was a numerous congregation, and 'tis thought there would have been more if timely notice had been given of his preaching. His Extraordinary Manner of Preaching gains him the Admiration and Applause of most of his hearers."

Whitefield's "Extraordinary Manner" consisted of an emotionalism usually regarded as unseemly by old-line Anglicans, and he scorched his listeners with horrendous descriptions of hellfire while blasting the conservative religious teachings of the traditional church. No account was kept of the converts Whitefield might have made in Virginia, nor any measure taken of his influence. It seems safe to say, however, that his hellfire and damnation evangelism would have made no significant impression on the ordered tranquillity of life at Byrd's Westover. Judging from the length of time (thirty years) before Methodist evangelists established themselves in the Colony, Whitefield exerted no great influence among the planter-merchants of substance.

Yet, the Great Awakening of which Whitefield was the precursor in Virginia, simultaneously with the spread of the new rationalism, represented the forces of spirit and mind stirring on the periphery of the plantation order when its patterns seemed fixed in perpetuity.

6

Byrd also seemed unaware — or certainly unaffected by — the shifts in the balance of power at the seat of government, where he had spent half of his life. Appointed to the Council, through his father's influence, in 1708, he had to wait until his sixty-ninth year to come into the highest honor of President of the Council. When, by seniority, he succeeded to this office in 1743, it was becoming little more than a titular honor.

In the thirty-five years that he had sat on the Council (Virginia's nearest equivalent of both the House of Lords and the King's Privy Council), this august body had declined in power in the General Assembly as the House of Burgesses rose in power. A seat on the Council still carried vast prestige, but the days were gone when only six Councilors could (as had the Carter-Blair-Ludwell-Harrison oligarchy) make decisions which affected the whole Colony without the support of the House of Burgesses.

The Colony was much larger, geographically and numerically, than in 1708, when Byrd first ascended to a Council controlled by the core of the oligarchy. When Byrd became Council President in 1743, the population had grown beyond 250,000 — the most of any colony on the continent — and twelve years later a careful survey estimated an expansion to 290,000, white and colored.

When Byrd had been born, just before Bacon's rebellion of 1676, the primeval forests were broken by such few and scattered clearings that a visitor said, "Virginia looked uninhabited." Byrd's birthplace had been a stonehouse (a fort against Indian attacks) at a trading post on the far edge of the frontier at the Falls, the head of tidewater in the James River. The first sounds he had heard were the howling of wolves and the shouted curses of the rough characters who drove his father's packtrains to the distant villages of the Cherokees.

Now, on land which Byrd himself had sold as urban lots, Richmond was growing up on the hills overlooking his father's old frontier trading post. Riverport towns were springing up, and stores, run by Scotsmen out of Glasgow, were competing with the trading stores — like King Carter's and the early Harrisons' and those Byrd had inherited from his father — where the big merchant-planters imported goods for the small freeholders in exchange for handling the shipping of their tobacco.

In those days there had been little settlement of the wilderness beyond the fall line of the great rivers — a line running north and south from approximately the present site of Washington to Richmond. "Tidewater," the water-drained land along the tidal rivers — Potomac, Rappahannock, York, and James — had been Virginia. Now families of substance operated plantations in the rolling Piedmont country, west of the head of the tidal water to the foot of the Blue Ridge. Settlers, many of whom came from other colonies, were taking up land west of the mountains, in the great Shenandoah Valley, and recently exploring parties had ventured into the Alleghenies — approaching the land claimed by the French.

Among the changes caused by this expansion was the spread of wealth. Although the rich planters were still a small proportion of the whole population, wealth was no longer concentrated in the hands of a few whose fathers had gotten there first (by or before 1670) with the most lands and slaves. The use of the slave labor forces, as a means of beating low tobacco prices and high charges with volume shipping, starting slowly in the latter part of the seventeenth century, spread from the turn of the century until every tobacco-planting family who had ambition, resourcefulness, and energy to advance their position in the colonial hierarchy operated with slave labor on a larger or smaller scale.

It was not, however, only those newly rising into the planter gentry who spread the wealth, with its concomitant political influence. A fundamental factor in the political changes was the numerical growth of the descendants of the individual fortune-founders of the seventeenth century. By the time of William Byrd's ascent to the Colony's highest honor, there were so many sons and sons-in-law, grandsons and nephews, of those early builders of personal empires that the Council could not begin to accommodate these younger planters entitled by birth and inherited property, by education and capacities, to serve in the Colony's highest councils.

Among those entitled to high place were dozens who felt a strong urge to assume the responsibilities in government which they accepted as inherent in their inherited privilege. As there was no room on the appointive Council, these intensely motivated Inheritors overflowed into the House of Burgesses, the elective body of the General Assembly.

Since the seventeenth century, there had always been a few planters of powerfully connected families among the Burgesses. But through the first decades of the eighteenth century the majority had always been maintained by "freeholders," most of whose tobacco-planting operations were on a modest or small scale. From the beginning, the bulk of Virginia's population had consisted of humble, hardworking tobacco-growers similar to the English class of farmer called "yeomanry." Their holdings were small, they did all the work themselves, and their unending struggle against the wilderness, taxes, and shipping charges (along with danger from Indians) had been dignified by their status as freeholders — independent, self-reliant freeborn English citizens, *on their own land*. Traditionally these settlers, the "people," had looked to the House of Burgesses, whose representatives they elected, for the protection and advancement of their interests.

Gradually, as more families turned to volume production with slave labor, the ambitious emerged out of this general run of the population and entered the "planter class." Technically, every tobacco-grower was a planter, but in general usage the word came to designate those who worked with slave labor and did not perform their own manual tasks. While countless of these so-called planters were less well-off than nonslaveholding families of some substance, they came to identify their interests with the planter class and to give their allegiance to the large merchant-planters, such as Byrd's friends the Carters and Harrisons. For the planter class held the social status of "gentry": not all planters were by any means gentry, but with few exceptions all gentry were planters.

Simultaneously with the siphoning off of the ambitious from the top of the small-scale tobacco-growers, the yeomanry lost numbers from the bottom as families gave up the struggle. Some worked as tenants and some as overseers; others, abandoning the land, moved into the towns for jobs or into the wilds to work as rangers; unknown numbers became vagrants, petty thieves, and whores. Some of the casuals and some respectable people drifted out of the Colony, or at least out of the settled regions. With the drop in numbers as well as the loss of the ambitious, the influence of the yeomanry declined in the

House of Burgesses concurrently with the rise of the numbers of the younger plantation masters representing hereditary position and alliances in the ruling class. When Colonel Byrd became the ranking Councilor, the House of Burgesses was becoming the dominant body in the General Assembly as the expanding ruling class, in effect, took over the whole of the General Assembly.

In this expansion, allowing for newcomers whose families had been unknown or not even in Virginia when Byrd was born, the core was still built around the fewer than a dozen families whose founders had won position in the primitive frontier before 1670. For fifty years beginning in 1722, only 110 of all the Burgesses who served were men of political consequence in Williamsburg. Of these, exactly one half, fifty-five, belonged to less than a dozen families: Beverley, Blair, Burwell, Carter, Corbin, Harrison, Lee, Ludwell, and Randolph. Of this fifty-five, one half (twenty-eight) belonged to three families: Randolph, eleven; Carter, nine; Beverley, eight. Among the representatives of other families, six had married into the Carter line, five into the Randolph, and four into the Beverley.

These same families were also represented in the Council. Of the ninety-one Councilors who served at one time or another between 1680 and the Revolution, twenty-nine — nearly one third — were members of nine families. Three each came from among those families who dominated the House — Burwell, Carter, Harrison, Lee and Ludwell. Three other families — Byrd, Custis and Wormeley — also had three members on the Council. The Pages, intermarried with the Carters and the Burwells, among others of the ruling class, had five Councilors.

In 1743 the thirty-nine-year-old man who was becoming the most powerful political figure in Virginia was connected with three of these families. John Robinson's grandfather was Major Robert Beverley, who, coming to the Colony as a lawyer, established his estate during the "reign" of Sir William Berkeley, and left nine children. Through John Robinson's mother, the youngest of Major Beverley's children, he was allied by kinship with the Randolphs and the Harrisons. His uncle, Robert Beverley II, was William Byrd's brother-in-law, and his father, a Councilor since King Carter's day, was a friend of Byrd's. As Speaker of the House and Treasurer of the Colony, John Robinson wielded more actual power than did Byrd, as President of the still prestigious Council. Yet Colonel Byrd's diaries never referred to the existence of Speaker Robinson, actually his nephew by marriage — a relationship that could be close in Virginia's small society. Byrd called "cousin" certain of his wife's in-laws.

Byrd's omission of John Robinson, personally a bland and persuasive character, would not necessarily indicate anything more than a failure of their social paths to cross. For, of all things, the elegant Byrd was a social being. But it would appear inconceivable that when he was younger, when he was actively seeking place, Councilor Byrd would have made no mention of the dominant political figure in his country's capital. When he first returned permanently to Virginia he had gravitated naturally to King Carter and Philip Ludwell, the dominant figures of their day, during the Public Times in Williamsburg when the General Assembly met. But they had been Councilors, and to Byrd the Council remained the body of interest.

All were gone of those seventeenth-century planter-political leaders who had strolled the broad streets of Williamsburg, dined and drank and gambled in the taverns after the day's business in the Capitol, and gathered in the Capitol yard to discuss tobacco prices and the "usury" of the British merchants who handled their shipments. Byrd alone was left of those proud men who had spanned the age when Virginia changed from a frontier, under the exploitive rule of the Stuart kings and their dictatorial Royal Governors, into the settled Tidewater community where, in their gracefully designed capital city, easy-mannered Governor Gooch worked in harmony and mutual affection with an evolved native ruling class.

Unintrospective Byrd never revealed any sentiment over the passing of those intimates whose lives had been intertwined with his. Philip Ludwell had been the uncle of his first wife, Benjamin Harrison II the long-lived grandfather of Byrd's friend and neighbor at Berkeley, and during the Public Times in Williamsburg, Byrd and King Carter had been one another's favorite drinking companions in the long hours from early afternoon dinner in a Williamsburg inn until bedtime. In Byrd's younger years, he had been no friend of Commissary Blair, the steely intriguer, although common interests and common loyalties had brought a surface cordiality during Byrd's middle years. During the last years, after aging Blair succeeded Carter as Council President, when Blair's deafness caused Byrd to conduct meetings for him, the two former enemies visited back and forth. Even then it was unlikely that the two old men talked of past times. To the end Byrd, a master of time, lived in the transcendent moment, here and now.

7

While not of a speculative turn of mind, and apparently untouched by the gathering forces of change, Byrd experienced troubled moments about the institution of slavery, upon which was built the whole structure of the Colony — economic, social, and political. Byrd was neither typical nor unique in recognizing the future threat of the black slave population. For decades the General Assembly had passed laws restricting or forbidding the further importation of Negroes as slaves, only to be overridden by the home government, which was dominated in its colonial affairs by merchant interests, including specifically the Royal African Slave Company. The colony of Georgia had prohibited the importation of slaves and rum, and in a letter to his friend Lord Egmont, one of Oglethorpe's partners, Byrd went to the heart of the psychological effects of chattel slavery.

Referring to Georgia, he wrote, ''I wish we could be blessed with the same prohibition. They [the traders] import so many Negroes that I fear this Colony will sometime or other be confounded by the name of New Guinea. I am sensible to many bad consequences of multiplying these Ethiopians amongst us. They blow up the pride, and ruin the industry of our white people, who, seeing a rank of poor creatures below them, detest work for fear it will make them look like slaves. . . . Another unhappy effect of many Negroes is the necessity of being severe. Numbers make them insolent and then foul means must do what fair will not. . . . These base tempers require to be rid[den] with a taut rein, or they will be apt to throw their riders. Yet even this is terrible to a good natured man, who must either submit to be a fool or a fury. . . . But these private mischiefs are nothing if compared to the public danger.''

Then developing the possibility of a slave insurrection, led by ''a man of desperate courage,'' which would ''tinge our rivers as wide as they are with blood,'' Byrd pointed out that ''besides the calamities which would be brought upon us by such an attempt, it would cost our

Mother Country many a fair million to make us as profitable as we are at present. It were, therefore, worth the consideration of the British Parliament, My Lord, to put an end to this unChristian traffic, of making merchandise of our fellow creatures. At least the further importation of them into our colonies should be prohibited . . . and I wonder the Legislature will indulge a few ravenous traders to the danger of the public safety.''

Byrd felt bitter about the New England ship captains who plied the Virginia rivers with slaves and rum, particularly about the rum sold to the poorer elements and illegally to slaves. ''With respect to rum,'' he wrote Egmont, ''the Saints of New England, I fear, will find some trick to evade your Act of Parliament. They have a great dexterity at palliating a perjury so well as to leave no taste of it in the mouth.''

To his friend Judge Benjamin Lynde of Salem, who had been a companion of Byrd's when they were law students at Middle Temple, he wrote, ''I wish you could live long enough to make all your countrymen honest by your righteous judgements and good example . . . I fancy your laws there are so tender that they put no knaves to death, but by a peculiar sort of banishment condemn [them] to sail about the world in sloops. . . . Some of these banditti anchor near my estate, for the advantage of trafficking with my slaves, from whom they are sure to have a good penny worth's. I am now prosecuting one of them, whose name is Grant, for this crime, and have evidence sufficient to convict him.''

Byrd's contempt for the ''foul traders'' of New England who sold rum was similar to the hatred felt by later Americans for the renegades who sold whiskey to the Indians, and his frequent reference to these traders as ''Saints'' might imply a disgust at the holier-than-thou attitudes of piety behind their traffic in fellow creatures. For Byrd could not justly condemn them for slave-trading, since he (like his unmentioned father before him) occasionally bought slaves for sale to other planters. While adapting to the prevailing customs himself, probably he felt it was one thing for English trading companies to bring in slaves as part of the Empire's mercantile policies and something else for individuals from other colonies to abet the traffic for their own profit.

In his attitude to the principle of slavery which he himself practiced, Byrd represented an ambivalence that was to be more in evidence in the generations following his. Since in Byrd's day little consideration was given to common humanity, his occasional queasiness about using blacks as slaves was less humanistic than realistic in appraising the *future* dangers to the society. While the necessary harshness (he would personally whip a sassy servant) sometimes went against his "good nature," Byrd was comfortable with the system as it was *in his own day*. In fact, he referred to the use of slaves very seldom, and likening himself to "a patriarch of old," never for a moment considered even the possibility of any changes that might affect the perpetual tranquillity of his own estate.

Yet, in pointing to the psychological effect of slave labor upon the white population, Byrd had located a source of unsoundness in the structure which appeared to be the best possible Colony in the best possible Empire in the best of all possible worlds. This psychological effect would, in a combination of factors, affect the economy.

In the preceding eighty years the spreading use of slave labor forces for the mass production of a money crop had on the whole worked successfully. The system had made possible the quick accumulation of wealth for the big merchant-planters. The bigger they were, the more successfully the system worked. In that period the presence of Negro slaves — while "blowing up the pride" and drawing the distinction between gentry and farmers — had not significantly affected "the industry of our white people."

Also in that period Tidewater land was plentiful for the replacement of acreage laid waste by tobacco. All through the settled regions new fields of tobacco were bordered by stands of second-growth pines — "old fields," as they were called. But, as Byrd's own favored life neared its end, planters were beginning to run short of new land in the settled regions at the same time that new lands opening in the boundless west lowered land values in the old regions. This changing condition demanded an adaptiveness precisely at the time when the psychological effect of the Negro slaves created a satisfaction with the static idyll that was the very antithesis of adaptiveness.

In the generations following Byrd's, there would be ambitious individuals whose industry and resourcefulness were not affected by the presence of slave laborers. By and large, these were men of relatively modest substance with a drive to move up among the real powers. Such were the sons of Captain Augustine Washington, who died in April of the year, 1743, of Colonel Byrd's ascension to the Council Presidency. But for the Inheritors who, like Byrd, desired no more than to live off their estates, the cracks in the whole system would make demands upon planter families which were not even imagined on the slumbrous riverside lawn of Westover.

Byrd, then, was among those who saw the slave population as representing the one cloud, small and as yet distant, over their paradise. Even he did not recognize all the implications of the then remote threat. In Byrd's time, planters of the generation following his — contemporaries of his Carter sons-in-law — gave no evidence of perceiving the cloud at all. Secretary John Carter had, despite his father's one unhappy venture in trading in slaves, acted as middleman in buying 145 Africans to be offered for sale.

It was not only the Africans being brought in who multiplied the slave population : even the smallest slaveowners bought females along with the stronger males in order to increase their number; and some of the larger plantations were practically breeding farms. ''Virginia-born'' Negroes brought higher prices, especially as domestics and skilled workers. On the surface, it looked like more blacks meant more wealth in a continuing spiral of prosperity, in which every planter with credit would be able to do in the future what King Carter had done in the passing generation.

The golden age was at a high noon, where the sun seemed to stand still over Westover and the great plantations in their perpetual thralldom.

Chapter Two

THE GENTLEMAN IN THE PALACE

As THE GOVERNOR, William Gooch (soon to be baroneted) was as typical of that benevolent era as was Byrd. Born in 1671, he entered that training school of Virginia governors, the British army, and rose to the rank of major. Without any considerable private fortune, Gooch played at times the London courtier seeking appointments, and was sent to Virginia in September 1727 as Lieutenant (or *de facto*) Governor. According to the then current custom, the titular Governor remained in England, drawing a salary but otherwise participating little in the Colony. As far as Virginians were concerned, Major Gooch was Governor, and the best they had ever known.

Every Virginian who met the Governor commented on his charm, his "easiness of manners," his courtesy, and his dignity. But what endeared all Virginians to this likable gentleman was the obvious sincerity of his interest in their welfare, his sympathetic understanding of their problems, and, ultimately, his identification with the people he governed.

To act on his sympathy with the Colony's welfare required Gooch to operate from the insecure footing of a tightrope. For while ideally, for the greater glory of the Empire, the interests of England and her colonies should have been one, Gooch had actually to serve two masters — the colonial government and the home government.

Since the practical attitude of the home government to the colonies was dominated by the English merchant class, England's policy to Virginia was fundamentally exploitive. Had Gooch acted strictly on his instructions, both in their letter and their spirit, he would have aroused rebelliousness in the General Assembly, and even such a strong and able governor as Spotswood had discovered that this was not a feasible situation. On the other hand, had Gooch ignored his instructions and given in to all the demands of the General Assembly, he would have been recalled.

Along with his pleasing personality and genuine sympathy, Major Gooch needed a cold-nerved adroitness to maintain continually a tenuous balance between the colonial interests of the English mercantile class and the interests of the Virginians, in private enterprise and in the Colony's well-being. Since the Governor maintained this balance through dealing with the law-making bodies of England and Virginia, each representing powerful private interests in undeclared conflict, Gooch showed himself to be a master at diplomacy and political maneuver, with surprising firmness beneath the affable exterior.

As with Byrd's perfection of the English-oriented dilettante's role in that precise time in Virginia, the cloudless era of general prosperity on both sides of the Atlantic permitted Governor Gooch to practice his gifts for flexible compromise without the distraction of critical problems. East of the Blue Ridge the once murderous Indian tribes, depleted and encompassed, had settled into apathy; pirates had almost entirely ceased to ravage the Chesapeake Bay areas, and scarcely a living person remembered when the last warship of one of England's enemies raided up an inland river. Although there was hardship among the humbler farming families (who couldn't compete with volume-produced tobacco), nobody suffered actual want where food could be supplied by the easily grown corn, untended hogs, game in the forests, and fish in the streams. Gooch found their lot better than that of the poorer classes in England. Most important of all, for his "harmonious" administration, Major Gooch inherited a working system of balance between the oligarchy controlling the General Assembly and the Whig ministry which had emerged to control the British government.

When Gooch had come in 1727 operations were turned over to him by Acting Governor King Carter, President of the then dominant

Council, and at home Sir Robert Walpole was in his sixth year as leader of the Whig oligarchy. The first Hanoverian, German-speaking George I, had died that year, and Gooch brought with him the announcement of the ascension of George II. An ill-natured figurehead without the inclination or qualification to rule, George II turned over the government to the ministry system evolved by Walpole.

The trend toward Parliamentary supremacy, which culminated in Walpole, had begun in the overthrow of the Stuart kings in the Glorious Revolution of 1688 and was paralleled in Virginia by the assertion of those rights in local government that led to England's recognition of the Carter-Blair-Ludwell-Harrison oligarchy. As the Crown was progressively weakened from William to George II, and the laws enacted in relation to the colonies promoted the interests of the merchants (represented by the Whigs) rather than the prerogatives of the Crown, there was a drift in all the colonies toward a nebulous division between internal and external affairs. During Gooch's administration, the laws passed by Parliament tended on the whole to confirm the colonial view that domestic legislation was exclusively the right of the general assemblies, and in 1750 Sir William Blackstone wrote that the colonial general assemblies ''are their houses of commons.''[1]

Yet there was an inconsistency, inherent with conflict, in the external-internal division. While the English authorities believed representative government was a right to be enjoyed, any behavior in any of the general assemblies which the home government regarded as aggressive or parochial caused a stress upon their subordination to what was termed royal authority and was in actuality their subordination to Parliament. All the colonies accepted this *de facto* subordination by submission to restrictive policies that protected mercantile interests.

The awareness of the submission, however, was blunted by a laxness in the enforcement of certain laws, within a practical policy which tacitly recognized the local conditions in the varying colonies. In New England, whose soil produced no money crop, the laws against manufacturing products for sale were lightly enforced; in Virginia these laws were strictly enforced. In all colonies, more or less smuggling was engaged in to circumvent the duties on articles which had to be imported through England, where duties were levied, even though

French or Dutch traders might offer the same goods for less and without the duties. The law which bore the hardest on Virginia required all tobacco to be exported to England, eliminating the buying competition of a world market, and this law was not easy to evade. As an extension of this restriction, the colony of shippers was forbidden to build ships except for inland river traffic; this law could not be evaded.

Virginians remained indifferent to the arbitrary distinctions between ''external'' and ''internal'' controls because of the success of and their obsession with the money crop of tobacco. Fur-trading also had been profitable to individuals, such as Byrd's father, and although this trade was on the decline, considerable money was still being made by shipping beaver and deer skins. A fair-sized trade was growing with the West Indies and other British colonies in food products and articles, such as barrel staves, which did not conflict with the interests of the English merchants. An agricultural community, with its own successful merchant-planters, Virginia felt no need of manufacturing; and any work, as in mills, that took place indoors — except for convivial tavern-keeping — was abhorrent to an outdoor-minded people. Then, as like attracts like, few skilled artisans were drawn to the Colony. People came to be landowners. Thus, although external controls forced the planters to sell on a restricted market and pay dear for imports, especially the silks and satins for ladies' clothes, these practices came under their unquestioning acceptance of ''what hath been the ancient custom.''

Then, from the beginning of his ministry in 1721, Walpole adopted a laissez-faire attitude to the Navigation Acts (restricting trade to English ships) and to details of internal government in the colonies. Commercial-minded Walpole represented the new moneyed interests rather than the small merchants, and to promote commerce generally he removed duties on more than one hundred articles. In attitude he reflected the pragmatism of the Whig party, which had supported the authority of Parliament over the prerogatives of the King.

Walpole, serving under two weak monarchs, developed the responsibility of the cabinet ministry with the supremacy of the ''prime'' minister in both the cabinet and the House of Commons. Remaining in the House of Commons, Walpole established the principle of a

House of Commons leader as prime minister, and established the cabinet system in which all ministers acknowledged his leadership. This cabinet system, by which England was to be governed, had not been in mind when William III signed a constitutional agreement after the 1688 revolution. It evolved largely through the personalities of titular kings and Walpole, a power-minded politician whose actions helped develop an efficient system among a people more adept at political practice than political theory.

The opposition attacked Walpole's practical politics for their corruption, and he certainly was open in awarding state offices and pensions to members of Parliament, as well as practicing bribery in "electioneering." However, his methods of retaining political power did not concern Virginians — especially as Walpole's Secretary of State for the Southern Department (of the colonies) shared his views on colonial trade. The Duke of Newcastle, Secretary from 1724 to 1748, opposed any new measures that would affect the good will of the colonies. Although Newcastle's object was to avoid injuring British trade with the colonies, the policy worked toward the harmoniousness of Gooch's administration.

2

While prosperity came generally to the colonies and England during Walpole's ministry, and his policies kept colonials from being vexed by the "externally" imposed restrictions, Gooch's instructions were drawn up by the Board of Trade. Officially "the Crown's" instructions to the Royal Governor, his orders entirely reflected the mercantile-minded colonial administrators and the influence of international merchants, who frequently attended the Board's meetings. As Gooch's regular correspondence, in reporting on the execution of his instructions, was directly with the Board of Trade, these gentlemen were in effect the Governor's immediate superiors.

Along with regular reports, Gooch was required to send copies of every law passed by the General Assembly. From the Board of Trade, these laws went to the King in Council and to the secretaries responsible for colonial affairs. The correspondence — from the Board of Trade, Privy Council, and the ministry — soon showed Gooch that a strict enforcement of his instructions in detail would protect England's merchants and manufacturers at the expense of the Colony. Not only would hardship be worked on the people but, in stifling Virginia's economic growth, the shortsighted, self-interested orders would hamper the Colony's growth as part of the British Empire.

More immediately, the execution of orders that placed the Governor in conflict with the governed would lose him the support of the Council and the good will of the House of Burgesses, and of all things he needed the cooperation of the House of Burgesses. The Burgesses controlled the expenditures of the Colony's revenues and habitually used their power of the purse strings as a weapon against governors. In their seventeenth-century struggle with the Stuart-appointed governors, no matter what other encroachments had been made, the Burgesses never yielded this power in the face of threats and bribes and royal abuse. By 1699, the House of Burgesses had won the right to appoint the Treasurer of the Colony, removing this office from the Governor's control, and at the least encroachment on any of their rights the Burgesses bristled with their obstructive weapon.

William Gooch was, as a successful diplomat must be, a realist. He did far more than merely avoid antagonizing the easily aroused Burgesses: he made a skillful use of his power to make appointments. For the passage of any legislation he particularly wanted passed, Gooch appointed Councilors and key Burgesses, along with their relatives and friends, to administrative offices. At election time he tactfully used his influence for Burgesses to whom (or to whose friends) he had given appointments.

From the beginning Gooch's expedient measures for harmony with the General Assembly included a sympathetic understanding of the Virginians' viewpoint in what amounted to self-protection against greedy practices of the mother country. In his opening address to the General Assembly, he won their hearts.

"As your observation and experience will suggest to you the best methods for promoting your own happiness, either public or private, be you so kind as to inform me of them, and then I will venture to promise for myself that as I have no other nor farther views than to approve myself by my royal master, such as I ought, and such as you may expect me to be, so you shall always find me in a disposition to receive you kindly, to advise you sincerely, to assist you faithfully in all your applications to me, and correspondence with me. And if to these we join what is my inclination, as well as obligation, and impartial justice in the administration here, and a fair and faithful representation of matters from hence, I shall then make no question, but by the blessing of God, which I shall always and earnestly implore, we shall see ourselves an happy and contented people.''

After his speech the General Assembly wrote to the King: ''We have no room to doubt but that his administration will always be acceptable to your majesty and easy to all your people here.''

After he had served for only seven months, the House of Burgesses gave him a present of £500 (though officially forbidden, he was the third governor so honored). ''[We] hope you will be pleased to accept of it as a special acknowledgement from the people of Virginia of the just sense they have of your regard for them and the interest and prosperity of this Colony.''

Then the House of Burgesses addressed him, May 22, 1730: ''So we shall upon all occasions endeavor to approve ourselves worthy of the care and favor of our sovereign and of that regard which in every part of your conduct you express for us and all the people of Virginia.''

The Speaker of the House of Burgesses said to Gooch in 1736 (August 6): ''We have long experienced your love and good will to the people of this country and observe with what readiness you exert it upon all occasions. . . . You have met them [the people] and heard their grievances in frequent assemblies and have had the pleasure of seeing none of them proceed from your administration. You have not been intoxicated with the power committed to you by his majesty, but have used it like a faithful trustee, for the public and with proper caution.''

Replying, Gooch said: ''The House of Burgesses may always depend upon my care to support them in their ancient rights and privileges.''

Two years later (November 4, 1738), the House of Burgesses complimented him. ''The long and happy experience we have had of your just and upright administration, the constant course of your conduct, and the readiness you have shown upon all occasions to promote the good and welfare of this colony, lay us under the strongest obligations to pay the utmost deference and regard to your advice. . . . You have given of your kindness and affection throughout the whole course of your administration. May you long continue to govern a happy and contented people.''

With all this affection between the Governor and the General Assembly, Gooch never wavered in maintaining the authority of his executive office as a representative of the Crown. Nor did he ever yield to the assertiveness that the proud members of the governing class kept insistently upon him. For the Governor also had a weapon: no bill could become a law until he signed it and sent it to the Board of Trade for approval, and he had the power of veto. While he sympathized with the Virginians over laws they regarded as unfair, and, unbeknownst to them, went from appeals to protests in his communications with the Board of Trade, he conscientiously enforced the laws — except where they were unenforceable.

Major Gooch blandly ignored the smuggling of goods into Virginia and of low-grade tobacco (which the planters were forbidden to sell) into England. The Church of England had long been determined to enforce in Virginia the rules covering the induction of ministers, who were supposed to be inducted by the Governor. As this would give the ministers tenure, the powerful parish vestries (controlled by the same families who controlled the General Assembly) refused to obey the law. Friendly Councilors soon convinced Governor Gooch of the unwisdom of following his instructions in making a fight which he could not win. As Gooch's evasion of this item concerned neither manufacturing nor commerce, the Board of Trade did not make an issue over it.

The laws forbidding home manufacturing gave Gooch more trouble. Although the influential planters, magnetized by tobacco, had never felt that manufacturing restrictions intruded into their internal affairs in the area of their primary interest, when tobacco prices fell, by 1730 the plight of the small farmers caused the General Assembly to pass a law encouraging the making of linen. Endorsing it, Gooch wrote that the act would be ''a benefit to the poorer sort of people and more especially at a time when the staple commodity of the country will not afford them maintenance and support.''

Gooch had to write apologetically to placate the English manufacturers. It was not that the manufacturers and merchants feared

competition in England from Virginians so much as a decrease in
colonial demand. Virginians were already buying steadily in extra-
legal trade with New Englanders, and the Scotch traders were operating stores which catered chiefly to the poorer people and the backcountry settlers. The Board of Trade even called Gooch's attention to
the violations of a small pottery maker in Yorktown. Apologizing for
him in 1732, Gooch wrote that his "coarse earthenware . . . is of so
little consequence that I dare say there has not been twenty shillings
worth less of that commodity since" he went into business. A few
years later, Gooch reported with relief, "The poor potter in Yorktown
is dead."

Gooch began to come out more forthrightly on the increase of
home weaving as continued low prices of tobacco forced the poor to
weave cloth for their own use and turned even big planters toward
weaving cloth for their own people. Gooch wrote that planters were
beginning to make shoes "with hides of their own tanning" for their
people, and humbler farmers also turned to tanning, although, the
Governor wrote, "the leather is very indifferent." He finally admitted
with some boldness that the new settlers west of the Blue Ridge were
not only turning out a good grade of linen but selling it up and down
the Shenandoah Valley.

By such tactics, indefinitely multiplied, Gooch stood between the
merchant-dominated controllers of policy and the welfare of the loyal
colonials. In some instances, the manufacturing interests simply circumvented Gooch as the Virginians circumvented impractical laws.
When he had first come, the only manufacturing in the Colony as an
end in itself (and this as a sideline to planting) was the operation of
five furnaces for melting iron ore. During Gooch's administration, the
manufacturers' protests to the home government caused a gradual
raising of the duty on imported pig iron until this enterprise in
central Virginia declined during Gooch's administration.

Although Gooch maintained the stalemate in the ceaseless tug-of-
war, England's tight supervision of Virginia's legislation could only
be interpreted as external controls by a people fundamentally contented — as reflected by Colonel Byrd — with their position in the
British Empire. After Gooch sent the laws he approved to the Board
of Trade, they were cleared through the Attorney General for an
opinion on their legality before being submitted to the King in

Council. Before 1720, if the Privy Council disallowed a law, the Colony was notified to discontinue it. In 1720 the "suspending clause" was introduced, in which certain laws did not become effective until allowed by the King in Council.

During the first fifteen years of its existence the "suspending clause," a source of potential conflict, was used only half a dozen times. From 1736 on, the suspending clause was used more frequently, always involving the type of colonial act — relating to trade, revenue, manufacturing, debts, and such — which touched on the interests of English merchants and manufacturers. Gooch frequently wrote appeals to the Board of Trade for the allowance of certain laws subject to suspending clause, but though he wrote strongly about acts which had been disallowed for the benefit of merchants, he could never force an issue with the distant powers who had to feel assured that their interests were being served.

In his adroit balancing performance, by which he pleased everybody, the remarkable accomplishment of Major William Gooch was that he remained his own man. As he became a Virginia convert, the Governor perfectly reflected that era with its harmonious duality of pride in English identification and passionate local attachment. He sent his son (his only child, who died in 1742) to William and Mary. In entertaining in the handsome, paneled oblong dining room, he and Mrs. Gooch showed a cultivated taste for local dishes. He particularly liked the flavor of bacon and ham, the product of lean, running hogs, and regularly sent the Bishop of London a present of "some Virginia hams." Although his intimate letters to his brother in England sometimes showed areas of concern, he was satisfied that he was doing a good job and proud of his people's love for him. Gooch could be described as a happy man enjoying a happy age in which to be alive in the plantation society.

3

During Gooch's administration, Virginia made its first participation in England's international affairs and for the first time sent troops to fight off the North American continent. The War of Jenkins' Ear was one of those events overlooked in the broad themes of history which exerted its effect on the individuals at the time. This war with Spain had its genesis, as did most things of consequence, in the assertions of the English merchants.

Although England enjoyed a healthful trade exchange with Spain, a commercial friction had been growing and English merchants — turning aggressive with the supremacy of the English navy — encouraged squatter operations on Spanish territory in the two Americas. English traders, mostly out of Jamaica, began to clash with the Spanish *guardacosta*, largely manned by pirates, based at Porto Bello on the Isthmus of Panama. These Spaniards were rough customers. By treaty Spain had the right of search for contraband, but in 1731 Capitan Juan de León Fandino went further with his *Isabel*. He boarded the *Rebecca*, commanded by merchant captain Robert Jenkins, bound from Jamaica to London, and, after searching for contraband, looted the ship of all valuable goods. Then, after some exchange between the two captains, Fandino had Jenkins' ear torn off, told him to carry it to the King with the message that they would do the same to him if he came their way, and set the ship adrift.

Nothing was known publicly about Captain Jenkins and his ear for seven years. Then, from 1736 to 1739, the merchants concentrated an attack on Walpole's peace policy, and in a dramatic stroke one-eared Robert Jenkins was exhibited in the House of Commons in March 1738, displaying what purported to be his missing ear. With this "cause," indignation was quickly aroused and "no search" became the nation's war cry. The House of Commons passed a resolution to require Spain to cease searching English ships, and Walpole perforce, in the summer of 1739, demanded that Spain relinquish the right of search. When Spain refused, war was declared in October.

As wars go, the War of Jenkins' Ear was a brief, dismal affair waged far from home. There was one successful operation, when naval Captain Edward captured Porto Bello, where Spanish galleons with silver cargoes gathered for provisioning and the dreaded *guardacosta* outfitted under the protection of the fort's big guns. After this triumph, the navy was driven off when it attacked Cartagena in New Granada (Colombia) and retired to Jamaica to gather an amphibious force. This is where Virginia came in.

The home government called on the colonies to furnish and equip an American regiment of three thousand soldiers, to be commanded by

Virginia's former governor, Alexander Spotswood. A British army colonel before coming to Virginia in 1710, Spotswood had had a strange colonial career: he battled to overthrow the oligarchy's power for ten years, then ended up by joining them. After the Board of Trade removed him in 1722 (validating the oligarchy's authority in local government), Spotswood settled on immense holdings he had acquired in central Virginia during his last years as governor, built a manorial establishment for his wife and family, and served with his customary efficiency as Postmaster General for the colonies. Far more international-minded than the colonials, or Gooch, he had long wanted to get at the Spaniards. He was commissioned brigadier general to lead the regiment and to serve as quartermaster general, a post similar to that he had held under Marlborough thirty years before.

Virginia, in filling its quota of four hundred troops, gave a demonstration of the Colony's practice of handling objectionable home government rulings while tacitly acknowledging England's authority. At intervals since the seventeenth century England had deported to Virginia batches of its jail inhabitants, ranging from unfortunates convicted for debt through petty thieves and vagrants to vicious, incorrigible criminals. The General Assembly protested no British ruling more strongly than this insult of England's dumping its undesirables on the Colony. England would halt for a while, but in 1740 several hundred recently delivered criminals were scattered through the Colony.

There were no jobs for them in an agricultural community, whose planters had long before discovered that deportees were as unwilling as unfit for hard manual work: they were troublemakers, stirring up restlessness, and produced numbers of bastards by black women. (The courts tried unsuccessfully to enforce the laws against miscegenation.) Virginia's Attorney General came up with the ingenious scheme of impressing for service all vagrants, except those in certain categories which could not apply to transient criminals. The result was that Spotswood gathered four hundred recruits at a training camp outside Williamsburg: England had its Virginia unit and Virginia was cleared of its undesirable element.

Spotswood journeyed to the Northern colonies to recruit through personal representation to the governors (several of whom followed Virginia's example), and ex-soldier Gooch, as lieutenant colonel, was left with the training of the mostly hardened characters. On his way north Spotswood fell ill and died in Annapolis on June 7.

Gooch was left in command of the Virginia unit, which was joined by several of the British gentlemen with military experience who had volunteered for the American regiment. Of the old-line families who dominated Virginia's ruling class, not one member volunteered; in fact, Byrd wrote an English friend in the Horse Guards advising him against serving in the hot country, where (as he correctly predicted) the toll from disease would be severe. But the young planters of the substantial gentry volunteered, including Lawrence Washington, of an ambitious family.

The Virginia unit under Governor Gooch sailed for Jamaica, where it joined the other colonial contingents and British regiments. In early March of 1741 the amphibious force approached Cartagena, chief port of the Spanish Main, and nothing went right. When the rainy season set in during April, men sickened by the thousands and died by the hundreds. Little more than one-third of the nine-thousand-man force was fit for duty. Captain Lawrence Washington contracted an illness that plagued him the rest of his life and shortened his days. His one gain from the adventure was a name for the new house he built after his father died: to honor the British naval commander, with whom he had become a friend on the expedition, he named his house on the Potomac Mount Vernon.

When the "war" ended by the summer of 1741, the war party in England did not encourage the people to linger over the details of the fiasco. The public's attention was directed to the new and bigger war nearer home, the War of the Austrian Succession. In any case, Walpole's power was gone. England's first prime minister went out of office in 1742, leaving his legacy of the cabinet system of ministers. For practical purposes this had superseded the Privy Council.

Governor Gooch limped back to Williamsburg, with wounds in both ankles from a twenty-four-pounder cannonball. The aftereffect of the unsuccessful assault on the Spanish American territory was felt more in Virginia than in England. The vengeful Spanish fleet attacked Georgia (formerly held by Spain) in 1742, and fear spread rumors across Virginia's coastal areas. Citizens went armed in the port city of Norfolk, where an Anglican rector preached with loaded pistols on the pulpit. The alarms gradually passed, but the historically unremembered intercontinental expedition was a precursor of the changes to come which, drawing the Colony out of its parochial concerns, threatened the perpetual tranquillity of the era.

4

Other portents of change occurred after Gooch resumed his residence in the Governor's Palace. The last of the seventeenth-century men of the oligarchy passed from the scene when Colonel William Byrd died in 1744, after one year as Council President. Something else also passed with Byrd, though none was aware of this at the time. As the archetype of the England-oriented Virginians, whose style and tastes were formed by British models, Byrd represented the declining few to whom the mother country meant ''home'' in its sense of personal associations. Some Virginians continued to go to school or college in England, and to study law at the Middle Temple (although their number was never large), but even to them Virginia was ''home.''

When Byrd had been growing up in England, his introductions into society were made by his mother's socially well-placed family — Byrd's maternal grandfather, uncles and aunts, and cousins his own age. Then he had reinforced familial ties by his marriage to an English lady. By the eighteenth century the family ties of students in England were mostly or entirely in Virginia.

More significantly to the majority, the element of time placed emotional distance between the mother country and the Virginians born in the eighteenth century. In their Virginian-English duality they might have thought of themselves interchangeably as Virginians and Englishmen; but while nationalistically identified with the mother country or the Empire, in the immediate associations of their day-to-day living they were becoming Virginians more than they realized. As the inconsistencies in the external-internal divisions were blunted by traditional practices and acceptance of the Empire's framework of authority, so the people's political and sentimental conditioning stifled any sense of separateness in the generations then mature or coming into maturity. Time, however, was unobtrusively weakening the physical links in the structure as it existed in Gooch's regime — time and character changes in the rising generation of the ruling class.

Now sixteen-year-old William Byrd III inherited Westover and the major properties developed by his grandfather, and the new master of the manor was neither dilettante nor prudent administrator of his estate. The young Byrd was the first Inheritor among the major families to squander a fortune in high living and reckless gambling. He was the prototype of the latter-day "idle rich" — illustrator of the theme of "shirt-sleeves to shirt-sleeves in three generations."

At the adjoining plantation, the third William Byrd's contemporary, Benjamin Harrison V, inherited Berkeley the year after young Byrd came home to Westover. Harrison's father, with two young daughters, was killed by lightning while closing an upper-story window during a thunderstorm. Twenty-year-old Ben Harrison was large, hearty, and affable, with a natural bent toward and gift for the political maneuvering at which the men of his family on both sides had excelled. His maternal grandfather, King Carter, and his Harrison great-grandfather had worked together in forming the core of the oligarchy, and his Harrison grandfather and father (both of whom died young), along with uncles and cousins, had been political powers in Williamsburg. The new master of Berkeley, not a mental type, had attended William and Mary, and soon after his majority entered the House of Burgesses. A skillful operator on committees, the fifth Benjamin Harrison would be conspicuous among those of the generation of unacquisitive Inheritors who devoted their main energies and talents to the Virginia General Assembly.

Since between the extremes of Harrison and Byrd there were many gradations in the behavior of the generation of the Inheritors, there could be no single type to characterize the full flowering of the golden age, as King Carter and the older Harrisons and William Byrd I had typified the generation of the Great Accumulators. Yet young Ben Harrison did typify those Inheritors who continued the responsible absorption in government of the earlier generations, and the third William Byrd led the vanguard of those who set the new fashion for extravagant and ostentatious living.

There had always been gentlemen in the Colony who enjoyed (by colonial standards) luxurious appointments and a vanity in display, occasionally straining their resources. In the generation of Inheritors

A horse race
Engraving from Richard Blome's Gentleman's Recreation,
second edition 1710 (Colonial Williamsburg Collection)

who came into maturity with William Byrd III there was a more widespread tendency toward splendor in the manor houses, in clothes (especially of the ladies), and in a baronial style of living. As it began to become commonplace for wealthy families to build showplaces, usually in brick, with handsomely carved interior woodwork, more and more planters imported fine furniture, silver, and glass and indulged in lavish entertainment of guests. Native horses ceased to be good enough for the informal races on private racecourses and, after a racetrack was laid east of the Capitol at Williamsburg, grandsons of the Great Accumulators began importing blooded studs to stand on breeding farms. William Byrd III was one of the breeders of blooded horses entirely for racing.

A significant difference between those few individuals of the seventeenth century who cultivated magnificence and the big spenders of the new generation was that these Inheritors began to live beyond their means, to live off capital and run into debt. While William Byrd II, for all his expectations of having life made "easy" for him, had known where money came from, his son — as prototype of the extravagant Inheritors — spent as if the source were inexhaustible. However, during Gooch's benign administration, the beginning of the spread of luxury spending merely brought more splendor into plantation life and more gaiety into Public Times in Williamsburg.

When the General Assembly met and General Court was held in Public Times during spring and fall, Williamsburg was transformed from the appearance of an English country town (as one visitor saw it) into a metropolis of the New World (as another visitor saw it). During the winter months, with few severe spells and usually some stretches of mild days, and during the stifling summers, when the breathless, humid heat gathered over the flat, water-drained lands of Tidewater, approximately fifteen hundred persons in Gooch's day lived as permanent residents in the "city" consisting of about two hundred and fifty buildings of all kinds (not including stables and carriage houses). During Public Times this number more than tripled, and five thousand people crowded into the inns, taverns, ordinaries, public houses, and private homes.

The families of the Councilors and the Burgesses comprised only a small proportion of this transient population. The families of consequence, who were not (or not then) in the General Assembly,

Slaves on a South Carolina plantation, about 1800. Artist unknown
(Abby Aldrich Rockefeller Folk Art Collection, Williamsburg, Virginia)

A family group. Painting by Charles Phillips, about 1745
(Colonial Williamsburg Collection)

came to town at the same time, for this was the social season in Virginia. Dinners and parties and balls were given continuously, as the ladies and gentlemen stored up the pleasures of human society to last them in the coming months. Also, back of the Capitol the merchant-planters gathered in the open Exchange, to discuss prices and conditions, to pay debts and contract debts, and to conduct various other matters of business.

The concentration of substantial citizens attracted all manner of lesser people — adventurers and whores, entertainers and promoters of entertainment, and those who came in to see the sights. Fairs were always held on the broad, grassy expanse of Market Square, where there were contests between strong men, fiddlers, dancers, and even a beauty contest. Footraces were run along wide Duke of Gloucester Street from the college to the Capitol, pigs with soaped tails were chased, fighting cocks were matched, and horses raced at the track. In the crowded taverns the drinking was heavy and sometimes boisterous, and gambling could run up comparatively high stakes.

In these Public Times when the sandy, rutted Duke of Gloucester Street crawled with planters' coaches-and-sixes, and there was an air of bustle around all the buildings, the impression Williamsburg gave of being a city was really false. Government was its only business, its reason for existence. Not a port, and without manufacturing, Williamsburg had been designed — with its straight streets on a mile-long rectangle — as a graceful, reposeful seat of government. Restrictions were enforced on the type of houses which could be built, the space to be occupied, and flower gardens were cultivated by most of the house owners.

When the crowds left after Public Times and the town returned to its slumbrous state, the important permanent residents were officials of the government and of the county (as Williamsburg was also the courthouse of James City County), and the faculty of the college. Probably the largest single group of inhabitants was composed of keepers of taverns, inns, ordinaries, and public houses, and the servants employed in them. There were the usual representatives of the professions: doctors and lawyers; there were apothecaries, who sometimes doubled as doctors, and dentists, who sometimes doubled as surgeons. There was enough year-round business to keep going the bakers and butchers, barbers and blacksmiths, goldsmiths and gunsmiths (the leading gunsmith built a charming house facing the Palace Green, which led from the Duke of Gloucester Street to the Governor's Palace), milliners and midwives, the printers who published the Colony's newspaper — the *Virginia Gazette* — and pamphlets, shoemakers and snuffmakers, tailors and tinsmiths, watchmakers and wigmakers. There were merchants and a few stores similar to the retail stores of a later date.

(In all the Colony, the Nelsons in nearby Yorktown were just about the only family of merchants — trade was their sole business and not an adjunct to tobacco-planting — who rose to power in the planter oligarchy during this period, and they married into the Carter and Burwell families.)

Since the acquisition of land was the abiding interest of nearly all planters of any substance, an important profession was that of surveyor, and the Surveying Office — which granted commissions to surveyors — was located at William and Mary. The place of land in the Virginian consciousness transcended the tobacco-growers' necessity for new land and the profits potential in speculation. Although land meant status, as to the English landowning gentry, it also meant something indefinably more. There was an adventure about the acquisition of land which drew men who had neither the need for more acres for tobacco-growing nor the cash from speculation, and whose status could scarcely be improved. At the same time, new land was the one answer to the tobacco-exhausted land in the old regions; also, its acquisition drew men on the way up, modest Inheritors making the ascent into the elite. Yet men went after land whether they needed it or not, and even when its acquisition served an immediate purpose, the chase — as when men who liked hunting shot game for their tables — absorbed them.

Governor Gooch himself, with no personal stake in land acquisition, was involved in the interests of friends in the General Assembly who were developing great land companies in the west. And it was these large-scale land operations west of the Tidewater, promoted by political forces from the old regions, that presaged the most fundamental change in the idyllic era of the golden age. For these westward expansions by land speculators encroached on territory claimed by the French and set in motion the events which shattered the self-sufficient parochialism of Virginia.

As time seemed suspended in Gooch's era, in space too the Colony seemed suspended above all the clashes of nations. It seemed to exist untroubled by international power confrontations in, almost literally, a world of its own. The change began in the year of Byrd's death, 1744, when Gooch effected another of the numerous treaties which colonial governors made with Indians.

5

When Major Gooch had come to Virginia, unlike his predecessors, he negotiated with Indian tribes in order to maintain peace between the Indians themselves rather than to protect the colonists. However, the existing treaties forbade the passage of out-of-state Indians only east of the Blue Ridge, and, as settlements began to scatter west of the mountains, they were threatened by raiding parties from the Six Nations. In 1744, Gooch negotiated a treaty with the Six Nations at Lancaster, Pennsylvania, which ensured peace — at least from systematic, large-scale marauding — on Virginia's opening northern and western frontiers.

The whole negotiation, including the payment of £200 to the Indians as a sign of good will, cost Virginia only £1,260, and the price seemed cheap for a treaty which would encourage the expansion of the populous areas and increase the Colony's trade. The immediate effect, however, was the opening of opportunity for individual wealth to politically connected men with the enterprise for land speculation on a vast scale.

The following year John Robinson, the Speaker of the House, received the permission of the Council — on which his father had succeeded Byrd as President — to obtain from the Governor a patent of 100,000 acres on the Greenbrier River. Later he incorporated this patent, in what is now West Virginia, into the Greenbrier Company.

The powerfully allied John Robinson, the dominant figure in the oligarchy for the next twenty years, from 1745 to 1765, has suffered a curious historical anonymity. As Treasurer of the Colony as well as Speaker, he became the central figure in a great financial scandal which shook the whole oligarchy. This scandal loosened the oligarchy's absolute control of Virginia politics and permitted young revolution-

John Robinson, Speaker of the House of Burgesses
Portrait by John Wollaston, about 1758
(Colonial Williamsburg Collection)

aries — some from *outside* Tidewater — to gain positions of authority. Robinson, a wealthy man, personally made no profit from his misuse of public funds to make unsecured "loans" to friends in the oligarchy. However, since the planter-politicians who benefited from Robinson's poor judgment were a cross section of Virginia's *Almanack de Gotha*, his own reputation was ruined rather than the reputations of those who had benefited. As the exposure came after his death, no general denunciation was made of him at the time. Francis Fauquier, then Governor, explained the loans as "the sensibility of his too generous heart." But later every effort was made to expunge his name from Virginia's colonial history. Nonetheless, the fact was that when heroes now known to every American schoolchild were nobodies, John Robinson controlled the political oligarchy that controlled Virginia.

The same year that Robinson's Greenbrier Company was founded, the English courts decided in favor of Lord Fairfax's claims for the extension of the Proprietary. Seven land grants made by Charles II during his exile had been acquired by Lord Culpeper in the 1680's and, through the marriage of Culpeper's daughter, went to the Fairfaxes as the (roughly) two-million-acre Proprietary in the Northern Neck. As the Proprietors, the Fairfaxes collected the quitrents (taxes) on the land which in other sections of the Colony went to the Crown.

Of the several Virginia agents for the Proprietary, the only successful one — both for the Fairfaxes and himself — was King Carter. During his second period (1722–32) as agent, Carter entered claims which tripled the Proprietary's holdings from under two million acres to more than five million.

In Charles II's original grants, made before Virginia had been mapped beyond the head of tidewater in the great rivers, the Proprietary's holdings were defined as "between the headwaters of the Potomac and the Rappahannock." In a long, single-handed battle with the Virginia courts, King Carter contended that the southern branch of the Rappahannock (later the Rapidan) constituted the veritable Rappahannock and that the headwaters of the Potomac originated in the Alleghenies.

It was only after the death of Carter, who had kept the claim alive, that Lord Fairfax bestirred himself to exert influence in England. Simultaneously he appointed his cousin, William Fairfax, to act as his agent in Virginia. Through Cousin William the Fairfaxes gained some important local support. William Fairfax became a Councilor and his daughter Anne married Lawrence Washington in 1743.

When the courts had awarded Lord Fairfax the audacious claims instigated by King Carter twenty years before, his Lordship seemed primarily aware of the two hundred thousand acres which Carter had patented for his own heirs, rather than sensing any gratitude for having his estate increased by more than three million fertile acres. In this, Fairfax reflected both the selfishly self-indulgent attitude of the nonproductive nobility and the assumption of the mercantile powers that the colonials existed for the enrichment of Britishers. However, an English title held great glamour in the Colony and, despite the gouge in tax revenues that Fairfax's Proprietary diverted from the Crown, it was a big thing when his Lordship shifted his residence to his Virginia domain. The validation of the Fairfax Proprietary, following Gooch's Lancaster Treaty with the Indians, seemed to act as an impetus to the formation of large-scale land companies to operate north and west and south of the Proprietary's boundaries.

Two years later (1747), Thomas Lee was the leader of a group who formed the Ohio Company to patent land to the north and west, in the vicinity of the present city of Pittsburgh. Thomas Lee, fifty-seven, had by circumstance come along at the tag end of the era of the Great Accumulators, although his grandfather, Richard Lee I, had come in the first wave of the fortune-builders back in the 1640's. It happened that Richard Lee II, Thomas's father, had been a scholarly recluse, and, while a leader in government as ranking Councilor, was content to conserve his inherited estate when his contemporaries and younger men were growing rich by aggressively acquiring then unsettled lands in Tidewater. As Thomas Lee was a younger son, his inheritance had been comparatively a pittance; also, though he had powerful connections through kinship, at the precise time of his coming into maturity no Lees held positions of influence in the Carter-Harrison-Ludwell-Blair oligarchy then controlling Virginia.

With only rudimentary education but (as they said) "of strong natural parts" and illimitable ambition, Thomas Lee started young to duplicate the rise of his grandfather, "the Emigrant" — who, along with founding a fortune as a merchant and planter, had served as Virginia's first Attorney General and as one of the most influential

Councilors in the days when the Council, with the Governor, ran the Colony. Thomas Lee had learned something about large-scale land grants when as a young man he acted briefly as agent for the Fairfax-owned Proprietary, between the two long agencies of King Carter. Like all the Proprietary's agents, Lee had been "his own best customer" — patenting choice lands for himself. Though he did not patent on the scale of King Carter, neither had he extended Fairfax's holdings. It was after his term as agent that Lee became a competitor of King Carter and developed his own extensive holdings along the Potomac, on which he built his massive baronial seat, Stratford.

The Lees were usually good marriers, and Thomas married an heiress of the old oligarchs, Hannah Harrison Ludwell. To them eventually came Green Spring, the manor house built in the 1640's by Governor Sir William Berkeley. Politically Lee rose to succeed his enemy, King Carter, on the Council in 1732, and in 1747 he was next in rank to President John Robinson, Sr.

Thomas Lee was not, however, close to John Robinson II, the *de facto* leader of the Tidewater oligarchy. An indefinable distinction, nothing like so definite as a division, was growing between the planter-entrepreneurs of "lower Tidewater" and the Potomac, or northern, side of the Northern Neck peninsula. Technically all the land drained by the tidal rivers was Tidewater, but the word was coming to mean the region between the Rappahannock and the James, and the eastern-most parts of the Northern Neck. Westward, where the Potomac took a northerly turn and was of great distance from the center of things at Williamsburg, a neighborhood was developing its own self-awareness within the customs and values of the older Tidewater, which had been settled around Jamestown.

In the Ohio Company, Thomas Lee joined neighbors of the Potomac region, including influential Colonel William Fairfax and Lawrence Washington. Despite his poor health after the Cartagena expedition, Washington was steadily growing in position in the Colony. Secretary Thomas Nelson, the Yorktown merchant, represented the Tidewater power — although he later shifted to the land company controlled by John Robinson's group. The Virginians shrewdly included powerfully connected Englishmen in their newly formed company, and in 1747 applied to Governor Gooch for their land grant.

Gooch refused them, giving the reason that the territory they planned to occupy would conflict with the French. Since it was suspected that Gooch's real reason was to protect John Robinson's group from competition, the Ohio Company had its English partners exert influence with the Board of Trade.

The Board of Trade ruled (September 2, 1748) for the grant, allotting two hundred thousand acres in the vicinity of the forks of the Ohio River, at the present site of Pittsburgh. When a fort was built there, and two hundred families settled, the Ohio Company would receive an additional grant of three hundred thousand acres. This half-a-million-acre grant was on the largest scale of granting public lands to private operators since Charles II's carelessly given rewards to his favorites a century before.

Before the grant was issued the following year, Gooch, acting with the Council, issued eight hundred thousand western acres to John Robinson's newly formed Loyal Company, independent of his more modest Greenbrier Company. This enormous grant, extending into what became Kentucky, was located far south of the Ohio Company's grant in order to avoid conflict between the rival groups. Although territorial conflicts were avoided, the rivalry between the two land companies was intense and laid the groundwork for continuous political maneuvering.

6

The Loyal Company, along with subscribers from the lower Tidewater, took in several extremely active members from the newly formed Albemarle County. At the foothills of the Blue Ridge, this rolling Piedmont country was the westernmost of the settled regions extending, parallel to the James River, from the older plantations in the area of the Falls at Richmond. This beguiling countryside was thinly settled in comparison to the older regions, and ambitious men were developing good-sized holdings of the fertile land. Two of the most ambitious who became members in the Loyal Company were the friends Peter Jefferson and Dr. Thomas Walker, both surveyors.

Peter Jefferson had grown up west of the Falls where his father, the son of an obscure yeoman, had developed fair-sized holdings and won acceptance among the scattered gentry in the then frontier community. Peter Jefferson, a man of enormous physical strength, had the abilities to support his ambition to advance his position beyond his small inheritance. Working his expanding holdings, he trained himself in the useful profession of surveying: this both provided an income and served as a means of discovering and patenting unclaimed lands. Developing himself personally, Jefferson was able to take advantage of his propinquity to neighbors from the ruling Tidewater families in the sparsely settled community.

William Randolph I, one of the Great Accumulators of the generation who were in Virginia by 1670, had established his home plantation at Turkey Island, upriver from the Westover-Berkeley-Shirley manorial row on the James. He and his wife, the former Mary Isham, had nine children who by marriage into families in the ruling order placed the Randolphs at the center of the interweaving dynastic families which formed the "web of kinship." As an illustration, William Randolph II, a slightly younger contemporary of William Byrd II, inherited Turkey Island and married Byrd's neighbor on one side, Anne Harrison, and a great-grandson married Elizabeth Carter of Shirley.

Thomas Randolph, the second son of William and Mary Isham Randolph (the Colony's Adam and Eve), was among the very first of the substantial gentry to move west of the Falls. He founded an estate called Tuckahoe on the river fifteen miles above Richmond. His son William returned to lower Tidewater for his wife, Judith Page. The daughter of Councilor Mann Page and granddaughter of King Carter, she had grown up in Rosewell, the first and most magnificent of the manor houses built after 1720. This William of Tuckahoe was five years younger than Peter Jefferson, and on the frontier the grandsons of the obscure yeoman and of the dynasty-founder became friends. Soon Peter Jefferson joined his line to the dynasty.

Thomas Randolph's younger brother, Captain Isham Randolph, was a merchant seaman (both merchant and ship captain), and spent more of his early years out of Virginia than at home. In London, Captain Randolph married an English girl, Jane Rogers, and then settled down on an estate, Dungeness, near his brother Thomas's Tuckahoe. The Isham Randolphs had a daughter, Jane, born about 1720, and this girl with the English mother and the seafaring father lived in the isolation of scattered holdings remote from the social life of her Randolph kin in Tidewater. Among her visiting neighbors was the powerfully built landowning surveyor Peter Jefferson, friend of her cousin William Randolph. When she was about nineteen and Peter Jefferson was thirty-one, in 1739, Jane married him.

After the birth of their son Thomas in 1743, when William Randolph died, according to an agreement Peter Jefferson moved with his family into Tuckahoe and supervised the management of that plantation for the next five or six years. By this arrangement, Thomas Jefferson spent several formative years of his childhood in the house with young cousins allied by blood with the Randolphs, Pages, and Carters. By inference rather than evidence, it would seem that the lordly young products of these privileged crosslines did not make a totally happy impression on Peter Jefferson's son. He was entirely his father's child, and the environment he claimed for his own was the rolling country of Albemarle to which his father returned shortly after he became a member of the Loyal Company.

Of the leaders of the Loyal Company who were actually in the west, Dr. Thomas Walker was the most active from first to last, and became the most powerfully connected politically. Not deliberately obscured by history as was his friend John Robinson, Dr. Walker never received the recognition due him as one of the truly protean figures of his generation — partly, perhaps, because along with others he became overshadowed by those who made Revolutionary reputations. Though Thomas Walker was a medical doctor, and a very good one (he was physician to his friend Peter Jefferson), the practice of medicine was almost incidental to his boundless activities: he was a successful merchant, a surveyor who acquired large land holdings, and an explorer, leading the first party into Kentucky; drawing on his mercantile background, he served as commissary general in the French and Indian Wars, and for thirty years was a member of the House of Burgesses.

Born in Tidewater, Walker studied medicine under his brother-in-law Dr. George Gilmer, who was established in Williamsburg as physician, surgeon, and apothecary. When licensed to practice medicine, Dr. Walker established himself in the new town of Fredericksburg, at the head of the tidal water on the Rappahannock, midway between Richmond and the Potomac. While gaining a reputation as an "eminent surgeon" and a teacher (training students who later became famous), he operated a store in Fredericksburg and then another store in Louisa County. For these he imported directly from England everything from gunpowder to clothing and household utensils.

Walker's trade was in the trend of the small mercantile establishments which were competing with the stores at the wharves of the big merchant-planters. In 1741, when twenty-six, Walker married a widow, Mildred Thornton Meriwether, through whom he acquired eleven thousand acres in Albemarle, part of a grant to the late Mr. Meriwether. After he came into this tract (on which he later built a manor house, Castle Hill), Dr. Walker began exploring trips over the mountains and down the valley to the southwest. These first trips seemed more in the way of adventure to a physically strong man with restless energy and widely ranging curiosity. The sort of person who had to get inside everything he did, Dr. Walker trained himself as a surveyor, and in 1749 he was appointed agent for the Loyal Company with the assignment of exploring the wilderness for the lands that were patented.

With this aggressive partnership in the field, the Loyal Company — and this also happened later in the Ohio Company — represented a strong working alliance between families established in the ruling class and families rising in the fluid hierarchical structure adapted from England a century before. It also represented the extension of the Tidewater oligarchy's interests into the new regions in the west, with implications for the future that none seemed to consider in the sudden rush to land speculation.

On the same day of the eight-hundred-thousand-acre grant to John Robinson's Loyal Company, two other grants went to applicants who had not formally organized companies. One of these was to Peyton Randolph, recently appointed Attorney General of the Colony. The son of the late Colonel Byrd's friend Lady Susannah Randolph, Peyton Randolph was a cousin of John Robinson, through their Beverley mothers, and, through his recent marriage, brother-in-law of young Benjamin Harrison. John Robinson, with the support of Gooch, used grants and partnerships in the land-grant companies both to reward the faithful in the old-line Tidewater clique and to gain or cement the alliance of supporters for his group in the political rivalry with the Potomac faction represented in the Ohio Company. Thomas Nelson shifted from the Ohio Company to the Loyal Company to align himself with the greater significance of Robinson's old-liners.

Outside the political implications, the stimulus of these huge grants started small-scale or would-be operators applying for patents, and grants of from two hundred to ten thousand acres were allotted continually. Surveying became suddenly an enticing profession through its association with western land speculation, and at least twenty Burgesses tried their hands at it.

Good Governor Gooch was not to experience any of the effects of the speculation craze which involved Virginians with the French. His tranquil and prosperous administration had been recognized by the bestowal of a knighthood, and, his health failing, Sir William Gooch felt that after twenty-two years he had earned a rest. Even while working on western grants, he had made his farewell speech to the General Assembly toward the close of the spring session in May, 1749.

". . . I am grown old and infirm, and the leave his Majesty has been graciously pleased to grant me of going home for the recovery of my health, was, I must confess, on my humble application; yet be assured, though supported by the comfortable hopes of relief, I shall not, without great reluctance, depart from a country, to which, by the sincerest affection, a long residence, and the changes and chances of this mortal life, I am so nearly allied."

He stayed on in the Governor's Palace until June, until signing the grant for the Loyal Company, and then left Williamsburg for England. Sir William had only a few years of retirement before he died. The era in Virginia which he had graced began to fade after his departure.

Although all the portents of change were present, the era did not end abruptly nor the new begin immediately. But changes did come fast, too fast for the generation which rose into power in the afterglow of warmth left by Gooch's residency in Williamsburg.

· 2 ·

End of an Era

Chapter Three

THE WAY FOR WAR

IF THERE WAS NO SINGLE TYPE in the generation of the ruling class who came to power at mid-century, there was one man, Richard Bland, whom the aristocrats themselves regarded as embodying what they liked to think of as typical of the best in Virginia. Of the Inheritors' generation, all born in the eighteenth century, Bland was one of the ablest — "the best constitutional mind in the House" — of those who, conserving their estates, gave their talents to government and made Virginia's General Assembly a breeding ground of political genius. Only as an Inheritor, and a prudent one, could Richard Bland have had the undistracted time to devote his single-minded attention to the study of theories of government combined with the practice of practical politics. The hardest-working member of the House of Burgesses, he was among the drafters (often the sole drafter) of nearly every important legislative paper, and the one to whom all turned for the articulation of any principle.

As the antithesis to Byrd's English-influenced elegance, Richard Bland had the carelessness about dress and formality which his contemporaries thought of as the best outward expression of the character of the Virginia planter. It suggested at once an aristocratic inner assurance and the habiliments appropriate to *landed* gentry, plantation gentlemen actively associated with agriculture. For Bland was, through his family connections, at the heart of the "web of kinship," and no man in the ruling class was more "one of them."

Also, unlike Byrd's dilettantism, Bland's learning was respected because it was applied to, and illumined, the political problems of the Colony. His peers complimented him as "learned" and as a "man of erudition and intelligence." Widely read, his area of specialization was English history, focused in the comparative study of English government and its relationship to colonial political developments. Since Bland's highly correlative intelligence, trained in the classics and law, served his fellow Burgesses as a continual source of guidance during the times of change, it was natural that the unpretentious and bookish doer came to represent (as was said of him later by historian H. J. Eckenrode) "that type considered characteristically Virginian — half practical farmer, half classical scholar and lawyer; genial, well-mannered, personally somewhat untidy and careless of dress."

Not only did this type represent what Bland's generation considered the best produced by their land-rooted society: with passing time, he became the prototype of the traditional Virginia planter. Not all who came after him, any more than all his contemporaries, were really practical farmers, and in many planters classical scholarship was superficial and even nonexistent. Richard Bland's type represented the ideal, and few Virginia planters deviated from the tradition in its outward manifestations — the well-mannered geniality of the responsible country squire. There was nothing English here at all, except the original of the landed gentry, and even this was forgotten in the frontier's mutations of the original, along with the purely native characteristics developed by many environmental factors, including specifically the casual habit of absolute authority.

By Bland's era, Virginians had accustomed themselves, as the English had earlier, to attitudes and activities based upon inherited wealth. After Byrd's generation (whose *fathers* had made the fortunes), it was possible to assume, as the English did, that wealth, with its concomitant position, had been there "always."

There was, however, one fundamental difference between the Virginian landed wealth and the English landed wealth. English management consisted chiefly of collecting rents, and the very rich hired subordinates to do even that. Virginian management required competence in the actual operations of the revenue-producing estates, mostly in tobacco-growing lands.

While most were aware of this difference, problems arose for the Inheritors' families where individuals were, for one reason or another, incompetent. There were not many like William Byrd III, who squandered in a lifetime all that their forebears had garnered, but the growing tendency toward splendor and high living was not always accompanied by sound commercial judgment. Then too, many highly placed planters who were not notably extravagant lacked the business acumen to meet changing conditions. English merchants visiting in the Colony found many of their customers to be "poor businessmen." Although these planters operated their plantations conscientiously and were on the whole responsible men, the emphasis was not on business: it was on style and politics.

Basically, the assumption that wealth, having been there "always," would always be there had assumed a static condition. As everything in the two decades of Gooch's administration had tended to confirm this expectation of continuity, there was nothing to announce to the newly planted aristocracy that the era of time suspended was passing.

Richard Bland, a prototype of his generation as the vastly acquisitive King Carter had been *the* prototype of the Accumulators' generation, was a sound manager of his plantation, living comfortably and usually debt-free. His Jordan's Point plantation was not among the great holdings, and he did not build on it one of the impressive manor houses. Nor had his Virginia forebears been among those who had acquired sudden wealth on an enormous scale. In the Bland line, there was a continuity of money extending from England — although earned rather than inherited money.

2

While the first Richard Lee was known to have been a kinsman of successful London merchants, and John Carter, the King's father, was believed to have been a kinsman of London vintners, Richard Bland's grandfather, Theodorick Bland, had been in partnership with his brother in an international mercantile house, and their families were established in high political circles in London. The Bland brothers had acquired the land of two James River plantations, Berkeley and Westover, after the original settlements had fallen into decay, and Theodorick Bland came to Virginia in the mid-1650's to develop the holdings commercially. With his mercantile background in England, he was quickly successful in Virginia, and "in fortune" he was "inferior to no person of his time in the country."

Fortunes in Theodorick Bland's time — before the general use of large slave-labor forces for volume production and before the growth of the population of small planters made riches for the wharf stores of the big merchant-planters — were not so vast as the wealth later acquired in King Carter's generation. Successful for his day, Theodorick Bland also possessed the stature as a man to place him in the then small group of political powers centered around the autocratic and aristocratic Governor Sir William Berkeley. After serving as Speaker of the House, Bland was appointed to the august Council, on which he had served seven years when he died, young, in 1671.

He left a widow, the daughter of former Governor Richard Bennett, and three small children. The family was befriended by the leading powers of Berkeley's cabal, including the Ludwell brothers, and the children came into a sizable estate. After Berkeley had been sold to the Harrisons and Westover to the Byrds, Theodorick's son, the first Richard Bland, established his own plantation at Jordan's Point. On the south side of the James, this was upriver from Berkeley, in Prince George County. The land there was very rich.

Richard Bland, Sr. (born 1665), a contemporary of King Carter, did not compete with the Accumulators of his generation for great wealth. He ran a prosperous plantation, on which he raised extensive livestock, and invested in other properties, including a lot on Duke of Gloucester Street in early Williamsburg. In the custom of his class of assuming political and community responsibility, Richard Bland, Sr., served in the House of Burgesses, as his county's justice of the peace, as a vestryman of Bruton Parish, and as a member of the Board of Visitors of William and Mary. Though not among the most prominent figures politically, Bland was personally an intimate of the ruling powers of his day, and frequently spent the night with William Byrd on his way to Williamsburg. He was on such terms with William and Mary Randolph, of Turkey Island, that he married their daughter

Elizabeth — one of the nine children who spread the Randolph strain.

Of this socially prestigious couple, Richard Bland II was born in 1710. His sister Elizabeth married William Beverley, the son of the historian Robert Beverley and Byrd's sister Ursula; his sister Anne married Robert Munford, whose son became Virginia's first playwright; and his sister Mary married Colonel Henry Lee. This Lee, a brother of Thomas Lee, founded the Leesylvania line of the family, which produced Robert Edward Lee. When the second Richard Bland was scarcely ten years old, his mother and father died within three months of one another, and he was placed under the guardianship of his uncles, William Randolph II of Turkey Island and Richard Randolph of Curles' Neck. (Curles' Neck had once been the property of Nathaniel Bacon, the Rebel, and young Richard's great-uncle Giles Bland had been hanged as one of Bacon's lieutenants in the civil war against Sir William Berkeley.)

As the firstborn son, he inherited the home plantation and thirty slaves. His uncles saw to it that the orphaned master of Jordan's Point received a sound education through the means then available in Virginia — tutors and small private schools, similar to Byrd's school at Westover where Bland's Beverley nephew died. As was the custom, he was also trained in the management of his estate and evidently enjoyed his work as a practical planter. When barely nineteen he married Anne Poythress, sixteen, and Bland had no trouble in amply providing for the twelve children she bore him.

His formal education was at William and Mary, where six professors instructed him in rhetoric, science, mathematics, and the classics, for which he formed an abiding love. Bland trained himself in the law, but evidently did not begin this study until after he had served as justice of the peace in his county — actually as a magistrate who sat on the local courts.

These courts, the dominant political bodies in their counties, were composed of the same type of substantial planters (frequently even the same men) who were sent to the Burgesses, and served as a training ground and steppingstone to the Capitol. Since the county courts had many legislative functions, assessed taxes and granted licenses and supervised highways, the members were close to the daily lives of the people and represented the oligarchic government at local levels. Appointed by option, the justices exercised their considerable influence — in the main — with the same responsibility as the members of the General Assembly, and when men like Richard Bland advanced to the House of Burgesses, they were ready to participate fully in its operations and to act on important committees.

Richard Bland served on the county court for four years, from the age of twenty-eight to thirty-two, before he went to the House of Burgesses. When he was admitted to practice law, four years later, at thirty-six, he had continued to work from his local base in gradually establishing political control of Prince George County. While the opportunity for such control was mostly restricted to men of families in the ruling class — or men at least associated with it, through marriage or some other connection — to gain control required both a command of practical politics and the *earned* trust of the freeholders. The acknowledgment that Bland was accepted as his county's leading citizen was made by his appointment as colonel of its militia. From then on his listings in the records change from "Richard Bland, Gent." to "Col. Richard Bland."

He was a lean, spare man who enjoyed good health and — judging from the work load the House put on him, the hours he spent in study, along with running his plantation and engaging in various side ventures — he must have exercised superb control of his energies. With a family of twelve children in the house, visits from his married brother Theodorick and his married sisters, Bland did not follow the style of the new grandees in ostentatious entertainment. Although he raised livestock, he did not gamble at the racetracks nor was he among those who imported blooded studs. His only extravagances seem to have been books and old Virginia documents, of which he became a famous collector.

Forty at mid-century, and coming into the fullness of his powers, Bland would work at Williamsburg in association with contemporaries who, like himself, had been influenced by the harmonious resolution of English and Virginian interests during Gooch's benevolent administration. Landon Carter, like Bland, had been seventeen when Gooch came during the political stability established by the old oligarchy, with Landon's father as President of the Council. Bland's first cousin, Peyton Randolph, had been only six, and Randolph's brother-in-law, Benjamin Harrison V, only two — with no memory of life beyond the idyllic era.

These were enlightened as well as powerful Burgesses, continually alert for any encroachment on colonial liberties and the rights of the General Assembly, but they had all been formed of the traditional attitude of Virginia's unchanging place in the British Empire. Implicit loyalty to the Crown was an article of faith in their security in the stable structure of the good society. Within this conceptual frame, their reactions and actions were governed — or at least influenced — by tradition, precedent, loyalties as British subjects, and acceptance of "what hath been the ancient custom."

In the changes that came with the new era, the oligarchy — with its power now centered in the House of Burgesses — sought to continue the relations with England as they had been under "our late Sir William Gooch . . . our great protector and benefactor." As the city officials of Williamsburg expressed it to the new Governor, Virginians had been fortunate in their recent governors and hoped that "we shall be preserved in our rights and privileges."

The working core of the oligarchy in the House, of which Richard Bland became the spokesman, was essentially concerned with no more than maintaining the existing relationships between Virginia and the home government. However, they were most passionately concerned with that, and, as their spokesman, Richard Bland started upon a career in a field never entered before by a Virginian. He became a pamphleteer, the most effective writer of polemical political essays of his generation and an incalculable influence on the generation who would join his in government during the next two decades.

The pamphlet in Virginia (as in the other colonies) was the most direct medium of communication of controversial material. In its day, the pamphlet alone served in the place of all present-day communications media — newspaper editorials and columns, television and radio commentators, magazines of opinion, and "timely" books rushed onto the market. The small sheets were easy to distribute and their concentration upon a single subject of current concern made the pamphlets references and guides for the political discussions in taverns and inns, at race meets and county courts, and, indeed — since political action was the continuing absorption of members of the ruling class — wherever men gathered.

Pamphlets had long been commonplace in England, written by professionals such as Daniel Defoe, a supporter of the rise of middle-class moneyed interests during Walpole's regime, and gentlemen amateurs such as Bolingbroke, the bitter attacker of the new England emerging in Walpole's ministry. In Virginia (as in the other colonies) pamphleteers were strictly amateurs. Also, all of Bland's pamphlets were directed to aspects of one single subject: the relationship of Virginia's government specifically, and by implication the colonial governments generally, to the home government. Beginning two years after Gooch's successor came to Williamsburg, Bland wrote the pamphlets which introduced what became a continuing debate over internal and external controls. With others, he brought into the open for analysis this tenuous division which had existed for so long in the pragmatic practices of custom.

With his personal involvement as a bulwark of the Colony's government, addressing himself to his countrymen and the royal governors on the fundamental principle of "preserving our rights and principles," Bland was not writing, as were the English pamphleteers, to open the floodgates of creative urges. Eschewing their hyperbolical and high-flown language, strewn with images and invective, he prepared his papers as a lawyer would prepare a case in equity. He arranged his arguments logically, based on reasonable propositions and historical precedents, in presenting the merits of the case. Though systematic, his pamphlets were not dry, and in one he used a deadly form of satirical humor. In their totality, the pamphlets of Richard Bland gave the first clear articulation of the nature of the political concepts — the germinal definitions — as developed among English people, transplanted to a new continent, who were being insensibly transformed into a new people, Americans.

Needless to say, the practical planter and scholar, constitutionalist and legislative drafter, who could give words to a people's inchoate assertions, would not be typical of any society. But in a society whose genius went into its government, and during a period of pivotal crisis, Bland was recognized as "the most learned and logical man of those who took prominent lead in public affairs, profound in constitutional logic." This was the judgment of Thomas Jefferson, whose generation took its place in the General Assembly in the 1760's with the natural impatience of young progressives toward an oligarchy (headed by John Robinson) who had controlled affairs for a quarter of a century. Long afterwards, Jefferson said that Bland "wrote the first pamphlet on the nature of the connection with Great Britain that had any pretension to accuracy of view on that subject.''

Richard Bland did not write anything at all, either for personal expression or publication (and evidently was a scanty correspondent), until he felt a threat to the happy, stable order left by Governor Gooch. At the age of forty in 1750, a conservative and preserver of the *status quo,* he had not been aroused to defense of the colonial point of view until Robert Dinwiddie had been Governor for two years.

3

Robert Dinwiddie assumed the office of lieutenant governor with a different background from all his predecessors: he had already lived in Virginia for a dozen years and had served as an ex officio member of the Council. In his position of Surveyor General of Customs for the Southern District of the colonies (the post once sought by William Byrd), he had insisted upon his right to sit with the Councilors when they acted as Advisory Council to the Governor. This was one of their three functions. Dinwiddie had not sat with the Councilors in their other two functions — when they acted as the upper house of the General Assembly and when they reviewed the inferior courts. Virginians felt that his familiarity with their government, gained during Gooch's ideal administration, assured them of no break in continuity. Also, Dinwiddie was an experienced veteran in colonial administration.

Born in Scotland of a mercantile family, Dinwiddie had begun his own career by forming a partnership with his brother in a Glasgow pottery company. At the age of twenty-eight, in 1721, he had gone to Bermuda in charge of admiralty affairs. He rose there to the post of Collector of Customs, with a seat on the Bermuda Council. After eleven years in the customs service, in 1738, he received his appointment as Surveyor General of the Southern District and elected to live in Virginia, forty-six miles from Williamsburg. During his association with the Council, he became close friends with Thomas Lee, leading organizer of the Ohio Company, and Colonel William Fairfax, the Proprietor's cousin and agent, and was generally well liked by all the Councilors. In the year of Gooch's retirement, 1749, Dinwiddie had retired from the colonial service and left Virginia to engage privately in trade.

Between Sir William Gooch's retirement and death, in 1751, no lieutenant governor was appointed, and three presidents of the Council served as acting governor. John Robinson, Sr., died after three months in office, and then Thomas Lee served for more than a year before he died. Lee was followed by Lewis Burwell, the grandson of King Carter who had caused the old man so much worry and heartache by his spendthrift ways and indifference to study while a student in London. When his grandfather's largesse was lost by Carter's death in 1732, Burwell returned to the Colony, settled down, and became a useful citizen. He held the office when Dinwiddie was appointed in July, 1751.

Returning to Virginia in November, Governor Dinwiddie made his formal entrance into Williamsburg where, with the background of some cannon salutes, he was met by dignitaries of the city, the college, and the church. Virginians enjoyed these ceremonials, and the fifty-eight-year-old Dinwiddie, paunchy and colorless, dutifully entered into the spirit of the thing. The new Governor looked what he was — all business, with a strong sense of "duty" (his word) and an inflexible determination. His plain-featured face had grown heavy, with a wide thin mouth cutting straight across the thick flesh, and the rolls that obscured his jawline ran into a pendulous double chin. Although he entirely lacked Gooch's charm and grace of manner, there was a reassuring forthrightness about him when he vied with the officials in exchanging compliments.

After he had settled into the now somewhat run-down Governor's Palace with his wife and two daughters — aged fourteen and eleven — the new Governor had to exchange more verbal bouquets when he met with the General Assembly in February, 1752. The Capitol had been burned in 1747 and, as the new building was not then completed, Dinwiddie's first meeting with the General Assembly was held in William and Mary. In his address Dinwiddie expressed his pleasure at being back among the people with whom he had "mingled in scenes of domestic felicity, and experienced the endearing reciprocations of friendship."

The Burgesses replied, "When we reflect on those social virtues, with which your Honor hath formerly distinguished yourself amongst

Robert Dinwiddie. Miniature, about 1750
(Colonial Williamsburg Collection)

us, we cannot but promise ourselves every pleasing aspect of an equitable and well-ordered government.'' With the aura of Sir William Gooch hanging over everybody, Virginians and the Governor (who said that Virginia was "now my country") were assuring one another that things would go on as before.

Already a course of events, in which Dinwiddie was personally involved, had been set in motion which would place the parochial tranquillity of Gooch's era in the past. The western land developments that had begun at the end of Gooch's administration had not expressed any of his interests. Grown old in office and with his health going bad, Gooch had not wanted to instigate change in the order any more than, say, had Colonel William Byrd II. Although potential conflict with the French was said to have been only Gooch's ostensible reason for not endorsing the Ohio Company's grants, it was true that in the year of his retirement a French force under Captain Celdron de Bienville was sent from Montreal to establish French claims to the Ohio River Valley and to cultivate relationships with the Indians.

The more vigorous Dinwiddie, both as a Briton (who gave his first loyalties to England) and as a governor interested in Virginia, regarded the French as intruders to be expelled. To him the settlement of the Ohio Valley was a necessity to Virginia's expansion and to the support of England's claims in the New World. The War of the Austrian Succession had ended in no more than a truce between England and France, and their rivalry for the country west of the Alleghenies was a reflection of their power struggle on the Continent. Since a link between the French settlements in Canada and Louisiana would limit England's American colonies to the coastal strip east of the Alleghenies, the Ohio Valley became the area of decision. With a continental, imperial perspective — the antithesis of Gooch's local view — Dinwiddie subscribed to the position defined by Council President Lewis Burwell:

"Notwithstanding the grants of the kings of England, France, or Spain, the property of these uninhabited parts of the world must be founded upon prior occupancy according to the law of nature.'' Since traveling parties staking claims could not constitute that right, but only "seating and cultivating the soil,'' it would be "highly for the interests of the Crown to encourage the seating of the lands westward as soon as possible to discourage the French.''

Dinwiddie, who had been involved in this race of settlers to win the territory before he became governor, held a personal stake in the expansion into the Ohio River Valley: he was a member of the Ohio Company, organized by his friend Thomas Lee. It was not only for the good of the Empire that commercial-minded Dinwiddie continued to stress the value of the ''skin and fur trade to be conducted'' in the opening frontier. When the Ohio Company was awarded its grant by the Board of Trade, Dinwiddie had worked closely with his friend John Hanbury, a rich London merchant and one of the English partners who used his influence in the Company's interests.

During Lee's tenure as acting governor, the Ohio Company began operations in the field. Where Wills Creek entered the Potomac (the present site of Cumberland, Maryland), 110 miles southeast from the forks of the Ohio River, a base was built — a two-story, log storehouse stocked with £4,000 of merchandise by Dinwiddie's London friend John Hanbury. Later this Wills Creek storehouse grew into the general headquarters, offices, and residence for the Company's agents, and a fort. Working arrangements were established with a group of pioneers in the area, and Christopher Gist, one of the frontiersmen who became renowned in the popular surveying profession, was dispatched on an exploratory expedition into the wilderness land claimed by the Company. Lee personally reopened negotiations with the Indians, with whom the agreements had become complicated as more English moved into the territory and the French made alliances with Indians in the Ohio Valley.

When Robert Dinwiddie efficiently, and without waste motion, assumed the administrative tasks, he continued the government's support of the Ohio Company's operations. Thomas Lee had been succeeded as the Company's president by Lawrence Washington, son-in-law of Dinwiddie's friend Colonel Fairfax.

Then in his early thirties, Washington was adjutant general of all the Colony's militia and rising in prominence among the younger men in Richard Bland's generation. His family had been in the Colony for a century, and his great-grandfather had been a man of position — prosperous planter, Burgess, and lieutenant colonel of the county's militia — in the then sparsely settled northern regions in the Potomac country. Through circumstances, the family's fortune had not advanced for a generation, and then Lawrence's father took over with surging ambition. A physically powerful and aggressive man, shrewd and contentious, Augustine Washington secured his part of an entangled estate, increased his holdings and put in a mill, and at his death, in 1743, left ten thousand acres and upwards of fifty slaves to be divided among his widow and three sons.

As the oldest, Lawrence, who had been educated in England, inherited the Potomac River property, on which he had built Mount Vernon after his Cartagena adventure. He was not the businessman his father had been. While engaging in land transactions, in production he was far from a big planter and his scale of living caused him to run up small debts. Then, too, his health grew steadily worse, and he was racked by a cough. However, Lawrence Washington possessed the personal qualities to inspire respect and trust in highly placed men, and he was, in his own right, as well as through his connections by marriage, a person of consequence.

In the general reorganization of the Ohio Company when Washington succeeded Thomas Lee as president, a group of Northern Neck and Potomac country stalwarts became members: George Mason; John Mercer and his son George; Robert Carter (the King's grandson), who established his Northern Neck manor seat at Nomini Hall on a magnificent open plateau near the Potomac; John Tayloe, whose Mount Airy on the Rappahannock was upriver from the Sabine Hall of Robert Carter's uncle Landon; and two nineteen-year-olds — George Washington, the younger brother of Lawrence, and Richard Henry Lee, a younger son of Thomas Lee, of Stratford Hall.

Before Dinwiddie and the Ohio Company could act on this settlement, the Governor learned in late June of the destruction of Pickawillany, the town of the friendly Miami allies. Charles Michel Langlade, a French trader, had led Chippewa and Ottawa braves on a sunrise attack, in which they killed (and boiled) a chief of such English loyalties that he was named Chief Old Briton. An English trader there was killed, and five others captured and sent to prison in France. "Remember Pickawillany" never became a battle cry, but this obscure disaster began the actions that led into the French and Indian Wars (a part of the Seven Years War, to England) to decide whether England or France would gain supremacy in North America.

What had begun as a westward push of the land speculators in the Ohio Company had become a conflict with a foreign power over

Young George Washington as a colonel in the militia.
Portrait by Charles Willson Peale
(Washington and Lee University, Virginia)

Virginia's territory in the New World. This included the present states of West Virginia, Kentucky and — in claims disputed by Connecticut and Massachusetts — Ohio, Indiana, Illinois, most of Michigan, Wisconsin, and parts of Minnesota. To Dinwiddie, Virginia's territorial claims meant a colonial assertion of his Majesty's claims. Transcending the Ohio Company and the Colony of which he was Governor, the French challenge was regarded by Dinwiddie as a threat to Great Britain's imperialistic purposes. In his vast correspondence, he petitioned the home government in terms of Virginia's part in a continental enterprise of England's American colonies.

4

Nothing moved very fast. When Dinwiddie wrote the home government for cannons with which to arm newly planned forts, his proposition ran afoul of bureaucratic analyses between separate agencies. Adjutant General Lawrence Washington died that year, 1752, and Dinwiddie sought to strengthen the militia by replacing him with four adjutants, each in charge of a district. Lawrence Washington's twenty-year-old half-brother George was appointed adjutant of the district south of the James River. This young Washington, coldly ambitious, was already a successful surveyor, using his earnings to invest in lands that had doubled the holdings of his modest inheritance of something over two thousand acres. However, George Washington knew nothing about military regulations, even the rudiments of drill, and he made no visits of inspection to the militia units in the district distant from his own neighborhood.

The following summer Dinwiddie finally received support from home, in a dispatch signed by George II himself. Advising the Governor that military equipment would be shipped to him, the King instructed Dinwiddie to send a representative to the French forces warning them that they were occupying English territory and demanding their withdrawal. Two parties were sent under pioneer-traders (one of them William Trent) with whom Dinwiddie had been working. Neither reached the French encampments. Then at the end of October, just as members of the General Assembly were gathering at Williamsburg, George Washington appeared and volunteered to deliver the message.

George Washington, whose fourteen-years-older half-brother had been like a surrogate father after the death of his own father when he was eleven, had enjoyed none of his brothers' advantages of education in England. Nor had he attended William and Mary at home. Although he had inherited ten slaves and three lots in the new city of Fredericksburg, along with the landholdings, he had availed himself of his brother's connections with the Fairfaxes to develop his own fortune through the avenues opened by surveying. Self-conscious about his lacks, young Washington applied an iron discipline to training himself for the great world.

Not yet twenty-two when he appeared before Dinwiddie, Washington already carried himself with a dignity and composure which, as he grew older, became imposing. He was six foot two, very tall for his day, and stood straight and lean (before later filling out). He had dark brown hair and blue-gray eyes and, as was said by George Mercer, later his aide and friend, "looks you full in the face." His skin was pocked by smallpox he had contracted when with his brother in the Barbados, his nose was large and straight, and his mouth was firmly closed over defective teeth. Not a handsome man, he had force and was developing a "presence."

Of all his contemporaries none was more aware than Washington of his own limitations, and like a knowledgeable artist he worked to develop his strengths. He was not a glib talker, not easy with the spoken word, and he lacked the humor that could lighten social exchanges. So, he concentrated on his demeanor and deportment, as well as studies for his self-improvement, and kept a notebook in which he carefully recorded the do's and don'ts of polite society. His rules showed an obsession with self-control, especially as he appeared to others, and he was very mindful of the shadings of behavior required in association with persons of different degree — superior, equal, inferior. In his own self-absorption and with work that kept him away from the Colony's social life, he was too far removed from the center of privilege to feel any obligations toward participating in government. He knew little about politics. However, on his meeting with the Governor, there was one common area between twenty-one-year-old Washington and sixty-year-old Dinwiddie: they were both men of business.

Unlike his brother Lawrence, George, with the acquisitiveness of his father and great-grandfather, was shrewd and a careful man with a penny. He liked to do well by himself, especially in clothes, and he enjoyed the good things in life as much as the most luxury-loving planter; at the same time he made sure he had the money, and he enjoyed the acts of earning it, like the men of King Carter's generation of Accumulators. Like them also, he intended to develop himself totally in proportion to his property-holding. When the tall young surveyor — recently appointed adjutant of a militia district through a position in the Colony won by his brother — appeared before the Royal Governor to volunteer, the hazardous duty in the wilderness represented an opportunity for advancement.

Dinwiddie immediately accepted the offer and had a letter written for the commanding officer of the French post. Washington was to demand a reply, as well as an escort back to the Virginia settlements. While at the French post, the militarily untrained young man was to appraise as far as possible the enemies' strength — in numbers, weapons, defensive alignments — and learn what he could of their plans.

When Major Washington rode out of Williamsburg, the convening Burgesses showed willingness to support Dinwiddie's plans by encouraging quick settlement of all the land west of the Alleghenies — the territory of the Loyal Company as well as the Ohio Company, and the more than six hundred thousand acres apportioned in other grants. The House extended from ten to fifteen years the settlers' exemptions from Colony and local dues, and petitioned the King to grant settlers exemption from the payment of quitrents for ten years. The Crown allowed this exemption. While settled families, forming potential communities, served the ''right of occupancy'' in the race with the French, there was in Williamsburg perhaps the stronger motivation of the advantage of settlers to the speculators in western lands.

Dinwiddie had disapproved of those large grants to individuals when he assumed office. But he was not long in Virginia before he observed that the large patentees *did* get the new land populated, and wrote to the Board of Trade in June, 1753, that the large patentees ''have been of service in settling the back parts of this Dominion, as they sell and parcel them out to poor people that came from other colonies to the north.'' However, when he first came, with his mind on getting all revenues due the Crown, Dinwiddie introduced a measure which so aroused the opposition of the House that the Burgesses would vote no money for military defense against the French in the Ohio country.

In Dinwiddie's view, exemption from quitrents and other fees applied only to new *settlers,* those actually living on the land. In expanding the Colony they were establishing England's claims to the territory. The Governor felt that the patentees of idle land, held for speculation, were avoiding fees and quitrents that belonged to the Crown. For this reason, he joined the Council in rejecting the Ohio Company's petition for an additional two-hundred-thousand-acre grant to the southward. In his determination to collect revenues from the large speculators on land, Dinwiddie was only doing his duty as he saw it. But he did not stop there. The new Governor tacked on a fee for affixing his signature on all patents, and this fee would go into his own pocket.

The fee was (as he saw it) "only" one pistole, a Spanish coin worth about sixteen shillings and eightpence. The motivations of Robert Dinwiddie in demanding this fee were most unclear. He was a rich man, at least by colonial standards, and in any case the aggregate of the fees he would collect would not come to any considerable sum. He was also an honest man. Possibly he was guided by lifelong habits of commercial practices which conditioned him to calculate, whether or not the advantage to him was important. But in his rather petty financial calculations he grossly miscalculated the reaction of the House of Burgesses, for his pistole fee touched the Burgesses on the sensitive spot of their right to control internal taxation.

By ill chance for his far-ranging plans, the new Governor aroused the House against him just when the French threat became a reality at Pickawillany in the summer of 1752. The pistole fee controversy loomed little larger than Pickawillany among the events that shaped Virginia's history, but it also was a beginning. It began the pamphlet-writing career of Richard Bland, who began the articulation of certain inviolable principles existing between the Colony and the home government. The definition of these principles — first by Bland, then by Landon Carter and others — revealed the temper of a conservative people who wanted no change *of any kind* in the tenuous balance between internal and external controls. This temper hardened as the statements of principles became broader and stronger, more far-reach-

ing in their implications, during the changes in which the fighting
with the French was central to all the changes that ended Virginia's
parochial idyll.

5

When Dinwiddie, while in London, had been appointed Lieutenant Governor, he made the customary agreement with the titular
Governor, then the Earl of Albemarle, to share with him half the
salary. But Dinwiddie agreed to divide a far larger salary than had
ever been allotted a Governor. The usual salary was £2,000, raised
from the tax of two shillings per hogshead on all tobacco exported
from Virginia. Dinwiddie, in agreeing to divide £6,600, committed
himself to sending Albemarle £1,650 twice a year, 60 per cent more
than the whole sum the office usually provided. He doubtless had in
mind making up the difference by various "perquisites," and with
this in mind he appealed to the Board of Trade for permission to
charge a governor's fee for signing patents.

In his petition, Dinwiddie obscured the point of the fee and concluded by mentioning the prudence of restraining "the governor and
council from granting exorbitant quantities to any one person — a
practice notoriously injurious to the inhabitants in general." This
practice was not "notoriously injurious," as Dinwiddie soon came to
recognize. Gooch had earlier described to the Board King Carter's
contributions in settling the new country between the heads of tidal
water and the Shenandoah Valley on the three million acres he
claimed for the Proprietary. Perhaps because of Dinwiddie's weak
presentation of his request to be allowed fees, or maybe simply the
inertia of a committee over a subject which touched none of its
members' interests, the Board of Trade made no reply to Dinwiddie's
petition.

When the new Governor arrived in Virginia, he found waiting in
the Secretary's office more than seventeen hundred patents for land
which required his signature, and another thousand "warrants of
survey" — surveyor's certificates. Under a warrant of survey, the
claimant of the land was not required to pay any quitrents until it
was actually patented. Perceiving that this practice deprived the

Crown of revenue, Dinwiddie adopted the policy of the Fairfax Proprietary, which required that patents be taken out immediately after the survey was registered. He declared that the arrears of quitrents due on lands held under a warrant of survey prior to April 22, 1752, must be paid before patents would be issued. This was dutiful, if somewhat highhanded, concern for the interests of the Crown. But, along with this dubious ruling on the payment of quitrent arrears, Dinwiddie included his demand for a payment of a fee to the governor for signing *all* patents.

Dinwiddie was not without disingenuousness in his approach to gaining this "perquisite." While the first session of the General Assembly was meeting in Williamsburg, the new Governor gave no reason for not signing the accumulated patents. The claimants assumed that other matters had kept him from getting around to affixing his seal and signature. When the time came in April for the Burgesses to leave for their homes, Dinwiddie then took his problem of charging a fee for his signature to the Council — which included several old friends.

This Council contained the usual members of the families early in power — Ludwell, Lewis, Corbin, Grymes, and Commissary Blair's nephew John. As a group these were not men of the force of those that composed the oligarchy forty years before, although John Blair was active and powerful on matters which aroused his interest. The other Councilors were new or relatively new to the Colony, with no line of descent from the oligarchy.

The Reverend William Dawson, a Councilor as well as president of William and Mary by virtue of his Commissary post (succeeding old Blair), was an amiable gentleman whose interests were essentially in the church and in the college. William Fairfax was a partner of Dinwiddie in the Ohio Company, as was Thomas Nelson, one of the two Nelson brothers on the Council. Their father, "Scotch Tom," was the merchant who had established his family in the ruling class entirely through trade — opening his Yorktown store in 1705. Son William was the businessman of the family, netting between £5,000 and £10,000 a year at the store, and the younger brother, Thomas Nelson, Jr., was the showpiece. He had studied law at the Inner Temple and married Elizabeth Burwell, granddaughter of King Carter and sister of Lewis Burwell, Council President before Dinwiddie's arrival.

All of these Councilors were agreeable to Dinwiddie's exacting a small fee for signing patents, and suggested one pistole. It would be impossible to estimate its value, about $3.60, in present-day currency: in 1752 it was three times more than the cost of a hundred acres (five shillings), or it was the purchase price of a cow and a half. It was a "trifling amount," as Dinwiddie called it, only to the well-to-do.

Dinwiddie's disingenuousness showed in his dealings with the House of Burgesses. Constitutionally he was under no obligation to clear his pistole fee with the Burgesses. However, since it was customary in Virginia for fees to be regulated by legislative acts, advising the House would have been, at the least, a political courtesy. But the Governor waited until the General Assembly had adjourned before announcing his imposition of a fee, along with the demand of quitrent arrears on land held under warrants of survey.

Reactions were generally slow to develop. The land speculators naturally did not like the measures, and groups discussed their opposition among themselves. But Dinwiddie professed to believe that the fee would have aroused no active opposition except for the personally motivated attack of Reverend William Stith.

A member of the Randolph clan and first cousin of Richard Bland and Peyton Randolph, Stith became one of the chief claimants to the triple post of Commissary, college president, and Councilor left vacant by Commissary Dawson's death in July, 1752. Stith, who held a master's degree from Queen's College, Oxford, and owned a considerable estate, had won a strong following when he taught in William and Mary's grammar school before becoming rector of the rich Henrico Parish. Dinwiddie, however, wanted Thomas Dawson to succeed his older brother as Commissary, and opposed Stith. Despite the Governor's opposition, Stith won part of the triple post when the Board of Visitors elected him president of the college. But Dinwiddie was determined to keep him off the Council. With the support of John Blair — who disliked Stith and was supporting Carter Burwell for the Council seat — Dinwiddie was able to persuade the Bishop of London to separate the other posts that previously went with the college presidency and to appoint Thomas Dawson as Commissary and Councilor. Dinwiddie accused Stith of retaliating, with the backing of the Randolph web of families, by stirring up the people against the pistole fee.

It could not have been so simple. Reverend William Stith had first spoken against the fee before Commissary Dawson's death, and Dinwiddie obviously held very strong feelings about the "high priest" in the Randolph combine. He wrote some harsh charges against Stith in letters to England. Unquestionably after Dinwiddie's opposition cost him a Council seat Stith became more outspoken in his attacks on the pistole fee, although temperately and always on the same point of the illegality of the "tax" — as opponents of the fee called it.

Then, when the General Assembly next met, in the fall of 1753, petitions from six counties — several far removed from Stith's demesne — complained of the "many hardships they labor under" and asked the House of Burgesses to give them relief from the new fee. Without any influence from Stith, the Burgesses resolved that the demand for the fee was "illegal and arbitrary," and was against the precedent established by the King's Privy Council in 1689. At that time, upon protests from the House of Burgesses, the Privy Council had disallowed a similar fee charged by Governor Lord Howard of Effingham. The House appointed a committee to draft a letter to the Governor — Richard Bland, the rich Charles Carter of Cleve, and his nephew Carter Burwell. Since Burwell was maneuvering for a Council seat, he needed to be in the Governor's good graces and manifestly was no ally of Reverend Stith.

The committee's letter to the Governor, very respectful in tone, addressed a direct inquiry: had the demand for the fee been made under his direction and, if it had, what was his authority for the demand?

Dinwiddie equivocated. "The welfare and happiness of Virginia I have very much at heart, and this great point has been the chief object of my attention ever since I had the honor to preside over this dominion."

Saying nothing about the income he needed for the payments to the Earl of Albemarle, and denying that he sought the fee for pecuniary gain, he stated that the fee was demanded by his authority according to his instructions (although the Board had not then acknowledged his specific petition) "and my conduct upon all extraordinary occasions has been regulated by the advice of the Council." He assured the Burgesses that he would always "show a just regard for the sentiment of the House of Burgesses, *in everything that properly lies before them.''* (Not his italics.)

Any internal levy was precisely a matter which the Burgesses regarded as properly lying before them. Immediately a reply was drafted. Comparison of it with Richard Bland's signed writings leaves no doubt that he was its author, and that in this letter — as in his later writings — he expressed the sentiments generally current in Virginia.

This letter began in the same respectful tone of the inquiry. ''We his Majesty's most dutiful and loyal subjects . . . are under the deepest concern, to find by your Honor's answer to our address, that the demand of a pistole, as a fee, for the use of the public seal, is made by your direction; and that we are under a necessity of making application again to your honor on that occasion.''

Then the address came straight to the point that was to be central in Bland's writings thereafter:

''We do humbly, but in the strongest terms, represent to your Honor, that it is the undoubted right of the Burgesses to enquire into the grievances of the people: They have constantly exercised this right, and we presume to affirm, that the drawing it into question, in any manner, cannot but be of dangerous consequence to the liberties of his Majesty's faithful subjects, and to the constitution of this government.

''The rights of the subject are so secured by law, that they cannot be deprived of the least part of their property, but by their own consent: Upon this excellent principle is our constitution founded, and ever since this Colony has had the happiness of being under the immediate protection of the Crown, the royal declarations have been, 'That no man's life, member, freehold, or goods, be taken away or harmed, but by established and known laws.'

''But the demand of a pistole, as a fee for the use of the public seal, being not warranted by any known or established law, is, we humbly conceive, an infringement of the rights of the people, and a grievance highly to be complained of.''

Bland's later line of reasoning was evident in his summation of the history of land-granting in Virginia. Dismissing the practice in the other colonies which permitted the governor to charge a fee, Bland concluded with the statement that the established procedures in Virginia "cannot be altered by the advice of the Council; and as your Honor's insisting upon the same will, in our humble opinion, be an infringement on the rights of the people, a great discouragement to the settling of the frontiers of this Colony, and a prejudice to our Majesty's revenue of quitrents, we think it our indispensable duty to desire that your Honor will recede from your demand."

On the principle that a soft answer turneth away wrath, Dinwiddie used diplomatic language in refusing to rescind the demand and unemphatically stated a sound legal principle: "The establishment of the fee complained of relates solely to the disposal of the King's land, and not a matter relative to the administration of government."

While legally his principle of the disposal of the Crown's land was sound, the Burgesses regarded the fee as a tax, and taxation was the prerogative solely of the House. On this point their acceptance of the ancient customs — which permitted them to abide the restrictions on the tobacco trade and manufacturing — was the factor behind their resistance to an act of the Governor which encroached on their "rights and privileges." The Burgesses unanimously passed resolutions condemning the Governor's fee and appointed a committee to draw up an address to the King protesting the action.

With Richard Bland and Charles Carter on this committee went Bland's cousin, Attorney General Peyton Randolph, and Randolph's brother-in-law, twenty-seven-year-old Benjamin Harrison V; Joshua Fry, a former mathematics professor at Williamsburg, then the Surveyor of Albemarle County; and Edmund Pendleton, the courtly and amiable protégé of House Speaker John Robinson. Pendleton, then thirty-one and in his first term as a Burgess, had been educated in the old apprentice system. Apprenticed to Robinson's uncle Benjamin Robinson, Clerk of Caroline County, Pendleton had been instructed "in all things belonging to a Clerk's office," and studied law on the side. Moving up fast among the powers, he had been taken in as a partner in the Loyal Company.

While this committee was drafting the petition to the King, the aroused Burgesses appointed Peyton Randolph as their agent to represent Virginia's position in England, and voted him £2,500 for expenses — more than the pistole fee would have earned Dinwiddie.

This got Dinwiddie's back up. Four days later (December 19) he prorogued the Assembly until the last Thursday in April, 1754. In parting, he addressed the Burgesses sternly, with some "marks of anger" (as he admitted in a private letter). Referring to their failure to vote any money for the defense against the French, he said that, "the friendship of the Indians" and the "designs of the French" and the "real prosperity of your country . . . should have been the fixed object of your attention." He advised them to return to their homes and "cultivate piety and morality."

In his home at Jordan's Point, Richard Bland went to work on his first pamphlet. One hundred miles away, at Sabine Hall on the Rappahannock, Landon Carter, in his first term as a Burgess, was also moved to begin a career in pamphlets and in short essays published in the forms of letters in the newspapers.

6

In Bland's *A Modest and True State of the Case* (frequently referred to as "A Fragment of the Pistole Fee"), he first traced the "mystery" of the patents in application remaining unsigned by the Governor until after the spring session of the General Assembly was over in 1752. Then came the fundamental principle upon which the Colony made its unalterable stand: "The rights of the subjects are so secured by law that they cannot be deprived of the least part of their property without their own consent. Upon this principle of law, the liberty and property of every person who has the felicity to live under a British government is founded. The question then ought not to be about the smallness of the demand but the lawfulness of it. For if it is against the law, the same power which imposes one pistole may impose an hundred, and this is not in one instance only but in every case in which this Leviathan of power shall think it fit to exercise its authority."

In strictly legal terms, since the question at issue was the Crown's lands, Lawyer Bland may not have been on the strongest ground in charging that the fee was "against law." It was against law according to the Colony's interpretation of the Burgesses' historic right to levy any form of internal taxation. For, even though the land was transferred to private ownership by the King and the levy was called a

Peyton Randolph (Reproduced through the courtesy of the Virginia Historical Society)

Edmund Pendleton. Portrait attributed to Charles Willson Peale (Colonial Williamsburg Collection)

"fee," it was the people who were paying without the consent of the Burgesses. This hairsplitting hit at the heart of the thus far loosely defined and pragmatic arrangement of internal versus external controls.

Neither Bland nor Landon Carter, in his pamphlet *A Letter from a Gentleman in Virginia, to the Merchants of Great Britain, Trading in That Colony,* defined this duality which lay as the source of the conflict between the Governor and the Burgesses. Bland did focus on the consequences of the imposition of royal authority upon institutions which "the ancient custom" imbued with constitutional rights as understood by the people.

"Liberty and property are like those precious vessels whose soundness is destroyed by the least flaw and whose use is lost by the smallest hole. Impositions destroy their beauty, nor are they to be soldered by patchwork which will always discover and frequently widen the original flaw.

"This shows the iniquity of every measure which has the least tendency to break through the legal forms of government and . . . the necessity of opposing in a legal way every attempt of this sort, which like a small spark, if not extinguished in the beginning, will soon gain ground and at last blaze into an irresistible flame."

Far from rhetoric to Virginians, Bland's warning confirmed them in their habit of resistance to any encroachment formed seventy years before during the reign of the Stuart kings. No personal motivations of Reverend William Stith were necessary to create a receptive atmosphere for Bland's ideas.

Yet Stith, who had been appointed chaplain of the committee writing the address of protest to the King, evidently did work on the feelings of some of the Burgesses. The House was in a mood of unseemly intransigence when circumstances forced Dinwiddie to convene the General Assembly on February 14, 1754, instead of waiting until April.

One month before the Assembly was called, on January 16, a somewhat attenuated George Washington rode into the Duke of Gloucester Street, turned off at Bruton Church into one of the muddy roadways flanking the Palace Green, and dismounted in the courtyard of the Governor's Palace. The letter he brought to Dinwiddie from the commander of the French post was not good news.

Writing in a courteous tone, Legardeur de St. Pierre stated simply, and flatly, that he had no intention of retiring from the territory to which his government ordered him to hold. "And I entreat you, Sir," he wrote, "not to doubt one moment, but that I am determined to conform myself to them [his government's instructions] with all the exactness and resolution which can be expected from the best of officers."

In passing, de St. Pierre justified Dinwiddie's faith in the young surveyor as an emissary. "I made it my particular care to receive Mr. Washington, with a distinction suitable to your dignity, as well as his own quality and great merit."

Dinwiddie, without military training, did not question the report of the equally untrained Washington, who had benefited by the services of Christopher Gist, the veteran frontiersman, as a companion and guide. Washington reported that de St. Pierre's force consisted of fifteen hundred well-armed troops, plus Indian allies, and — on the basis of his counting more than two hundred newly built canoes and observing others blocked out — he believed the French planned a spring advance.

Of all times, Dinwiddie now needed the support of the prorogued Burgesses — and he had hardened their spirit by dismissing Peyton Randolph from his Attorney General's post as soon as Randolph sailed for England as the Burgesses' agent. He also recognized the need of rushing troops to the area of the forks of the Ohio River, but no law authorized the Governor to pay out money to volunteer troops. For an emergency act, Dinwiddie turned to his young friend Washington.

Washington's area as an adjutant had been shifted to the Northern Neck, which he had wanted from the beginning. Geographically, the Northern Neck did not extend west of the head of tidewater on the Rappahannock, but as King Carter's successful claim for the Proprietary had interpreted the boundaries, the Northern Neck legally embraced Augusta and Frederick counties in the Shenandoah Valley. Since these counties were nearest the point of the French threat, Dinwiddie authorized Washington to raise a force of a hundred troops from their militia. At the same time Dinwiddie authorized William Trent, with whom he had earlier contracted for the building of a fort at the forks, to raise a company of a hundred men from the three hundred traders active in the threatened area.

Before Washington left for the Valley, Dinwiddie planned to use his report to arouse the Burgesses to raise an additional force of four hundred men and to allot the money by then desperately needed for equipping and supplying the force in the field. He also wrote the governors of other colonies for military aid against the French.

A month later a discouraged Washington returned and reported, "You may, with equal success, attempt to raise the dead to life again, as the force of" the Shenandoah Valley counties. Lord Fairfax, who had established himself at Winchester in Frederick County and, according to custom as its leading citizen, been appointed colonel of its militia, did not even have the ghost of a force. Outraged, Dinwiddie called in his friendly Council and proposed, in effect, to draft the militia or invoke the penalties provided in the law. The Councilors called the Governor's attention to the proviso that the militia could not be compelled to serve outside the borders of the Colony, and the Ohio forks represented dubious territory. Pennsylvania as well as Virginia claimed the area, although the Pennsylvania Assembly was lax in pressing the claim which would require their colony to supply military aid against the French.

A reconvened House of Burgesses had to be handled. On the opening day, Dinwiddie gave in his own words a substance of Washington's report on the French threat, with the warning of a spring advance during which the French would solidify their hold by building forts along the Ohio. In his appeal for funds to supply forces of defense, the Governor tried to stir the Burgesses by vivid descriptions of the terrors frontier warfare would bring to the settlers.

The Burgesses listened without response. His appeal was referred for study to the committeee of the whole. In the following debate, it was evident that many Virginians did not wish to break out of their self-sufficient thralldom by military entanglements with the French. Some Burgesses showed themselves to be completely without feeling for supporting Great Britain's continental claims: a few of these went so far as to deny the existence of any real danger, and one said the territory belonged to the French anyway. Others, their minds on the rivalries of the land companies, claimed the whole report was a scheme to promote the interests of the Ohio Company.

Among the Burgesses who believed the danger was real enough, and supported the Governor's appeal, were two of his chief opponents over the pistole fee — Richard Bland and Landon Carter. They were among the more enlightened who tried to convince their provincial-minded fellows that at least the funds should be allocated. Dinwiddie himself joined the discussions and suggested every argument he could think of.

Finally, without any emotional support, the Burgesses voted £10,000. But the unsettled pistole fee — then being argued out in England — motivated the legislators to make some encroachments of their own into the Governor's customary prerogatives. The House voted the money with the proviso that a committee of fourteen of the Colony's prominent men should determine how the money would be spent.

Dinwiddie was torn between accepting the funds with a proviso which he, with justification, regarded as "unconstitutional and derogatory to the prerogatives of the Crown" or in venting his rage by proroguing the hostile Assembly. He compromised by doing both. He accepted the emergency funds, proviso and all, and then immediately (February 23) prorogued the Assembly. Perhaps remembering the ill effects produced by his parting words to the previous session, he confided his feelings to a letter. "I am sorry to find them [the Burgesses] very much in a republican way of thinking."

Dinwiddie revealed no awareness of the correlation between his encroachment on what the Virginians regarded as their constitutional guarantees and their assertion of a "republican way of thinking." While the Burgesses were not at their responsible best in their retaliatory encroachment, Dinwiddie seemed to miss the political nuance in his having stimulated what amounted to a reflex in the House.

As Dinwiddie saw it, preceding governors had been wrong to yield to the republican way of thinking, and the cold-eyed Scotsman was going to show the Virginians that he would hold to the point of the Crown's prerogatives regardless of the consequences. He evidently gave no thought to the Virginians' definition of principles that represented an immediate consequence. If he ever saw the pamphlets of Richard Bland and Landon Carter he never mentioned it.

Dinwiddie revealed a basic detachment from the *life* of the people — unlike Gooch's Virginia identification — by his concern over the attention the pistole fee affair attracted in London newspapers and coffeehouses. This public airing of the controversy over a "tri-fling" fee presented him in an unfavorable aspect at home. Two months after he prorogued the brief Assembly, he wrote to a friend, "I must confess to you, if I had [known] that this affair would have created so much uneasiness to me, and trouble to my friends at home, I would not have taken the fee." To the Virginians, he refused to show any signs of his "uneasiness."

7

After the Burgesses had departed from the capital, Dinwiddie turned from politics to a late-life surge of interest in military affairs. Though he had no natural instincts to compensate for his lack of knowledge, the sedentary Governor began to enjoy the use of his authority as commander-in-chief of Virginia's armed forces. He wrote his merchant friend John Hanbury, to have "Scott, my tailor, to make me a proper suit of regimentals" to "be here by his Majesty's birth day." The celebration of the King's birthday was a big social event in Williamsburg, when the Governor became a leading figure at a ball. "I do not much like gaiety in dress," Dinwiddie confided, "but I con-ceive this necessary" — for his appearance as "a military officer" at the grand affair.

Along with turning himself out as a soldier, Dinwiddie developed a passionate absorption in the details of organization. After giving up on the counties' militia units as a source for an expeditionary force, he arranged to recruit three hundred volunteers in six companies. Two hundred thousand acres were allotted to be divided among the men, according to their merits, after they had erected a fort at the mouth of the Monongahela, and they would be exempt from quitrents on their portions for fifteen years. During their service, the recruits would receive the customary fifteen pounds of tobacco (about eightpence) daily allowed foot soldiers.

Officers had to be selected on the basis of character and famil-iarity with the backcountry. As colonel of the regiment (which became the First Virginia), Dinwiddie appointed the ex-mathematics pro-fessor and Albemarle County Surveyor, Joshua Fry. Fry possessed the status qualifications of being a landowner and a learned gentleman; he was mature and had the frontier experience of a surveyor; and, a natural leader, he won the respect of all classes of men.

For second in command Dinwiddie chose twenty-two-year-old George Washington, who was given the rank and pay of a lieutenant colonel. Washington had sought the post himself, going directly to the Governor. On returning from his first mission, Washington had ended his report to Dinwiddie with a true statement of his objectives: "I hope what has been said will be sufficient to make your Honor satisfied with my conduct; for that was my aim in undertaking [the mission] and chief study throughout the prosecution of it."

The ambitious young surveyor did not stop with asking Dinwiddie for a command in the new regiment. He might have been politically naïve, but from the intimate associations he had enjoyed with the Fairfaxes through his brother, he knew his way around in the area of obtaining appointments. He approached the most influential older men he knew, through his family, and won the support of Councilor Richard Corbin. A member of an English-Virginian merchant family which had been established among the early powers in the days when Sir William Berkeley arranged his own colonial court, Corbin was a kinsman of the Lees in the Ohio Company.

After Dinwiddie had the officers, the men (on paper) and some money, he began the actual plans for arming and supplying the troops in the field. However, the former customs duty expert made civilian assumptions about those gritty details known as "logistics" and "liaison." Fascinated by command of a military force, daily writing instructions and exhortations to the men in the field, the efficient administrator at his desk could not sufficiently grasp the day-by-day reality of logistical problems to be aware of his limitations.

His chosen officers, principally Fry and Washington, had much to learn about the difference between ordering an individual to assemble wagons and teams at a given point and the actuality of the wagons, laden with supplies, being ready to roll from that point on a given date. By mid-April Washington, impatient at the delays, started northward with half the force and ten wagons of the seventy-four promised — and those with such sorry teams the men had to help pull the wagons up hills. It was probably just as well for his future.

When he reached the Ohio Company's base at Wills Creek on the western Maryland border, a young officer, Ensign Edward Ward, rode up with the news that the unfinished fort at the forks had surrendered to a French force numbering more than a thousand. William Trent, the trader to whom Dinwiddie had assigned the contract of building the fort for the Ohio Company — along with various chores related to supplying the column — had flitted about, completing no task, and was not even at Fort Trent when the French appeared. The French completed the fort, naming it Fort Du Quesne, and Dinwiddie lost the race to occupy that crucial site.

Dinwiddie learned of this melancholy turn from young Ensign Ward, who reached Williamsburg on May 4. Undismayed, the amateur military chieftain went more zealously at building a force to carry the undeclared war to the French. While the governors of most of the other colonies had been unmoved by his appeals for aid in the continental struggle, and none had shown any enthusiasm for intercolonial action, New York and North Carolina were unhurriedly arranging to send a regiment each. South Carolina's governor, James Glen, who delighted in showing his superiority to Dinwiddie in epistolary exchanges, had actually dispatched a company of regulars.

In late May Dinwiddie was cheered by hearing that Washington's half of the Virginia regiment had encountered a French force in a collision fight and handsomely defeated the enemy. Ten French soldiers were killed and twenty-two captured, one of whom was wounded. (The high proportion of killed to wounded was accounted for by Washington's Indian scouts, who were very quick to take scalps from fallen men.) In his report, Washington wrote, "I heard the bullets whistle, and, believe me, there is something charming in the sound." The Governor could only conclude that his young appointee had found his métier.

When, at the end of May, Colonel Fry died from injuries suffered in a fall from his horse, Dinwiddie commissioned Washington full colonel in command of the First Virginia Regiment. However, he brought in a Scotch friend, Colonel James Innes, to assume command of all the forces. Innes had military experience, including his service as captain in the American regiment during the Cartagena campaign.

The South Carolina Independent Company of regulars arrived under Captain James McKay, and McKay, commissioned by the King, refused to act as a subordinate to a "colonial" colonel. Dinwiddie had to quiet Washington over the conflicts in rank, as he had earlier dealt with Washington's haggling over pay. Despite his personal grievances, Washington was thirsting for glory, and Dinwiddie warned him not to "make any hazardous attempts against a too numerous enemy."

Since Dinwiddie was always sending admonitions about something, Washington did not heed the warning. The loyalty of his Indian allies was suspect, and Washington's ambition caused him to rationalize that aggressive movement toward the French would bind the Indians more strongly than the depressing delays over supplies and the arrival of Colonel Innes, with the troops from New York and North Carolina. In June he put his Virginia regiment, the South Carolina company, and the Indian allies on the rocky trail across western Pennsylvania, widening the road as they advanced toward Du Quesne.

Two days' march from the French fort, he learned that a large French and Indian force was ready to move out against him. At a council of war, the officers agreed the point of wisdom was to retreat to the Wills Creek fort. Washington's force could not make it.

Food ran low. Animals collapsed from exhaustion and then men collapsed from the labor of moving the guns over the rough terrain. Fifty miles short of Wills Creek, in the Great Meadow in western Pennsylvania, Washington's force reached the flimsy and incomplete fort they had started as a potential base on their way out. By then desertions had decreased the force to four hundred, and, with the bread all gone and the meat of the cattle too tough for nourishment, only about three hundred of these were in condition to function. Those three hundred did what they could to strengthen the palisado, named by Washington Fort Necessity. Their Indian allies deserted during the night.

The French and Indian force of more than seven hundred surrounded the fort and shot from behind trees that gave better protection than the thin walls of the fort. Washington's men fought for a day in a dismal downpour, losing one third of their effective force — thirty killed and seventy wounded. The next day, July 4, 1754, Colonel Washington surrendered his first force.

Dinwiddie felt that Washington's ambition had made him reckless. In justifying himself, the Governor translated his cautionary advice to Washington into an order forbidding him to attack until his whole force was joined. However, with no ax to grind, William

Johnson, an English agent of broad experience in dealing with Indians, wrote to a friend that Washington had not "acted with prudence and circumspection." Johnson wrote, "He should have avoided an engagement until all our troops were assembled, for march in such a close country . . . by detachments will never do." He blamed Washington's glory-hunting and the inexperience which caused him to place too much credence in the stories of French deserters — "which show him not at all the soldier."

Dinwiddie's choice was certainly not a soldier at that stage, except in potential: he had the courage and resolution and, as he wrote, "My inclinations are strongly bent to arms."

Dinwiddie did not blame Washington as strongly as did Johnson and an Indian ally, Half King. Half King said that the white man had made a mistake in building the feeble fort, after earlier wasting a month during which sufficiently strong fortifications could have been built to beat off the French. Dinwiddie took into consideration the failures of the suppliers, particularly Trent's brother-in-law, George Croghan. Very shrewd in promoting his own interests, Croghan had contracted to deliver fifty thousand pounds of flour in fifteen days, and kept putting off the troops with promises he never kept. Dinwiddie also reproached the other colonies for not sending their allotments: the New York and North Carolina units — the latter half-armed and unsupplied — only began arriving in late July.

Dinwiddie placed the blame everywhere except on his own inexperience. This prevented him from ever seeing that the whole invasion plan was doomed by the lack of a military organization. The businessman and the ambitious young surveyor had simply been a poor combination for mounting a military offensive against professionals.

Still undaunted, Dinwiddie only increased the size of his plans, heartened at last by the full cooperation of the House of Burgesses.

8

In a brief session in the lingering heat of summer from August 22 to September 5, the Burgesses showed a sense of responsibility about the French on their border, after the defeat of Virginians *east* of the

Alleghenies, and voted £20,000 for military expenses. At the same time, they showed their intransigence about the pistole fee by attaching a rider to the bill which called for the £2,500 for their agent, Peyton Randolph. The Council, which remained split with the lower House over the Governor's fee, rejected the rider, even though this defeated the emergency military appropriation.

Dinwiddie prorogued the Assembly with a speech which, Landon Carter recorded, "carried all the venom and all the falsehood of an angry passionate man. . . . Every Burgess, I am sure, retired full of revenge . . . and I wrote a paper published in Maryland setting the matter in a true and faithful light, which has met with much applause."

With the passing of the hot weather, the men's tempers cooled, and the Burgesses were in a reasonable mood when they returned to Williamsburg in the bland, blue weather of October. Also, when old friends met in the taverns, they exchanged the reassuring news that had come from England about the settlement of the long pistole fee controversy. The Board of Trade had found for the Governor in the dispute over the fee itself, but the detailed conditions which the Board approved would work no hardship on the people.

No fees would be charged for patents of one hundred acres or less (protecting the small settlers) nor for land "beyond the mountains," which excluded all the land involved in the big speculations. Also, no fees were to be charged on the warrants of survey submitted before April 22, 1752, the date on which Dinwiddie had taken his stand over the thousand warrants waiting in the Secretary's office when he became Governor. The Board ruled against him on quitrent arrears and, anyway, in the scuffle over the fee, this potential revenue for the Crown had been forgotten.

Since it was by now evident that Dinwiddie was sick to death of the whole thing, the most ardent defender against the Royal Governor's encroachments into the House's "rights and privileges" could not suspect that he would try to take any advantage of his technical victory or make other encroachments. The Board also forced Dinwiddie, to the debasement of his authority, to reappoint Peyton Randolph as Attorney General. To keep things on "a very good footing," Dinwiddie approved the Assembly's payment to Randolph of £2,500.

In response to this, John Robinson sought an audience with the

Governor, in which the persuasive Speaker apologized for (as Dinwiddie reported) "the great ill manners" shown him by the House
and, presumably, for Robinson's own angry threat to pay Randolph
without the consent of Governor or Council. Dinwiddie granted the
requested pardon and harmony was restored. The House voted £20,-
000, even though a poll tax had to be levied on the poor to raise the
revenue. This time there were no riders, except again the proviso that
a committee should supervise disbursements. Seeing no vindictiveness
in the proviso, Dinwiddie accepted it in good spirit.

Also, members of the extraordinary committee — Richard Bland
and George Wythe, another scholarly lawyer, then thirty-six, Speaker
John Robinson and Charles Carter, and Dinwiddie's object of outrage
in the pistole fee controversy, Peyton Randolph — had proven themselves to be responsible men about Virginia's territorial involvements.
Richard Bland particularly had shown his capacity for hard, clearsighted work. He was unaffected in fulfilling his duties by his constitutional opposition to the fee (which, indeed, he regarded as one of his
duties) or by the narrow-minded provincialism and self-interest with
which some of his fellow Burgesses had obstructed the measures of
support for Dinwiddie's military plans.

Bland served as the commissioner to an Indian trade scheme
designed to neutralize hostile tribes, on the committee to settle the
entangled accounts of the Colony's militia, and on the committee "to
enquire into the conduct of the officers and men" in the disastrous
expedition. Mostly he was put to work drafting statutes. In the
friendly glow following the settlement of the dispute, the House
selected Bland as their representative to wait upon the Governor to
ask his permission for establishing a guard for the Powder Magazine
in the Public Square in Williamsburg.

While everybody was anxious to put the pistole fee controversy
behind them, there was never going to be for the charmless Governor
Dinwiddie the affection that the Burgesses had given Gooch, nor was
he ever to make Gooch's identification with the Virginians. They could
respect Dinwiddie and, after William Stith died the following year, he
had no active opponents.

Yet the Board of Trade's validation of the Governor's principle
of the fee had been based upon the legal assumption that the House of
Burgesses was a subordinate legislative body, upon whom the Crown's

rulings were supreme, regardless of colonial custom. This assumption negated the arguments which Peyton Randolph had presented in England: although the Burgesses accepted the supremacy of the Crown, a governor — even with the consent of the Council, his royal instructions and orders from the authorities in London — could not modify or abridge the customs and practices of Virginia's constitution. The ruling against that argument, lying in the pragmatic area of internal versus external controls, could have been seen to represent that "least flaw" in the "precious vessel" described by Bland in his pamphlet.

At the time, Richard Bland and Landon Carter, and other Burgesses who had viewed the Governor's fee as a flaw in the vessel of liberty, apparently were too occupied with the problems on the Colony's western border to ponder the implications of this "imposition" on the "beauty" of Virginia's relationship with the mother country. But Bland had recorded the words that such an imposition could not be "soldered by patchwork, which will always discover and frequently widen the original flaw."

Dinwiddie, engrossed in his broadening war, certainly was not the man to philosophize over the possible future consequences of his insistence upon what he interpreted as the prerogatives of the Crown. When the mild autumn faded with the first cold snaps of late fall, the Governor was drawn into closer contact with the Crown, as Great Britain took over "Virginia's little private war" (as Governor Glen of South Carolina referred to the territorial clash with the French).

Back in the summer, in June, Dinwiddie had made no effort to send representatives from Virginia to a colonial congress in Albany, New York. He gave as his reason the heavy costs of the military campaign, which disinclined the Assembly to load "the country with more expenses." Judging from the lack of cooperation which he had received from the governors of the other colonies, Dinwiddie probably felt the congress would accomplish nothing toward containing the French. He repeatedly made known his belief that the job could not be done with the limited revenues available and the poor cooperation between the colonies. New York and Pennsylvania were trade rivals in the west, Pennsylvania and Virginia in the Ohio Company country, and Virginia and South Carolina over the Cherokee trade.

When England sent troops, supplies, and trained personnel to the support of the colonials, war was not officially declared against

France. Neither country wanted war, though both would overestimate what the other would take in order to keep the peace. With the arrival of the first contingents from England, Dinwiddie began an active cooperation with everyone representing the Crown — even though this, subordinating his position as Virginia's commander-in-chief, placed a blight on his belated military career.

Governor Horatio Sharpe, of Maryland, was given a commission by the King and placed in command of the combined forces for a new, larger, and more thoroughly organized expedition. Dinwiddie himself suggested that all Virginia officers, including Washington, be demoted to captain, where they would be outranked by the officers who were commissioned by the Crown to the same rank. Washington discussed this subordination to British officers with, Landon Carter wrote, "a number of us his friends, and we one and all advised him not to serve on such dishonorable terms." Washington resigned, and Dinwiddie made no effort to assuage his sensitive pride.

Now that Virginia was drawn into Great Britain's imperialism, the businessman in the Palace gave priority to the Crown's interests in the long-enduring power struggle with France.

Chapter Four

THE MAN AND THE HOUR DID NOT MEET

WHEN THE BRITISH took over Virginia's war in 1755, and expanded it into a continental war, Dinwiddie was not as happy as he had expected to be with the presence of his own countrymen. First superseded in command, with his late-life aspirations to military glory squashed, then placed in an anomalous secondary position by the arrival in the colonies of a new and ambitious titular Governor, the conscientious careerist began to suffer nerve strain which broke his health. Harassed in mind and unwell in body, Dinwiddie — who had begun his administration with an assertion of the King's prerogatives — finally found himself allied with the General Assembly in common cause in protecting Virginia's interests.

In this gradual shift, Dinwiddie made no more complaints about the House of Burgesses' "republican way of thinking." For their part, the Burgesses continued a tendency to be occupied with small details of local concern — to the neglect of the emergencies of war — which, in Dinwiddie's view, was obstructive in effect, and very trying to the Governor. As the members were often divided among themselves and of changing humors, the impatient Governor found them "tedious in doing business." However, the deeply needed support given him by its leading members bound his interests permanently (long after he had returned to England) with Virginia's.

From the mid-1750's, when the British came, the General Assembly entered its phase of the full political flowering of Virginia's golden age. By then controlled completely by the ruling class in an aristocratic order, the General Assembly addressed itself to its business without regard to political considerations in the sense of following constituents' demands.

The freeholders in a deferential society elected men in the trust that their chosen representatives were qualified to represent their values and their interests without guidance from the voters. In turn, the Burgesses made no speeches designed to show their constituents that they were in Williamsburg thinking of their counties every minute. In any speeches made during debates, the kind of oratory designed to appeal to emotions or to obfuscate issues by a cloud of highly charged words was almost unknown. Indeed, such oratorical flights would have been as out of place as at a modern corporation's board of directors meeting. The art of oratory to them was the oral expression of logic, and their meetings were for serious discussion — if not always on weighty subjects.

In the relatively small oblong room for the seating of the hundred-odd men, facing one another on the long sides, the points of difference were reasoned out by equals who, in a homogenous society, were familiar with one another as neighbors, friends, and kinsmen. The points of difference were reasoned out as by members of a board of directors of a company or a club. While individuals and groups of course had their special interests, there were no blocs of voters to form a basis for special appeals. No matter what amount of time was spent on the trivial concerns which exasperated the Governor, the Burgesses, unless they were acting in deliberate intransigence, eventually got on with the business that needed legislation for the whole Colony.

2

In the mostly responsible cooperation the Burgesses began to give Dinwiddie during his nerve-racking troubles with the British in America, his staunchest supporters had been leaders of the opposition over the principle of the pistole fee. Landon Carter, Richard Bland's fellow writer of antifee pamphlets, had by 1755 become one of the most prominent members of the General Assembly. Exactly the same age as Bland, forty-five, Carter was personally the antithesis of the oligarchy's constitutionalist in the House. While Richard Bland was the representative whom the ruling class regarded as typical, Landon was the class's "character" — the nearest thing to an eccentric among the leaders in the General Assembly.

Landon Carter was distinguished among the older generation of Inheritors as the first who *felt* overshadowed by his father. At least, he was the first of the well-recorded Inheritors who was known to have been motivated by the drive to live up to the model of his father. The younger generation of Inheritors — as William Byrd III and Landon Carter's own children — were inclined to take their positions for granted, and it was largely that generation which produced the extravagant spenders, high-stake gamblers and, occasionally, wastrels. Among Landon Carter's approximate contemporaries — Richard Bland, his older brother Charles, and his nephew Benjamin Harrison V — who devoted their energies to government, these other Inheritors also took their estates for granted, although as trusts for which they were responsible. Among them all, Landon Carter stood alone in aspiring to be the man his father had been, and knowing that he could never be.

No one could have been in the mid-eighteenth century what King Carter had been in his day. The times were too different. According to the opportunities available in his time, Landon Carter was a very successful planter. Handsomely endowed by his father with several working plantations, he was among the few Inheritors who increased their original holdings. He owned land in a dozen counties, stretching west to the Shenandoah Valley, with which, following his father's pattern, he was able to provide all three of his sons with sizable holdings. Four hundred slaves were quartered at his home plantation, Sabine Hall, and 181 others worked on eight separate plantations. This placed him among the largest slaveowners of his day. Virginians, despite the legends and unlike the later cotton kings in the lower South, seldom worked with huge slave-labor forces. Fewer than fifty planters owned more than a hundred slaves and fewer than a hundred planters owned more than fifty: no one approached the approximately one thousand slaves of King Carter.

Landon had started on his own at twenty-two, either shortly be-

fore or immediately after his father's death in 1732. Then he had
married Elizabeth Wormeley, daughter of his father's lifelong friends
of Rosegill, and moved to what became his home plantation thirty-odd
miles upriver from Corotoman on the Rappahannock. There he built
his gracefully roomy Georgian mansion, Sabine Hall, on a plateau
from which a series of terraces dropped to his wharves on the river
about a mile from the manor house.

When he had first come home from school in England — where he
showed more love of learning than any other of King Carter's boys —
he had lived at Corotoman with his widower father, and, bright and
attractive, had studied his father's methods of operating the vast
planting-shipping-trading complex. The agricultural aspect appealed
most to him. Along with his genuine interest in volume-production
farming, he brought to his own operations the same absorbed attention
to details that had characterized his father's successful planting and
immense accumulations. Economically, unless he were to devote his
life entirely to moneymaking, Landon Carter could scarcely have done
better in his time.

In his class and generation, an income-producing estate was regarded as the necessary support for the fulfillment of his responsibilities to the community — principally in government at local and
Colony levels. These responsibilities he fulfilled from an early age.
Beyond this, on the model of his father, his position was the base for
the cultivation of the whole man.

With his genuine love of learning (his mind receptive in youth to
teachings in the classics) and his lifelong desire for the companionship
of books, Landon Carter probably surpassed his father in breadth of
knowledge and intensity of engagement with the life of the mind. He
wrote scientific observations, at least one of which was praised by a
scientist of the day, and he developed in writing a number of scientific
approaches to agricultural problems. He showed an unusual interest in
studying and treating the sicknesses that came to his children and
people, and was very scientific in recording symptoms and remedies.
The pamphlets he wrote on constitutional problems between Virginia
and the mother country were learned and fully developed arguments.

Yet Thomas Jefferson (of Carter's younger children's generation), who praised Bland's writings, said that Carter's were "dull,
vapid, verbose, egotistical." This was an ungenerous judgment by a

revolutionary-minded young intellectual who came to the House of Burgesses in Carter's later years and was bored by the older man's speeches. Those speeches, Jefferson said, like Carter's writings, were "smooth as the lullaby of the nurse, and commanding, like that, the repose only of the hearer."

Landon Carter's political pamphlets did lack compactness and conciseness; his speeches were long; and while it was harsh to call his writings and speeches "vapid," both lacked the sharpness of making a point: both lacked "spark." Nothing aroused the hearts of the hearers. But Jefferson's charge of "egotistical" — only superficially accurate in the sense in which he meant it — got close to the source of Landon Carter's inner insecurities caused by comparisons with his father.

Humility, as nonegoism, was scarcely a characteristic of the giants of Virginia's golden age, including Jefferson himself. In Jefferson, however, as in King Carter, there was an inner assurance which directed the energies in an objectivity that transcended self-awareness. Landon Carter was an extremely subjective-minded man, preoccupied with perfecting an impossible self-model. Very much aware of his exalted position in the colonial society, and very proud, he suffered no abashment at delivering himself fully of his ideas, either in the House or in his pamphlets. In doing this, Landon Carter was fulfilling his obligation to the community in giving his fellow Virginians the benefits of his cogitations on their behalf, but his manner of presentation could appear to be egotistical.

His personal behavior could make an even worse impression. In the high standard he set for himself, the virtues of moderation and reason ranked at the top, along with responsibility to the community. Of all things, he wanted to think of himself as "a reasonable man" who, doing his duty to his fellows, scorned the base courting of popularity. Yet, his inner insecurity was revealed by his need of praise, combined with a touchy reaction to criticism or even disagreement. Thus, while his ideal demanded a lofty detachment from the popular throng, his inner needs demanded continual external reassurances. Since the resulting unstable behavior — often regarded as "arrogant" — brought him few of the external assurances, he was that unhappy man in conflict with himself.

Well before the time he came to the House of Burgesses in 1752,

Landon Carter was characterized by what would today be diagnosed as paranoid features. While he did not suffer the delusions of persecution of the fully developed paranoiac, he magnified and dwelt upon slights, regarded the frailties of his fellows — in relation to himself — as expressions of ill will toward him, and reacted to differences of opinion as to personal attacks upon his honor. Opposition to his will caused in him the most violent reactions, and as he grew older he began to seem close to actually suffering feelings of persecution.

Where the other face of paranoia is the delusion of grandeur, in Carter the paranoid element was an assertion of imperial omnipotence. An English visitor had made the observation that the big planters could scarcely bear the thought of another's will imposed upon them, but Carter's touch of paranoia made it unbearable for another's will even to be made known, no matter how trifling the circumstances. Over these injuries he both brooded in silence, recording in his diary reflections on the baseness of man, and erupted into retaliatory actions.

His quarrels and rages (for which he suffered in repentance for the lost ideal of moderation) were matters of gossip in Richmond County, and occasionally his feuds involved the whole county. When the Reverend William Key preached a sermon on "Pride," which Carter took to be aimed at him (as it may well have been), he vowed he would "clip the wings of the whole clergy in the Colony." Arousing a majority of the vestry to his support, Carter had the pulpit boarded over and the windows and doors of the church boarded up. The majority of the communicants rallied around Key and broke open the church, permitting the rector to hold his service. Further enraged by this effrontery, Carter and his friends seized the glebe in which the rector resided, leased the holding to three men, and drove off the parson's cattle.

Though temporarily dispossessed, Key carried his case to the courts and sued for damages. The jury awarded him the sizable sum of £30 sterling. Carter could not comprehend the reality of being bested by a mere clergyman, and he carried his appeals all the way to the Privy Council. This body upheld Key and charged Carter with the costs.

With such eccentric behavior, Landon Carter had made lasting enemies in his home county. Although he had served diligently and

Landon Carter of Sabine Hall
(By courtesy of Mr. Carter Wellford)

intelligently as a magistrate of Richmond County, the majority of freeholders were slow to be convinced of his dependableness as a representative at Williamsburg.

Candidates were not elected to the Burgesses merely because of their wealth and social position. Landon Carter's nephew, Robert Carter, whose Nomini Hall overlooked the Potomac, was ignominiously defeated in his county in 1752 and 1754. Robert Carter III had spent much time in England, married an heiress from Maryland, and, newly settled in Westmoreland, was simply not a familiar person to the freeholders. (His peers solved the problem of his low vote-appeal by appointing him to the Council.)

Landon Carter was defeated three times for the House of Burgesses before his election in 1752. At voting time, either in the courtroom or on the courthouse green, the freeholders came face to face with Carter and the other candidates. The candidates sat at a long table with the sheriff, justices of the peace, and the clerks, who had a numbered poll sheet with the name of their candidate at the top. Each voter approached the table as the sheriff called his name, spoke his choice, and that candidate's clerk wrote the voter's name beside a number. When a voter named his choice, that candidate arose, bowed, and gave his thanks. In this very personal business, the bold-featured Colonel Carter, with a deep cleft in his knob of chin, looked on with a touch of melancholy rather than any of the arrogance that might seem to be associated with his imperious behavior.

Landon Carter had known his share of personal tragedy. His first wife died when he was thirty, and his second wife, the young Maria Byrd, lived only three years after their marriage. A year after her death, when he was thirty-six, he married Elizabeth Beale, of the same county, and two of their four children died young. He had a daughter, Maria, by his second wife, and four children by his first marriage, with the oldest of whom, Robert Wormeley Carter, he was experiencing a clash of wills.

Robert Wormeley Carter, twenty-one in 1755, was among those of the younger generation addicted to high-stake gambling, racing horses and betting on them. Although he never came close to ruining his estate, the future master of Sabine Hall did display in his youth the love of pleasure and lack of mental cultivation which his father regarded as the symptoms of decay in the aristocracy. Yet, while seeing the "trifling" habits of his son's generation as a general symptom, Landon Carter developed the persecutory sense that Robert Wormeley Carter was acting entirely out of disrespect for his parent and all the parent's values. The two of them engaged in some acrimonious scenes, and Landon Carter made some very bitter private entries about his heir. The growing unhappiness in his homelife may have contributed to that touch of melancholy in Colonel Carter's countenance, but his troubles did nothing to mellow the violent-tempered eccentric.

By 1752, when he was forty-two, Carter's neighbors had evidently come to accept his vagaries and a majority of the voters placed their trust in him as their representative in the House. Among the Burgesses, his equals, Carter's ready assumption of responsibilities, his strong, articulate stand on the pistole fee controversy, and his active, intelligent support of Virginia's involvement in the war caused his personal idiosyncrasies to go largely unnoticed. He was quickly appointed to important committees, and there was only one for which he privately expressed distaste. On a committee to draft an address to the Governor, Landon Carter decided that literary efforts were better done by a single hand than in committee: he let the veteran composer of such documents, Richard Bland, write it himself.

By his own family connections, Landon Carter would naturally have taken a place in the oligarchy controlled by John Robinson. His brother Charles worked actively with what Landon Carter referred to as "the Party"; their nephew, Benjamin Harrison V, was a stalwart of that group at the age of thirty; and young Harrison's brother-in-law, Attorney General Peyton Randolph, a cousin of Richard Bland and of John Robinson, was second in power only to Speaker Robinson himself. When Landon Carter's daughter married Robert Beverley, he would be allied by marriage with Robinson and Peyton Randolph. However, Landon Carter operated independently of the party, and of everybody else, acting completely on his own convictions.

In fact, he referred slightingly more than once in his diary to "the famous Mr. Bland," of whom he was evidently jealous, and cited him as an example of political inconsistency in the interests of political expediency. To Carter, "consistency" ranked among the highest of those unalterable virtues which formed his self-model. Among the vices to be avoided was a lust for power — although this was an inconsistency in the image based on the model of his father, for no more power-minded man ever rose to dominate a period in Virginia than King Carter. Landon Carter believed that the greatly loved John Robinson, whom he referred to (not entirely in admiration) as "a jewel of a man," was motivated by a lust for power in his domination of the House of Burgesses.

It was not that Landon Carter suspected the oligarchy of not acting for the good of the community — though he disapproved of some of their maneuvering in the House — but in his unwavering conviction that everything should be subordinated to "the benefit of the community," he bore down hard in his stress on judging by merit and not by friendship or that contemptible ephemera, popularity. Since he somewhat irrationally demanded that other men live up to his model of virtue, he was in little danger of being tempted by popularity.

Sometimes hurt by the lack of the scorned popularity, he retired to his library and fields. He had little capacity for diverting himself with the usual pastimes of his fellows. He entertained dutifully rather than from the pleasure of companionship, and was frequently put in a bad humor by his son's friends bringing out the cards after dinner. In Williamsburg, he never seems to have joined jovial groups in the taverns after the work was done in the Capitol. His brother Charles and Peyton Randolph induced him to go with them one night to the theatre, where Lewis Hallam's "Select Company of Comedians" — direct from London — was performing. He reported in his journal on the "stupidity and nonsense delivered from the mouths of Walking Statues."

With all his complexities of personality and his loner's role in the General Assembly, Landon Carter's principles transcended personalities, and he completely realized his own self-model in his devotion to Virginia's interests and political liberties. He was one of the leaders in the General Assembly of whom it could truly be said that the planter's pride gave a "high aristocratic spirit" to liberty. At an early stage of his Burgess career, he became a friend and supporter of young George Washington and showed that, when his insecurities were not threatened, he had a great capacity for loyalty and generosity. When the coming of the British complicated things for poor Dinwiddie, Landon

Carter emerged as one of his steadfastly clearsighted supporters in the major issue involved in Virginia's troubles with the world outside her borders.

3

Dinwiddie's fellow countrymen at first brought him every reassurance of the British efficiency, which he had missed. They complained of the same uncooperativeness between the colonies, which he had fretted about, and immediately set about to establish unity of action. The first to arrive in early January was Sir John St. Clair, a regular-army major, sent to act as deputy quartermaster-general of the forces in America. With the local rank of lieutenant colonel, businesslike St. Clair rode winter roads to the supply depot and concentration point at Wills Creek, renamed Fort Cumberland. While reviewing the local commands, St. Clair showed the colonials how British methods worked in gathering packhorses (instead of depending on the promises of conniving traders), in establishing hospital facilities for the local troops who fell sick in droves from camp diseases, and in bringing an atmosphere of order to the whole operation never seen during the days of Dinwiddie's Virginia appointees.

While Fort Cumberland was being prepared as a sound base of operations, on February 19 three British ships dropped anchor off Hampton, the old port city which fronted on Hampton Roads. The officers of the two British regiments on board gave the natives a glimpse into the hard-drinking social high life enjoyed by the gentlemen in the regular army. Later in the month Major General Edward Braddock, his Majesty's Commander-in-Chief of all the forces in North America, was driven up the peninsula to Williamsburg, to be received at the Palace by fellow Britisher Dinwiddie.

At that time sixty and stout, Braddock was a comfortable presence, more at home (like Dinwiddie) at the desk than in the saddle. Although his father had been a lieutenant colonel in the Cold Stream Guards and Braddock had spent forty years in the regular army, he had served mostly in administrative branches and had advanced so slowly that only recently had he been promoted above the rank of colonel. His brisk approach to coordination of colonial efforts was entirely to Dinwiddie's liking and, with no troublesome General Assembly in session, the Governor enjoyed a period — which turned out to be brief and illusory — of participating in preparations for a decision with the French "intruders."

In March, General Braddock, his military family and the two regiments of British regulars sailed for Alexandria and the final planning stage. In April Governor Dinwiddie followed the military to the new port city on the upper Potomac, where he was joined by the governors of Maryland, Pennsylvania, and Massachusetts — Sharpe, Morris, and Shirley — and where Braddock was joined by a new aide-de-camp, George Washington.

Washington, after resigning from his command of the Virginia troops, had recognized the road to opportunity opened by service directly with Braddock. Now twenty-three and experienced in the ways of obtaining appointments, Washington did not apply directly to the British military commander for a place on his staff: he let it be known at Braddock's headquarters that the physically tough Virginian, with experience on the frontier, was available for service. Staff work had not then developed into specialized compartmentalization, and Washington was appointed captain and aide-de-camp, along with other young men. In the absence of any such office as chief of staff, Captain Robert Orme, a likable and persuasive personality, seemed to be the most influential with Braddock. Washington established a friendship with Orme and with Braddock's military secretary William Shirley, son of the Massachusetts governor.

In the various conferences, Dinwiddie participated in the big scheme for evicting the French from their holdings along the western borders from Lake Champlain to Virginia. The three major movements would be directed at Crown Point on the southern shores of Lake Champlain, at Fort Niagara on Lake Ontario, and at Fort Du Quesne. With the plans completed, when portly Braddock took carriage to be driven across the mountains to Winchester — and eventually on to Fort Cumberland — Dinwiddie returned in early May to Williamsburg for a session of the General Assembly.

After his high-level conferences with fellow Britishers, dealing in continental concepts, Dinwiddie's patience was tried by the Burgesses' long discussions over matters having nothing to do with the urgent business of raising money for the war. When they did get around to talk of revenues for military expenses, Landon Carter described the genuine embarrassment of some of the Burgesses. In making their last large appropriation by the imposition of a poll tax, the Burgesses had pleaded poverty and accepted the new tax as a heavy burden. If now they should vote another large appropriation, they might seem to have been talking poor mouth, when the truth was that droughts (along with the usual high charges attached to shipping tobacco for sale) made money scarce and times hard. From the smallest to the largest, planters were buying necessities on credit.

The Burgesses got around the dilemma by appropriating the small amount of £6,000 (small in comparison with the needs of the military operations), which would be raised by a lottery. Although the Governor got far less than he wanted, the Burgesses satisfied their consciences by making *an* appropriation and, by avoiding a tax, supported their claims of the Colony's poverty.

Humiliated before his British cohorts by the General Assembly's feeble support of the war, Dinwiddie personally got into Braddock's black book. One of Dinwiddie's Shenandoah Valley contractors failed in his promise to deliver cattle to Fort Cumberland in late May, at just about the time it was becoming evident that neither the Colony's government nor soldiers could lure back the Indian allies who had deserted after the fall of Fort Necessity. The general lumped the Governor with the Virginians in ineptitude — "the folly of Mr. Dinwiddie and the roguery of the Assembly," he wrote Pennsylvania's Governor Morris. "I have been deceived and met with nothing but lies and villainy."

Unsupported at that stage by his General Assembly, and dismissed as incompetent by the British professionals, Dinwiddie was outside the operations when he learned that (on June 9) Braddock had started his advance from Fort Cumberland to Fort Du Quesne. The British general had a combined force of the two regiments of regulars, three independent companies, one company of militia each from North Carolina and Maryland, and nine companies of Virginia militia. A detachment of regulars served the artillery pieces and a naval detachment handled the block and tackle for moving the heavy siege guns.

In one month to the day, July 9, Braddock met the enemy and disaster. Eight miles from Fort Du Quesne his strung-out force was caught in the woods, in front and on both flanks, by French troops and their Indian allies. The British regulars, unaccustomed to fighting an invisible enemy, broke, carrying the colonial militia with them in a rout. Braddock, the desk general, died of wounds. His young secretary, Governor Shirley's son, was left dead on the field, and Captain Orme was wounded. Captain Washington, who rode unscathed through the hail of bullets and arrows, won admiration for his coolness and courage in rallying the shattered troops.

When this information was brought to Dinwiddie, the Governor learned of an alarming and almost incredible consequence of the military disaster. Before Braddock died, whether or not suffering from failing faculties, he turned over the command to Colonel Thomas Dunbar with the orders to destroy all supplies and retreat. By July 20, regular army Dunbar had brought back the troops to Fort Cumberland, from where — in the middle of summer — he talked of going into "winter headquarters" at Philadelphia. Despite the outraged protests of Virginians, on August 2 Dunbar put his regular regiments and two of the independent companies on the road to Philadelphia. He left behind four hundred sick and wounded and the remnants, scarcely two hundred, of the militia companies. These leaderless survivors faced the road which, having been built at such expense and effort toward Fort Du Quesne, now served as a passageway for the French and Indians to the Virginia frontier.

Dinwiddie set about with practical-minded determination to pick up the pieces left by the professionals who had scorned him. Fortunately for him at that time Governor Shirley succeeded temporarily to the command of the North American operations, and the two civilians could work together in mutual respect and understanding. As Dinwiddie wrote the Massachusetts governor, "I acknowledge I was not brought up to arms, but I think common sense would have prevailed not to leave the frontiers exposed after having opened a road over the mountains to the Ohio, by which the enemy can the more easily invade us." However, despite the spirit of cooperativeness between the two governors, Shirley instructed Dunbar to take his regulars to the New York frontier for the campaigns planned in the north. (The northern campaigns, without any disaster such as Braddock encountered, also failed of their purpose.)

It was when Dinwiddie and the Virginians faced the menace on the Colony's frontier, with no British professionals to rely on and no other colonies to call on, that the Governor and the House of Burgesses began to work together. The emergency had little to do with England's continental ambitions or, immediately, with Virginia's claims to the western lands. Their frontier exposed to a "barbarous and inhuman enemy, flushed and elated with their late success" (Dinwiddie to the General Assembly) was all too clearly a present danger.

Even while the emergency meeting of the General Assembly was in session, during the smothering heat of August, Dinwiddie acted on the assumption that appropriate amounts of money would finally be allocated. Forgetting the past differences with George Washington, he again commissioned him colonel of the Virginia regiment, but this time with a significant difference: Washington was also to be "commander-in-chief of all the forces now raised and to be raised for the defense of this his Majesty's Colony," with full authority to act defensively or offensively according to his discretion. At twenty-three the ambitious ex-surveyor, who had found that service to his country happily opened the way to advancement, was recognized as the top soldier in his part of the world.

A force of fourteen hundred men was to be raised to serve under Washington, and Dinwiddie planned for an extensive building of forts and blockhouses along the frontier. At the beginning, Washington's discretion would be limited to desperate defensive measures for the protection of the hundreds of isolated families against whom France's Indian allies were already moving.

4

With the session of the General Assembly which convened on August 5, 1755, the House of Burgesses began a series of measures involved with supporting the war on the border. These measures completed the transformation of Virginia from its self-sufficient parochial idyll into entanglements with problems, internal and external, that were to characterize the life of the Colony during the remainder of its existence.

Neither the people nor their leaders recognized the cause-and-effect progression of separate events — incidents, issues, and decisions — which from later perspective appear to unfold with historical inevitability. That the events did lead to an apparently inevitable consequence was largely because Englishmen in positions of power failed to diagnose a trend in the colonials' reactions. Gathering momentum, the reactive trend developed the progression, which, however, was not at all apparent in the early stages.

When Dinwiddie read his opening day message to the General Assembly in the Capitol, he needed no exhortations to arouse the Virginians to legislate money for defense. With no dissenting vote, the Burgesses allocated £40,000, the money to be raised by a poll tax of one shilling a year on every tithable for the next four years and a tax of fifteen pence per year for the next four years on each one hundred acres of land. Dinwiddie could boast that Virginia had raised for defense a sum almost double that produced by all the other colonies together, and confidently predicted recruiting a force of twelve hundred men.

The recruitment of men and the strengthening of militia was not going to be as simple or as easy as raising money. It was over these measures dealing with the personal liberty of freeholders that Dinwiddie found the Burgesses most trying in their discussions, their hair splittings and compromises. While young Washington began to develop some curbs on his awesome temper and some patience in handling the incomprehensible vagaries of his fellow men in the militia, terrible tales drifted from the Shenandoah Valley to Williamsburg about the massacring of families "with all barbarous circumstances, and unheard of instances of cruelty." Young women were carried off into concubinage by "lawless savages," and "the smoke of the burning plantations darkens the day."

It was not that the lawmakers in Williamsburg were unmoved by these horrors, or by the report that the frontiers had been "contracted in many places to 150 miles and are still drawing nearer and nearer the center." But the laws governing militia and conscription were involved with freeholders' "privileges," with tradition and custom. While legislation was not determined by popularity, the Burgesses found it difficult to unite on courses which aroused understandable protests in the communities.

Dinwiddie's running troubles over raising the desired force and maintaining militia on the frontier caught him when he was physically suffering, and he might have been less than normally attentive to other factors that were distracting the people's representatives in Williamsburg. After an early drought had heavily damaged the tobacco crop, a later drought hurt the harvest in Indian corn, the main staple of the farm animals as well as the people. There was no record of citizens starving, although food was scarce in many households, but according to Reverend James Maury, "vast numbers of stock, of all kinds, perished."

The Reverend James Maury, a rector and classical scholar, was in a strategic position to observe the condition of the people in the mid-Colony area between Tidewater and the frontier. His parish in Louisa County extended across the county line into Albemarle, and his three churches and a chapel were scattered through the physically large parish. In traveling the countryside, Maury mingled with "all sorts and conditions" of people — including his wife's uncle Dr. Thomas Walker, the highly placed surveyor of the Loyal Company. To feed his own brood of eight children, Maury added to his burdens by opening a Greek and Latin school (to which, in 1758, went fourteen-year-old Thomas Jefferson). Mr. Maury recorded, "Our people are loaded with debts and taxes. Money is much scarcer than it has been for many years."

It was to the problems caused by the scarcity of money in the pinched times that the members of the General Assembly turned their attention when they met in special session in October, 1755. The so-called Two Penny Act, then passed as an emergency measure, led to the first real wedge in the relationship between Virginia and the mother country. It was in debate over this act, passed for the relief of the people generally, that the conflicts of interests between the Colony and the British government were openly articulated with a passion that went far beyond the reasoned constitutionalities of Bland's and Carter's pamphlets over the pistole fee.

5

There were actually two of the Two Penny Acts, the first enacted for ten months and the second for one year. In this way, the emergency measures would serve their purposes without running afoul of the "suspending clause" by which each new law could be disallowed at the Crown's discretion. The purpose of the 1755 Two Penny Act was to spare the citizens from paying their debts and meeting contractual obligations at the exorbitant market prices to which tobacco had been driven by the poor crop. With tobacco quoted at twenty-six shillings per hundredweight, the act established the fixed rate of sixteen shillings and eightpence per hundredweight (or twopence a pound) for the payment of all debts or contracts made in tobacco. The obligation could be discharged either in money or in tobacco.

These figures represented the net price of tobacco in Virginia, not on the London market. On tobacco shipped to England, various duties amounted to 7.3 pence per pound. The tobacco-grower, after paying the duties and shipping charges, had to get tenpence per pound in London in order to net twopence. When the prices went higher in London, the big planters could make the big money that compensated for their risks. It was the small planter, the independent farmer, paying his bills and taxes in tobacco, who was hurt by paying at a high rate of tobacco prices. The Two Penny Act was one of the clearest illustrations of the great planters, like Landon Carter, acting in the Burgesses to protect the average citizen.

Fixing the local price at twopence per pound, while protecting the taxpayer, did work some hardship on certain classes of salaried persons and on persons holding contracts. Where small amounts of tobacco were involved, the hardship was not significant. In the case of clergyman Maury, whose annual salary was "upwards of 17,000 weight of tobacco," the difference would come to approximately £80 — a considerable sum to a hard-pressed householder. Maury, however, was typical of the majority who accepted the necessity of the act, of which Richard Bland had been one of the drafters. Maury recorded, "Each individual must expect to share in the misfortunes of the community to which he belongs."

When this legislation was passed in the special session of October, 1755, Dinwiddie wearily dissolved the House after two weeks, as the Burgesses' minds were not on the pressing matters of the war. Dinwiddie was absorbed by it. He maintained a continuous correspondence with the governors of the northern colonies, out of which the only intercolonial action mounted was an effort made by two commissioners Dinwiddie appointed, Peter Randolph and William Byrd III, to enlist the aid of the Catawbas and the Cherokees against the French and the Shawnees. However, although the first Two Penny Act went into law with hardly a ripple, while the nerve-racked Governor was concentrating on the war, a small protest movement contained the seeds of divisiveness.

At that time the professors at William and Mary were clergymen, and four of them, all native-born Englishmen, had been educated at either Oxford or Cambridge. John Camm, William Preston, Thomas Robinson, and Richard Graham, without roots in the Colony, had no sympathy for the causes behind the act which reduced the cash value of their salaries. These four professors petitioned Commissary Dawson to call a convention of the clergy to make a representation to the Bishop of London. Dawson had then succeeded Stith as college president and held the traditional three offices (Commissary, college president, and Councilor) ; but, not among the power-motivated, he was an easygoing gentleman who found his triple post too burdensome as it was. In fact, the Bishop's Commissary in Virginia began to take to drink. To avoid trouble, Dawson evaded calling a public gathering and sent a private letter to London.

This was not enough for the professors. Led by John Camm and Richard Graham, they enlisted six other clergymen to their cause and sent in their own protest to the bishop. Among the clergy who signed was the Reverend Patrick Henry, Scotch-born uncle of a nineteen-year-old namesake who was then struggling to support his wife and growing family on a three hundred-acre farm. Although the petition had no effect on the 1755 Two Penny Act, their action led to a split between the laity and the established church, the repercussions of which played a part in ending the tranquillity of the era. As the split widened and deepened, involving the whole Colony, it came to provide the issue in the first impassioned declaration of the conflict of fundamental interests between Virginia and the home government.

At first the split was small and confined largely to the four protesting professors and the leaders of the oligarchy. Needless to say, Peyton Randolph, John Robinson, and Richard Bland, with Thomas and William Nelson, were authoritative members of William and Mary's Board of Visitors. Their reaction to the protest was, in effect, to discharge the four professors. As Dinwiddie particularly disliked two of them, Preston and Robinson, he supported the Board's accusation of

their drunkenness. Those vanished from Virginia: Robinson died and
Preston went with his family back to England. But Camm and
Graham began a legal fight for reinstatement, with payment of their
back salaries, which they carried all the way up to the Privy Council.

This took years and, becoming involved with their protests
against the Two Penny Act, grew into the crucial issue in which the
emotions of the Virginia people were aroused against home rulings.
However, when the four professors began their opposition after the
1755 Two Penny Act, little notice was taken amidst the larger troubles
over scarcity and tight money, with the uncontrolled terror on the
frontier and the freeholders' resistance to the government's claims on
their military services.

In all the woes, Dinwiddie remained primarily concerned with
filling his quota for service in the border warfare. He complained to
the Board of Trade in February, 1756, about the freeholders' insistence "on their privileges" to the General Assembly. Finding in the
colonials "the want of a martial spirit," he wrote, "I was never
among a people that have so little regard for their personal safety."

The frontier people *were* concerned about their safety in a primal
way — guarding their homes rather than going off in military units.
Then, since all colonials looked to England for protection against the
mother country's enemies, in the six generations of the Colony's
existence there had never been anything of a standing army to awaken
a martial spirit. With this background, the Virginians' faith in the
army regulars of the mother country had been shaken by Braddock's
rout — which Dinwiddie himself wrote had aroused "very great con-
sternation" among the people — and by Dunbar's irresponsible withdrawal of his Majesty's troops from the exposed frontier. The factors
of the freeholders' sense of personal rights about military service, the
frontiersmen's unwillingness to leave their families, the shaken confidence in regular army troops, all contributed to a native prejudice
against the regimentation of army life and against men being removed
from their own counties even when their communities were not threatened. Where a well-connected George Washington might find in
military *leadership* a path to glory very much to his personal tastes,
the men who would leave their crops to serve in the ranks found — in
a land-centered country where the armed forces were not an established profession or livelihood — little inducement to turn soldier.

Dinwiddie believed that the danger to part of their Colony should serve as inducement enough. Landon Carter, with his unenthusiastic opinion of his fellow men, was pessimistic about such appeals speeding the deliberations of the Assembly. Their constituents were parochially minded, rooted in their neighborhoods, and there was evidently reflected among them the suspicion, advanced by members of the House, that the border turmoil was the result of land speculators' greed and England's power struggle with France. That beyond these soundly based suspicions was the reality of French control of the western borders — which would limit the American colonies to a coastal strip bounded on three sides by the hostile French and Spanish powers — was not the type of consideration to stir the minds of an agricultural people then absorbed in making ends meet.

That concern over money problems was the primary consideration was shown by the people's representatives when the House next convened in March, 1756. The Burgesses, with the quick approval of the Council, allotted £25,000 for the defense of the border — again to be raised by an increase of the tax of tithables and each one hundred acres of land. But to make the money immediately available, the Burgesses committed themselves to the long-debated practice of issuing treasury notes. The first treasury notes had been issued the year before, and with the £30,000 issue of 1756 the Colony was in the business of paper money. It was issuance of paper money, more than the intrusions of military demands on the freeholders' privileges, that completed the end of the "life in thrall" idyll within the golden age.

Landon Carter had found little support for his recommendation of treasury notes — in anticipation of levied taxes — when he introduced the subject only two years earlier. But once committed, the General Assembly began turning out paper money regularly for the expenses of the war until, in round figures, £540,000 of treasury notes were issued. Always the paper money was supported by taxes, levied specifically to cover the notes, extending into the future and placing a heavy, increasing burden on all classes. The burden fell very hard on those large landowners and slaveholders already in debt to British merchants. Tithables liable to the poll tax were all male whites over eighteen and all Negroes over sixteen. Besides the poll tax and the land tax and license taxes, direct and indirect taxes were placed on imports and exports.

Unlike the times of high charges and low tobacco profits when volume tobacco production with slave labor could bring wealth to a few, there was no expedient for beating burdensome taxes that accrued during lean years of tobacco production. Then planters struggled against worn-out lands while the new lands to the west were blocked off by the French and Indians, and expensive habits of living were fixed as the standard for all who had emerged above the middle bracket of the planter gentry.

While Dinwiddie was not unaware of the hardships borne by the colonials, his fixation on the one idea of protecting the border — with some help from George Washington's letters — finally aroused the Assembly to pass legislation for building up the military forces. Dinwiddie presented to the Burgesses letters from Colonel Washington and other officers calling for the assistance desperately needed to prevent the enemy from attacking the Shenandoah Valley town of Winchester, the center of military operations in the shrunken frontier. The Assembly passed laws governing the militia and at last came to terms with military conscription: if volunteers could not be induced to raise the provincial force to fifteen hundred, single men would be drafted from the militia.

It was not only the Assembly that responded to the threat to Winchester. When Dinwiddie ordered half the militia in ten counties contiguous to the three frontier counties to rendezvous at Winchester, "great numbers voluntarily offered themselves," recorded James Maury, who went along as chaplain, "although it was a season of the year when men could least be spared from home, and, indeed, when a long continuance of duty must have blasted all expectations of a crop in those who had no slaves to labor for them." At least in that part of Virginia, Maury observed — contrary to Dinwiddie's complaints about the want of a martial spirit — a "general spirit of patriotism, and the resentment against the common enemy, which seems to have diffused itself through every rank of men."

Maury might have viewed the patriotic spirit a little too optimistically (Washington wrote that "the spirit of desertion" among the militia when they did arrive injured the morale of his regiment of regulars) just as Dinwiddie and Landon Carter had been too pessimistic about the Assembly's deliberations in consideration of the freeholders' lack of martial spirit. However, there seemed clearly a swing toward willingness to serve in aiding the frontier communities — certainly in those counties near the exposed Valley.

With money for support of the border warfare at last assured and a new spirit about recruitment, and with England having officially declared war on France (while the Assembly was in session in March), Dinwiddie's personal troubles were only just beginning — and they were not caused by Virginians. They were brought from "home."

6

When the French and Indian War merged, in 1756, into the Seven Years War, England was joined by Frederick's Prussia against an array of France, Austria, Sweden, and a few small Germanic states. With England's attention diverted to the Continent, the direction of the colonial war was entrusted to a new commander-in-chief, John Campbell, the Earl of Loudoun. With the coming of Loudoun to the colonies — he arrived in New York on July 25, 1756 — the personal troubles of poor Dinwiddie reached an intolerable climax. For Loudoun was also the new full Governor of Virginia. Unlike the late Earl of Albemarle, who, as titular governor, had been content to share Dinwiddie's salary, Loudoun acted as Dinwiddie's immediate superior and was the rightful occupant of the Palace in Williamsburg.

After Albemarle's death, Dinwiddie had hoped to be appointed full Governor and halt the drain on his salary. The appointment of Loudoun, a fellow Scot, was a cruel disappointment to him. As with peers who had come to the colonies before, his Lordship could be very engaging with his intimates, and he had attracted to his staff Colonel William Byrd III, who had been living with kinsmen in England when Loudoun planned his expedition. But by an indifference to the feelings of others and an irresponsible carelessness about correspondence, Loudoun treated Dinwiddie with a callousness which was cruel in its effect.

Dinwiddie wrote his Lordship on the first of July asking when he might be expected in Williamsburg. Saying that his family would vacate "the government house" (Palace), he wrote, "I shall take care

to have the House ready for your reception, and rent a house for
myself and family.'' Loudoun did not reply until September, when he
said he did not know when he would come. As it turned out, the new
Governor never came to Virginia, but Dinwiddie remained unsettled
and uneasy.

Long before that, back in May, from the time he heard of
Loudoun's appointment as Governor and American commander-in-
chief, Dinwiddie began to complain more continuously of his health.
He had been ''fatigued in mind and body these six months,'' he wrote
in late May. In September he was ''seized with a paralytic disorder,''
which affected his handwriting. By October he was applying to
Loudoun for permission to write ''home'' for a leave of absence on
account of sickness. As the normally vigorous Dinwiddie lived to a
hearty seventy-eight, his ailments through the middle months of 1756
would appear to be of psychic origin. The long stress, on which
Loudoun placed an intolerable additional strain, somatized in various
physical disorders, including exhaustion.

In truth, Dinwiddie had gotten in over his head in trying to
direct the military operations on the frontier. In his conscientiousness,
he fretted himself over details to an extent to agitate the officers,
especially Colonel Washington. As his instructions were often contradictory, Washington, growing edgy, wrote some sharp replies to him,
and the rapidly rising younger man and the sick older man entered
into an acrimonious, profitless exchange.

George Washington had grown edgy for more reasons than the
unending, temper-trying problems of defending the frontier families
with inadequate manpower and a militia whose performance he found
undependable. His advance in responsibility and in mastery of the
profession of arms, which caused him to recognize Dinwiddie's limitations, had broadened his vision beyond the controls and directions
emanating from the Governor's Palace in Williamsburg. Since his
service with Braddock, Colonel Washington had begun to relate himself to the commander-in-chief of the American colonial forces. At first
this was Governor Shirley of Massachusetts.

Washington had early revealed a gift for attaching men of consequence to the advancement of his career: in addition to the loyal
support of Landon Carter, he had that of Landon's brother Charles
and their nephew Robert Carter Nicholas. With Governor Shirley he

had used what could have been merely an unpleasant incident to bring himself favorably to the commander-in-chief's attention.

Washington had run into another problem of command with an officer holding a commission from the King, Captain John Dagworthy of Maryland. Washington was surer of himself than in the McKay episode, and after Dinwiddie tried and failed to obtain royal commissions for him and his officers, he asked permission to take up the matter personally with Governor Shirley. It was a long ride on a horse from Winchester to Massachusetts, but Washington not only got Commander-in-Chief Shirley to silence Dagworthy but also improved his time in travel by establishing an acquaintance with the governors of Pennsylvania and New York.

In New York, Washington, then twenty-four, also tried to improve his personal fortunes by the standard method of marrying an heiress. Being what might be called "a man's man," Washington had never been successful with women. In his teens, his unrequited infatuations with young ladies — identified only as "Sally" and "the Lowland Beauty" — had inspired him to struggle to express his sense of rejection in verse that was unusually bad even for the mannered sentiments of his day. Then, in his early twenties, he had addressed himself seriously to Betsy Fauntleroy, daughter of William Fauntleroy, a consequential Rappahannock River neighbor of Landon Carter. Fauntleroy was one of the few Inheritors who concentrated on the commercial enterprises of shipping and trading rather than planting, and though his landholdings were not large, his wealth was. Betsy very firmly turned down the marriage proposal, the first Washington is known to have made.

It is possible that Washington, at home in the rough camp life where most of the available women were the poor drabs who served soldiers, was not at ease with ladies of the social class in which he established himself. And, although he was winning fame, he was not rich nor a member of a powerful family. In New York, however, he had the advantage of his friendship with a powerful Virginia family, that of Speaker John Robinson. Robinson's son Beverly had married Susanna Philipse, heiress of the founder of a Hudson River manor, and it was natural that the Robinsons of Yonkers should put up the visiting Virginian.

As a guest, Washington was delighted to discover Susanna's

sister Mary, co-heiress of the Philipse estate. That the twenty-six-year-old Mary (called Polly) was attractive was doubtless less persuasive to Washington than her possession of something over fifty thousand acres. To a rising young man of ambition, thoroughly inculcated with the lust for land that prevailed in his Colony, Polly's Carter-sized holdings made her irresistible. Unfortunately, despite his gallant squiring of her to the amusements of New York, she had no trouble in resisting him.

Despite this failure in his otherwise triumphant journey, Washington profited by his association with persons of consequence outside Virginia, where he had become habituated to close association with the grandees. On his return, he showed no hesitation in bringing himself personally to the attention of the new commander-in-chief, the Earl of Loudoun. At the same time he showed that his judgment of men needed to mellow. Suspecting that his differences with Dinwiddie (and perhaps also his frequent bypassing of his former commander-in-chief) would influence the Governor, he wrote asking Dinwiddie if he would recommend him to Loudoun.

Dinwiddie had already given Washington a fine recommendation without any prodding. He also assured the young colonel that he would invite him to meet Loudoun when the commander-in-chief came to Williamsburg, so that Washington could describe the conditions on the frontier. Pragmatic Washington then wrote directly to Loudoun, and told him his presence in Virginia offered the only hope for improving the military situation.

When Loudoun delayed coming to the colony of which he was Governor — and before it was suspected that he would never come — Washington wrote him of the specific problems in Virginia, and ended with a disingenuous appeal for greater rewards than he was receiving for his sacrifices as a soldier who had responded to "the solicitations of the country." Saying that his nature, "open and free from guile," scorned flattery, Washington laid on some heavy-handed compliments. Not having met the affable earl, Washington had no way of knowing that Loudoun was lax about acknowledging letters and slipshod in all his dealings. Also, having made up his mind to concentrate his military efforts in the northern theatre, the commander-in-chief had no interest in action relating to Fort Du Quesne.

Washington, in going around Dinwiddie to Loudoun (as he was

accustomed to going around him with prominent members of the General Assembly), was acting on what had become a general recognition of Dinwiddie's limitations in military affairs. To accomplish the purpose assigned to him — through which, of course, he would advance himself in colonial affairs — Washington had to circumvent the sick, harassed man in the Governor's Palace. Dinwiddie, although he could not turn loose his preoccupation with military details, had his own troubles caused by Loudoun in which, for the Colony's good, he handled himself well under oppressive conditions.

7

The year before Loudoun came to New York, in March of 1755, Dinwiddie on his own initiative had placed an embargo on the shipping of Virginia produce which might reach the French. In fact, the provisions from Virginia which might aid the French were not considerable: Dinwiddie was actually worried about the heavy, profitable trading some of the northern colonies engaged in with the French settlements in the West Indies and the St. Lawrence Valley. The economy of Massachusetts and Rhode Island was dependent upon molasses, as the raw material for the rum industry, and traded — among other items — provisions which were very useful to the French. Until war was formally declared in 1756, this trade was not illegal, but Dinwiddie felt that the enemy should not be supplied by these northern colonies and by provisions which came through New York and Pennsylvania. After forty vessels, mostly from Massachusetts, Rhode Island, and New York, were reported in the French port of Louisburg at the mouth of the St. Lawrence, he wrote the Board of Trade.

". . . Many vessels with flour, bread, pork, beef, etc., from the British colonies, proceed to Lewisburg . . . where they . . . barter their provisions for rum, sugar, and molasses, the products of the French sugar islands." In another letter he wrote, "The feeding of our enemies may in some cases be deemed a Christian duty; but surely these enemies that commit the most barbarous cruelties and unjust actions, can have no pretensions" to be supported "in their horrid murders and barbarities. . . . But the lucrative dastardly views of some traders have no restraint." He stressed "the concern and trouble

I am under in providing provisions for our forces, when the French are supplied with necessaries from the very people they are invading.''

After Dinwiddie laid the embargo largely to establish a precedent for other colonies, his example was followed by the governors of Maryland, Pennsylvania, New Jersey, New York, and Massachusetts. However, they were not applied simultaneously and, as each was temporary and none strictly enforced, the embargoes were not very effective. When Loudoun came to the colonies, he immediately imposed a colonial embargo. Only Dinwiddie seemed to enforce it conscientiously.

When by September the planters were faced with the loss of forty thousand bushels of Indian corn, which would spoil if not shipped, a clamor reached Williamsburg from all over the Colony. The Council advised the removal of the embargo, and Dinwiddie wrote Loudoun (October 6) asking for permission to remove it. Loudoun replied evasively that he would look into the matter. When Loudoun next wrote he said nothing about the embargo.

In the next spring, 1757, Dinwiddie wrote desperately for permission to remove the embargo, especially on tobacco — which could scarcely be said to be victualing the enemy. Again Loudoun replied that he would get around to the matter, and then sent a circular letter to all the colonial governors placing another embargo on the ports.

By then the General Assembly had met (April 14) with a House of Burgesses that was at last giving Dinwiddie their unqualified support. Richard Bland and Landon Carter and the other leaders, who had supported the Governor's tired appeals to the Burgesses to recognize the shortsightedness of undersubscribing for defense, were not needed in the two months' session to get action on money allotments and on new laws for defense. Eighty thousand pounds were voted, in treasury notes, and the House passed the necessary laws for protecting the frontier and strengthening the militia of which Colonel Washington so bitterly complained. Richard Bland, as the Assembly's chief drafter of important acts, went to work on the new bills. Bland and Peyton Randolph were also selected to draft a message which held an element of sadness.

Dinwiddie had told the Burgesses that his ill health made it necessary for him to request his recall to England. With manifest sincerity he assured the then friendly Burgesses of his regard for "this Dominion" and made the promise (which he kept) to work for the Colony's good at home. Overnight Bland and Randolph wrote the House's official reply to Dinwiddie's resignation, and the following day Bland (despite his limitations as a speaker) read the message in a voice to convey the affection and respect Dinwiddie had won among Virginia's governing class.

With this aura of good feeling, the Burgesses and the Governor united to remove Loudoun's embargo. In response to the House's May 3 resolution that the people could not pay the high taxes, caused by war expenses, unless they could ship their tobacco and foodstuff, Dinwiddie wrote to his superior (May 6) that Virginia was lifting the embargo. With this act, Dinwiddie finally aroused an immediate response from the Earl of Loudoun : he was infuriated.

As Governor Sharpe, on hearing of Virginia's action, had lifted the embargo in Maryland, Loudoun wrote Dinwiddie that his removal of the embargo had the "very bad consequence" of breaking "the concert of action with the other provinces, and destroys that confidence which is so necessary for the good of the whole." Loudoun had held to the point that removing Virginia's embargo would look like partiality from him, as nominal governor, and had never heeded the Virginians' argument that this "impartiality" actually caused the Colony to be discriminated against.

That the Virginia Lieutenant Governor heeded these arguments so embittered Loudoun that he convinced himself that Dinwiddie "had done this for money." In a letter to a friend in England he wrote, "As he has desired leave to resign [he] is determined to get all he can in any shape before he goes." Loudoun may have been influenced in this judgment by malicious gossip, lingering overtones of the pistole fee controversy.

Not knowing of Loudoun's suspicions about his motives, but feeling the sting of his superior's rebuke to him, Dinwiddie wrote a dignified and seemingly forthright answer. By implication denying his sympathy with the Burgesses' resolution to lift the embargo, he advanced sound arguments which indirectly referred to the tussle over the pistole fee. The House of Burgesses was entering, he wrote, "into a dispute of the legality of laying the embargo, which I endeavored to prevent, and thought it more eligible to take off the embargo than to admit of any dispute in your power in ordering it." Also, the Bur-

gesses threatened not to vote any money for the war until the embargo
was removed.

Then the ill-used man, having announced his retirement from
colonial office, spoke out about Loudoun's failure to reply to his letters
on the embargo. "At the time . . . that I never received an answer to
the letter I wrote you . . . it was then noticed that the embargo was
taken off in New England . . . which gave me room to believe that
your Lordship approved of the steps I had taken." As a clincher,
Dinwiddie concluded by quoting from a letter of Lord Holderness,
Secretary of State for the colonies: "Without any regard for the
embargo to order every vessel loaded with grain, etc., for Britain,
Ireland, and the British plantations, to be cleared outward."

Dinwiddie's letter, and time, quieted his Lordship. He wrote,
"As to the embargo being taken off in New England, previous to your
doing it, I have never heard it before, but I will own that these
governments did never keep it well; for several of their small smuggling vessels got out during the whole time of it." As for his anger,
"The truth is that I was extremely hurt at the time, but it is now all
over, and I have forgot it."

Loudoun's difficulties with other colonial officials did not end so
happily. He never forgot his feud with Governor Shirley of Massachusetts and made no friends in the colonies. As Dinwiddie and
Braddock had discovered before him, the colonies showed little enthusiasm for working cooperatively in the common cause of Great Britain, and Loudoun's lack of diplomacy in dealing with the governors
did nothing to promote unified action. Without this, his campaigns
against the French — concentrated in the north — needed military
genius in the field to have a chance of success. Since he showed no
particular aptitude, he failed against Montcalm and was recalled in
1758 — without ever having visited Virginia.

Before Loudoun sailed home from New York, long-suffering Dinwiddie and his family had left Williamsburg, January 2, 1758. He
seems not to have been the sort of man to experience any satisfaction
over the failure of the discourteous earl, who had received the Governor's appointment which Dinwiddie deserved and, as commander-in-
chief, reduced him to a secondary role even in Virginia. Judging from
a letter he had written the previous summer and from his continuing
interest in Virginia, Dinwiddie felt mostly a pride in his achievement

as Lieutenant Governor, particularly through winning the support, first of the leaders of the opposition to his misguided pistole fee, and then of the formerly intransigent, local-minded Burgesses.

He wrote his letter in June to William Pitt, who, then a new cabinet minister, was to be the dynamic force in pushing England's war in America. "I must inform you that they [the Virginians] have been more attentive to his Majesty's commands and supporting his just rights, than any other colony on this continent." By then, the new issue of treasury notes had brought to approximately £200,000 the money the Burgesses had allotted for war defenses: eighty block-houses and stockades for families had been built in the Valley, the chief of which, Fort Loudoun at Winchester, served as Washington's headquarters; and, along with the strengthening of the militia follow-ing Richard Bland's draft, Washington's regiment was finally grow-ing toward the desired complement of twelve hundred. According to his purposes, Dinwiddie had reason to feel proud.

In Williamsburg, where the winter's quiet had settled, the re-spected though never loved Governor had left latent consequences of his war measures — especially in the disrupted economy — which would be realized only after he was back home, and other governors would confront conditions that would have been unimaginable when Dinwiddie first arrived after Gooch's benevolent administration.

As the continental-minded administrator during Virginia's en-tanglements outside the Colony's former range of interests, Dinwiddie had done nothing unnecessary that affected the security of Virginia's future in making the transition from the era of "life in thrall" to the era of international involvement. However, his one unnecessary act, the pistole fee — unrelated to Virginia's border war and resulting expenses — had resulted in the first articulation of colonial principles. And these principles would be applied, in stronger language and in more direct appeal to the people's emotions, to the consequences of the economic disruptions caused by the high taxes for war expenses, when they fell in seasons of poor crops and during the shifts of property values in the old lands.

Totally unrelated to Dinwiddie, but central to the interests of wealthy Virginians in the French and Indian War (Seven Years War), would be the disposition of the western lands in which the prominent speculators were involved.

The disposition of the western lands would be another factor in the differences between those interests of Virginia and of Great Britain which came into the open as a consequence of the Colony's entanglements beyond its parochial interests.

That the actions initiated by Dinwiddie would cause more or less inevitable reactions was not suspected by the governing class when several Councilors — who had never joined the Burgesses' opposition to the Governor — accompanied the Dinwiddie family to Yorktown to see them off. And to his stoutest opponents over the pistole fee — Bland, Landon Carter, and Peyton Randolph — that controversy, then in the past, seemed to have no significance in a present that absorbed them in the new problems rising out of the changes to their community.

When John Blair, as President of the Council, became acting Governor until Dinwiddie's replacement arrived, Virginia's General Assembly could only feel that they had been well served by the business-minded Scotsman. If some, like Landon Carter, were aware of changing values in the younger generation, the men in government did not record any prescience that an era had begun to pass during Dinwiddie's stay in Williamsburg.

· 3 ·

The Changing Character of the Golden Age

Chapter Five

THE NEW WAVE FORMS . . .

OUTWARDLY THE QUALITY of the Gooch era seemed to be recaptured when Francis Fauquier moved into the Palace in June of 1758, six months after Dinwiddie's departure. This elegant gentleman, patron of the arts and felicitous companion, made friends with the planters of the ruling class, cultivated men of brains, and immediately identified himself with Virginia's interests.

The political conflicts during the decade of Fauquier's administration — in which Virginia openly clashed with the mother country — made impossible the harmony that had characterized Gooch's age; but the advance in political thinking by the stalwarts of the oligarchy, along with the emergence of new leaders in Williamsburg outside the oligarchy, created an atmosphere of intellectual-political ferment in the aristocracy that made Fauquier's era the most golden of the golden age in the flourishing of the Colony's genius for government. His time saw the full flowering of Virginia's cultivation of government by a minority of "those presumably best qualified to govern."

Fauquier's decade in the Palace also reflected the golden time in its social life, although the tranquillity of the parochial idyll was forever lost. The new Governor had style, the urbane manners of the great world, grace in conversation, and he entertained with a casual magnificence which exemplified the social ideal of the planters in their turn to extravagant splendor.

Along with the cosmopolitan elegance of his tastes, which was so admired by Virginians, Fauquier was a man of erudition, and the high-ceilinged, panel-walled parlor became the scene of learned conversations. He was also a musician, and in the evenings performances were given by talented amateurs: Peyton Randolph's brother John was a violinist, and Robert Carter of Nomini Hall, who took a house next to the Palace after his appointment to the Council, played on the harpsichord and German flute.

Another trait that endeared Francis Fauquier to the pleasure-minded planters was his love of high-stake gambling. There was a story that he was appointed to the governorship through the influence of Lord Anson, to whom (the story went) Fauquier lost his whole patrimony in a single night's play. The story was probably apocryphal, but no other explanation was given for Fauquier's leaving his life of ease and cultivation in England, at the age of fifty-four, to take an administrative post in the colonies.

His father was a French Huguenot, a doctor, who with his sisters and brothers had sought sanctuary in England. In England John Francis Fauquier seems not to have practiced medicine. Getting a post in the Mint under Sir Isaac Newton, he was promoted to be deputy master of the Mint and was elected a director of the Bank of England. He had married an Englishwoman, and his children were born in London. One of John Francis Fauquier's brothers, William, became a successful overseas merchant, a director of the South Sea Company, and, an avocational scientist, was elected a fellow of the Royal Society. At his death in 1747, William Fauquier left his estate and his honors to his nephew Francis, who became a director of the South Sea Company and a fellow of the Royal Society.

Nothing seems to be known about the education by which Francis Fauquier received his grounding in the classics; his scientific interests, which included observation of natural phenomena, evidently were shared by the whole Fauquier family. He served in the army until about the time of his marriage to Catherine Dalston, of a fine county family (her father was a baronet), after which he settled comfortably into the life of a country gentleman. In assuming his uncle's directorship in the South Sea Company and a Fellowship in the Royal Society,

Francis Fauquier
Portrait by Richard Wilson, 1760
(By courtesy of the Thomas Coram Foundation for Children, London, England)

Fauquier showed himself to be well qualified to take a position among the great merchants of his day as well as among the philosophically minded. Also, he attracted the attention of influential members of the government by a paper he wrote in 1756 addressed to England's problem of public debt which, accumulated during earlier wars, would be enlarged by financing the operations in America and India.

His pamphlet, *An Essay on the Ways and Means for Raising Money for the Support of the Present War without Increasing ʿthe Public Debts,* went into three editions, and his theories of a graduated income tax were later adopted in doctrines which formed the basis of the modern methods of financing wars. He had been encouraged to write this essay by Lord Anson, First Lord Commissioner of the Admiralty, who had been impressed by the ideas Fauquier expressed in brilliant conversation. While it has been considered that his enlightened ideas on financing the Seven Years War, rather than a gambling loss, won him the appointment as Virginia's governor, this too is a surmise and nothing explains why he accepted the appointment.

However, from the day of his arrival, his acts and his attitude showed that he entered into the assignment wholeheartedly. Even after his wife Catherine, growing bored with colonial society, returned to England, Fauquier continued to enjoy life among the Virginians as though born to it. At his death, the *Virginia Gazette* editorialized that his administration had been "much to his own honor and the ease and satisfaction of the inhabitants."

In appearance, he was a dandy. At fifty-four he had none of Dinwiddie's bejowled heaviness. His lean, firm cheeks slanted to a pointed chin, and under arched brows his dark eyes were bright and alert. With his engaging looks to set off his admired style and respected mind, once Fauquier showed his commitment to Virginia's interests, he was in an ideal position to use diplomacy — with strength when required, with flexibility when indicated — during the conflicts that shook the foundations of Virginia's relations with Great Britain.

2

All the causes of conflict between the Colony and the home government were close to the surface when Fauquier came. The specific issues of potential dispute — Virginia's burdens from the expenses of war and the rights to the western lands over which the fighting had begun — were there to be exacerbated. Also, when Fauquier moved into the Palace, Virginia had passed beyond the most urgently troublesome and confusing problems brought by the war and the people generally could begin to turn toward concentration on their internal affairs.

Even before Fauquier's arrival in Williamsburg, the war leadership of Pitt was bringing the decisive military action in the colonies that had been lacking during Dinwiddie's struggles, and the British were on their way to evicting the French without the necessity of Fauquier's deeply involving himself.

Pitt had recognized that in England's world power fight, the conquest of Canada and the western fringes of the American colonies were primary objectives. Leaving the war in Europe largely to Frederick of Prussia, Pitt himself took over the direction of a three-pronged campaign in America to be made by British regulars, with support from colonials. Major General James Abercromby, who succeeded the deposed Loudoun, was nominally commander-in-chief of the American expedition, and responsible only for the move against Fort Ticonderoga. For the move against Louisburg, as an approach to Quebec and the major thrust at Canada, Pitt appointed Colonel Jeffrey Amherst, promoted to major general. Colonel John Forbes, promoted to brigadier, was given the assignment of taking Fort Du Quesne.

This centralized planning was all very orderly, thorough and large-scale, with no dependence upon the efforts of individual governors and commanders to effect intercolony cooperation. In March of 1758, Council President and acting Governor of Virginia John Blair had received his copy of Pitt's letter to the colonial governors announcing the new command structure, and General Abercromby wrote the acting Governor asking Virginia to furnish two thousand men to Forbes's campaign against Fort Du Quesne. With the consent of the Council, Blair convened the House on March 25 for a brief session.

Though a few years ago Dinwiddie had been forced to plead and finagle to recruit two hundred men and raise £10,000, the Burgesses quickly voted £26,000 for recruiting and supplying two thousand, plus £6,000 for their Indian allies. Each recruit was promised £10, and the two regiments were rapidly raised.

Colonel George Washington remained in command of Virginia forces, including his First Virginia Regiment, and the Second Virginia went to Colonel William Byrd III. Not yet impoverished by his excesses and at the peak of his social prominence, Byrd was at this time regarded as a man of potential. Fourteen years after the death of his father, who personified the tranquillity of ''life in thrall,'' he was leading Virginia troops in a world war — involving America, Europe, and India, where Robert Clive was establishing English dominance on the eastern coast by defeating the native rulers allied to the French.

When Fauquier arrived, he wrote home that he found the Virginians ''very zealous in his Majesty's service and very strenuous to support the common cause.'' It was as if, after all the halfhearted starts, the divided sentiments in the General Assembly and divided authority in the field, the momentum of support of the war in Virginia began to gather simultaneously with the single-minded, clear-purposed direction from London and the unified command by qualified professionals in the field.

It was true that Virginia's number one military hero, Colonel Washington, was at odds with Brigadier General Forbes over the road to take to Fort Du Quesne. From Washington's long experience in frontier fighting, and the memory of Braddock's disaster, he was not presumptuous in believing that the latest British regular was making the wrong approach. However, conditions of command were changed and Washington's usual methods of appeal were fruitless. After writing to Speaker John Robinson a tirade against the stupidity of the British generals, he wrote a temperate letter to Fauquier stating what he called the ''obvious facts'' about Forbes's delays.

Fauquier did not allow himself to be drawn into the dispute. It was a military decision, to be made by Forbes, a veteran of infantry command and an intelligent Scotsman with vision, initiative, and the ability to win cooperation from civilian officials. Very ill during the campaign, and crusty, Forbes finally told Washington that he was satisfied with the advice he was getting from others about the road to Du Quesne and, in effect, he didn't want to hear any more about the Virginian's preferred route. For, along with his road-building, General Forbes was operating in another area. He had persuaded Pennsylvania officials and Sir William Johnson, the Indian authority, to open negotiations with Indian tribes toward the end of alienating them from the French.

Forbes believed that the Indians would side with the winner, and the English representatives evidently convinced the Indians that they were backing the side doomed to lose. A conference of many chiefs at Easton, Pennsylvania, in late October led to a treaty by which some of the Indians signed themselves to loyalty to the English. Forbes had endured the delays against which Washington had protested in order to eliminate the fighting of the Indians on their own chosen terrain of densely wooded mountainous ground. He was not repeating Braddock's mistake.

Barely one month after the Easton treaty, Forbes led his troops to a bloodless occupancy of Fort Du Quesne. When his force arrived at the fort on November 24, five hundred French soldiers had so recently evacuated it that the ashes of the buildings they had burned were still smoking. A large number of Indians, some near the abandoned fort and most safely on an island in the river, were waiting to greet the conquerors peaceably.

George Washington, after his years of bitter schooling in border warfare, at last shared in the prize victory as little more than a spectator. In missing the glory, he stubbornly clung to his theory that his proposed route to the fort had been a better one. He wrote Governor Fauquier that ''we can not attribute'' the possession of the fort'' to more probable causes than weakness, want of provisions, and the desertion of the Indians.''

Although his long campaigning ended in something of a personal anticlimax, and his health had suffered grievously from the hardships of the frontier and camp diseases (especially dysentery), the twenty-six-year-old Virginia soldier emerged from the war among the prominent citizens and big planters of the Colony. In July he had been elected a Burgess from Frederick County, when he did the unheard of thing of not personally appearing at the polls. But he had in the Winchester region of the Shenandoah Valley, as in Tidewater, powerful friends to work for his election and to represent him at the voting. Out of his pocket he paid in round figures £40 to provide the entertainment which freeholders expected of all candidates: forty gallons of rum punch, twenty-eight and a half gallons of wine, and six gallons of the best Madeira wine; thirteen gallons of beer and thirty gallons of strong beer; one hogshead and one barrel containing twenty-six gallons of the best Barbados rum; and sundry dinners.

Four years before his election to the Burgesses, in 1754, he had become master of his late brother's estate, Mount Vernon, by leasing it from his sister-in-law and her second husband, George Lee. This Lee was a grandson of Richard Lee II — and nephew of the late Council President Thomas Lee — whose father, another Richard Lee, had established himself as a merchant in England and married an Englishwoman. George Lee, born and educated in England, had come to Virginia as an adult and married Nancy Fairfax Washington. The George Lees leased Mount Vernon to Washington for the yearly rental of fifteen thousand pounds of tobacco, at the established rate of twelve shillings sixpence per pound — something less than £90 currency. This rent included the use of slaves on the property and a gristmill, and at his sister-in-law's death the estate would be Washington's.

With the border fighting over, Washington at last completed the perfect arrangement for assuring a more profitable cultivation of the estate than had his brother: he successfully proposed marriage to one of the richest widows in Tidewater Virginia. Martha Dandridge Custis came from a family of gentry long established in New Kent County (whose shipping plantations fronted on the Pamunkey River) and, amiable and common-sensical, had married wealthy Daniel Parke Custis.

As the heir of the eccentric John Custis, Daniel Parke Custis also inherited the litigation that had dogged the husbands of Colonel Parke's daughters, John Custis and William Byrd II. While Colonel Byrd had finally managed to pay off the debts he had acquired from the estate of his raffish father-in-law, John Custis had been unexpectedly confronted with claims presented by the illegitimate offspring of Daniel Parke in the Leeward Islands.

Among the licentious Colonel Parke's mistresses had been a Mrs. Catherine Chester, whose daughter Lucy — one year old at the time of Parke's murder — she claimed had been sired by her lover. When Lucy grew up, she married a Thomas Dunbar, who changed his name to Dunbar Parke as a means of making his wife's claims more legitimate. For Colonel Parke, though reckless of his reputation, had been exceedingly vain of his name, and provided that his male heirs all change their last names to Parke. Custis, who had gotten nothing but trouble from his wife's share of the entangled estate, never considered changing his own name, and this omission was a basis for Dunbar Parke's claims.

When John Custis died, the suit was still dragging through the courts, and Daniel Parke Custis accepted the suit along with the lush acres of his plantation, the White House, on the Pamunkey, and a handsome house in Williamsburg. Like his wife Martha, Daniel was of an amiable disposition, uninterested in politics, and having been governed by his autocratic father until nearly forty, he was content to live in quiet splendor and do well by his home-loving wife. When he died at forty-five, in July of 1757, the suit (a part of litigations which had been going on for nearly half a century) was being prosecuted by the Dunbar Parke estate, grandchildren of the long-dead Colonel Parke and Mrs. Chester.

This legal complication was in turn inherited by Martha Dandridge Custis, along with an estate valued at £23,000. This nagging legacy of a forgotten amour was the smallest cloud on the prospects of the widow, with two small children, when George Washington went courting in the spring of 1758, less than a year after her husband's death. After the gentle Martha had agreed to marry Washington (who was eight months younger than she), her prospective husband showed in the most positive of all ways that he was not in love with her.

George Washington had given a number of small indications that he cherished a secret love for Sally Cary Fairfax, the highly literate wife of his friend George William Fairfax and daughter-in-law of Washington's powerful supporter on the Council. After his engagement to Martha Custis, Washington received a letter from Sally Fairfax, the first in some while, and this aroused in him a need to know, before his marriage, if she shared any of his long-concealed feelings for her. Referring to Sally in the third person he wrote:

"I feel the force of her amiable beauties in the recollection of a thousand tender passages that I wish to obliterate, till I am bid to revive them. But experience, alas! sadly reminds me how impossible this is —" that is, for her to bid him to revive his memories. Instead, he believed "that there is a Destiny which has control of our actions, not to be resisted by the strongest efforts of human nature." She was married, to all evidence happily, and he was going to be; *but*, "You have drawn me, dear Madam, or rather I have drawn myself, into an honest confession of a simple fact. Misconstrue not my meaning; doubt it not, nor expose it. The world has no business to know the object of my Love, declared in this manner to you, when I want to conceal it. One thing above all in the world I wish to know.'' With circumlocutions that would obscure the meaning to any reader of the letter except her, he wrote, in effect, that she was the only person who ''can solve me that'' — the nature of her feelings for him.

With all its deliberately obscuring language, Washington's letter was so unguarded in its skirting of the society's conventions, and so naïve in expressing romantic hope where no reason existed for him to entertain any, as to suggest that his feelings for his friend's wife ran very deeply within an unsophisticated emotional nature. Discreet Sally, obviously uninterested in him except as a friend, answered with a gossipy note in which she made no reference to his sentiments or question. Washington's forlorn love hopes died hard. ''Do we still misunderstand each other's letters?'' he wrote her. ''I think it must appear so, though I would feign to hope to the contrary as I cannot speak plainer without. But I'll say no more, and leave you to guess the rest.''

With these parting words to ''the object of my love,'' the new Burgess and soon to be ex-soldier went ahead with his plans to marry the agreeable heiress.

Compared to Sally Cary Fairfax, Martha Custis would scarcely have been a dazzling romantic object. While Sally was slender and patrician, with a cultivated mind and grace in the higher life of the plantation society, Martha was small and comfortably plump, with little education and no interest in the mental life, and her tastes ran to homemaking. With her light-brown hair and hazel eyes, she was considered to be attractive in ''person,'' and even her demanding father-in-law had praised her character. But Martha, according to the custom of plantation widows, whether rich or poor, was not looking for a Tristan any more than Washington was seeking a love substitute for his lost Isolde. A story went that she accepted Washington's proposal because she wanted a good manager for her estate, and this sentiment would be in character with her practical turn of mind. If so, both she and the young Virginian on his way toward the top each got what was wanted.

When George Washington left off his completed tasks in the

Martha Custis Washington
Miniature by Archibald Robertson, 1791-1792
(Colonial Williamsburg Collection)

border fighting and prepared to assume his seat in government, the war began to recede from Virginia's frontier. The main theatre became Canada, the conquest of which was completed two years later (September 8, 1760) with the fall of Montreal. Clive had then established dominance in India, and England, the undisputed mistress of the seas, became the world's chief colonial power. In Europe, England's ally, Frederick of Prussia, made his own rise and established a new continental power.

Although the world position of the mother country did not affect Virginia directly, Fauquier inherited the consequences of Virginia's part in the colonial war, both in the problems of paper money and in the changed temper of the people. After the fall of Fort Du Quesne, the Colony was forced to keep men under arms in prolonged fighting with the Cherokees, and this continued the tax burden and caused the issuance of more paper money. The first consequence of the war's effects confronted Fauquier on his first meeting with the General Assembly, in September, 1758. This was the occasion of the passage of the second Two Penny Act, whose repercussions would, more than any other single event, bring the underlying conflicts into the open — and show Fauquier's sympathy with Virginians.

3

The second Two Penny Act was passed for the same reasons as the first: short crops brought high prices which, with planters of all sizes burdened by taxes, again worked a hardship upon everyone settling contracted debts. Richard Bland wrote the new act, again fixing payments in tobacco at sixteen shillings and eightpence per hundredweight, and also fixing prices on certain grains. And, as before, the Burgesses passed a temporary law (twelve months) for the Governor's approval in violation of his instructions. He was instructed not to approve without the consent of the Crown any act which ran for less than two years, and to approve no act which repealed another act without including the suspending clause. Fauquier, as had Dinwiddie, ignored his specific instructions on this point in responding to the emergency.

Although Dinwiddie's superiors at home had given him no reprimand for violating the sixteenth article of his instructions, so quickly were conditions changing that the Privy Council now sent Fauquier a severe rebuke. The Governor was threatened with recall if ever again he signed the passage of a law which did not contain the suspending clause.

At this time the Privy Council was under pressure from both British merchants and powerful British clergy. The merchants' complaints had been growing since 1751 when a law, passed in Gooch's last year to protect debtors, went into effect. By this law debts owed in sterling were permitted to be paid in Virginia currency — based upon tobacco certificates — at an advance of 25 per cent above the equivalent amount in sterling. Even when this law went into effect, however, British merchants claimed that the true rate of exchange was an advance of 33 per cent. And by 1759 — when the Virginia treasury notes were multiplying — it was estimated that sterling was worth 65 per cent more than Virginia currency. While there was certainly justification in the merchants' complaints, there were hardships among the debtors aggravated by the tax burdens caused by war. With all the other factors involved in the unremitting struggle for profit and advantage between the Virginia tobacco-growers and the British merchants, at bottom neither wanted to bear the consequences of an economy disrupted by war.

Fauquier, the avocational student of the economics of war, could shrug off the protests of the merchant bloc as routine in the scheme of things in a nation built upon trade. But the pressure brought by the clergy emanated from Virginia. Although the second loss in salary was a justifiable cause for the Virginia clergy's protest against the Two Penny Act, a visiting English clergyman, the Reverend Andrew Burnaby, wrote that the leaders of the protest went about it with a "violence of tempers," to create antagonism to them among other Virginians.

The protest was started by Dinwiddie's old gadfly John Camm, who called another convention of the clergy. This was attended by about one third of the Anglican ministers, most of them English-born, and they petitioned Fauquier to refuse to sign the act which had been passed in the General Assembly. After the Governor refused to overrule the Assembly, Camm sailed for England near the end of the year to plead his case. Fauquier wrote the Board of Trade that Camm was "a turbulent man who delights to live in a flame."

However, Camm presented himself convincingly to the Archbishop of Canterbury, who supported his appearances before the Board of Trade and Privy Council. Camm also persuaded the Bishop of London, whose diocesan authority embraced the colonies, to accept as facts a garbled misrepresentation of the Two Penny Acts and the motives of the lawmakers who passed them. The bishop wrote the Board that the Two Penny Act was part of a movement designed "to lessen the influence of the Crown and the maintenance of the clergy." The following year, 1759, the King in Council disallowed the Two Penny Acts, along with other acts relating to the salaries of the clergy. As a slap at the General Assembly, and the Governor who approved the act, the King gave John Camm the welcome duty of delivering the official documents to Williamsburg.

For some reason — perhaps the enjoyment of his triumph among friends in London — Camm did not appear with the documents at the Palace until ten months after he had been given them to deliver. The urbane Fauquier was overcome with rage when he looked at the "worn" and "dirty" pages delivered him, and accused Camm of sending copies of the orders to his clergy allies in Virginia six months before he presented them to the Governor. It was a true accusation, as was Fauquier's charge that Camm had lied about him in England. Then Fauquier ordered him out of the house and told him not to come back.

As Camm was leaving the palace with Reverend William Robinson, Fauquier called to them to halt. Gathering his Negro servants in the front hall, he pointed Camm out to them. "Look at this gentleman," he said. "Look at him that you may know him well and if he ever attempts to come hither do not suffer him to enter my gates." Robinson privately wrote, "There was something peculiar in this last indignity, for it is the greatest affront that can be put upon a freeman here to give orders concerning him to his slaves."

Camm had accomplished incomparably more than arousing Fauquier's lasting antagonism. His successful part in getting the Two Penny Acts disallowed encouraged clergymen in various parishes to sue their vestries for the difference between the payment of their salaries at the fixed rate of sixteen shillings eight pence per hundredweight of tobacco and the market price. With these suits the clergy aroused an ill feeling in the people generally that was comparable to Fauquier's toward Camm.

When Fauquier had signed the Two Penny Act he had said that if the clergy received their salaries at high market prices when crops were short, "animosities would exist between the clergy and the laity every scarce year of tobacco." Also, in defending his signing of the bill, the Governor had said that the attachment of the suspending clause would have nullified the purpose of the bill in meeting an immediate emergency. Since both houses of the General Assembly had been almost unanimously in favor of the Two Penny Act, he did not see how he, "an entire stranger to the distress of the country, [could] set his face against the whole Colony and refuse to pass a law for which he had a precedent for passing." Furthermore, to have acted against the manifest welfare of the Colony would have cost him the cooperation of the House and the Council, with whose members he had quickly established an accord.

To the Governor, the successful petition of the Camm-led clergymen, followed by individual suits against the vestries, gave the Anglican clergy in Virginia the appearance of indifference to the people's emergency and to the will of their elected representatives. As his personal rage against Camm did not soften, Fauquier shared the disapproving attitude of the majority of Virginians against the clergy of the church of which he, as Governor, was the titular head in the Colony. While his official position forbade him from taking an active stand against those of the clergy represented by Camm, he suggested that his new friend Landon Carter take up the issue with his pamphlets. "I long to see you in print, as the conversation of the clergy is revived by the arrival of Mr. Camm. He treated me as usual with indignity, and I in turn forbade him my house."

Carter had heartened the Governor by publishing a pamphlet in December, 1759, when copies of Camm's orders — including the Bishop of London's advisory letter to the Board of Trade — had been circulating in Virginia before Camm returned. Titled *A Letter to the Right Reverend Father in God, the B[isho]p of L[ondo]n,* Carter's pamphlet (which was published in London as well as in Williamsburg) expressed his long-standing resentment of the Virginia clergy by a denouncement of the bishop's impugning the General Assembly's motives in passing the Two Penny Act. The bishop had stated that the purpose of the act was to subvert the royal prerogative. Carter, acknowledging that the Two Penny Act had skirted the letter of the law, pointed out that "there were exceptions in all cases," and that "justice to the people and charity to the poor" made the Two Penny Act such an exception. By taking this position, Carter believed that he had "given the first breath of liberty in America."

Also before Camm's return, in March, 1760, Richard Bland joined Carter's attack on the clergy in general and the bishop in particular with a more reasoned, though no less indignant, pamphlet which extended the argument into the realms of royal prerogative. It was actually the later popularization of Bland's principles that produced the first outspoken opposition to a Crown which supported the clergy against the welfare of the rest of the population.

The Reverend William Robinson confirmed Bishop Sherlock in the views inculcated by Camm by writing him about the applause with which the pamphlets were received in Virginia. This "showed to what a pitch of insolence many are arrived at, not only against our most worthy Diocesan, but likewise against his Majesty's most honorable Privy Council."

The fight against the clergy took five years — from the passage of the second Two Penny Act in September, 1758, to the county court case at the end of 1763, when the impassioned protest against the King broke into the open. During this span, when Virginia's diminishing external entanglements were involved mostly with the warring Cherokees — with the then old problem of keeping men under arms and financing their maintenance with more treasury notes — the private war of words conducted by Bland and Carter against the combative John Camm did not make a large impression on the population generally. It was like a minor refrain unobtrusively mounting to a climax while the minds of the people and their government were concentrated on the immediate problems of living.

Making ends meet was the concern of the average freeholder, and meeting the expenses of grander scales of elegance occupied the big Inheritors, or the Inheritors (like George Washington) with big ambitions. There were also the immediate issues between Williamsburg and the Crown which, unending, would not reflect any drift from day to day, although the drift was there, simultaneously with the growth of the animosities in the "Parsons' Cause."

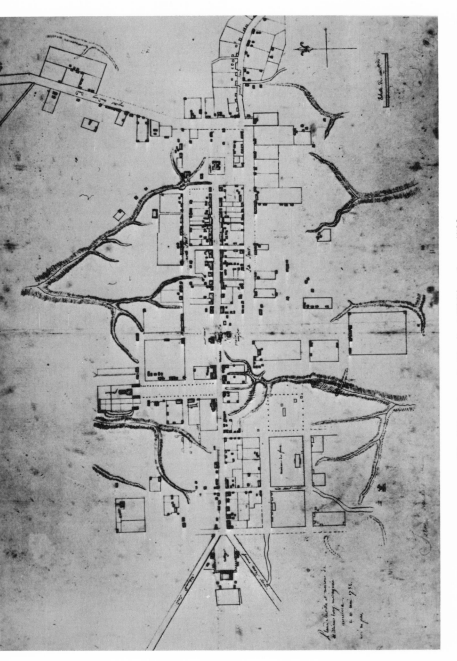

The *"Frenchman's Map"* of Williamsburg, 1782

Duke of Gloucester Street runs east-west, the College of William and Mary at its western end and the Capitol at the east. (Earl Gregg Swem Library of the College of William and Mary)

4

The seat of government had been completed back in Gooch's time as it was to endure as the colonial capital, and the few additional houses, retail stores, and artisans' shops, along with the rebuilt Capitol and a new theatre, effected no change in the character of this essentially rural center of a plantation society. Where the shipping-trading center of Boston had grown into the largest English city outside the British Isles, and the trading center of Philadelphia was a cosmopolitan metropolis, Williamsburg, with neither industry nor trade, remained a charmingly designed country town which twice a year blossomed as a gathering place for the families of consequence and fashion.

With the meetings of the General Assembly serving as an excuse as well as a reason for the gatherings, the ladies and gentlemen entertained at all hours in the overflowed private and public places, and their carriages and horses clogged the broad Duke of Gloucester Street — "one of the most spacious in North America," observed the English visitor Burnaby. As the story went, a Virginian would walk a mile to catch and saddle a horse to ride a hundred yards, and the dust sprays or splashes of mud along the main thoroughfare did not encourage walking by ladies and gentlemen turned out in their town finery.

Although the rich were the most conspicuous, a cross section of the Colony's whole population came to town during Public Times. A British officer who was a prisoner of war during the Revolution gave his impression of the different classes whose social structure had not changed from Fauquier's decade. Since the "first class," by whom the officer was entertained, were similar to his own background, he accepted its members without much scrutiny. "More respectable and more numerous here than in any other province," he wrote home, "for the most part they have liberal educations, possess a thorough knowledge of the world, and with great ease and freedom in their manners and conversation." According to his observation, every gentleman kept his own stud "as well as sets of handsome carriage horses."

It was the "second class" which fascinated and puzzled him. These slaveholders (technically "gentry"), ranging from uneducated men and women who had recently risen out of the yeomanry or artisan class, through families of professional men and merchants, to the well-to-do on the outer circle of the ruling class, were "such a strange mixture of characters, and of such various descriptions of occupations, that it is difficult to find their exact criterion or leading feature. They are, however, hospitable, generous, and friendly; but for want of a proper knowledge of the world, and a good education, as well as from continual intercourse with their slaves, over whom they are accustomed to tyrannize, with all their good qualities, they are rude, ferocious and haughty; much attached to gaming and dissipation, particularly horse racing and cockfighting; in short, they form a most unaccountable combination of qualities and principles directly opposite and contradictory . . . and notwithstanding this inconsistency of character, numbers are valuable members of the community, and very few deficient in intellectual faculties."

He found the "third class" to be "fewer in Virginia, in proportion to the inhabitants, than perhaps in any other country in the world. Yet, even those who are rude, illiberal and noisy, with a turbulent disposition, are generous, kind and hospitable. We are induced to imagine there is something peculiar in the climate of Virginia, that should render all classes of so hospitable a disposition. . . . They [the third class] are averse to labor, much addicted to liquor, and when intoxicated, extremely savage and vengeful . . . [and] their amusements are the same with those of the middling sort, with the addition of boxing matches, in which they display such barbarity, as fully marks their innate ferocious dispositions."

These observations, made from the vantage point of Colonel Randolph's upper James River plantation of Tuckahoe, showed something of the British view of the class system. He particularized on the second class's attachment to gaming and dissipation, especially horse racing and cockfighting, and mentioned that the third class — as "noisy" as were their kind everywhere — also shared these amusements. But his friends among the first class were also addicted to gaming, and the noise of their all-night card games in Williamsburg kept other guests in the tavern awake and resentful. Though rich enough (or with sufficient credit to maintain extravagances on debts) to breed racehorses with their own frequently imported studs, the gentlemen attended the races and cockfights along with those of the

*The Capitol, Williamsburg
(Colonial Williamsburg Photograph)*

*The Governor's Palace, William
burg (Colonial Williamsburg
Photograph)*

The Raleigh Tavern, Williamsburg (Colonial Williamsburg Photograph)

Wetherburn's Tavern, Williamsburg (Colonial Williamsburg Photograph)

middling and lower sorts, and placed bets of a size that at least one parent (Landon Carter) felt to be outrageously irresponsible.

To an English gentleman this was not worth mentioning in the upper class. However, what he was observing was a whole people who, under similar environmental influences, shared certain of the same characteristics, most noticeable among which were a love of drinking, gaming, and horses — horses to ride, to swap, and to talk about, to watch race and to bet on, and, where circumstances made it possible, to breed.

There were of course men and women in all the classes who did none of these things. Some were devoutly religious, even in Virginia, and a response was growing, largely in the broadly inclusive "second class," to the New Light evangelical movement. Landon Carter and Richard Bland were, if not typical, not unique in scholarly habits which precluded interest in gaming and horse racing, and the book business done by the *Gazette* office on the Duke of Gloucester Street indicated habits of book-buying by others than the big shipping-planters who imported books with their cargoes. Presumably, as in any society, families who were neither scholarly nor devout eschewed the racetracks and the card tables and imbibed occasionally rather than by addiction, simply out of a preference for quiet living.

However, since all the individuals who lived what might be called privately would be less noticeable to visiting observers, the British officer was supported by all evidence in finding pleasure-loving a dominant characteristic among Virginians, and the crowds in Williamsburg at Public Times gathered to revel. According to a French visitor, the sounds of merriment made his stay intolerable. To the colonials, briefly liberated from the isolation of their plantations, the boisterousness which disturbed the Frenchman were like the welcome sounds of a party to party-givers.

The most famous public dances were given regularly during the meeting of the General Assembly at Henry Wetherburn's tavern. Wetherburn, probably the most celebrated publican of his day, had first become known in Williamsburg as the operator of the Raleigh Tavern. For unknown reasons he was evicted from the Raleigh in 1743, near the end of Gooch's administration, and the new establishment, which opened across the street, won immediate favor with the big spenders of the day. Dinwiddie was given his welcoming entertainment there and the land speculators of the Ohio Company held meetings in one of Wetherburn's spacious rooms.

The tavern, on property originally owned by Richard Bland's father, was a broad frame building, one and a half stories, with gabled windows in the sloping roof of the upper half-story and a low brick-walled basement which raised the main floor five steps above the ground. Wetherburn had demonstrated that advantageous marriages could be made outside the ruling class by marrying in succession the daughter of one Williamsburg tavern-keeper and the widows of two others. Through the accumulated "hoard," he furnished his tavern with the finest mahogany pieces, pier glasses, brass candlesticks, delicate china, and prints on the paneled walls. His hostelry was famous for its liquors and he experimented with brandied cherries. That he aimed strictly for the carriage trade was indicated by the half a pistole fee he charged for a ticket to the "Ball for Ladies and Gentlemen."

Wetherburn's dances were evidently large social events, for the Reverend Mr. Burnaby found Virginia ladies to be "immoderately fond of dancing . . . Toward the close of an evening, when the company are pretty well tired with country dances, it is usual to dance jigs. . . . These dances are without method or regularity: a gentleman and a lady stand up, and dance about the room, one of them retiring, the other pursuing, then perhaps meeting, in an irregular fantastical manner."

The visiting observers made no comment on the theatre, but theatregoing was one of the main diversions of members of government and their families. In the early Fifties Lewis Hallam's "Select Company of Comedians," direct from London, had (though failing to amuse Landon Carter) made many friends in Williamsburg. After Hallam's death, the company returned in 1760 under a new manager and star — David Douglass, who had married Hallam's widow, the leading lady. Mrs. Douglass's sons, Adam and Lewis Hallam, Jr., were regular members of the troupe, with Lewis's wife Sarah and Mrs. Douglass's niece Nancy, who was described as "bewitching." This popular company played in Williamsburg's second theatre, beyond the capitol, during spring and fall, off and on, for more than a decade, and attendance at its plays was something of a social event.

5

At the Capitol, Governor Fauquier himself started the business of each day in high style. At noon he arrived with pomp in a carriage drawn by six bays and, after his liveried footmen had opened the door, stepped out in a London-made velvet suit. With his unfailing grace, Fauquier bowed to the crowd gathered to watch his arrival, and moved lightly into the building and up the stairs to the second floor, where he was robed for his meeting in the Council chamber.

Fauquier worked easily with the House and the Council on the legislation concerned with England's conquests and maintenance of the western borders from Canada to Florida, encompassing the continuingly insoluble relations with the population of Indian nations. The Burgesses, in their ground-floor chamber, applied themselves to the discussion of the multiple bills introduced by representatives of localities. The most trivial local items received their full share of the Burgesses' attention, and many of these comparatively trifling matters revealed — more than the important acts — political alignments within the ruling class. Beyond these debates, the real work was done in those powerful committees controlled by John Robinson's oligarchic allies.

In the open Exchange beyond the Capitol, members of the General Assembly gathered with friends, business associates, and merchants to conduct business transactions which would normally require weeks of correspondence. They also discussed those personal affairs which revolved around crops and tobacco prices, the buying and selling of land, and the currency, which included tobacco certificates, paper money, and private bills of exchange. (The big planters, whose credit was established with an English mercantile house, could draw on the merchant for cash; and although the cash was usually an advance against a tobacco shipment, the bill of exchange was used much as a check drawn upon a bank.) Increasingly, in 1760, the talk in the Exchange turned to debts owed to British merchants.

There was a rising refrain of resentment against the "usury" of merchants. They began to be blamed for all the financial troubles which beset those high-living planters whose tastes for luxuries were not always accompanied by tastes for the commercial dealings required to support a manor seat on a grand scale. While the British merchants came of a class trained for and dedicated to making profits out of commerce, and while they could be very sharp traders and certainly looked to their own advantage, they operated in a competitive world market where it was elementary for every man to look out for himself. In the earlier generations of the fortune-founders, whose resourceful combination of planting-shipping-trading reached their acme in King Carter (1663–1732), the acquisitive men of commercial enterprise did not expect the British merchants to be in business for the accommodation of Virginia planters, and they had matched any London merchant in cold-minded, ruthless bargaining.

Carter, in the last year of his life early in Gooch's administration, did write privately his conviction that the merchants were becoming too inclined to make a one-way street of their colonial trade. He predicted to the old Perry firm that ''I must profess it beyond my comprehension to foresee what will be the consequence of . . . the oppression of the merchants . . . who are daily increasing their oppressions upon us.'' During most of Carter's business lifetime, Perry and Lane had been the largest and most influential firm of merchants trading in Virginia, and Carter had enjoyed four decades of close association with Micajah Perry. After the death of the elder Perry, the business began to deteriorate and was dissolved shortly after Carter's death. In his letter to the younger Perry, Carter wrote, ''It is an old adage that oppressions make a wise man mad: what our madness will produce, I can hardly promise myself to live to see the end of.''

The ''madness'' first took a turn evidently different from what King Carter had expected. The attitude of the debtors in the Inheritors' generations was to grow more dependent upon the merchants while, in the atmosphere of proudly assertive independence of spirit, cursing them for their oppressions.

Beginning in Gooch's administration, changes in the marketing system gradually undermined the positions of those merchant-planters, like Carter and the first William Byrd, whose stores and wharves and warehouses constituted a shipping center where the big entrepreneurs acted as exporters for the small-scale tobacco-growers. The small tobacco-growers shipped more and more from one or another of the forty public warehouses established during Gooch's time, and from the port cities which came to supplant the private wharves as shipping centers. At the new port cities and on into the backcountry, the small tobacco-growers began to buy direct from stores. Most of the stores were operated by young Scotsmen working out of Glasgow, but a growing number of the new stores were operated by native Virginians.

A young country boy named Patrick Henry, whose early marriage had already brought three children, was struggling with his second store, where he was failing by trying the British merchants' methods of extending credit. The young Scotsmen kept to themselves, for fear that fraternizing with the colonials would make them soft in extending credit. They would not even employ native Virginians, although the tendency to give credit was not listed among the reasons. One of the Scotsmen wrote home that the Virginians' background created ''a resistance to confinement and drudgery . . . [and] they have too many passions to sacrifice before they can be of service to anyone.''

As the new shipping points and the spread of stores eliminated the private commercial centers, the generations of Inheritors became *only* planters and not, as the founders had been, merchant-planters. Where an Inheritor was, like Landon Carter, genuinely interested in maintaining a successful operation and keeping out of debt, he could do both; and although without the commercial foundation he could never amass on the scale of his father, he demonstrated that strictly as a planter a tobacco-grower need not be at the mercy of merchants.

While there were other Inheritors like Landon Carter, and enterprising newcomers such as George Washington, all too many planters were supported in their pretensions by the willingness of the British merchants to extend credit. As the merchants seemed actually to encourage credit, the luxury-minded planters were confirmed in the attitude which accepted debt as inherent in the system based on land and slaves. Perhaps the more naïve about the world of business actually felt betrayed when merchants revealed that they had not extended credit in a spirit of benevolent approbation of the young planters' style of living.

The merchants extended credit partly in a greedy belief in the tobacco Eldorado and partly because they themselves were caught in the practices of the system. Merchants were always reluctant to press for debts owed by any planter with good connections in family, friends, and political associates. The planter's offended pride at being hounded could lose a merchant a whole bloc of customers. Also, merchants hesitated to take legal action against even the middle-sized debtor because the case would be expensive on its tortuous course through the Virginia courts and the merchant's reputation would become that of a Shylock. Then, as the merchants collected interest on the debts, most were inclined to share the planters' sense of security in land: if things came to a pinch, a parcel of acres could always be sold off.

There was another element that existed largely in intangibles. Between a large planter and a merchant, the relationship was essentially personal. When their business association became long established, a mutual regard could develop, as it had between King Carter and Micajah Perry. If a merchant established a representative in Virginia, real friendships would be formed.

Flowerdewe and Norton, a firm rising in prominence since the collapse of Perry in the 1740's was represented in Virginia by young John Norton. He married Courtenay Walker, of Yorktown, and, raising a family in that port city, was elected to the House of Burgesses. When Fauquier came, Norton, then forty, was himself established among the Virginians in influence. Later, in 1764, when Flowerdewe died and Norton became head of the firm, he moved his family to London and his twenty-one-year-old son, John Hatley Norton, became the second-generation representative in Virginia.

The younger Norton would become so indulgent in extending credit to his friends that his father, the former Burgess, warned him of danger to the firm. "You . . . seem to be desirous of appearing to the people of Virginia as a person capable of relieving all their wants, in which you may meet with their applause." By this definition of his son's motivation in extending credit, the businesslike merchant provided an insight into the nature of personal motives involved in the whole structure of the system, as well as revealing the expectations of those planters whose life-styles assumed that credit would gratify their extravagant predilections.

Fauquier, alarmed at the increase of imports (with a large proportion of luxuries and liquors) over exports, wrote the Board of Trade that he could think of no way to change the balance, because "the generality" of Virginians "obstinately shut their eyes against" the gritty realities of commerce. Receiver General Richard Corbin, of one of the very oldest Virginia-English planting-merchant families, wrote of his fears for the generation unless they would curtail their extravagances. Others on the scene believed curtailment was impossible. Nathaniel Savage wrote to John Norton that "frugality . . . is a potion scarcely to be swallowed by Virginians brought up from their cradles in idleness, luxury and extravagance."

As with all the generalities about the people, these observations expressed a growing tendency among what Fauquier called "the generality" of Virginians, and by no means included every planter family. However, the habit of debt was becoming widespread among planters of all degrees, from the largest to the smallest, and it was also becoming a habit to attribute to the merchants the consequences of their practices.

While the system of consigning tobacco shipments to English merchants clearly favored the merchant, and they were certainly in business to exploit any advantage, the reputable firms, such as Norton, were cooperative and considerate; and, although Norton netted £4,000 a year off the Virginia trade even in the hardest times that were to come, he took enormous risks, and in the 1770's the debts on his books were to reach £40,000. As a class, at the operational center of the system, the merchants were not the villains they were increasingly made out to be in the planters' discussions in the Exchange and in the taverns, and ultimately in the public mind.

It was a case of

> *In tragic life, God wot,*
> *No villain need be! Passions spin the plot:*
> *We are betrayed by what is false within.*

Those planters who took the easy way of credit as a means of keeping up in the race for splendor were betrayed by their own vanity and a pride which blinded them to the realities of the business they were in through inheritance. It was inevitable that the baronial masters would look elsewhere than at their own weaknesses for the causes of their insecurely based grandeur, and the merchants were handy for the role of the heavy. Also the merchants reflected a mother country against whom the growing offspring felt an assertive impatience of restraints and controls.

6

All the factors of potential division and conflict between England and the Virginia colonials (which existed with only differences in detail in almost all the colonies) were accepted in 1760 Williamsburg as no more than chronic grievances. Although there was an unspoken, sub-surface drift toward a deepening resentment of these grievances — a forming resentment of the very nature of the political-economic relationship out of which these grievances arose — the minds of the men in the capital were centered on the operations of the Colony's government and, with time allotted for the pleasures of social life, on their own advancement within the structure as it existed.

The new Burgess, George Washington, was as typical of the general attitude as any, even though in his ambitions for personal advancement he was cut from the pattern of the earlier generations of acquisitive planters. He might go into debt to buy slaves and luxuries, but he did not expect credit to support his style of life with Martha at Mount Vernon. Like his older friend Landon Carter, he was one of the planters genuinely interested in agriculture and determined to make it pay. Industrious and systematic, he gave (as did all the really successful planters) personal attention to every detail and was very businesslike about extracting the highest yield from his acreage. He rented out portions of his land, grew heavily in corn as well as tobacco, and, when he discovered that his land would not produce top-grade tobacco, turned to large-scale planting in wheat and to milling.

Coming into the General Assembly in the February session of 1759, around the time of his twenty-seventh birthday, he made no presumption on his military reputation nor on his friendship with such oligarchic leaders as Speaker John Robinson. With his recognition of his own limitations, he did not attempt any speechmaking. Quiet in the noisy sessions, the ex-soldier observed carefully the operations of those men — Robinson, Peyton Randolph, Richard Bland, the Carters, and others — who were master players at their own game of politics. To help his own understanding of the nature of his political responsibilities, he read analyses of the English government, and he read in a broad area of interests in the self-cultivation of a country gentleman. Washington seemed to find the deepest pleasure in reading history and plays (he was a regular theatregoer when in Williamsburg), and the ideal literature was Addison's *Cato,* in which history and drama merged.

Since he was newly married and the Williamsburg house of Martha Washington's late husband had not then been sold, the probability is that the colonel and his lady stayed in the house built by the eccentric John Custis. At times the new Burgess joined friends in the east room of Henry Wetherburn's tavern, relaxed among male friends and played cards for low stakes. He was careful with his money.

In that first session, Washington set the pattern that his conduct would follow as a member of the General Assembly : he became known for his ''majestic'' walk, his careful dress, his magnificent figure on a horse, the impressiveness of his attentive silences in the House, and his modesty and formality rather than for participating either in the high social life of the capital or in the transient issues handled by the Burgesses. He took no stands. However, the positions he took later showed that the publicly shy Washington, with no adeptness for maneuvering in committees, was learning with his customary thoroughness about the fundamental issues which it was the responsibility of the General Assembly to confront.

Washington's contemporary, Richard Henry Lee (born January 20, 1732), who was elected to the Burgesses in the same year, 1758, was the antithesis of the military hero in his immediate, self-assured participation in the House's discussions and in readiness to talk. This Lee had the advantage over Washington in coming of a family who had been prominent in the Colony's government for more than a century. His father had been President of the Council, his brother was a Councilor, and his cousins were scattered through the House. Having been born at the top, in the third generation of Inheritors, Richard Henry Lee possessed none of Washington's acquisitive drive nor commercial interests. At the same time, he was not among the extravagant high livers. His drive was in political ambition, and his political thinking was much more advanced than Washington's when he came to Williamsburg. Lee was, in fact, an embryonic revolutionary — the first to emerge from what was by then the hereditary ruling class.

7

As the third son of Thomas Lee and Hannah Ludwell Lee, Richard Henry Lee inherited no stake in Stratford Hall, the massive manor seat on the Potomac. This went to his older brother, Councilor Philip Ludwell Lee. Lee was educated at home and for seven years — from twelve to nineteen — at the academy in Wakefield, England. Since his two older brothers were studying law at the Middle Temple during his last years in Wakefield, it can be presumed that he was being prepared either to join them or to enter one of the universities; but the death of his father brought all three sons back to Stratford Hall.

For the first few years back in Virginia these older three of the six Lee boys lived a bachelor idyll in the splendid rooms of the manor house and on the wonderland of the estate. Richard Henry and firstborn Philip Ludwell enjoyed the companionship of affectionate opposites. Philip Ludwell was the plantation master of the legend, with the inherited wealth to support his style of living: he provided generous hospitality, loved parties in the great hall of Stratford and in the homes of friends, liked fox-hunting and all outdoor sports, and was, among those whom he accepted as his equals, warm and spirited. To those whom he considered his inferiors, he could be overbearing and rude, with an ''arrogant, haughty carriage,'' and he generally showed an excessive pride of family — a trait not unique to Philip Ludwell among the Lees.

Richard Henry was a throwback to his grandfather, Richard Lee II, the austere scholar. To the typical devotion to the classics among the educated planters of his day, he added (unique for his time) the study of English, and Shakespeare and Milton took their places with Virgil and Horace. But, as one of the members of the governing class who prepared himself for public life as any professional would prepare himself for a career, Lee was most absorbed in history and in the theories of government. He possessed a most intimate knowledge of those principles of John Locke which had exerted an influence on Virginians as early as the turn of the century. Richard Henry Lee enjoyed half a dozen years of quiet seclusion at Stratford for the studies which prepared him for his leading role in the General Assembly.

In 1757 he married Anne Aylett and set up his establishment at Chantilly, on a point of land overlooking the Potomac several miles above his birthplace. His unpretentious frame house was anything but baronial and, although he had inherited forty slaves, his indifference to agriculture (or to any income-earning endeavor) made his plantation an unsuccessful operation.

Before Richard Henry Lee set up his own home, an episode when he was twenty-three may have exerted a profound effect on his political philosophy and career in the General Assembly. When General Braddock came to Virginia in 1755, Lee felt a passing impulse toward military action and, as a captain in the Westmoreland County militia, marched a company of the somewhat dubious patriots to the British general's headquarters. Braddock took one look at the farmers, led by the lean, ascetic-looking scholar, and contemptuously declined their services. Then, not recognizing one colonial from another, the general left Lee standing alone on the shore when he and his officers climbed into a small boat to be rowed out to the commodore's ship.

To Richard Henry this was not merely the insult of a British general to him, a colonial: it was the insult of a representative of the British Empire to a *Lee.* Many Virginians were offended by fat Braddock's contemptuous attitude to colonials, and this undoubtedly was one of the multiple contributions to the later changes in their attitudes toward England; but Richard Henry Lee was the only member of the planter class who (by record) harbored a rankling at an insult taken personally.

There was another element in his background when he went to Williamsburg that probably effected his evolution into a revolutionary, especially in those revolutionary aspects in which he turned against his own class. His father, Thomas Lee, as the chief founder of the Ohio Company, had been challenged in western land expansion by the Tidewater group headed by John Robinson; and, more personally, when Thomas Lee had served as Council President, the real power was wielded by Speaker Robinson and his Tidewater cohorts. When Richard Henry himself came into a General Assembly that soon was to include six other Lees, the real power was still held by Robinson's Tidewater oligarchy.

There was no speculation about where Lee stood in regard to Robinson. Soon after he took his seat among the Burgesses, when they voted on the (by then, largely ritualistic) election of their Speaker, Lee voted against Robinson. Later, he became one of the most determined investigators of Robinson's financial entanglements as Treasurer.

Despite his opposition to Robinson, the Speaker appointed Lee to some of the most important committees in the House, and the Tidewater oligarchs on those committees gave every recognition to the talents and desire for responsibility of the young newcomer. The oligarchy's custom of encouraging initiative in anyone in whom merit was encountered might have, in Lee's case, included the practice of the principle of making allies of the opposition; if this were so, it did not work on Lee.

His opposition to Robinson's allies aroused the lasting enmity of his cousin Benjamin Harrison V, whose Harrison and Carter lines (the King was his grandfather) formed the oldest continuity in the Tidewater oligarchy. The old rivalry between Thomas Lee and King Carter would not of itself account for Harrison's antagonism to Richard Henry. The large, affable Harrison, anything except a grudgeholder, was noted in the Assembly for the infectious, sometimes bawdy humor by which he relieved tensions in committees and generally eased the strains of legislation. Then, Harrison's uncle, Landon Carter, was an intimate of Richard Henry's brother Francis Lightfoot Lee, the real planter of the Lee family in that generation, and a genial man of a humorous turn of mind (as well as a scholarly mind) who was liked by everybody; Harrison's cousin Robert Carter of Nomini Hall was an intimate of Philip Ludwell Lee, himself as regal and old-line as the most conservative Tidewater baron.

But Richard Henry, tall and spare and humorless, had a touch of righteousness and more than a touch of imperiousness in the zeal of his opposition first to the oligarchy and then to the oligarchy's position in relation to England. Lee's Puritan-type zealousness was made harder to bear for hearty, gregarious men like Harrison because of the carefully reasoned eloquence of his speeches. In the House where some

Richard Henry Lee
Portrait by Charles Willson Peale, 1784
(Independence National Historical Park, Philadelphia)

of the oligarchy's leaders were poor speakers and where some of the Burgesses (like Landon Carter) talked too much, Lee, with a mellifluous voice, was known as a "harmonious" speaker. Although he lacked the passion and feeling for humanity to stir the hearts of his listeners, he was impressive in combining logic and learning, and quick in an impromptu debate.

Yet one of his most famous speeches held both a dubious motivation and a cloudy generality. Before he entered the House, in 1756 when the Burgesses were raising money for war, a 10 per cent duty was placed on the purchase price of slaves. This was an act much favored by the established planters, since it discouraged the competition of new rivals by making the price of slaves in volume prohibitively high. "The Squabble," as Governor Fauquier termed it, over this duty, came to a head between the established planters and the ambitious planters who wanted the duty removed during February and March of 1759 — the first session attended by George Washington, although he had been elected the year before, when Lee entered the House. In supporting the duty, Richard Henry Lee was not going against his interests as the owner of forty slaves. But his speech has been taken as showing prescient perspicacity.

"And well I am persuaded, sir, that the importation of slaves into this Colony has been, and will be attended, with effects dangerous, both to our political and moral interests. When it is observed that some of our neighboring colonies, though much later than ourselves in point of settlement, are now far before us in improvements, to what, sir, can we attribute this strange, unhappy truth? The reason seems to be this: that with their whites they import arts and agriculture, whilst we, with our blacks, exclude both."

The moral effect on the white population had been pointed out by William Byrd, among others, of the earlier generation, and it was commonplace among the enlightened of Lee's generation to deplore the evil effects on both races. As for Lee's practical points, in the "arts," since Virginia's arts were expressed in government and political theory, and secondarily in the style of social life (including some fine indigenous architecture in the plantations' manor houses), *as of at that precise time,* judging the Virginia civilization by its own intention, it was inaccurate to say that other colonies have "greatly . . . outstripped us." In agriculture, the generations of the fortune-founders had not been outstripped by anybody through the use of slaves as labor forces in planting, nor were individuals who concentrated on agriculture (such as George Washington and Landon Carter) suffering by comparison with individuals in other colonies.

What was happening was that a large proportion of Inheritors expected loosely supervised slave labor on indifferently managed plantations to provide them with the security with which to follow their own pursuits — as Richard Henry Lee himself in public life. Agricultural development was suffering because the Inheritors assumed the prerogatives of a leisure class on the assumption that they were independent of the need of attention to the source of income. The practices of Lee's contemporaries were making a leisure generation while undermining the source necessary for a continuing leisure class.

This is in no way to enter that timeless argument as to whether or not the use of slave labor was *in itself* effective economically, and certainly none can argue against the baleful effects of the institution on both races — and increasingly on the planters through the stifling mental climate created by the slavery defenders of the nineteenth century. It is to point out that in Lee's generation, while the presence of slave labor caused a large proportion of the Inheritors to neglect agricultural (and commercial) developments, the very attitude, which took income through slave labor for granted, made possible the development of the Colony's genius in government, as Lee's own life course demonstrated.

In the King Carter era, when Lee's father was building himself into a position of wealth and political influence, the great entrepreneurs could extend (without thinning) their attention and energies to encompass vast agricultural-commercial enterprises and the exercise of knowledgeable responsibility in high places in government, while still enjoying the cultural uses of their minds. Richard Henry Lee was a conspicuous representative of a generation which, assuming the benefits of their progenitors' accumulations, concentrated in depth on a single objective which had only been one facet of the protean figures of the preceding generations. Political scholarship, centered in studies designed to fit an individual of the ruling class for responsible leadership in government, could and for some had become an end in itself.

It was not that the use of slave labor *per se* militated against agricultural developments. The *effects* of slave-owning on Inheritors such as Lee caused them to neglect the economic bases of theirs and the Colony's security. Lee, sometimes referred to as the Cicero of the General Assembly, represented a generation of a class that assumed the attitudes of the Roman aristocracy (also based on slave labor) without an economic foundation which could endure with that attitude. However, their *assumption* of an enduring ruling class of the landed gentry did make possible the full flowering of the political genius of the golden age in Fauquier's enlightened era.

It might be asking too much of Richard Henry Lee, or any of them, to have perceived this. Such a perception, however, would have truly revealed the prescience for which his speech has been praised by after-the-fact evaluators holding different perspectives on the whole institution of slavery from those prevailing in the English-speaking world of his day.

In the prevalent attitude of his day, when New England fortunes were being made in the slave trade, Lee was neither unique nor particularly perspicacious in voicing apprehensions about the effect of the blacks upon the whites. He would have been unique indeed if he had perceived that the black slaves exerted any ill effect upon *him*. For they made possible the sequestered sanctuary in which, untroubled by agricultural or commercial enterprises and developments, he followed his own bent in preparing the speeches that dazzled his fellow Burgesses. The question Lee might have asked was this: why did the black slave-labor forces cause him and the others to neglect the source of their own and their Colony's economic well-being? After all, Landon Carter, far richer than Lee and politically as busy, continually conducted agricultural experiments. But the austere Lee was at his most human and least logical when he took his part in establishing the precedential procedure of viewing the problem of the blacks by their effects upon *others*.

It was obvious that the effect of slave-labor forces *was* to discourage the immigration of whites who would bring new methods of working the land. But somewhere, unconscious rationalization took over as the inheritors of agricultural land continued outworn methods on land becoming exhausted — with a factorage system of marketing unchanged since the first few merchant-planters established their shipping centers more than a century before — and found personal justification in the arts of governing they brought to Williamsburg.

The ultimate question of whether black slaves justified this golden age in politics was, most definitely, not in the air the Virginians breathed in their hours on earth.

8

Two of Richard Henry Lee's future fellow revolutionaries came to Williamsburg in 1760 — Thomas Jefferson and Patrick Henry. Henry, then twenty-four — four years younger than Lee and Washington — was in town temporarily to take an examination permitting him to practice law. Seventeen-year-old Jefferson was in residence, starting in March, as a student at William and Mary. Neither at that stage seemed to have anything in common with the assured, eloquent Lee, nor with one another.

Patrick Henry has been so frequently pictured as an ''uncouth rustic'' and a ''shambling plebeian'' that it must be stressed that to be born outside the ruling class was not necessarily to be the opposite of the aristocrat. In the graduations of the plantation society, Henry's family on both sides belonged in the gentry and were strongly placed in county politics. His father was a graduate of King's College, Aberdeen, and became a magistrate in the gently rolling, fertile country of Hanover County, north of Richmond. His father's brother, the Reverend Patrick Henry who had joined John Camm's protest against the Two Penny Act in 1755, had migrated to Virginia at a different time from John Henry and settled in the same community. John Henry married a widow, Sarah Winston Symes, whose own family and whose first husband's family were well-connected county people and, while in modest circumstances in comparison to the rich, were as comfortably fixed as the average farm family.

The young Patrick Henry was, except for some years at ''a common English school,'' largely tutored by his father, from whom he learned Latin and a smattering of Greek. At fifteen he was trained for a year in one of the new crossroads stores, and the following year his father was able to set him up in a store of his own. Henry liked talking to people too much and was too generous with credit to make much success as a merchant, and in a year the store failed. When he was eighteen he married sixteen-year-old Sarah Shelton, whose father was in a position to start them in life with a three-hundred-acre tract and six slaves. Young Henry was even less well suited for farming than for storekeeping and at twenty-two, the father of three children, he opened a second store while continuing his losing struggle with the farm.

After two years he gave up the whole thing — store and farming — and moved his family in with his father-in-law in the large, prosperous tavern which Shelton owned in Hanover Court House. As Henry, while living with him, sometimes helped at the bar, in the "plebeian" picture he was described as a "bartender" for this brief period of his formative years. Actually he was studying law during those months with his father-in-law.

A casual glimpse of the slim, slouched figure in the tavern could well have suggested a young drifter without much on his mind. Good-natured, he always liked sociable gatherings, and, if a party got going, he would help out with his fiddle. Typical of boys raised on a farm in a lightly settled country, he enjoyed hunting and fishing and was much at home in the woods. But those indigenous pleasures would not make him the "forest Demosthenes" of the legend any more than his companionship with persons of no consequence made him an untutored idler. As a matter of fact, he was very ambitious.

Not of an intellectual cast of mind, he enjoyed reading, and, while no one would have taken him for a scholar, Henry had a cultivated intelligence. The point was that before he turned to law, during the failure at farming and storekeeping he had not found the way in which his ambition could use his particular kind of intelligence. He was not of a mind that would have its potential developed, as was Richard Henry Lee's, through contemplative hours with books. Patrick Henry's mental gifts were unselfconsciously developed through studying the people of "all sorts and conditions" — *including* "plain people" — with whom he passed the hours in talking. Henry was learning, by absorption, what the "harmonious" Lee never had, a knowledge of the hearts of men and women. He learned what people were thinking outside of Williamsburg.

When Patrick Henry came to town, he was plainly dressed after the manner of the country people of his neighborhood, and his utilitarian attire would have contrasted with the tailored coats and breeches, brocaded waistcoats and neckpieces of linen ruffles in which

George Wythe. Portrait by an unknown artist
(Colonial Williamsburg Collection)

the stylish adorned themselves in Public Times. Personally he remained indifferent to dress and, even after he became familiar with the styles, preferred simpler clothes. Also, since he was a highly effective actor, Henry might have retained his comparatively plain dress as a distinguishing characteristic. (Young Jefferson, who also came plainly dressed to Williamsburg, soon outfitted himself according to the prevailing fashions.)

The purpose of Henry's first trip, passing the bar examination, was almost not realized. He was examined by four of the most eminent lawyers of the day, who were also very formidable gentlemen. Huge Peyton Randolph, Attorney General, and his brother John, who would succeed him, had both been educated at the Inner Temple; Robert Carter Nicholas, King Carter's grandson, would succeed John Robinson as Treasurer; and courtly George Wythe, then in his early thirties, would assume the first chair of law at the College of William and Mary. These distinguished men of law generally felt that Henry was inadequately prepared. Many stories grew about the examination, but the end of it was that George Wythe and John Randolph were willing to sign the certificate which admitted the unprepossessing applicant to the practice of law in Virginia.

Academically Henry was inadequately prepared — or, at the most, on the borderline and he never became learned in the law. But he had an instinct for his own gift: he could sway juries as no other lawyer of his time. He knew the people who composed the juries. When he rode his lean horse out of Williamsburg with his precious certificate, he was going toward a career which would return him to Williamsburg, in the House of Burgesses, practically by the popular acclaim of the people, who recognized his knowledge of their hearts.

9

There was never any question of Patrick Henry's going against his class when he later joined Richard Henry Lee as a revolutionary: he was not born in the ruling class. But Tom Jefferson was a Randolph — at least, by blood strain and by his acceptance of the privileges inherent in the connection. However, Jefferson was not formed by an environment characterized by the attitudes and assumptions of hereditary members of the ruling class. Although aware of the advantages of belonging to the Randolph clan, he was not as an individual molded by his sense of the importance of his family. In the sense that Richard Henry Lee was quintessentially a Lee, Tom Jefferson was only peripherally a Randolph.

His maternal grandfather, Isham Randolph, was that son of the founding couple, William and Mary Randolph, who spent much of his life at sea and finally settled, with an English wife, on a plantation in the then unsettled James River country west of the fall line at Richmond. Jefferson's half-English mother had grown up in this semifrontier neighborhood far by travel from the Tidewater plantation seats and — since her father's political career was brief and inconsequential — from the social life of Williamsburg. Her most eligible suitor had been the physically powerful, ambitious surveyor Peter Jefferson, entirely a product of the newly opened country where plantation manor seats were few.

When Tom Jefferson was a child, the family moved farther west, to the new county of Albemarle, where his father began to concentrate on planting his holdings. Peter Jefferson became a citizen of importance in the new county, serving at times as magistrate, as county surveyor, two terms in the House of Burgesses, and as lieutenant in the militia until his death. Since, like his father-in-law, he took no real part in the Colony's government, his son knew about Randolph kinspeople holding high place rather than having casual familiarity with persons of consequence.

The young Jefferson was entirely his father's son. When Peter Jefferson died when his son was fourteen, Thomas Jefferson was already completely formed. He was a product of the new county in which his father had established himself rather than of the old Tidewater, although from his teens he viewed the world beyond geographic boundaries and his receptive mind was totally cosmopolitan. Where his father's rise in the new county most significantly affected Jefferson was in his lasting respect for and belief in the men of agriculture who brought vitality to the society and perpetuated that high sense of individual responsibility which characterized the best in the ruling class. Jefferson developed the conviction that these qualities, epitomized by his father, sustained a true and vital aristocracy in contrast to the aristocracy of property (with its social trappings) which could produce self-inflated drones and the inertia of the self-satisfied.

Jefferson's mother seems to have exerted no influence on him and his scant references to her do not reveal any great esteem. From all accounts, she was a homebody of pleasant disposition, and there was no evidence of any friction between her and her most gifted child among six children — Tom had a younger brother and four sisters. While Jefferson, as an adult, was always solicitous of his mother's welfare, Jane Randolph Jefferson simply was not interested in those things of the mind that drew her firstborn son from his earliest days.

Peter Jefferson, while not in the class of the great landowners, left his wife and children substantial property, including more than sixty slaves. Jefferson's mother had for her lifetime the home plantation, with sufficient slaves, horses, cattle, and hogs to maintain its operation. Called Shadwell, this plantation was situated on the Rivanna River, a small stream which was later opened for navigation by light boats — bateaux — in an operation for the removal of obstructions inaugurated by Thomas Jefferson when he was twenty-two. After all the other children were provided for, Tom on his twenty-first birthday would come into a tract of 2,650 acres on the Rivanna (on which he later built Monticello), another approximately 2,500 acres of scattered holdings, and twenty slaves. As well as leaving his family well provided for, Peter Jefferson left friends — particularly Dr. Thomas Walker, his physician and fellow holder of shares in the Loyal Land Company — who acted as mentors as well as very prudent executors of Thomas Jefferson's estate during his minority.

Tom Jefferson was practical-minded about his inheritance. After he came of age, he gradually consolidated his landholdings, increased his slaveholdings, was systematic in his farming and operated a mill. Unlike Richard Henry Lee and others whose family fortunes were older and on a vaster scale than Peter Jefferson's, Tom Jefferson did not take the flow of income for granted. However, in later life, he fell into the same kind of financial difficulties that had overtaken William Byrd II and the Custises, when he assumed the debts of his father-in-law along with an estate containing 135 slaves and 11,000 acres. It was when his wife's inheritance doubled his own holdings that Jefferson entered into a grandiose style of life, while interest accumulated on the debts held by implacable British merchants. The mixed blessings of this inheritance dogged Jefferson with debts in his later years. But during his early life he lived within his means — except for occasional extravagances — and when he came to Williamsburg as a student at seventeen, Jefferson seems to have possessed a contented outlook based upon a realistic appraisal of his limited privileges.

He was privileged in the society of his day to be in Williamsburg in college at all; he had the cash he needed for clothes and the books he bought; and he had good connections. For his closest friend he gravitated to John Page, great-grandson of King Carter and heir to Rosewell, the first and grandest of the baronial manor seats. John Page, one year younger than Jefferson, was a cousin of Jefferson's cousin Thomas Mann Randolph. It was his Tuckahoe plantation that had been managed by Jefferson's father after Randolph's father died, and where Tom Jefferson had spent several years of his childhood with his richer contemporary kinspeople. Later Jefferson often visited Page's great house on the York River which, evoking comparisons with his parents' home at Shadwell (and making even the Randolphs' Tuckahoe seem comparatively modest), might well have contributed to the aspirations of grandeur he ultimately realized at Monticello.

Like Patrick Henry and Richard Henry Lee, Jefferson was ambitious, although not with the obvious objectives held by his seniors. His ambition, centered in the uses of his mind, was more for personal distinction, for honor. In the notebook in which he copied maxims that impressed him, he wrote:

> *But if it be a sin to covet honor,*
> *I am the most offending soul alive.*

While the continual growth of his mind developed in him a sense of the power of knowledge, all his life he was drawn to study for its own sake. His father had not been a learned man (his library consisted of only forty volumes), but was among those who, deprived of educational advantages and having limited intellectual interests, determined that his son should be given every opportunity and encouragement to develop his mind. When Tom Jefferson came to Williamsburg he had already formed habits of self-discipline as rigidly as the new Burgess, George Washington, eleven years older.

Blessed with a sound physical constitution, with an extraordinary natural resistance to disease, he practiced daily habits to insure his health and the flow of energies that kept his mind sharp and clear for uncounted hours of study and reflective reading. He took walks and ran, of course rode, swam in season, and each morning bathed his feet in cold water. Jefferson believed these morning ablutions were the preventive which kept him from ever having a cold — and they might have contributed to his immunity, especially since he *believed*. However, as he never suffered from any serious ailments, and also kept every tooth in his head until great age, his freedom from upper respiratory ailments could more likely be attributed to the generally careful regimen with which he treated the healthy system he inherited. For it was fundamental with Tom Jefferson that nothing distract him from following the high demands he placed upon his mental development.

"I was a hard student," Jefferson said of himself, and his companion John Page said that he "could tear himself away from his dearest friends, to fly to his studies." Dr. George Gilmer, a nephew of Dr. Thomas Walker, was a contemporary of Jefferson and later his physician and friend; Gilmer's son Francis grew up in Jefferson's community as a lifelong admirer of Albemarle County's great citizen, and wrote that "much of his success must be ascribed to methodical industry. . . . His application from very early youth has not only been intense but unremitting."

From these observations, it would appear that the lean, sandy-haired young man from the Piedmont did not burst upon the college in Tidewater as anything of a prodigy. He was well grounded in the classics, from Mr. Maury's school, when he came, and probably had already developed his receptivity to the study of mathematics, which he found "peculiarly engaging and delightful." He would certainly have been recognized as the intellectual type rather than a man of action: he was shy and sensitive, and would remain thin-skinned even after decades in the political arena. Though of an amiable disposition, he was deeply reserved; he would never become a good speaker or like to speak in public.

As an intellectual type, however, the young Jefferson at William and Mary did not appear particularly aloof or "indifferent." In his schooling for polite society, he had learned all the dances of his day — minuet and reel and country dances — and had become a competent performer on the violin, which he enjoyed playing immensely. (While Patrick Henry fiddled by ear, Jefferson studied and learned the notes, and copied in his music books the notes even of the tunes of country dances.) After he had been in Williamsburg several years, he relaxed a little on his self-disciplines when he first discovered girls, and for a time some of his frolics were indistinguishable from those of the average college student.

Yet, even at seventeen, Jefferson was essentially not only attracted to the world of ideas but some quality in him attracted thoughtful, scholarly older men. This was most fortunate for Jefferson at William and Mary, for the personal interest he aroused in Professor William Small, and the attachment that developed between them, availed the student of companionship with the only first-rate mind then at the college.

10

Jefferson entered William and Mary after the Board of Visitors had dismissed the clergymen faculty members who led the protest against the Two Penny Act, and before John Camm had won their reinstatement. In the interim the drinking of President Thomas Dawson had gotten out of hand and it was reported to the Bishop of London that his Commissary "was accused . . . of being a Drunkard." He showed up drunk at Bruton Parish Church, and the Reverend William Robinson wrote, "I have seen him so intoxicated by nine o'clock in the morning as to be incapable of doing business; he was likewise accused of seldom or never attending College Prayers, of being much addicted to playing at cards, and that in public houses." Poor Dawson, who wanted only to avoid disputes, acknowledged his sins to the Board of Visitors. On his promise to turn over a new leaf, and with the support of his friend Fauquier, he was permitted to continue his downward course until released by death in December, 1761.

In addition to its alcoholic president, the college had one professor in the grammar (preparatory) school, one for the eight Indians in the Indian school, two in the divinity school, and in the philosophy (liberal arts) school which Jefferson attended there were only William Small and a clergyman, Jacob Rowe. Six months after Jefferson entered, Reverend Jacob Rowe and Reverend Goronwy Owen, the poetical master of the grammar school, themselves took on too many glasses and led the restless college students into a hassle with the town boys. The result was the exit of two more clergymen from the faculty, and William Small became Jefferson's only teacher for the next year.

In the classroom Small was a brilliant lecturer in his own fields of mathematics, physics, and metaphysics — grouped as natural philosophy — with, as Jefferson later wrote of him, "a happy talent of communication." He became equally illuminating in handling the departed Rowe's subject of moral philosophy, which embraced logic, rhetoric, and ethics. Evidently the merrymaking Rowe had skimped on teaching the rhetoric and ethics aspects of his courses, for Jefferson said that Small gave the first lectures at the college in ethics, rhetoric, and belles lettres.

It happened that in Small's own academic training, rhetoric and logic were closely allied, and in the teachings of his mentor, William Duncan at Aberdeen University, mathematics (a passionate interest of Small) was treated as the purest expression of logic. Thus, the combining of his own subjects in natural philosophy with Rowe's subjects in moral philosophy became under this well-grounded natural teacher a single correlated course in the scientific-philosophical development of the mind. As well as promoting the logical rhetoric in which Jefferson came to excel as a writer, Small offered a new and ordered intellectual approach to the whole phenomenon of life. He, Jefferson wrote of his great teacher, "probably fixed the destinies of my life."

Small was himself only twenty-six when Jefferson first came into his class at William and Mary. Born in a hamlet a few miles north of Dundee, Scotland, the son of a minister, Small had graduated ("laureated") from Marischal College, Aberdeen University, in 1755. Coming to Virginia for reasons unknown, he attended his first faculty meeting in the colonial college in October, 1758, and was a relative newcomer when he met the intent seventeen-year-old Jefferson. The bachelor was probably a little lonely in the overgrown village, which only periodically became a city, and a natural affinity quickly sprang up between him and his mental-type student.

"He," Jefferson wrote, "most happily for me, became soon attached to me, and made me his daily companion when not engaged in the school; and from his conversation I got my first views of the expansion of science, and of the system of things in which we are placed.'' He undoubtedly got also from ''Dr.'' Small the introduction to a book, which had an incalculable influence on his own written expressions in logical rhetoric. Although he nowhere mentions William Duncan's *Logick,* Jefferson owned a copy of the book, and it would seem unlikely that Small, in their intimate conversations, would not mention this work of his own mentor.

In the typically eighteenth-century logical reasoning in Duncan's *Logick,* one point of his own was that in the ''abstract ideas of the Mind . . . Judgements are grounded in *intuition,* and the Manner of Reasoning is by demonstration.'' This was in differentiation from natural knowledge, where judgments were by experience, and reasonings by analogy and induction; it also differed from historical knowledge, where testimony was the ground of judgments and reasoning was by criticism and probable conjecture. In the abstract ideas, Duncan regarded intuition as the recognition that the ideas incorpoated in a proposition do actually exist in the relationship which the proposition declares. Then comes the reasoning by demonstration through syllogism — the major premise, the minor premise, the conclusion.

What evidently made the impression on Jefferson (even if in his subconscious) was that by this process the intuitive judgments were recognized as truths *in their own right,* which in turn yielded derivative propositions which were equally truths. In this relation between the certainty produced by intuition and demonstration, Duncan defined the intuitive judgment as the ''self-evident proposition or perception.'' He developed that: ''When any proposition is offered to the View of the Mind, if the terms in which it is expressed are understood . . . the Proposition is said to be *self-evident,* and admits not of any proof, because a bare Attention to the Ideas themselves produces full Conviction and Certainty.''

Sixteen years later, in the exercise in logical rhetoric for which he won his greatest fame, the student of Duncan's former student, with a perfect illustration of ''demonstration'' by syllogism, wrote, ''We hold these truths to be self-evident, that all men are created equal, that they are endowed by their Creator with certain unalienable rights, that among these are life, liberty, and the pursuit of happiness.''

To any eighteenth-century Englishman, this proposition — at

least as theory — would fulfill Duncan's dictum of being "self-evident," in that it needed no proof, because the ideas themselves produced conviction. In his conscious synthesis of ideas which were prevalent in Virginia and in the English-speaking world, when Jefferson, at thirty-three, presented his logical rhetoric for the world, he may have forgotten the Duncan seed planted by Small when he was in his late teens.

It occurred in the most impressionable period of Jefferson's always intensely sensitive mental life, when he was literally absorbing a whole new world of ideas undreamed of on the simple plantation on the Rivanna River. Jefferson never forgot the influence of the "beloved professor" (as John Page called the young Scotsman) and never wavered in his affection for the not too happy man who left Virginia two years after Jefferson left the college. When the Bishop of London restored the deposed professor of moral philosophy, Reverend Jacob Rowe, in 1764, William Small resigned in an involved dispute. Returning to his home country, he died when only forty-one — a year too soon to learn of his former student's Declaration of Independence.

For Jefferson's mental enlightenment he had arrived at the college at precisely the one period when the liberal-minded Small, with "correct and gentlemanly manners," could act as his personal tutor and give him the guidance of a father. Their friendship did another thing for the young Jefferson: it opened doors in Williamsburg to other influences which were as profound as Small's. As the lone noncleric on the faculty, Small found his intimates among the town's enlightened laity. One of his friends was George Wythe, the eminent lawyer who signed Patrick Henry's license to practice law, and, through Small, Wythe would become Jefferson's law teacher in 1762. Wythe was a friend of Governor Fauquier and, through Wythe and Small, Jefferson was introduced into the cosmopolitan evenings in the Palace. There he played his violin in the musical group which included his mother's first cousin John Randolph, the other signer of Henry's law license.

When, in 1699, the General Assembly had planned to shift the capital from Jamestown to the straggly settlement at Middle Plantation, where the new city of Williamsburg would be designed and laid out eastward from the focal point of William and Mary, a petition from the college had pointed out the advantages the students would derive from being located at the seat of government and business. No student among the distinguished roster of William and Mary men in colonial public life took such advantages of living at the seat of government as Thomas Jefferson. When he left William and Mary, after a little more than two years, to study law, his extracurricular activities included attendance at the General Court and sessions of the General Assembly.

From Jefferson's arrival in Williamsburg, through his years as a college student and law student, he was a spectator of the rift between the Anglican clergy and the prominent laity, whose reasoned positions reflected the feelings of much of the population. The student's view was naturally colored by the liberalism of his mentor, Small, and of the urbane Fauquier; and Fauquier's antagonism to the clerical element represented by John Camm was made understandable to Jefferson by the goings-on he saw while at the college and by the dissensions he was aware of there when he was studying law in Williamsburg. What he was witnessing was a rising feeling against the outwardly imposed authority *represented* by the Church. The feeling was rising to a climax against the Virginia clergy — and all it represented of British controls — over the Camm-led campaign to recover the loss in salaries caused by the emergency Two Penny Acts. This too would influence Thomas Jefferson.

Chapter Six

... AND A NEW TIDE COMES IN

AT ABOUT THE TIME Thomas Jefferson entered William and Mary, and shortly after Washington and Richard Henry Lee began their service in the House of Burgesses, the General Assembly made two moves which began a redefinition of the Colony's relationship to the Crown. When the members of the Assembly read the King's official disallowance of various of their acts — including the emergency Two Penny Act — and heard of the threatening rebuke Fauquier had received for signing the twelve months' Two Penny Act without a suspending clause, a joint committee of the House and Council was formed in October, 1760, to write a petition presenting their case to the King.

In originally passing the Two Penny Act for a self-limiting twelve months period, the General Assembly had been aware of deliberately evading the King's instructions to the Governor about the suspending clause by enacting a law whose purpose would be served before it could be subjected to the Crown's approval or disapproval. Fauquier, as had Dinwiddie before, connived in this evasion. The writers of the petition, however, were little concerned with a technicality of evasion of the King's prerogative. They were concerned with establishing the prerogatives of their own needs according to the doctrine Richard Bland was developing since his *A Letter to the Clergy* pamphlet.

Bland and the other petitioners advanced their theories in a paper based on denial of the Bishop of London's charges about the General Assembly's motives in passing the act. The petition presented those facts which John Camm had omitted when he persuaded the church officials to accept his biased account. In accepting Camm's version, the Bishop of London had reported to the Board of Trade that the passage of the Two Penny Acts, without the suspending clause, was part of a design "to lessen the influence of the Crown and the maintenance of the clergy" — with great emphasis upon the subversion of the clergy's position.

The petition pointed out that the acts were far from being aimed at the clergy: fixed prices in money, for debts owed in tobacco, applied to the salaries of church janitors and county clerks as well as ministers, and to all civil officials; to grants for the support of the parish's sick and needy; for rents and for contracts with merchants, architects, and builders. In sum, the whole Colony was affected.

As for the clergy specifically, the clergymen in the Shenandoah Valley counties of Augusta and Frederick (which Washington represented), where little tobacco was grown and that far from market, had themselves petitioned as early as 1738 for salary payments in money at the very low rate of three farthings per pound of tobacco. When, in 1753, rising tobacco prices and rising costs made this fixed rate too low even for the simpler life in the Valley, the General Assembly granted a petition that the rate be raised to a penny and a half per pound — less than the twopence per pound of the emergency law which the English-born Virginia clergy convinced the Crown was aimed at them.

Then, in 1755, on the low ground in the area of Norfolk, the Colony's largest port, tobacco quality was so poor that two counties successfully petitioned the Assembly to be allowed to make payments in cash, at a rate which should not go below one and two tenths pence per pound. These accommodations to local needs for the past twenty years seemed, to the petitioners, proof of the absence of any intention by the Assembly to abuse the Crown's prerogatives or subvert the clergy in the passage of the Two Penny Acts designed solely to relieve the distress of the total population.

That the acts could be regarded in any other light, the Councilors stated, could only have come about "through the artful misrepresentation of designing persons." Though moderate in tone, it was a strong statement of position, and the Assembly did not stop with sending the petition to the King: it took measures to propagandize its position, along with other Colony interests, in London.

Ever since the House of Burgesses had sent Peyton Randolph as its agent to represent the Colony in the pistole fee controversy with Dinwiddie, the House had wanted to be represented in London by an agent other than James Abercrombie, who was responsible to the Council and the Royal Governor rather than to the Colony's elected representatives. In 1759, the members of the House obtained the agreement of a majority of the Council to appoint an agent for the whole General Assembly, who would be entrusted by and responsible to a Committee of Correspondence. (This joint committee, from the House and Council, was in no way associated with the later inter-colonial Committees of Correspondence that grew up immediately before the Revolution: it merely had the same name.)

Originally composed of twelve members, four Councilors and eight Burgesses, the Committee of Correspondence represented the core of the Tidewater oligarchy. From the Council were the Yorktown merchant William Nelson, chairman of the committee, and his flashier brother Thomas, the Colony's acting Deputy Secretary; Surveyor General Peter Randolph, first cousin of Peyton Randolph and John Robinson (and of Thomas Jefferson's mother); and Receiver General Philip Grymes. From the House came Speaker John Robinson, Attorney General Peyton Randolph, and Richard Bland; three Carters — the brothers Landon and Charles, and their nephew Robert Carter Nicholas; Benjamin Waller, and Governor Fauquier's lawyer-friend George Wythe. As of 1759, when the Agent's Act was passed for Fauquier's signature, those twelve Assemblymen constituted the most powerful political alignment in Virginia.

James Abercrombie predictably protested to the Board of Trade against having another Virginia agent in London, and the Board asked Fauquier if he was sure that signing the Agent's Act was well advised. Fauquier, in reassuring the Board, gave it his opinion that the Assembly would revise the act to meet the Crown's objections. It is possible that the Governor advised his Virginia friends to make the necessary changes in the act, as in October, 1760 — when the petition to the King was drafted — the Assembly passed an amending act which explained that the agent was appointed by the House and the

Council jointly, and only with the Governor's approval. Major Edward Montagu, a lawyer of the Middle Temple, was confirmed as the agent of the Committee of Correspondence, and the Virginia government had established something like its own foreign office.

The October action on the Committee of Correspondence and the petition to the Crown could be seen as reflections of the doctrines expounded in Richard Bland's *A Letter to the Clergy* pamphlet published in March. Following, as it had, Landon Carter's outraged memorial by only four months, and appearing when members of the governing class were resentful of Camm's circulating the Crown's orders before the Governor received a copy, Bland's pamphlet made an impact on the minds of literate Virginians.

Marshaling facts (which were more fully developed in the petition) to disprove the bishop's "invidious and insolent charge," Bland used his countercharge as an introduction into an examination of the principles underlying the whole question of "prerogative."

"The Royal Prerogative is, without doubt, of great weight and power in a dependent and subordinate government: like the King of Babylon's decree, it may, for aught I know, almost force the people of the plantations to fall down and worship any image it shall please to set up; but, great and powerful as it is, it can only be exerted while in the hands of the best and most benign sovereign, for the good of his people, and not for their destruction. When, therefore, the Governor and the Council (to whom this power is in part delegated) find, from the uncertainty and variableness in human affairs, that any accident happens which general instructions can by no means provide for; or which, by a rigid observation of them, would destroy a people so far distant from the royal presence, before they can apply to the throne for relief; it is their duty as good magistrates, to exercise this power as the exigency of the state requires; and, though they should deviate from the strict letter of an instruction, or perhaps, in a small degree, from the fixed rule of the Constitution, yet such a deviation cannot possibly be *treason,* when it is intended to produce the most salutary end, the preservation of the people: in such a case it deserves commendation and reward."

Then Bland advanced his *salus populi est suprema lex* doctrine — "The Colony must consider its own interests even at the expense of constitutional forms" — that was to have profound effect on Virginians' thinking and was to form the idea for the first verbal explosion against the Crown.

"The royal instructions ought certainly to be obeyed, and nothing but the most pressing necessity can justify any person for infringing them; but, as *salus populi est supreme lex,* where this necessity prevails, every consideration must give place to it, and even these instructions may be deviated from with impunity: This is so evident to reason, and so clear and fundamental a rule in the *English* Constitution, that it would be losing of time to produce instances of it."

Addressing the clergy, he made the irrefutable statement:

"You were of this opinion, I believe, when you petitioned the Assembly, in the year 1755, for an alteration in your salaries; and, I am persuaded, if you had been lucky enough to have had them fixed in money to your satisfaction, we should have seen strong advocates for such a law, notwithstanding it would have been as manifest an infringement of the royal instructions as the law is which these memorialists complain of. We should then have had no representations against us for *assuming a supremacy inconsistent with the dignity* of England; we should have been *an orderly and well-regulated Colony, and the clergy would have been respected and well used by the people.*"

While addressed to the Virginia clergy, Bland's pamphlet was the first declaration in the colonies of the principle of necessity taking precedence over the Crown's prerogatives. Its effect in changing the Virginia attitude went incomparably further than any direct results it achieved as the basis for the position taken in the Assembly's petition. For soon that principle would be popularized in oratory which touched the hearts of men and women everywhere in the Colony. Patrick Henry read Bland's *A Letter to the Clergy* and his mind began to translate its principles into visceral arguments that would reach the people where Henry knew they lived.

2

In the mythical aspects of Henry the "rustic plebeian," he is presented as an "obscure country lawyer." He was a country lawyer in that he did not practice in one of the few cities; but, as Virginia was a rural community, a lawyer handling clients in the county court-house towns was typical of his times. He was obscure only in compari-son to those of the older lawyers who had been in practice long enough to establish large reputations in their communities. However, since "obscure" holds an implication of "unsuccessful," the word gives an entirely false impression. Patrick Henry became a very busy lawyer almost immediately after leaving Williamsburg with his license in the summer of 1760.

First engaged by friends and kinspeople of the spreading branches of the families of his mother, stepbrother and father-in-law in Hanover County, the twenty-four-year-old lawyer soon attracted clients without family associations in his own county and in the ad-joining county of Goochland. Then he developed an ever widening circle of clients in counties to the west — Cumberland, Louisa, and Jefferson's Albemarle. It was significant that he gravitated to the new country beyond the old Tidewater, and never tried a single case in Henrico County — the long-settled region to the east and south of Hanover, where Richmond was growing slowly as a shipping-mercan-tile center. By 1763, his third full year in the practice of law, Henry handled nearly five hundred cases and his books listed more than £600 in fees. Roughly £225 of this had been collected by the end of that year, and, as in the preceding year Henry had collected £300 of the £310 owed him, he could reasonably expect to collect a large per-centage of the remaining fees.

This might be a long way from the eminence enjoyed by Peyton and John Randolph and George Wythe at the capital, but it was also a long way from obscurity. At the end of 1763, Patrick Henry was at least modestly established in his own community, when his chance came to move in a single leap into Colony-wide prominence.

During the years he was building up his country law practice, the Reverend John Camm and four other clergymen (including Henry's uncle, Patrick Henry the Elder) had brought suits against their vestries for the difference in their salaries for the year 1758–1759, when the disallowed Two Penny Act had been in force. Taking a hint from Fauquier, all the vestries' lawyers except one defended on the ground that the Two Penny Act had been "repealed" rather than "disallowed," since "repeal" implied that the act had been legally in force before the Crown's decision. On this ground, the county courts found against the clergy and so did the higher courts — the General Court at Williamsburg, composed of Councilors. Camm followed his usual procedure of taking his case to England, and there, eventually, the Virginia courts were sustained.

If that had been the anticlimactic end of Camm's fight against the laws of the Virginia General Assembly, he and his English-born clergy supporters would have aroused a good deal of antagonism to no practical purpose. But the Reverend John Camm, not a large figure in history books, had in all unawareness set in motion forces which, wholly outside his own narrow intention, shaped the course of history.

While Camm and his three fellow clergymen were carrying their losing fights through the courts, the case of the fifth clergyman-plaintiff took a different turn. This was the Reverend James Maury, whose Fredericksville parish extended into an edge of Albemarle County and who, at his small private school, had won the respect of Thomas Jefferson for his classical teaching. Nothing of the self-interested troublemaker such as the contumacious Camm, Maury had supported the first Two Penny Act in the conviction that all citizens should share in sacrifice. Also, unlike the English-born clergymen, Maury had been brought to Virginia as an infant by his Huguenot parents. He had received all his education in the Colony, attending William and Mary, and would be considered a Virginian.

The scholarly, public-spirited Maury was probably driven to joining the plaintiffs by actual need of his large family, for the difference in what he had received at the rate of twopence per pound of tobacco and the market price would amount to more than £200 — a larger amount than had actually been paid. By such a homely motive as providing for his children, Maury, himself a minor footnote in history, provoked the "incident" that released the flood of historic forces.

Fearing that his case against the Fredericksville vestry would not get a fair hearing in Louisa County, in which his parish was located, Maury brought his case to trial in adjoining Hanover County. On November 5, 1763, the case opened in the court of Colonel John Henry, father of Patrick Henry. Maury had engaged the most famous lawyer in the area, Peter Lyons, and the defendants had engaged a well-known, mature lawyer, John Lewis. In Colonel Henry's court the two attorneys did not argue over those points of "repeal" versus "disallowance" on which the other four cases had been decided for the defendants. Lewis's defense was based on his clients' compliance with the law, as represented by the Two Penny Act, and Lyons's case was based on the claim that the Two Penny Act had never been validated as a law. Unlike the other magistrates, Colonel Henry decided for the plaintiff, on the ground that the Two Penny Act was null and void from the beginning.

By this ruling the brave Henry, going in the face of popular opinion and the other decisions, inadvertently did his part to give his son the opportunity to use the Maury "incident" as the opening of the door into public life — which also opened the floodgates to release the gathered forces.

The December term of court was selected for the second part of the trial, in which a jury would fix the amount of damages to be awarded the Reverend James Maury. With the principle of the case decided against his clients, John Lewis then withdrew from representing the Fredericksville vestry any further. The vestry replaced him with the young lawyer Patrick Henry, who had been trying cases in their county and who had many friends in Hanover County.

When the sheriff selected a jury, the eminent Peter Lyons was dissatisfied by the absence of prominent citizens among the jurors. Patrick Henry claimed that they were all honest men without blemish on their characters. True, two of the jurors had been prosecuted for permitting a New Light minister, John Roan, to preach in their homes, but the plaintiff's counsel could not well make a point of this, as Hanover County was known for its many dissenters from the Church of England. More than twenty years before, the Presbyterians in Hanover County had formed small "reading-room groups" allied with the New Side Presbyterian movement, and in 1747 the county had become the chief preaching area in Virginia for the Evangelical Samuel Davies.

It would seem that the Reverend Mr. Maury had lacked the ability for cold scheming of his friend John Camm in holding his trial in a county where so much dissidence from the Established Church existed. If Maury missed the anticlerical mood prevalent in the county, the new lawyer for the defense counted on it.

In the large crowd that gathered that December day in the courthouse town (where the tavern in which Patrick Henry had tended bar faced the courthouse across the road), Henry's uncle, the Reverend Patrick Henry the Elder, climbed stiffly down from his carriage. His namesake hurried up to the old clergyman and fervently urged him not to attend the trial. The reason he gave was that his uncle's presence would restrain him in his opposition to the clergy. What the young lawyer did not tell his uncle was that the case he had prepared went far beyond opposing the clergy, as represented by family man Maury: his case was an attack on the clergy of the Established Church as *it* represented the will of the King.

For Henry was not basing his case upon the law at all, but upon the principles defined in Richard Bland's *A Letter to the Clergy*. The Reverend John Camm, by his misrepresentations of the General Assembly's motives to the Bishop of London, indirectly provided Henry with his ammunition: it was in Bland's indignant denial of the bishop's false charges that he developed the fundamental principles which Patrick Henry made into his own "harangue," as Maury termed his inflammatory speech to the crowded courtroom.

On that occasion Patrick Henry did arise to address the bench and the jurors with at least the appearance of shuffling embarrassment. Whether he was actually unsure of himself or, as an actor, assumed the awkwardness, his father was convinced of his son's uncertainty, for the judge sank down in his chair "in evident confusion." Then Colonel Henry's son began to talk. All the appearance of awkwardness fell away, and he spoke as one transformed. And the men in the court listened as though spellbound.

Maury, enraged at the spellbinding, wrote Camm, "This harangue turned upon points as much out of his depth, and that of the jury, as they were foreign from the purpose." The points were by no means foreign to Henry's purpose. The country lawyer was defending his client by attacking the authority, the King, who had disallowed an act for the people's protection. After developing Bland's line that the people's representatives had the right to pass their own necessary legislation without interference from the Crown, Henry declaimed, "A king, by annulling and disallowing acts of so salutary a nature, from being a father of the people, degenerated into a tyrant, and forfeits all rights to his subjects' obedience."

When such words for the first time rang through the court of an

English colony, Maury reported that "the more sober part of the audience were struck with horror." Peter Lyons, the distinguished counsel of the plaintiff, waited for the judge to reprimand the lawyer who "had spoken treason." But Colonel Henry was himself lost in the same rapt attention with which the jurors and spectators watched the impassioned speaker.

From the King he turned to attack the clergy in general, without referring to Maury. In their greed, he shouted, they snatched "from the hearth of the honest parishioner his last hoecake, from the widow and her orphan children their last milch cow! the last bed, nay, the last blanket from the lying-in woman." There was not a sound as he then turned directly to the jurors.

Unless they were "disposed to rivet the chains of bondage on their own necks" they should "make such an example of him" — referring to Maury for the first time — "as might hereafter be a warning to himself and his brethren not to have the temerity" to dispute the validity of laws "authenticated by the only authority which . . . could give force to laws for the government of this Colony — the authority of a legal representative of a Council, and of a kind and benevolent and patriot Governor."

Not only had such treasonable words never before been heard in a colonial court, but such persuasive speechmaking had never before been heard in the Colony, where political speechmaking had been developed as an art. Later Thomas Jefferson, when no friend of Henry, said he was "the greatest orator who ever lived." He had talked for an hour. When the jurors were released from his spell, they were out five minutes. They awarded poor James Maury, with all his mouths to feed, one penny as the amount the vestry was compelled to pay him above what he had received by the Two Penny Act.

In all the milling around after the excitement of the trial, Henry made his way to Maury and apologized for his attack on the clergy. He had made his attack, Maury reported to Camm, "to render himself popular."

Then Maury went to the very heart of the matter in his letter to Camm, the instigator of it all. "You see, then, it is so clear a point in this person's opinion that the ready road to popularity here is to trample under foot the interests of religion, the rights of the church, and the prerogatives of the Crown."

3

Patrick Henry was right in his opinion, though not precisely as Maury worded it. The difference between what the Church of England clergymen said and the country Virginia lawyer meant defined the breakdown in communication between the Colony and the home government that would never be re-established. To Maury, for the Colony to assert the validity of its own emergency legislation was "to trample under foot . . . the prerogatives of the Crown." The fine distinction of Henry's argument was that the Crown's prerogative must not be blindly obeyed without regard to the Colony's welfare.

This was Bland's *salus populi est suprema lex* doctrine developed to the personalized emotionality of characterizing the King who would insist on his prerogative at the expense of the people as a "tyrant" who "forfeits all rights to his subjects' obedience."

This was what the people could understand, and Patrick Henry was right in his opinion that he gave voice to the unspoken words in their hearts. The people acclaimed him as their own champion, and at the very next vacancy the citizens of Louisa County sent him to represent them in the House of Burgesses. He was on his way to becoming the most popular figure in Virginia, with a popularity among the people in general that had never before come to any Virginian. Discounting the brief, turbulent, and controversial career of Nathaniel Bacon nearly a century before, Patrick Henry was beginning to emerge as the Virginia people's first hero.

In beginning his ascent as the people's idol, Patrick Henry was in no conflict with the ruling class. For not only had he popularized doctrines already propounded by aristocrats, but the very issue which served as his springboard — the Two Penny Act — had been legislation evolved by the oligarchic inner core of the ruling class. This point is of extreme significance, because in the Henry myths he has been pictured as the unlettered choice of the *people* with the implication that he represented the people's interests as opposed to the interests of the ruling class. As it happened, members of the ruling class, in collaboration with the English Governor, first evaded the Crown's rulings in order to enact the legislation for the people's welfare (including, of course, their own) and in defending their position developed the arguments which Henry simplified and dramatized.

Patrick Henry appealed to the people because, in his simplification of the issues, he had gone directly to the heart of the matter. Voicing their own spoken assertions against controls imposed from a distance, in his treasonable identification of the King as a "tyrant," he had articulated the sentiment among the people generally that the King symbolized factors alien to their interests. It was in this appeal that Patrick Henry was differentiated from the ruling class in government and advanced beyond them in comprehending the temper of the people.

By the time of his entrance into the House of Burgesses, he was advancing beyond any man in public life in his feeling for the temper of the people and in the directness of his approach to confronting the growing differences between the Colony and the home government. This directness, going head on at the emotional center of the issue, was what essentially differentiated the newly rising figure from the entrenched powers in the General Assembly.

To the spokesmen of the ruling class, Landon Carter and Richard Bland, the King symbolized the mother country to which they gave implicit loyalty in their identification as Virginia English. But to them the King did not symbolize the whole established system with which Virginia interests were in conflict. The members of the ruling class in the General Assembly, through the nature of their correspondence with England and their relationship with Governor Fauquier, understood that the Crown meant for them the Board of Trade, the Privy Council, Parliament, the influential bloc of merchants, the powerful ministers — and the King.

As lawmakers, the Burgesses had inherited a pragmatic system of operating with the Crown (in all its aspects), and all of their governors within memory had known when to look away from the violation of unenforceable laws (as Northern governors had ignored the large-scale smuggling). What the ruling class was trying to do was to establish limitations on the Crown's prerogatives, in which the General Assembly could not be overruled on such totally internal affairs as the still rankling pistole fee and emergency legislation for the welfare of the population.

In this shift in the nature of the Virginia government's demands, it was inevitable that communication would break down — when each transatlantic exchange of correspondence required upward of five months — over such a dubious doctrine as Richard Bland's. The King either had his prerogatives or he didn't. If the Colony could deny the King's authority on the grounds of emergency, and the General Assembly was the judge of what constituted an emergency, there was no end to the emergencies which could be declared. The members of the General Assembly, aware of the honorableness of their motives and their loyalty to the King, knew they were not advocating a doctrine designed to undermine the Crown's authority. They wanted the right to legislate in emergencies for what Landon Carter had called "exceptions," and the gentlemen in the ruling class sincerely meant only exceptions. To them this was a constitutional recognition of long-standing pragmatic practices.

But, whatever the nature of their intentions, Bland's *salus populi est suprema lex* doctrines could certainly be seen as a contradiction of the Crown's authority — if the authority could be denied according to the needs of the people. However, with all of Bland's ingenious constitutionality, the reality in the strained relationship between Virginia and England was that Bland's doctrine won acceptance among members of the ruling class. For the doctrine placed in governmental theory a conviction on which the General Assembly *wanted to act:* it expressed a changed attitude in the Colony's governing class.

This change was missed, or was ignored, in the breakdown of communication. It was a quiet, unrevolutionary change made among an aristocracy who could have appeared, from a distance, to be doing no more than increasing the demands made for nearly a century toward more autonomy in internal affairs. Only it went deeper. It was becoming, in essence, a demand for the General Assembly to govern as a coequal to Parliament.

The change and all its nuances was missed, or ignored, precisely at the time when England, at last freed of its wars by the Treaty of Paris in 1763, turned its attention to the colonies with fresh impositions of controls that aroused fresh resentments in Virginia and in the Northern colonies. The new controls were not at all political in nature: concerned with postwar economics and the policy of maintaining an expanded world empire, the controls expressed no purpose of the Crown to impose authority for its own end. The new rulings, however, for whatever purpose, did impose authority from the outside on a people experiencing a rise of assertive resistance to any laws not originating with themselves.

England's bad timing in executing the colonial details of her imperialistic policy gave Patrick Henry his good timing in making his popular appeals to the people's emotions. For the people among whom Henry was to emerge as hero were, to begin with, not as English-oriented as the Tidewater ruling class.

From Hanover County on westward through the Piedmont to the Blue Ridge, the rise of Evangelical religions broke the strong link which the Church of England had always provided with the mother country. In those areas, too, the planters seldom shipped on the consignment system with the English merchants, and thus lacked the commercial ties of the big planters who shipped on the tidal rivers east of the fall line; and their sons, not going to school or college in England, did not continue the cultural ties that existed in Tidewater.

Further west, in the Shenandoah Valley, large proportions of the colonists were Germans and Scotch-Irish, with no ties of any kind to England. Westward from Tidewater, where the large plantations grew progressively fewer until in the Valley the dominant economic unit was the small farm, the population became progressively more "democratic" in the social sense and, hence, more remote from — actually alien to — the transplanted English social structure in the early settled regions along the tidal rivers.

These western Virginians had never had a real voice in the government controlled by John Robinson's oligarchy. Another element in Patrick Henry's timing was his simplification of Bland's theories into emotional appeals understandable to these people precisely at the time when the westerners were ready to assert their right to be heard in Williamsburg.

Everything came together for and with Patrick Henry. When England inaugurated its new imperialistic policy in 1763, there was a king whose desire to "rule as well as reign" could make him appear to be the tyrant of Henry's personalization of the English side of the governmental conflict. While Maury and Camm became no more than footnotes of the times, George III, with exquisite timing from Patrick Henry's viewpoint, blundered with his government to loom larger than, in actuality, he ever was.

4

George III had been fourteen years old at the death of his father Frederick, Prince of Wales, the greatly disliked son of George II. As the heir apparent of his grandfather, the young boy came under the influence of his mother, Princess Augusta of Saxe-Gotha, who, having suffered humiliations as the wife of the King's despised son, expected to compensate through her own son: "George must *rule.*" She brought in as his adviser Lord Bute, a thirty-nine-year-old Scottish earl, who reinforced the mother's influence on the malleable boy while establishing himself, an ambitious mediocrity, as a loyally regarded mentor. George III was twenty-two when his grandfather the King died on October 25, 1760, and delayed his coronation until the following year.

In person he was most attractive: very fair, with blue eyes and auburn hair, and a well-proportioned figure that moved with grace. Inwardly he was warm, showing tenderness to family and friends, but, in accordance with the self-concept developed under the influence of his mother and Bute, he was beginning to show a hard exterior. Fundamentally, he was a young man in conflict with himself. Having incorporated his mother's ambition for him to be a strong ruler, George III had an image of himself as a "Patriot King" supported by loving subjects. Actually, raised in his mother's home and educated by private tutors, he was immature, knew nothing of getting along with the people, and the reality of his image was that he was an amateur blundering into the pragmatic world of British politics.

To be the ruler of the concept fostered by his mother and Lord Bute, he had first to break the system established in peace by Walpole, and used in war by Pitt, of a responsible, united cabinet, led by a Prime Minister dependent upon majority votes in the House of Commons. In breaking this system, George III wanted to recover the royal powers, in which the Prime Minister would become an instrument of the King's will and the cabinet would be reduced to the actuality of "King's servants." To do this he had to get rid of strong-man Pitt, of whose power he was intensely jealous, and to remove from the Whig oligarchy the power of patronage by which members of the House of Commons were bribed. Pitt, "the Great Commoner," was something of a supraparty man operating by his own autocratic methods.

George III
Portrait attributed to Allan Ramsay, about 1770
(Colonial Williamsburg Collection)

With England then having emerged victorious from the Seven Years War, George III removed Pitt from the House by elevating his wife to the peerage, as Lady Chatham, and settling a pension of £3,-000 a year on the ex-Commoner. The new Lady Chatham belonged to the powerful Grenville family. Her brother, George Grenville, was appointed Secretary of State in 1762, and Lord Bute, who had been made George III's first Secretary of State, was elevated to Prime Minister in May, 1762. This mediocrity, though he had the King's loyalty, was too unpopular to form a strong government, and Bute resigned (April, 1763) after serving scarcely one year. Then, apparently in a move to appease the deposed Pitt, George III appointed Pitt's brother-in-law, George Grenville, to succeed Bute as chief of the ministry in the office of Chancellor of the Exchequer.

Then fifty-one, a squat, stolid man, rude and tactless, Grenville brought to the position a driving love of personal power. In Grenville's government, George III's Tory supporters, with whom he was supplanting Whigs, were the King's personal henchmen rather than truly Tory partisans and no serious match for Grenville. Unable to handle Grenville, the young King had a nervous breakdown. He burst into tears during conferences with him and other ministers, in a foreshadowing of his later insanity. Obsessed with authority, he was struggling, against what nature had fitted him for, to fulfill his mother's model of himself.

The reign of George III was in this condition in 1763 when the Treaty of Paris formally acknowledged England's world dominion and the British government announced its new continental policies for the American colonies. England's policy was designed to meet the need for peace with the vast Indian populations in the lands west of the Alleghenies, to protect the northern and southern flanks, and to devise means of raising revenues in the colonies to help the home government (with its enormous war debt) defray the expenses of maintaining the frontier.

To implement the first part of the policy, a proclamation of October, 1763, which announced the establishment of new governments in Quebec and the Floridas, fixed "for the present" the Allegheny watershed as the western boundary of the English settlements. To the English government this was a reasonable long-range policy. A centralized control over the expansion of the separate and competitive colonies into the western lands would make the Indian problem more manageable, as well as cutting the expense of maintaining garrisons against hostiles when the flanks now had to be protected.

As things had stood before the proclamation, Pennsylvania, by the Easton Treaty of 1758 (which led to the bloodless conquest of Fort Du Quesne), had already ceded lands west of the Alleghenies to the Indians. In New York, westward expansion had stirred up trouble with the Mohawks, and South Carolina's expansion had brought on the long wars with the Cherokees which continued the expense to England and the other colonies of maintaining men under arms. Forbidding Virginians to settle in their own west was all part of the total controls and, in the larger view of England's new international policy, the human "rights" of the Virginians could be ignored for the time being.

The Virginians saw it differently. What became the Seven Years War had begun when Virginians, in pushing westward into territory claimed by the Colony, had clashed with the French; and Governor Dinwiddie, involved in the interests of the big speculators, had interested the Crown in supporting "Virginia's War." When men left their families to fight the French and Indians on Virginia's borders, one of the inducements had been land in the west, and unknown numbers of these veterans had already settled on grants earned by their military service. Now suddenly they were ordered to evacuate.

Also ordered to vacate their homes were other families who had bought tracts of land beyond the line allowed by the 1763 proclamation and considered themselves permanently settled. Speculators in land, from Thomas Jefferson's father to George Washington's brother, had left in their estates stock in the western land companies, and Tidewater grandees had vast holdings they had waited a decade to settle. Resistant to any controls imposed from England, Virginians naturally resented an order which deprived them of the rewards for which Dinwiddie had first dispatched young Washington to the Ohio country.

Now himself a big landowner and responsible member of the government, Colonel Washington revealed in a private letter how the most conservative Virginians reacted to the ill-timed proclamation. As pragmatic as the British themselves, Washington wrote that he regarded the proclamation "as a temporary expedient to quiet the minds of the Indians,'' which in no way would deter him from his intention of acquiring some of the most valuable lands in the restricted territory. He suggested that desirable lands be ''immediately surveyed, to keep others off,'' for he believed that ''after a while, notwithstanding the proclamation that restrains it at present,'' the lands could be taken up.

Washington was saying in effect that the proclamation would not be enforced if no fuss was made about it, and unknown numbers put into practice his plan of quiet evasion. But, along with practical adjustment to the proclamation, a great fuss was made. Virginians felt — reasonably, from their viewpoint — that while England imposed controls to protect *her* winnings from the war, Virginia was denied her rewards from the war which she had originated and which was fought in part of her land. The reaction in the Colony made a deep impression on the traveler, Reverend Andrew Burnaby. He wrote:

''The public or political character of the Virginians corresponds with their private one: they are haughty and jealous of their liberties, impatient of restraint, and can scarcely bear the thought of being controlled by any superior power. Many of them consider the colonies as independent states, not connected with Great Britain otherwise than by having the same king, and being bound to her by natural affection. . . . In matters of commerce they are ignorant of the necessary principles that must prevail between a colony and the mother country; they think it a hardship not to have unlimited trade to every part of the world [and] they consider the duties upon their staple as injurious only to themselves. . . . However, to do them justice, the same spirit of generosity prevails here [Williamsburg] which does in their private character; they never refuse any necessary supplies for the support of government when called upon, and are a generous and loyal people.''

The Reverend Mr. Burnaby, on the scene, actually caught here the crux of the colonial–mother country relationship, which was missed in the unstable government of George III. Burnaby's observation held the basic contradictions in the changing relationship: the Virginians were a ''generous and loyal people'' who were bound to Great Britain by ''natural affection''; but many considered ''the colonies as independent states,'' and could ''scarcely bear the thought of being controlled by any superior power.''

It was not only the ruling class which, in its lordliness, was coming increasingly to resent external controls. The people in general, as Patrick Henry was discovering, were "jealous of their liberties" and "impatient of restraint." Nor did Virginians react only to the impositions of external controls on the Colony; the General Assembly reacted strongly to coercive acts against other colonies. For, as each action must cause its reaction, England's centralized control of all the colonies as a continental dominion developed in the separate colonies a sense of common interests in their larger identity as an American dominion.

Virginia made a particular identification with Massachusetts the following year, 1764, when, as part of the Revenue Act, England passed a Sugar Act with dire effects on New England distillers. The Molasses Act of 1733 had carried duties on rum, molasses, and sugar (designed to protect the British sugar islands), but little hardship had resulted since royal governors winked at the heavy traffic in smuggling. But Grenville's Sugar Act of 1764, which amended the lightly enforced Molasses Act, had teeth in it; released warships were to patrol the waters to prohibit smuggling and force the collection of duties. While, among other changes, the duties on sugar were halved, there was still a lot more than the little-to-nothing formerly paid in times of unmolested smuggling. A protest committee of the Massachusetts House of Representatives formed to study the constitutionality of the new act, and its chairman James Otis, declared that the Sugar Act would "deprive the colonies of some of their most essential rights as British subjects, and . . . particularly the right of assessing their own taxes."

Massachusetts, like Virginia, was not on the soundest constitutional ground, since England's right to tax through duties had been accepted as long as the duties could be evaded in practice. But both colonies, in their profound change since the spirit of self-assertiveness engendered by the French and Indian Wars, were hardening against the postwar British policy which showed an intention of finding more sources of revenue from the colonies to apply to Great Britain's colonial expenses. In this hardening, the colonies' tortuous constitutional arguments were expressions of fundamental demands for equality in government. As Thomas Jefferson later wrote of Richard Bland, in the principles he was propounding, libertarian meant that the colonies were not subservient to the mother country — and, hence, not to be coerced on matters where taxes (whatever called) involved the economic well-being of the citizens.

In the failing communication between the colonial governing bodies and the governing bodies of the Crown, the offices in charge of colonial affairs as well as Parliament simply seemed to have grown impervious to protests from the colonies. Not recognizing the change of temper behind the protests, the English bodies dismissed them as no more than chronic complaints. However, had there been any alert sensitivity to colonial developments in George III's government at the end of the war, expressions of the changing temper could have served as warnings.

5

Even before the bitterly resented proclamation forbidding Virginia the fruits of the long war borne on her borders, the British merchants won the support of the Crown in their effort to force the planters to pay their debts in sterling. As far back as 1759, when Virginia (the last colony to issue paper money) had been issuing paper money for only four years, the merchants had prevailed upon the officials in charge of colonial affairs to send additional instructions to Fauquier. He was to urge the Burgesses to amend the statutes of 1757 — which provided for the depreciation of Virginia currency in payment of debts owed in sterling — so that all debts contracted before 1757 would be payable in sterling and local currency would be acceptable only if the merchant-creditor chose to accept it.

The Burgesses rejected that proposition out of hand, as the Governor had probably expected them to. Later he overrode the Council in supporting the Burgesses in passing four more issues of paper money in the next three years. Then, in May, 1763, further instructions forced Fauquier to address the House on the King's recommendation for the security of the merchants being paid in paper money, and to tell the surprised Burgesses that continued evasion of the King's recommendation would put them ''deeper in his Majesty's displeasure.''

This startling announcement from their friend came at a time when the British merchants had driven down tobacco prices, when families were being forced to live on one fourth of their income of a few years before, when planters of proud names had their bills of exchange protested and families of great prestige were hounded by creditors, when the General Court was crowded with creditors, and the sheriffs were becoming reluctant to deliver judgments against honest workers threatened with jail. With all the justices and injustices on both sides of the planter-merchant tug-of-war, and with many planters paying for their business naïveté and personal vanity to the hard-headed commercial men who had encouraged them to go into debt, again it was bad timing for the Crown to admonish a people burdened with war-incurred taxes to give satisfaction to the merchants whose profits came out of their labors.

The House of Burgesses responded by appointing two committees to investigate the basis of the King's recommendation for security of the merchants' debts. The committee — formed of two stalwarts of the oligarchy, Richard Bland and Benjamin Harrison, and the self-confident newcomer Richard Henry Lee — discovered that taxes backing the notes far exceeded the amount of the notes. In other words, according to their method of supporting the paper issues with taxes, the paper money would steadily be retired.

Of course this did not satisfy the merchants, who had long complained at the rate of exchange for debts owed in sterling. The Burgesses, looking to their interests from their viewpoint — as the merchants did the same — deeply resented the Board of Trade's censure and the threat of the King's displeasure over currency which Virginia had been forced to issue in order to conduct the war. Nothing showed more strongly the government's temper than the statement of the second committee — composed of Charles Carter, lawyer George Wythe, and John Robinson's protégé, the courtly Edmund Pendleton.

"Our dependence upon Great Britain we acknowledge and glory in as our greatest happiness and only security; but this is not the dependence of a people subjugated by the arms of a conqueror, but of sons sent out to explore and settle a new world, for the mutual benefit of themselves and the common parents: It is the dependence of a part upon one great whole, which, by its admirable Constitution, diffuses a spirit of patriotism that makes every citizen, however distant from the Mother Kingdom, zealous to promote its Majesty and the public good." The statement further made it clear that the General Assembly of Virginia held the right of determining "the public good" in *its* part of the whole.

This strong statement of position made the usual lack of impression in London, even though it was followed in January, 1764, by an ingenious rebuke to the Crown. Governor Fauquier had called a special session to pass on to the Burgesses an appeal from General Amherst for five hundred troops for defense against Indians. Three lawyers — Bland, Pendleton, and Peyton Randolph — along with Richard Henry Lee drafted a "humble address" to the Governor. Actually intended for English eyes, the address explained why Virginia could not comply with Amherst's request to raise troops. The expenses of raising troops could only be met by issuing paper money, and they had been warned of the displeasure of the Crown and the merchants over their paper currency.

This, of course, did nothing to appease the merchants. In 1763, this bloc had persuaded Parliament to pass a Currency Act which prohibited the use of any colonial currency issued after September 1, 1764, for payment of debts. Although this act applied to the colonies generally, and this type of prohibition had been enforced in New England since 1751, the merchants' new show of strength through the home government struck heavily at Virginia.

New England was not affected and — a galling fact to Virginians — some of the colonies with the soundest currency enjoyed their good position because of their failure to contribute substantially in either men or money to the war. In other colonies that were affected, New York and Pennsylvania, the legislatures made official protests, and John Watts, a New York merchant, wrote, "We have no resources upon an emergency, except in paper money." In the growing intercolonial community of interests, he stated that "the loss on Virginia paper was honestly acquired, by the government exerting itself" during the war. Richard Jackson, the agent of Pennsylvania, predicted that "under the present . . . restraints, we shall, in a few years, be without a necessary medium of trade."

This was not an alarmist's warning. Difficulties grew cumulatively in the middle colonies over the lack of a medium of exchange acceptable to England, and in Virginia the problem soon became crucial. When Virginia's paper money reached the date of retirement, that issue was removed from circulation and the legal tender burned, and in less than a year after the Currency Act became effective (October, 1764) Fauquier reported that as "circulating currency" had "grown very scarce, the people were really distressed for money of any kind to satisfy their creditors." Since the burning of legal tender received for taxes would continue as the notes matured, he predicted — also correctly — that the troubles would multiply.

However, while Parliament and the Board had been listening to the exhortations of the merchants — who, after all, represented the lifeblood of the trade on which Great Britain was growing into the premier world empire — members of the home government continued to neglect the words being written in Virginia and the other colonies. Early in 1764, Landon Carter published his first pamphlet — written the preceding October, before Henry's courthouse speech — on the subject of the King.

"I say then it is a virtue in a Prince to acquiesce at all times in the agreement of his subjects among themselves, in any part of his dominions, when that agreement does not affect his own *royal right* in any *sensible* manner, or the rest of his subjects of his Kingdom in any manner *whatever*." On the other hand, prerogative carried too far could "be construed to the destruction of the Prince's virtue . . . [of] that goodness which inclines him to encourage and enjoy the peace of his subjects, mutually settled between themselves."

Later in the year, apparently encouraged by the reception given his friend's pamphlet, Richard Bland published an essay originally written for his own "amusement." The contumacious John Camm (who was never to be quieted during the remainder of the colonial period) had not then accepted defeat on his Two Penny fight, and Bland's essay had started as an ironical attack on Camm's activities as a parish rector, titled *The Colonel Dismounted, or the Rector Vindicated in a Letter Addressed to His Reverence.* Passing from satire into a dissertation on the constitution of the Colony, Bland's essay was the historic testament of Virginia's evolved political principles. Regarded both by men then on the scene (as law student Tom Jefferson) and later historians of the period as the initial paper of the revolutionary movement, *The Colonel Dismounted* defined the nature of governing principles between the mother country and the colonies as Virginians had come to regard the interdependence of their relationship.

"If then the people of this Colony are born free, and have a right to the liberties and privileges of English subjects, they must necessarily have a legal constitution, that is, a legislature, composed, in part, of the representatives of the people, who may enact laws for the INTERNAL government of the Colony, and suitable to its various circumstances and occasions; and without such a representative government, I am bold to say, no laws can be made.

"The common law, being the common consent of the people from time immemorial, and the 'birthright of every Englishman, does follow him where ever he goes,' and consequently must be the GENERAL LAW by which the colony is to be governed. . . . From these principles, which I take to be incontrovertible, as they are deduced from the nature of the English constitution, it is evident that the legislature of the Colony have a right to enact ANY law they shall deem necessary for their INTERNAL government."

Here at last the General Assembly's leading constitutionalist took a straight, steady look at the tenuous division which had so long existed between the vague concepts of "external" and "internal." After nearly a century of more or less satisfactory compromises between the principles of the Crown and the practices of the colonies, Bland's statement was a declaration of the end of satisfaction with pragmatic evasions made with the connivance of benevolent governors. The local governing body wanted, demanded, the constitutional guarantees of principles recognizing the validity of internal government "suitable to its various circumstances and occasions." With Landon Carter's stricture against indiscriminately used prerogatives of the King, the doctrine of "consent" was being advanced.

While these theories were sifting into the consciousness of Virginians, and growing as subjects of conversation among the more literate, the ministry put together by George III could not have moved more insultingly against the temper of the people if Grenville had deliberately determined to give a contemptuous slap at the pretensions expressed by colonials in pamphlets written by high-ranking members of the ruling class and petitions presented by carefully selected committees of the House of Burgesses.

Thick-skinned Grenville, his mind obsessed with the facts which he was a master at amassing, actually regarded his Revenue Act of 1764 as an isolated expedient for drawing additional revenues from the colonies in the total postwar policy. Virginia and the other colonies saw it — as it was — as the first law ever enacted to raise money directly from the tax-paying citizens of the colonies. This was the Sugar Act, which hit New England so hard, but it encompassed far more than a tax on the sugar and molasses used by distillers. Duties went up on some imports, were placed on formerly duty-free imports used in all the colonies, and doubled on such foreign goods reshipped through England as hides, raw silk, iron, and so on. Nor was that the worst.

When Grenville had presented his act to Parliament, he added that it would also be "proper to charge certain stamp duties" in the colonies. Parliament agreed to this principle, and when the news reached Williamsburg in May, 1764, the Virginians got the impression, correctly, that the Crown was ready to impose a stamp act as soon as Grenville prepared it.

Except for Dinwiddie's misadventure with the pistole fee, which applied only to persons patenting more than a hundred acres of land and the end of which had still not been heard, Virginians had never been taxed directly by the mother country. The jealously guarded right to control the Colony's revenues had been the Burgesses' traditional weapon against encroachment from governors since the days when the Stuarts sent their high-handed colonial administrators. The right to legislate their own taxation and expenditures was the ground on which the original oligarchy, of King Carter's era, had defeated the tough and skillful Spotswood in the battle over who would rule Virginia — the Crown's representative or the ruling class. And now after one hundred and fifty-seven years of evolving representative government while building a civilization on a naked continent, now after articulating their evolved principles of government which they believed would promote the public good of the whole of Great Britain, now with resentment already mounting at England's postwar policy and with self-assertiveness running high, they were to be taxed like a conquered province. They were to be taxed as if their General Assembly did not exist.

Right there the lines were drawn. No one in George III's government seemed aware of it, and in Virginia few men recognized the finality of the cleavage except Patrick Henry.

With him the recognition transcended the constitutional principles articulated chiefly by Richard Bland and Landon Carter. Incorporating those principles into the emotionality of his thinking, the people's spokesman recognized that Bland's position represented only the constitutional rationale behind the people's feelings: they felt the cleavage in their hearts.

6

Most of the measures of the new continental policy which England imposed on the colonies, and all the impact, came to Virginia after Henry's speech in the trial at Hanover Court House. Maury's trial in Hanover County had been a very local affair, and Henry's turbulent, treasonable words had been heard by only a few country people. Since there were no court reporters to record his speech, only the general sense of his attack on "tyranny" had spread through the counties where he was known as a trial lawyer. But when men and women talked of their young neighbor, his words specifically on the Two Penny Act seemed prophetic of the whole course the Crown was following with the tax-burdened citizens. The remarkable aspect of Henry's speech — made as a means of gaining popularity — was that it was prophetic.

Between his speech in a county courthouse and his first appearance in the Capitol at Williamsburg, the Crown seemed to insist on fitting Henry's description of a king who, "from being the father of the people, degenerated into a tyrant, and forfeits all rights to his subjects' obedience." Although what the Colony called the Crown then consisted mostly of roughriding Grenville and a Parliament influenced by merchants, since Henry's constituents were remote from the operating structure of the government under the King, Henry thought in terms of the simplified dramatic appeals to which the country people responded. He came to the House of Burgesses, then, confirmed in the position of passion he had assumed to win popularity during a courthouse trial.

As he had proclaimed that a king forfeits all rights to his subjects' obedience by disallowing "salutary" acts (such as the Two Penny Act) for the people's welfare, he progressed to the position that the new externally imposed taxes — whether in the form of duties or the direct tax represented by the threatened stamp act — forfeited the subjects' obedience. In Hanover Court House the subjects had refused civil obedience in spirit when the jury awarded the Reverend Mr. Maury one penny on damages of between £100 and £200. In Williamsburg, Henry carried the same spirit to the more sophisticated assemblage. It was in that spirit of readiness for civil disobedience that he differed from those enlightened Burgesses who had earlier drawn the lines of their stand against external controls. They gave no ultimatum, but Henry believed the people he represented were ready for eventualities.

George III's government evidently paid no attention to either. But George, who must rule, had invited disharmony in the whole Empire when he replaced the farsighted if egotistical Pitt and the effectively operating Whig oligarchy with ineffective, unpopular Bute, and followed him with power-hungry Grenville, as egotistical as Pitt but lacking both his vision and his humanity. None of these people in George's government, including the fair young man who wanted to be the beloved "Patriot King," was acting tyrannically. They were too busy with the new problems of a nation in sudden expansion into a world empire to give thought to the changing feelings and convictions of distant colonials who formed (as they saw it) an appendage to Great Britain.

Naturally the colonials did not view themselves from the same perspective. While to Virginians the Colony was not the center of the universe, it was the center of their lives. Having participated in a successfully waged war which they started in their own interests (and indirectly in England's), they were experiencing a surge of independence of spirit that bristled at any controls imposed as upon a subservient people. From the democratic-minded, self-reliant frontiersman at one end of the Colony to the aristocratic-minded baronial planter at the other end, the people could view very personally such offhandedly imposed controls as those violating the traditional practices of their government and depriving them of their fruits of war on their borders. They were not thinking of England's problems any more than Grenville's ministry was thinking of theirs.

In this failure of communication, the one difference between the home government and Virginia's government was that the General Assembly was trying its best to communicate. The indifference with which their communications were received opened the way for the visceral appeals of Patrick Henry. For in 1764 the bad timing of England's postwar controls on the colonies was the intangible outside the calculations of a Grenville and George's Tory henchmen. But when timing became of the essence, it was Henry's gift to be a genius at seizing the opportune moment.

Chapter Seven

THE EMERGENCE OF THE REVOLUTIONARIES

RICHARD HENRY LEE had begun to feel the pinch of cash for his growing family as he neglected his plantation for his studies and intense participation in politics. It was a time when fluctuating tobacco prices — frequently low except for the very best tobacco and not consistently good even for that — were causing such a hardworking, systematic planter as George Washington to fail to meet expenses. Even the fine-grade tobacco shipped from the rich land in the Custis estate, bringing ten and a half pence per pound in London, could not net enough to compensate for the losses on the poorer tobacco grown at Mount Vernon.

When one shipment of 12,600 pounds of Custis tobacco brought £555, and £384 of that (nearly 70 per cent) went to the British government in duties, after shipping charges were paid, Washington netted £145, about 25 per cent. Accepting the impossibility of making a go of it with the high duties and the grade of tobacco of Mount Vernon, Washington turned to growing wheat, which he milled, and marketed his own flour. Richard Henry Lee turned to his older brother Philip, the Councilor, for the use of his influence in getting an appointment to a vacancy on the Council.

The still prestigious Council was on the wane in active political power and was beginning to act as something of a body of inertia. Its character seemed to be colored by the Nelson brothers, merchants of Yorktown, by men of large affairs like Robert Carter of Nomini Hall and of large self-esteem like Philip Lee. The Council had become as interested in sound money (sterling) as the British merchants trading in Virginia. Had Richard Henry Lee won the appointment, he would have been the only Councilor who actually needed the £600, *sterling,* a year salary that went with the post of honor. He would also have lost the effectiveness of the political force he could bring to bear in the more flexible, less conservative House.

As he did not get the appointment, Lee became in point of time the first active revolutionary in the House of Burgesses. This was in the autumn of 1764, before Henry entered the General Assembly in the spring of the following year. The imperious gentleman from the Northern Neck revealed that he — like the country lawyer — was one of the few men in Virginia who recognized that the lines had been drawn between the colonies and the mother country.

The recognition came to him during the summer after he had read in the Revenue Act of Grenville's declaration of intent to impose direct taxes through a tax of stamps. From his secluded plantation on the Potomac, Lee wrote his reactions to a friend in London. Following Bland's line of the "illegality of taxation without consent," Lee went further: "Possibly this step by the mother country, though intended to oppress us and keep us low, in order to secure our dependence, may be subversive of this end. Poverty and oppression, among those whose minds are filled with the ideas of British liberty, may introduce virtuous industry with a train of glorious and manly sentiments, which, when in future they became supported by numbers, produce a fatal resentment of parental care being converted into tyrannical usurpation."

Now Grenville, as Chancellor of the Exchequer with the powers of chief minister, was concerned not with oppression but with retiring Great Britain's huge war debts. However, the idea of tyrannical usurpation had come into the minds of Virginians — in Lee's through intellectual processes while Henry's came through emotionalism. In their reactions, Henry's threat was civil disobedience, whereas Lee's threat was more generally ominous, in the future, and actually more final: "a *fatal* resentment," he had written. He may or may not have heard of Patrick Henry's speech in the county some distance from his own. The likelihood would be that he had not heard of it — or certainly no more than in generalities related to a test case in the Two Penny Act — and that the two dissimilar men had arrived independently at the same conviction.

Feeling as he did about the threatened taxation without consent — and he felt very strongly — the hard-pressed Lee then took a strange turn in his career. When he arrived in Williamsburg for the fall 1764 session of the General Assembly, he encountered a resentful apprehension over the threatened imposition of taxes.

The Burgesses, gathered on the facing benches in their long oblong room, sat impatiently through the Governor's opening address on October 30. The bland Fauquier was very businesslike about items on his agenda. After a couple of weeks he got around to the by then chronic complaint from London about the payment of planters' debts in sterling. As whenever he was forced to execute distasteful instructions, he became a little stiff; he warned the Burgesses that their continued refusal to change laws would bring down upon them the displeasure of the Board of Trade. With no dissenting votes, the Burgesses politely told the Governor that they continued to refuse. Their minds were not really on the items advanced by Fauquier.

Shortly after the House convened, on Thursday, November 1, John Robinson laid before the Burgesses a letter which he had received, in his capacity as Speaker, from the Massachusetts House of Representatives. The letter advised the Virginia General Assembly that the House of Commons in a committee of the whole had voted on passing certain stamp taxes on the American colonies and that voting the bill into law only waited on the next meeting of Parliament.

On the following Thursday, the 8th, the Speaker instructed the Committee of Correspondence to lay before the House letters from their London agent. A letter from Montagu dated April 11 warned the committee that the House of Commons "appeared so unanimous of opinion that America should ease the revenue of this annual expense [maintaining the frontier] that I am persuaded they will not listen to any remonstrance against it." There appeared to be such a determination by "Government that this money be furnished by America by some means or other [that] pleas of incapacity will scarce avail. . . . I should conceive it would be extremely worthy of your serious attention what may be the consequence of introducing such a precedent as the imposition of a Stamp Tax by British Parliament.''

The ''pleas of incapacity'' arose from all the colonies. Caught, like England, in a postwar fall in the economy, and with their trade restricted to Great Britain, the more mercantile colonies also struggled against burdensome taxes, scarce money, high duties, and the very dear cost of British manufactured imports. Unlike Virginia, they felt the pinch in the form of rising unemployment. Commercial houses failed in Boston, where unemployed artisans began to forsake the city; Rhode Island real estate was selling for half its former value, and hard money had disappeared from the colony; in New York land went for a pittance in forced sales and creditors drove their debtors into bankruptcy. William Livingston of New York wrote, ''It seems as if all our American world must inevitably break, and Lord have mercy on the London merchants.'' It was not only the Virginia planters, with their extravagance and unhealthy dependence on credit, who felt the clutch of English merchants.

These were the matters that engaged the ''serious attention'' of the Burgesses. As soon as they were finished with the Governor's business, the members of the House turned to act on the subject that occupied their thoughts and conversations, and accepted Landon Carter's suggestion to draft protests to the King, the House, and the Lords.

It was somewhere in the two weeks between the time when Speaker Robinson laid before the House the warning letter from Massachusetts and the Burgesses' selection, November 14, of a committee to draft the protests, that the revolutionary-minded Lee made a personally pragmatic decision. Since Great Britain seemed certain to impose a stamp tax on the colonies before spring of the following year, he decided to get in on the ground floor of its operation. ''Early in November'' (in his own words), Lee applied for the post of collector of the stamp tax in Virginia.

He did not make his application generally known, and its disclosure was later used against him in a bitter public argument with the successful applicant. When Lee defended himself in that 1766 exchange, he stated that he had become convinced of his error in applying for the collector's job within a few days and he appealed to the ''many worthy gentlemen with whom I served in the General

Assembly . . . who would know what part I took'' in the papers the House committee drafted in opposition to the proposed tax. Lee, however, did not state that he had withdrawn the application. Although he was apparently willing to profit from the collector's post if and when the bill passed in Parliament, he followed his principles by joining his fellow Burgesses in making a strong protest against the measure.

2

When the committee was formed to draft the three petitions — one to the King, one to the House of Lords, and one to the Commons — Lee, as lucid in writing as in speaking, was placed on the committee with such of the oligarchy's regulars as Peyton Randolph, the chairman, Benjamin Harrison and Landon Carter, and the learned lawyers Edmund Pendleton and George Wythe. For some reason, constitutionalist Bland did not serve on that committee, perhaps because his old friends expected to do little more than rephrase his doctrines for an English audience.

Richard Henry Lee, however, expected to go beyond a restatement of those doctrines of Bland that were already well known in the Colony. Since the lofty stands taken by the oligarchs on the Colony's ''rights'' and ''liberties'' seemed to change nothing in England, the younger Lee wrote intemperate words designed to attract attention in the ''Address'' to his Majesty and in the ''Memorial'' to the House of Lords. The older men, grown accustomed to their way of doing things, spent considerable time toning down the utterances they felt were unseemly or inflammatory. Apparently George Wythe was chief among Lee's unwanted collaborators, applying a restraint natural to his temperament, and Wythe himself wrote the ''Remonstrance'' to the House of Commons.

The three papers were completed after a month of group effort and compromise, along with whatever unrecorded wrangling went on behind closed doors. Benjamin Harrison, one of Williamsburg's most adroit soothers of ruffled feelings in a committee room, may well have been less than gentle with the Lee cousin whom he disliked, for Big Ben had at his command a hearty humor which could turn the tide of an argument but which would not sit well on the ascetic scholar. Lee could still take pride for his part in the finished papers, but he emerged from the collaboration confirmed in his hostility to Robinson's Tidewater oligarchy.

As it was, the resolutions (finished on December 13) were strong enough — "very warm and indecent," Fauquier found the terms — for the Governor to write an advisory letter to the Board of Trade. "I have been told by some Gentlemen of the Committee . . . that their whole study has been to mollify them [the resolutions], and they have reason to hope there is nothing now in them which will give the least offense."

Wythe was certainly one of the gentlemen who told Fauquier of the behind-the-scenes maneuvers. Not only was the lawyer an intimate of the Palace, but he often spoke for the Governor in the House.

The burden of all three documents was the by then standard colonial line against taxation without consent. In effect renouncing the past's pragmatic practices across fuzzy definitions of internal and external, the colonies generally took a strong position on limiting taxation to those internal affairs for which their *representative* legislatures were responsible. This was the genesis of the later rallying cry "No taxation without representation." Although all the colonies entered their protests, only New York took as hard a line as Virginia on defining the issues behind their opposition to the stamp tax.

The address to his Majesty was an appeal that he protect the people of Virginia "in the enjoyment of their ancient and inestimable right of being governed by such laws respecting their internal policy and taxation as are derived from their own consent, with the approbation of their sovereign or his substitute [their governor]." The memorial to the House of Lords stated, "Your memorialists conceived it to be a fundamental principle of the British constitution, without which freedom can exist nowhere, that the people are not subject to any taxes but such as are laid on them by their own consent, or by those who are legally appointed to represent them." Following this line of representation for all the colonies, the memorial stated that taxation by a legislative body in which they were not represented "must necessarily establish this melancholy truth, that the inhabitants of the Colonies are slaves of Britons from whom they descend."

Wythe's remonstrance to the House of Commons got more down-to-earth, in an indirect appeal to the mercantile interests. With Virginia already oppressed by war debts, a stamp tax would reduce the people to such "extreme poverty" that they would be "compelled to manufacture those articles" which they were then buying from England. This veiled warning had been put more succinctly in a letter by Pennsylvania's Benjamin Franklin to an English friend. "What you get from us in taxes you must lose in trade. The cat can yield but her skin. And as you must have the whole hide, if you first cut thongs out of it, 'tis at your own expense."

The Virginians, acting in a concerted move by the colonies — with an awareness of being *American* colonists within the structure of Great Britain — felt they had done all possible in laying their case against a stamp tax before the British government.

Although history usually is concerned with acts of commission, a historical turning point in the developing strain in the colonial–mother country relationship was an act of omission. The reasoned petitions on which the best brains in Virginia had, to the neglect of the Burgesses' own affairs, worked for a month were totally ignored, along with those of the other colonies. After Virginia went to the expense of printing and circulating it in London, the House of Lords did not even have the memorial read to their Lordships. Some persons must have glanced at the papers, for Grenville was sufficiently aware of reports of the colonies' opposition to be annoyed. But nobody was sufficiently interested to discuss the colonies' resistance when the stamp tax bill was presented in the House of Commons. Its passage through was routine, like any bill.

Making Dinwiddie's pistole fee look like the good old days, this new act required a stamp for every piece of paper which carried printed matter. Beginning with newspapers and individual advertisements in newspapers and ending with packs of playing cards, stamps were required on every conceivable contract, on bills of sale and bills of lading, pamphlets and almanacs and calendars, land survey orders and college diplomas.

The act was incredible to the colonials. It was also incredibly bad in its timing.

The omission made by the British government in not reading the colonies' petitions did not result only in the negligent passage of a bill in indifference to the "consent" demanded by the American colonists. It resulted in deepening communications between the colonies, especially Virginia and Massachusetts, where the Virginia petitions *were* read.

Until well into the French and Indian Wars, the colonies had gone their separate, competitive ways, aware of one another only to the extent of jealousy. The attempts, made largely by British governors in the colonies and British generals, to develop cooperative efforts during the war had accomplished little in practical results. But their cumbersome gropings toward some community of interests had awakened the colonies' awareness of one another, even though each remained essentially self-centered. It was England's postwar policy, which treated the colonies as a single colonial entity (without regard for their different social and economic systems, their different needs and aspirations), that promoted the sense of a communality of interests as American colonials in a gradual transcendence of their continuing self-centered concerns. The disregard of their petitions drew them together for potential community of *action*.

For the intercolonial exchanges of 1764 and 1765 were not instigated by British governors; they were spontaneous exchanges between peoples united in common cause. Unlike the war, this was not a cause that was involved with the intercontinental expansions of the British Empire. This was very local, very personal, and the British government became the common oppressor, whereas the French and Indians had never presented a singleness of threat to all the colonies.

Grenville's government never meant to be insulting by ignoring the protests. His money-minded ministry was too indifferent to what the colonials thought to bother to be insulting. After all, the stamp tax had been successfully imposed in England, yielding a large revenue, and it was not as if the colonies were expected to help defray England's £140,000,000 debt. Grenville expected no more than £60,000 from the colonies as a contribution to the £350,000 yearly cost of maintaining British troops in North America. And the ministry had allowed a sufficient interval between the declaration of intent and the passage of the bill to allow the colonies time to get used to the need of providing additional revenue, during which interval the Chancellor of the Exchequer was open to proposals from the colonies for a tax of their preference. The colonies had offered no feasible substitute.

By then, however, the colonies and Grenville's government were talking about quite different things. Grenville regarded it as reasonable for the colonies to supply *revenue* to help defray the expenses of American garrisons which protected the flanks of the colonies; the colonies were fixated in their opposition to the *principle* of a tax imposed without their consent.

During this crucial failure in communications, George III, the symbol, was out of it entirely. He was ill — said to be temporarily deranged — when his Chancellor of the Exchequer introduced the stamp tax bill. The character of the government was Grenville's. A highly intelligent man, with an orderly mind that was adroit in handling facts, he was a master of marshaling statistics in debate. Also an insensitive man, he — in effect representing the Crown — did not include the feelings of the American colonists among the pertinent facts. This intangible element, not chartable in his statistics, was the overlooked root of the matter.

It was bad enough for the colonies to be inflicted with such a broad tax burden in the hard times; it was worse that the imposed tax violated their ancient right of legislating their own taxes; it was unthinkable that these things were done to them with a total disregard of their feelings about it. The people, of all kinds and degree, were outraged at the prospect of the tax which would go into effect the following year.

3

When the gardens of Williamsburg flowered in the spring of 1765, the General Assembly gathered somewhat reluctantly for a session on May 1. This was a busy season for planters, and except for some continuous legislation over tobacco that needed to be resolved between the House and the Council, there were only routine items to be disposed of. No news had reached the Colony of any action taken by Parliament on the Stamp Act, and in the four preceding months of winter and early spring the planters' attention had been absorbed with growing tobacco.

Unknown to the men settling themselves in Williamsburg's houses and inns, the House of Commons had passed the bill on February 27, the House of Lords on March 8, and in the continued absence of the ill King, royal assent was given by commission.

As the dull session progressed through the radiant weeks of May, rumors began to grow about a matter of more intense local concern than the tax bill against which the Burgesses had made their stand before Christmas. There was talk about a mysterious loan of £240,000 sterling to be floated in England, to be paid off by tobacco taxes. With £100,000 Virginia could retire the paper money that had caused such controversy, and a ''loan office'' would be established with the remaining £140,000 to advance money to some of the larger planters against the security of their landholdings. Since the proposed loan was supported by John Robinson's oligarchy, the whisperings hinted at some irregularity in the accounts of Speaker Robinson's office of the Treasury in which some of the biggest names in the Colony were said to be involved.

Landon Carter did not attend that session. His brother, Charles Carter of Cleve, had died the year before, and Landon was executor of the estate, which had some debts against it and other complications. Charles Carter, Jr., had been elected in his father's place, and he wrote his uncle Landon, ''The scheme proposes something in the nature of a loan office . . . I esteem you a principal member of the Legislature and therefore have put my hand to paper — you know best whether it will be worth your while to attend.''

The talk was kept quiet, for not only was Robinson the most powerful man in the House but one of the most likable. ''An excellent man,'' Jefferson said of him, ''liberal, friendly, and rich.'' Robinson was indeed too rich to have needed any money for his own estate and was known as well for his generousness as for the equanimity with which he conducted the House.

Tom Jefferson, in his third year as a law student under the Governor's intimate George Wythe, might well himself have heard some of the rumors, for he was a regular attendant at those routine May sessions of the House. Then twenty-two, Jefferson was using the study of law chiefly as a basis in the preparation for the business of life: proceeding thoroughly, without haste, he was engaged in what might be called self-designed graduate studies.

He had come into his own estate by then and was managing the farming of his property. He also began to take part, as the man of the family, in the supervision of the finances of his mother and sisters in the family place of Shadwell. Though this property would not come to

Jefferson until his mother died, Shadwell remained his house, where he stored his growing library. Since he was on no rigid schedule in his law studies with George Wythe, Jefferson journeyed back and forth between Shadwell and Williamsburg. He rode alone, unless occasionally accompanied by Jupiter, a slave his own age, who was that combination of the times — a companion–personal servant. Usually Jupiter followed the horseman in a one-horse cart which carried their luggage.

Most of the youthful frolics Jefferson had indulged in when he first left William and Mary were behind him — including a blighted romance. For the object of his first love, the young man from Albemarle had aimed as high as could be reached in the Colony. Rebecca Burwell, the second cousin of his friend John Page, and the great-niece of Charles and Landon Carter, was the daughter of the late Council President Lewis Burwell, who had been the favorite and most troublesome grandson of King Carter. After the death of her parents when she was young, Rebecca had been raised in the family of her uncle by marriage, Councilor William Nelson, the Yorktown merchant.

Of course "beautiful" — all the belles who figured in the lost loves of colonial Virginia were beautiful — Rebecca Burwell was serious-minded and a devout communicant of the Anglican Church. Perhaps her lack of frivolousness appealed to the likewise serious-minded young Jefferson, but, alas, he was not as brave in trying to win Rebecca as he had been in selecting her. Never a facile talker, he foundered in his prepared speeches when he attempted to make anything like a proposal. Finally, he gathered his courage to the point of telling her about a planned trip to England, with the implication that on his return he would address her *the* question.

This was much too vague for a young lady as desirable as Rebecca Burwell, who might not have been too interested in the first place. Shortly before his twenty-first birthday, Jefferson learned that his love object had become engaged to the older Jacquelin Ambler, whose family — in an enormous brick house — dominated the remnants of the community in the decaying city of Jamestown.

As a rejected suitor, Jefferson showed himself to be an emotionally immature twenty-one. Becoming a cynical misogynist, he bought Milton's works and copied in his notebooks disparagements of women he found in Milton and other poets. From Virgil, he copied, "Cruel love, to what extremities doth thou drive the hearts of men," and from David Mallet:

> *O 'scap'd from love, O safe on that calm shore,*
> *Where sin, and pain, and passion are no more.*

If Jefferson believed this last line when he wrote it, he must have been suffering from self-delusion, for he was not a man given to the passions of the emotions. Most likely he had suffered injury to his pride, his surging male ego, and he caught the real essence of his transitory cynicism in a doggerel from Latin. "Trust the winds with your bark, but do not trust the girls with your heart, for you can put your confidence more securely in waves than in women."

(When Jefferson married at twenty-nine, these apostrophes of youthful disillusion were far in the past; but until the end of his long life — though he enjoyed the state of marriage and fatherhood — friendship with men remained the most important of human relationships and one of the most important elements in his life.)

By the May, 1765, session of the General Assembly, the wounds of adolescent love apparently had healed, and Jefferson, with some emotional maturity gained, was absorbed in the political activities which were to become the center of his broadly ranging mind.

A person of Jefferson's class who craved personal honors had no choice outside public life, for that alone was the pathway to distinction in Virginia during the golden age. As it was also an obligation for those who accepted the responsibilities implicit in their inherited privilege, it would not be a case of Jefferson's consciously deciding that his career would include serving in the House of Burgesses; rather it represented an eventuality he would take for granted. In this way, his attendance at the sessions would be less a conscious preparation for his future than a manifestation of his interest in the activity which dominated Virginia life. That the spring 1765 session made a lasting impression on Jefferson was revealed by the clarity of his memory for details of the events when he was an old man.

The mysterious business about the great loan to be floated in England was not introduced until near the end of the session, Friday, May 24, just a few days after Patrick Henry made his late appearance in the Burgesses. While his fame had spread through his own neighborhood following his courthouse speech, his admirers had had to wait until a vacancy occurred to elect him to the House, and he took his seat on May 20.

4

The face of the newcomer was long and thin and angular, with sallow skin and dark brows, and in no way could he be seen as a handsome man, nor, in repose, an impressive one. Lean of build, he wore the often described plain clothes — of "coarse apparel," some said — and did not carry himself with the authority of such a Tidewater grandee as the hugely fat Peyton Randolph. Henry was amiable of manner as well as of disposition, and he was as quiet as the massive Washington during the first days that he sat at the bench among the handsomely tailored gentlemen most of whom were total strangers to him.

Jefferson had made Henry's acquaintance during the Christmas season of 1759–60 when, on his way to college, he had spent the holidays in the Hanover County home of Colonel Dandridge. Henry, a near neighbor, had dropped in every day and — though the seven years' difference in their ages was considerable at that stage of their lives — they had enjoyed one another's company during, as Jefferson recalled, "the festivity of the season."

When Jefferson wrote about Henry in later life, he showed an understandable ambivalence. After the Revolution they broke politically, and Jefferson came to distrust everything Henry stood for as a molder of the independent commonwealth. While he never ceased to give Henry credit as the leader of Virginia's revolutionary movement — "He was far before all men in maintaining the spirit of the Revolution" — nor ever withheld praise of his unequaled gifts of oratory, he became harsh in his judgments on Henry's indifferent legal learning and mental laziness, and took some pretty savage cuts at Henry's character.

Praising him as "the best-humored man in society I almost ever knew," and attributing to him "a consummate knowledge of the human heart," Jefferson scorned him as a "man of very little knowledge of any sort. He read nothing. . . . He wrote almost nothing; he *could* not write." He was "ignorant . . . all tongue, without head or heart . . . avaricious and rotten-hearted. . . . His two great passions were love of money and fame." Of his spellbinding oratory, "When he had spoken, and I myself had been highly delighted and moved, I often asked myself when he ceased, 'What the devil has he said?' "

While these judgments were far in the future when Jefferson listened to the House debates, these later evaluations colored his remembered impressions of their first meeting when he recorded them more than half a century after that Christmas country season. "His manners had something of the coarseness of the society he had frequented," Jefferson wrote; "his passion was fiddling, dancing, and pleasantry. He excelled in the last and attached everyone to him. The occasion, perhaps, as much as his idle disposition, prevented his engaging in any conversation which might give the measure either of his mind or his information."

"The idleness of his disposition" was a later judgment, based largely on Jefferson's scorn of Henry's lack of mental discipline, particularly in the law, where he continued to try (and to win) his cases on emotional appeals rather than on the legal issue involved. During a holiday season, in the midst of fiddling and dancing, the boy approaching seventeen would scarcely attribute to an idle disposition the social pleasures enjoyed by a married man in his mid-twenties. Perhaps as Jefferson thought in later years of when Henry had been the most popular political figure in the Colony, he may have felt some jealousy at the easy "pleasantry" which "attached everyone to him."

However, Jefferson felt only admiration, even awe, for Henry's first action in the House, and never minimized the tremendous effect made upon him by Henry's boldness and revolutionary spirit. "He left us all far behind."

Henry made his first impact on Jefferson and on the Burgesses when he broke his silence on Friday, May 24. The loan office had then been proposed and Speaker Robinson's friends were advancing, in lukewarm debate, the reasons for supporting it. As Jefferson recalled their reasons, it was claimed "that from certain unhappy circumstances of the Colony men of substantial property had contracted debts, which, if exacted suddenly, must ruin them and their families, but with a little indulgence of time, might be paid with ease."

Patrick Henry
Portrait by Thomas Sully, painted in 1815 from an earlier miniature
(Colonial Williamsburg Collection)

At this point in the debate, the new Burgess from Louisa County arose and exclaimed to the startled oligarchs: "What, sir, is it proposed then to reclaim the spendthrift from his dissipation and extravagance, by filling his pockets with money?"

On that sour note, the debate ended and the vote was taken. Robinson's supporters had the votes, but Henry had stirred up something. When the resolutions were sent up to the Council, the bill's supporters appointed a committee to confer with the Council, which was done only when the Burgesses expected opposition. Despite the conferring committee, the Council rejected the loan and the Robinson group let the matter die.

Henry's words, which had suddenly changed the whole temper of the debate, were, Jefferson wrote, "indelibly impressed upon my memory." Although supporters of the bill included Jefferson's cousins, he apparently saw with a fresh vision the potentials of abuse held by a landowning oligarchy long in power. Henry's dramatizing phrases had "laid open with so much energy the spirit of favoritism, on which the proposition was founded, and the abuses to which it could lead, that it was crushed in its birth."

Here again Jefferson was making after-the-fact interpretations in attributing to the energy of Henry's indictment the crushing of "the spirit of favoritism." Robinson's friends "of substantial property" did not want any close investigation of the proposed loan, and what Henry's graphic words had done was bring out into the open the suspicion that there was something fishy about the whole loan.

There was something fishy indeed, and long before the loan proposal Richard Henry Lee had been trying to discredit John Robinson, his father's rival, by unearthing some damaging irregularity in the Treasury accounts. As early as 1759 Lee had been behind the formation of a committee to examine all notes turned over to Treasurer Robinson, and to burn only the paper money redeemable before May, 1765. The following year Lee tried to introduce a measure to burn all paper money paid in for taxes. Naturally these moves were opposed by Robinson and his friends, as impugning his character. Then, in 1763, Lee climaxed his moves with an outright accusation. As a member of an *ad hoc* committee to audit the Treasury books, Lee reported to his fellow Burgesses a deficiency of £65,000 and demanded an immediate investigation.

Robinson made a bold countermove. He created a committee to make the requested investigation with Lee as a member, and placed Lee on the committee to report to the Governor and to those British merchants who were renewing their attacks on Virginia currency. The investigation discovered a deficiency of nearly £40,000 caused by several sheriffs' delinquency in tax collection. The House exonerated Robinson, and Lee drafted a reply to the merchants which stated that existing taxes were sufficient to redeem all paper money in circulation.

This was all official action, a matter of record, but there may well have been more than suspicion that some trickery — such as not actually destroying the paper money claimed to have been burned — covered large loans from public funds to prominent planter-politicians among Robinson's friends. Lee kept up his demands for investigation, and in the May session, when the loan was proposed, a committee composed of Robinson's friends delivered a report completely clearing the Treasury office. Lee was not present. He had learned that John Robinson had come into possession of the facts about his applying for the post of collector of the Stamp Act taxes, and this was not something he wanted aired in the House of Burgesses by the Speaker he had been trying to undermine.

Lee did gain a future ally in Henry, for the newcomer to the House sensed that he had touched upon a sensitive spot. Not long afterward he joined Lee in forcing investigations, which could not be whitewashed, into the accounts of Robinson's Treasury office.

5

On the Saturday and Sunday following the debate on the loan office, the Burgesses began to leave Williamsburg for their homes and their interrupted planting. On Monday and Tuesday the House continued to dwindle as routine matters were disposed of and the Council returned the bills it concurred with. Before adjournment on Tuesday, the Stamp Act was scheduled for consideration the next day.

Since the final action on this tax bill, the royal assent, was not taken until March 22, only a copy of the bill as it passed in the House of Commons had — as Fauquier said — "crept into the House." His verb "crept" was apt, as whatever discussion there was about the copy of the bill was insufficient to hold the departing Burgesses in Williamsburg. George Washington for one had left on the long journey to Mount Vernon, to look after his wheat.

On Wednesday, May 29, when the Stamp Act was scheduled for consideration, only thirty-nine of the hundred and four Burgesses were in their seats. Having said their say in formal protests, the majority evidently felt that since the bill had passed anyway, it was pointless to discuss it further.

At this stage, testimony is abundant on the happenings that began Wednesday morning, but as it is a compilation from different sources, none of which is in itself complete, the chronological details are not always clear.

One incontrovertible fact was that on the morning of May 29, Patrick Henry presented to the House five resolutions he had written on the Stamp Act. On the back of a page containing a copy of the resolutions, Henry later wrote:

"The within resolutions . . . formed the first opposition to the Stamp Act and the scheme of taxing America by the British Parliament. All the colonies, either through fear, or want of opportunity to form an opposition, or from influence of some kind or another, had remained silent.

"I had been for the first time elected a Burgess a few days before, was young and inexperienced, unacquainted with the forms of the House, and the members that composed it. Finding the men of weight averse to opposition, and the commencement of the tax at hand, and that no person was likely to step forth, I determined to adventure, and alone, unadvised, and unassisted, on the blank leaf of an old lawbook, wrote the within."

After Henry had written the five resolutions, he then showed them for discussion to two other Burgesses outside the Tidewater clique, George Johnston, a lawyer from the northern county of Fairfax, and John Fleming, a lawyer of Cumberland — one of the counties west of his own Hanover where Patrick Henry had built up his law practice. No one mentioned precisely when the three men met in "conclave" — as it was called by Paul Carrington, another Burgess, who knew of the meeting.

After Fleming and Johnston had conferred with Henry on his five resolutions, the three Burgesses agreed to add two more resolutions which were much stronger than Henry's five. The sixth called directly for civil disobedience and the seventh denounced as "an enemy to his Majesty's colony" any person who asserted that anyone except the General Assembly could impose taxes.

These added resolutions were not Henry's. He made no claim to them and they were not in his handwriting. That they followed the line of his court speech of eighteen months before could either indicate that his words had circulated or that the ideas were in the air outside of Tidewater, or both. In any event, Henry obviously knew the two men he approached were of like mind. Henry, Fleming, and Johnston agreed that Henry should present only his five resolutions first. According to the House's reaction to those, the collaborators would then decide whether or not to present the more inflammatory added resolutions.

On Wednesday morning the House met at ten o'clock, and routine matters dragged along without Speaker Robinson or any of the oligarchy showing any inclination to introduce the Stamp Act for consideration. Then George Johnston moved that the House go into committee of the whole to consider "the steps necessary to be taken in consequence of the resolutions of the House of Commons . . . relative to the charging certain stamp duties in the Colonies . . . in America."

The motion was immediately seconded by Patrick Henry.

Peyton Randolph took the place of Speaker Robinson as the presiding officer. Randolph's large, globular face, with its projecting double chin, could hold an expression of grave hauteur. Once he was at ease with a person, the Attorney General was genial and warm, and he was generally liked as well as admired. But the English-trained lawyer had been one of the examiners who felt that Henry was inadequately prepared to practice law and, after the newcomer's outburst against Robinson's loan proposition, it would scarcely be imaginable that Randolph's countenance lost any of its reserve when Henry — and not Johnston — arose to address the House.

There was nothing intemperate in Henry's manner as he read, from the scribbled-on blank pages of a lawbook, his five resolutions.

"Resolved

"That the first Adventurers and Settlers of this his Majesties Colony and Dominion brought with them and transmitted to their

Posterity and all other of his Majesties Subjects since inhabiting in this his Majesties said Colony all the Privileges, Franchises & Immunities possessed by the People of Great Britain.

'' [defaced]

''That by two royal Charters granted by King James the first the Colonists aforesaid are declared intituled to all the Privileges, Liberties & Immunities of Denizens and natural-born Subjects to all Intents and Purposes as if they had been abiding and born within the Realm of England.

''Resolved

''That the Taxation of the People by themselves or by Persons chosen by themselves to represent them who can only know what Taxes the People are able to bear and the easiest Mode of raising them and are equally affected by such Taxes themselves is the distinguishing Characteristick of British Freedom and without which the ancient Constitution cannot subsist.

''Resolved

''That his Majesties liege People of his most ancient Colony have uninterruptedly enjoyed the Right of being thus governed by their own assembly in the article of their Taxes and internal Police, and that the same hath never been forfeited or any other way given up but hath been constantly recognized by the Kings & People of Great Britain.

''Resolved

''Therefore that the General Assembly of this Colony have the *only and sole exclusive* Right & Power to lay Taxes & Impositions upon the Inhabitants of this Colony and that every Attempt to vest such Power in any Person or Persons whatsoever other than the General Assembly Aforesaid has a manifest Tendency to destroy British as well as American Freedom.''

As soon as he sat down, the debates began — ''violent debates,'' Henry said. The chief opponents to the resolutions of Henry's group were Richard Bland, his cousin Randolph, his cousin Speaker Robinson, and the Governor's voice George Wythe. These were not violent men normally. Bland, the scholar, was low-voiced and deeply courteous and not quick to debate on the floor. Robinson was usually persuasive, though he could show force, and Wythe given to the moderation of an approach by reason. Randolph was the most likely to grow heated. The oligarchy's most effective and relentless debater, Edmund Pendleton, was among the Burgesses who had already departed.

Some of the lesser-known members, not included in the accounts of either Jefferson or Fauquier as among the leading opponents, may have spoken the "threats" which Henry said were "uttered," although Henry included (what he called) the whole "party of submission" as casting "much abuse . . . on me."

Jefferson, recording nothing about threats or abuse, remembered Henry's "torrents of sublime eloquence, backed by the solid reasoning of Johnston." A French visitor, who happened to come in that day when the debates reached their climax, wrote in his journal, "I was entertained with very strong debates."

Burgess Paul Carrington, in his memo on the debates, reported that the first four resolutions passed "without violent opposition," and it was only the fifth resolution which brought forth a "most bloody" debate. However, never referring to Henry's opponents as a party of "submission," he noted that they did not disagree with Henry and his allies "as to the grievances complained of." Since the Burgesses had seen only a copy of the stamp tax bill that went through the House of Commons, Henry's opponents preferred to wait for an answer to their earlier petitions which "possibly might rend[er] the proposed proceedings unnecessary."

While that was Carrington's opinion, it could well have been one of the factors in the objections of the leading Burgesses. Waiting on England belonged in the House's tradition of presenting reasoned protests and then sitting back. However, if the passage of the bill in the House of Commons had been followed by passage in the Lords, then the bill was already *law*. In either case there were also personal factors. First, Patrick Henry was not one of them. Then his first four resolves were no more than rephrasings of doctrines advanced for a decade by their accepted constitutionalist Richard Bland. In their capacity as members of the Committee of Correspondence, Henry's opponents had given representations of their position which the new Burgess knew nothing about. The committee had written Montagu, the

General Assembly's agent in London, the way they wanted their protests presented in England.

". . . That no Subjects of the King of great Britain can be justly made *subservient* ["subject" erased] to Laws without either their personal Consent, or their Consent by their representatives we take to the most vital Principle of the British Constitution; it cannot be denied that the Parliament has from Time to Time, where the Trade of the Colonies with other Parts was likely to interfere with that of the Mother Country, made such Laws as were thought sufficient to restrain such Trade to what was judg'd its proper Channel, neither can it be denied that, the Parliament, out of the same *Plenitude of its Power,* has gone a little Step farther & imposed some Duties upon our Exports; but to fix a Tax upon such Part of our Trade and Concerns as are merely internal, appears to us to be taking a long & hasty Stride & we believe may truly be said to be of the first Importance. Nothing is farther from our Thoughts than to shew the least Disposition to any Sort of rudeness, but we hope it cannot be taken amiss that we, apprehending ourselves so nearly concerned, should, at least whilst the Matter is in Suspence, humbly represent against it, & take every Measure which the Principles & Laws of our Constitution appear clearly to justify, to avert a Storm so very replete with the most dangerous Consequences."

Finally, the language of Henry's fifth resolve went farther than they wanted to go if the bill was already the law. The learned, legally trained members of the oligarchy, with their long experience in protecting Virginia against any move which they considered a threat to their liberties, simply did not believe "that every attempt to vest" the power of taxation in any person "other than the General Assembly aforesaid has a manifest tendency to destroy British as well as American freedom." They felt such intemperate utterances were "rash" and disrespectful to the King.

Time soon proved that the oligarchy had insensibly grown conservative in its protection of Virginia's rights and liberties. Stands that had been advanced in their reasoning and in their vigor ten years before had already become a part of a younger generation's consciousness. While the Tidewater leaders never stood still, they appeared to be holding a fixed position in comparison with the advances in boldness and defiance made by the upcountry Burgesses who, with less sentiment of allegiance to the Crown, were taking off from the positions established by Bland and Landon Carter.

With only thirty-nine members in the House, Henry found enough supporters among the "young members" (as Fauquier said), all of whom represented areas beyond the old Tidewater, to get the first four resolutions passed by a vote of 22 to 17. The fifth, the most controversial, squeezed by in a 20 to 19 count. Peyton Randolph stormed out of the room, passing his young Jefferson cousin in the doorway. Whether speaking to Jefferson or merely muttering to himself, he said, "By God, I would have given one hundred guineas for a single vote." One vote would have brought the tie, which Speaker Robinson could have broken.

The next day, May 30, the resolutions were reported to the House. According to the French visitor, it was on this day that the debates grew so warm over the fifth resolution that Henry rose to defend this point to which all the other resolutions led.

Speaking extemporaneously, he became carried away by his theme of the threat of tyranny presented by the King and Parliament, and not Virginia's representatives, exercising the power to tax. Jefferson, as transfixed as the rest of the silent audience, said, "He appeared to me to speak as Homer wrote." Paul Carrington, saying that the "manly eloquence" surpassed anything he had ever heard, could write of the actual arguments that they were "beyond my powers of description."

Then, as in the courthouse speech, Henry seemed caught up in the flow of passion. "Tarquin and Caesar each had his Brutus, Charles the First his Cromwell, and George the Third —"

"Treason!" interrupted Speaker Robinson.

"Treason," other Burgesses muttered, "treason."

Henry was an actor and he knew when he had made his point. Going on as if this was what he had intended to say, he concluded:

"— may profit by their example. If this be treason, make the most of it."

Robinson was a parliamentarian and he did not intend to let Henry off so easily. He said, according to the French observer, that "he was sorry to see that not one of the members of the House was loyal enough to stop him before he had gone so far."

But it was Henry's day. He had the momentum and he knew how

to keep it. He made a lip-service apology for anything he had said which might have affronted the Speaker or the House and declared he "would show his loyalty to his Majesty King George the Third at the expense of the last drop of his blood." Then, adroitly returning to his theme, he added that "what he had said must be attributed to the interest of his country's dying liberty which he had at heart." If, however, "the heat of passion might have led him to have said something more than intended," again he would beg their pardon.

There was nothing even the skillful Robinson could say to that, not when numbers of the Burgesses rallied around Patrick Henry in support. The issue of treason was dropped, without censure, and the resolutions were adopted by the same vote of the day before, to be entered into the *Journal*.

6

The next day, Patrick Henry pulled on his leather breeches, mounted his horse, and picking his way among the carriage-and-fours and carriage-and-sixes, rode out of Williamsburg. With the satisfaction of accomplishment, he was going back to his farm. During the eighteen months since he had told Reverend Mr. Maury that he made the address to the jury to win popularity, Henry had been confirmed in his opinion that he was voicing views which the people wanted to hear. While he unquestionably enjoyed his popularity — found anywhere from the smallest social gathering to the acclaim of strangers that would come with his spreading fame — he also developed a passionate spirit of those liberties of assertive individualism felt intuitively by the people he knew in the upcountry and along the frontiers.

With all the legends of Henry as the backwoods Demosthenes, when success came he did continue to associate with plain people — simple farmers, hunters, and trappers — and spent more time than the average Burgess in hunting and fishing trips. He did not associate with these woods companions exclusively, nor did he shoot and fish all the time (he was very busy in his law practice), but he maintained close communication with the feelings of those inarticulate democrats who were uninfluenced by the values and unfamiliar with the thought patterns of the Tidewater planters long accustomed to ruling the Colony by traditional methods.

Younger men, the upcountry had no memory — as did Bland, Randolph, Robinson, Benjamin Harrison, and Landon Carter — of the idyllic era of "life in thrall" under the benevolent administration of Major Gooch during Walpole's live-and-let-live ministry. Henry himself had been in his teens when Dinwiddie stirred up the Colony and stimulated the first pamphlet-writing with his pistole fee. Since he was twenty Henry had known the atmosphere of war and taxes, paper money, and merchant-inspired complaints by the Crown, and he had won his first important case on the issue of the Crown supporting English-born clergy against the General Assembly's emergency laws for the people's welfare. By his identification with the country and his forest companions Henry was, in his way, as far removed as they were from the constitutionalist principles of the General Assembly in the intricate shift of their relationship with the Crown.

In simplifying the issues to the emotional appeals to which the upcountry people responded, he may have begun by seeking popularity through speaking what they wanted to hear — and for a certainty he never lost his love of fame nor the power which it brought him. But in voicing their sentiments, he came to embody their spirit.

It was this spirit that went abroad in Henry's name. For his resolutions actually made less impact, far less, in the General Assembly than among Virginians outside the ruling class and especially in the Northern colonies.

On the day that Henry rode home, thinking his work finished, the oligarchy rallied its forces and bore down on what Jefferson called "the more timid" members to expunge the resolutions adopted the day before. Henry's supporters held together on the first four, but their ranks broke on the fifth resolution — the crucial one to Henry's party — and this was expunged from the records.

According to the French observer, it was on this last day, May 31, that Henry's supporters (presumably Fleming and Johnston) introduced the explosive sixth and seventh resolutions:

"Resolved

"That his Majesty's liege people, the inhabitants of this Colony, are not bound to yield obedience to any law or ordinance whatever, designed to impose any taxation whatsoever upon them, other than the laws or ordinances of the General Assembly aforesaid.

"Resolved

"That any person who shall, by speaking or writing, assert or maintain that any person or persons, other than the General Assembly of this Colony, have any right or power to impose or lay any taxation on the people here, shall be deemed an enemy to his Majesty's Colony."*

There was considerable discussion, the Frenchman recorded, over the proposal "that any person that would offer to sustain that the parlement of Engl'd had a right to impose or to lay any Dutys whats'r on the american Colonys, without the consent of the inhabitants thereof, Should be looked upon as a traitor, and Deemed an Enemy to his Country." It was not so much a majority opposition to the idea expressed as that "the whole house was for Entering resolves on the record but they differed with much regard the contents or purport thereof."

"While some were for shewing their resentment to the highest degree," Speaker Robinson's controlling group — who came to be called, without entire accuracy, "the conservatives" — opposed any statements in the nature of an ultimatum. It was in drawing back from an ultimatum that the so-called conservative party basically differed from Henry's party of revolutionaries.

Habituated to winning compromises by strong stands on grounds

---

* While all accounts agree that the debates took place over the two days, May 29–30, during which the five resolutions were passed by the House sitting in committee of the whole and then adopted, no account traces the chronology of the debates. No journal was kept for the committee of the whole, and the recordings of the adopted resolutions in the *Journal of the House of Burgesses* were reticent to the point of evasiveness. The House's clerk was Peyton Randolph's brother John, a Tory-minded aristocrat who became a British loyalist during the Revolution, and he omitted even any mention of the fifth resolution, which had been adopted before being expunged.

As for the sixth and seventh resolutions, the anonymous French traveler was the only observer who mentioned discussion of the seventh resolution, which he placed on the 31st, after Patrick Henry had left. The Frenchman's account appears in the *American Historical Review*, vol. 26 (July 1921), pp. 746–747, as a small segment of the *Journal of a French Traveler*, pp. 726–747. A summary of the available material on Henry's Stamp Act speech and the resolutions appears in the footnote on page 746 of this article; in Robert Douthat Meade's *Patrick Henry*, pp. 175–181; and in Douglas Southall Freeman's *George Washington*, vol. III, appendix III–3, pp. 592–595. Dr. Freeman concluded, "The puzzle cannot be solved on the basis of the evidence submitted."

of reason and constitutionalities, their purpose in *any* protest was to obtain accommodation within the existing structure of the Empire. Holding a deep feeling for the Empire and their part in it, the oligarchs wanted to *preserve* what they considered to be their rights as they had existed traditionally before Dinwiddie's pistole fee. Their efforts were designed to restrain the home government from changing the relationship to Virginia's disadvantage and by measures which violated their fundamental principles. As Richard Bland had written in his first pamphlet on the pistole fee, they were committed to "opposing in a legal way."

With this attitude, they by no means represented the dead force of inertia. They were not inflexible in their position: they had continually moved, according to circumstance, and would continue to move. There should be no connotations of the Old Guard, certainly not of "reactionary," to the group in the ruling class who were, precisely as of May, 1765, unwilling to go with Henry's party on threats of civil disobedience. In *The Colonel Dismounted,* Bland stressed the rights felt by the English citizen "if he lives in an obedience to its [the constitution's] laws." They *were* politically conservatives by the definition of operating within the existing order — to *conserve* it as the order had operated for what they considered the public good.

There were reactionaries in the General Assembly and in the ruling class, men who became English loyalists when the split came, and the big planters whom Henry might well have had in mind when he wrote of those who, "from influence of some kind or another, had remained silent" about the Stamp Act. But not one such was among the members of the oligarchy who, opposing Henry's resolutions, managed to have the fifth expunged and the last two suppressed — the three resolutions which defied and, hence, threatened the traditional order.

In doing this, those labeled "conservatives" reacted far less strongly against Henry's resolves than leaders in other colonies who later became associated with the Revolution. John Morin Scott, soon to become a radical of radicals in New York's Sons of Liberty, and James Otis of Massachusetts, who had been advanced in defining libertarian principles, both denounced the Virginia Resolves as treasonable, and Benjamin Franklin advised Pennsylvania not to follow Virginia's rash example.

In Virginia, Henry's revolutionaries and Robinson's conservatives favored different means to the same end. Since the privileged members of the oligarchy — as well as Northern leaders — were remote from the people to whose hearts Patrick Henry had his ear, they did not discover the degree to which the bumptious newcomer had spoken for the people of all the colonies until they learned, gradually, of the response to all seven of the resolves.

7

The Virginia Resolves were first published in the *Virginia Gazette,* including the preamble.

"Whereas, the honorable House of Commons in England have of late drawn into question how far the General Assembly of this Colony hath power to enact laws for laying of taxes and imposing duties, payable by the people of this, his Majesty's most ancient colony : for settling and ascertaining the same to all future times, the House of Burgesses of this present General Assembly have come to the following resolves. . . ."

By June 24, the Resolves were reprinted in the Newport *Mercury,* on July 1 in the Boston *Gazette,* and on July 4 in the Massachusetts *Gazette* and the Maryland *Gazette.* A curious version of Henry's speech appeared in the *General Advertiser for the New York Thursday's Gazette.* A private letter written in late June from Virginia to England appeared in the *London Gazeteer and New Daily Advertiser* on August 13, 1765. "Mr. —— has lately blazed out in the Assembly, where he compared —— to a Tarquin, a Caesar, a Charles the First, threatening him with a Brutus, or an Oliver Cromwell; yet Mr. —— was not sent to the Tower : but having prevailed to get some ridiculous violent Resolves passed, rode off in triumph. Some of the Resolves were passed one day and erased the next; and the G[overnor], advised by the Council, thought proper to dissolve the Assembly." This was picked up in the New York paper on October 31.

Lest the British government neglect these straws in the wind, official letters were sent by Governor Fauquier and Commissary Robinson to the Board of Trade and the Bishop of London. What gave significance to these letters was the totally divergent positions held by the Governor and the Commissary, who personally could not abide one another. Reverend Mr. Robinson, the first native-born Virginian to hold the office of Commissary, had been appointed against Fauquier's violent opposition to succeed Dawson in 1761. He had not been given the other offices — a seat on the Council and presidency of the college — that usually went with this position, and as Commissary he did little more than routine administration. But he was sufficiently alarmed by the resolutions and speechmaking of Henry, the clergy's critic, to write an outraged account of the goings-on to his bishop.

The urbane Fauquier seemed mostly embarrassed in having to report to the Board of Trade the resolutions made by an "outsider." "In the course of the debates, I have heard that very indecent language was used by a Mr. Henry, a young lawyer who had not been a month a member of the House; who carried all the young members with him; so that I hope I am authorized in saying there is cause at least to doubt whether this would have been the sense of the Colony if more of their representatives had done their duty by attending to the end of the session."

For Francis Fauquier, then in his sixties, things were moving too fast. His intimate Virginia world was composed of those substantial planters who were by the nature of their position conservative in temperament, with much the same feeling as his about the sanctity of the Crown as the symbol of the constitutional order of Great Britain. Two of his social intimates, Robert Carter of Nomini Hall and John Randolph — both of whom shared the personal associations of having lived in England — were politically conservatives without the flexibility of the House's ruling group. Some of Carter's fellow Councilors, who met with the Governor in Advisory Council, were politically conservative in its Old Guard connotation. With his personal friendships and sympathetic knowledge of Virginia's needs, Fauquier understood — if he did not always approve — the orderly processes of protest presented by his friends in the House. But this Mr. Henry was more appalling to him than to the Tidewater oligarchy.

A cosmopolitan of Fauquier's intelligence comprehended the implications of Henry's appeal more than did Robinson's group. In his letter to the Board he played down the presence of what Burgesses called "Henry's party," as if to prevent the episode of the resolutions from calling the home government's unfavorable attention to the

General Assembly. When a continental congress assembled in New York that October, Fauquier sent no representatives from Virginia's General Assembly.

Like the ruling class as a whole, Fauquier's concern was in preserving harmony between the Colony and the Crown, although none of his interest in Virginia could have caused him to tolerate for a moment any disrespect to the King. It was on this last point that he was careful to give the impression that Henry's ''indecent language'' did not represent the General Assembly.

Another Britisher in the colonies reported to Secretary of State Conway the effect of the circulation of Henry's resolves in the Northern colonies. General Thomas Gage, commander of the British forces in North America, wrote that the Virginia Resolves ''gave the signal for a general outcry over the continent.''

Despite all the publicity given the Resolves, and the reports from British officials in America, Grenville's government did neglect the straws in the wind.

Even more ominous than the newspaper accounts and the officials' reports was the attitude of the people as discovered by the Frenchman traveling in Virginia. Moving westward from Williamsburg, he heard ''a great deal about the Noble Patriot Mr. Henry'' in his home county. ''The whole Inhabitants say publicly that if the least Injury was offered to him they'd stand by him to the last Drop of their blood.'' If it came to the worst they would call the French to their succor. As for the British Parliament, ''If they were in Canada'' they ''would as soon be Dd. as offer to do what they do now.''

In a tavern, the French traveler talked with two prominent citizens about Henry's speech. Not among Henry's ''plebeian'' companions of idle hours in the woods, these two gentlemen were well informed about the debates in Williamsburg. One of them summarized his reaction by saying, ''I'll sooner die than pay a farthing and I am sure thaat all my countrymen will do the same.''

Literally meaning *I'll sooner die than pay a farthing,* this typical citizen of the backcountry was expressing that uncomplex assertion of individual liberties which was alien to the experience of the British ministers and which, by its acceptance of the personal consequences of defiance, was not clearly understood — *then* — by the most enlightened protectors of Virginia's interests in the ruling class. Nor did the constituted defenders of Virginia's liberties, with their security in the traditional order and their warm memories of the idyllic era of harmonious relations, perceive the actual hostility toward Great Britain that had developed in the backcountry. The primal (as opposed to constitutional) resentment of outwardly imposed controls by the parent country had brought an element of hatred which was totally foreign to the great planters' imperious rejection of the imposition of another's authority.

Patrick Henry, neglecting his lawbooks and the classics in his preference for the association with simple people in country pleasures, was indeed ''far ahead'' of the intelligent, responsible, patriotic, middle-aged Virginians of Speaker Robinson's group in recognizing that to the people the lines had been drawn. The backcountry people were beyond memorialized protests which established their principles, and they were way beyond compromise. With no sentiment about the traditional order, they had taken their stand on the line laid down by Patrick Henry, and they were ready — some even eager — for the eventualities of ultimatum. Henry was speaking for activists.

· 4 ·

The Era of the Revolutionaries

Chapter Eight

THE CRISIS

Patrick Henry and Richard Henry Lee were dissimilar allies drawn together not only by their revolutionary approach but by their shared aggression toward the Tidewater oligarchy. While Lee had come to Williamsburg with a chip on his shoulder in facing the entrenched rivals of his father, Henry had ''blazed out'' as a spokesman for the upcountry citizens who had never made their voices heard strongly in the Robinson-controlled House.

Anything pertaining to conscious motivation in Henry's speaking for this previously muffled bloc can only be conjecture about that largely intuitive man. He enjoyed a natural affinity with those Burgesses from outside Tidewater, and those without Tidewater alliances such as had been made by George Washington. They represented neighborhoods similar to his own; they shared his revolutionary views in expressing the sentiments of his neighbors, and — of equal importance — they shared the political outsider's urge to break the power of the party in control. Most likely Henry, the master of timing, had spoken as the voice of the upcountry and then discovered (as after his courthouse speech) that he had a good thing. Not to impugn his motives, it is to stress that Patrick Henry welcomed the political leadership extended him by the previous outsiders.

His alliance with Richard Henry Lee quickly formed the basis for a new party rising, at last, to challenge the absolute control of an oligarchy which had endured as long as the memory of any man then living in Virginia. The new party was in no sense another political party, as Whig and Tory represented opposed parties. It was rather a new power rising within the General Assembly (or, specifically, in the House of Burgesses) that would force the oligarchy to share its control.

As with all such rises of new powers, Henry's party needed the favor of fortune in the turn of events which they could neither direct nor foresee. The new party got the favorable turns in the death of Speaker Robinson in little more than a year after the Virginia Resolves, and in two scandals that shook the ruling class. In the realm of the unpredictable, they also gained an unexpected ally in the unlikely person of the Randolphs' sandy-haired young cousin Tom Jefferson, studying law with the conservative George Wythe and himself a frequent guest of the socially brilliant Governor in the Palace.

2

As with the fiddle, which Henry played by ear and Jefferson by notes, Patrick Henry *absorbed* the feeling of the people by companionship with them, and Thomas Jefferson *studied* the elements composing the political atmosphere of his day. For all his identification with "democratic" principles, Jefferson was personally aloof from the people in mass and had nothing of Henry's common touch. For all his later denigration of the aristocracy of property — referring to certain "ciphers of the aristocracy" among the powers when he was young — Jefferson was temperamentally himself an aristocrat.

By the combination of intense individualization, illimitable self-assurance, and a vision of life-styles beyond the Tidewater, Jefferson could appear a nonconformist, and he could certainly never be called a conformist in the way he set his own styles (as in architecture) and developed his own thinking rather than follow the existing patterns. Yet, much of Jefferson's divergence from existing patterns was caused by the individual concepts that grew in his unceasing mental life which, with his sense of power in his knowledge, produced an unfettered creative urge to change things according to his vision.

These developments belonged in the restless experimentation of a type of genius rather than deriving from any repudiation of the aristocrat within himself.

He was a very fastidious man, formal in address, and Cousin Peyton Randolph at his most reserved was no more remote from intimacies. Embracing every privilege of the aristocrat, he found his friends and wife among the ruling class, and when his own estate was doubled by that of his father-in-law he built an establishment which, for all its originality, was on the scale of magnificence of the Colony's greatest grandees. This hilltop mansion, Monticello, was remote from the main highways of travel when he moved there. Later, when summer travelers to the springs took to tarrying as guests, he built a distant retreat where he could enjoy his necessary privacy. Although he was generous in his hospitality, Jefferson, as the antithesis of Patrick Henry's sociability, was a very private person.

Although many of Jefferson's recollections of his early years were refracted through the self-image of the person he became, the potentials for all the intellectual powers he realized were actively present and forming the shape of his mind when he studied the historical and philosophical background of the political conflict whose emergence he observed as a law student. Yet, it can only be presumed that his enthusiastic recollection of Henry's "blazing out" in the House implied his approval of Henry's viewpoints when he heard them. This presumption would be supported by the nature of the thought that formed a changed mental climate, along with the changes in Virginia's isolated self-sufficiency, since the death of William Byrd II — the year after Jefferson was born.

In the two decades since the "life in thrall" of Byrd's era, there had been a growth in the influence of Newton's concept of a law-governed universe. As Sir Isaac Newton, John Locke, and Lord Bacon were the Olympians to Jefferson, he would have been receptive — certainly since the days of Small's influence — to the doctrines of the mathematical law of cause and effect. In this, man, as a part of the rational system, could understand the cosmos by his own reason without the necessity of divine revelation. In following this, Jefferson read the Scriptures with the same critical analysis which he brought to other writings. Pursuing knowledge with the rationalism which promised to liberate man from superstition and the awe of authority,

Jefferson partook of the humanistic theories which denied that the poor, afflicted, and dispossessed were objects of God's will. As products of their environment, men had the power through science and education to improve their condition by control of their environment, and to mold their own destinies — realizing the Kingdom of Heaven on earth. In the political world which Jefferson inhabited, these rational explanations of the universe applied to institutions, constituted authority, and fixed degree.

Within this background, Jefferson was of course aware of the rise of the stress on natural rights implicit in the doctrines of the consent of the governed, as promulgated in the writings of Richard Bland and Landon Carter, and in the fiery speeches of Patrick Henry. However, approaching the colonial relationship to Great Britain through reason, Jefferson developed a different vision from Henry and Richard Henry Lee, the revolutionary leaders when he first responded to the new spirit in the General Assembly.

In Henry the implication of natural rights took the form of emotion directed against England, reflecting the backcountry's hostility to the controlling parent country. In Richard Henry Lee, with all his scholarship, there was also an antagonism toward both Great Britain and the Tidewater oligarchy, expressed in a revolutionary attitude toward the established Virginia-English order. Neither Henry nor Lee were to become constructive in the formation of the nation that followed the overthrow of the order. Both showed themselves to be fundamentally local in their revolutionary bent.

Jefferson's more intellectual approach was a rethinking of man's whole condition under the influence of the conviction, propounded from Locke to Montesquieu, that physical and social environment was the determining factor in shaping institutions. In this conviction the capacity to change was inherent with a concept of progress. He gradually focused on the Virginia–mother country conflict a political philosophy, applicable to that conflict, which he distilled from his studies of the written works of the minds that formed the mental climate. With all the excited approbation he later remembered feeling for Henry's words, the young law student was not at that stage of his development a committed radical. Just as he had not burst upon William and Mary as a prodigy, so he did not suddenly emerge as a political revolutionary.

Thomas Jefferson
Portrait attributed to Bass Otis, about 1800
(Colonial Williamsburg Collection)

In his evolution into a revolutionary (an evolution which, in later life, continued his humanistic liberalism into "democratic" principles undreamed of in the little British colonial capital), again Jefferson stood in sharp contrast to the intuitive Patrick Henry. Where the great trial lawyer had suddenly appeared as the spokesman for the unarticulated sentiments of the upcountry people, Jefferson slowly evolved as a synthesizer of the enlightened thought of the English-speaking world.

In his early twenties, he had none of Henry's and Lee's hatred of the British, and considered himself a loyal subject of the King. His tastes and his manners were being cultivated by association with Fauquier's London-style elegance and he was aware of how much his broadening horizons owed to the conversations he was privileged to sit in on with the Governor's learned intimates. With his English-educated cousins in the higher circles of the Tidewater oligarchy as well as among Fauquier's friends, Jefferson was observing the gathering clash from a position quite unlike Henry's and Lee's — from the inside of the Virginia-English ruling powers. From this position, he moved slowly.

Though his drift was continuously toward new concepts of liberated man controlling his environment, and in time he was to push the principles of the Enlightenment to the very ultimate in practice, in 1765 he was still very much in a learning process. He later described this period as a time when he was "bold in the pursuit of knowledge, never fearing to follow truth and reason to whatever results they led, and bearding every authority which stood in the way."

In his commonplace book, in which he wrote ideas which impressed him from published works, Jefferson made more entries — twenty-seven — during his twenties from Montesquieu than from any other writer. Charles Louis le Secondat, Baron de Brède et de Montesquieu, published *The Spirit of the Laws* in 1748, and his political philosophy exerted great influence when Jefferson was studying law. When Jefferson was old (after the new nation had been formed), he developed decided reservations about Montesquieu, with "his predilection for monarchy and English monarchy in particular." It is significant, however, that when he read Montesquieu around the time of the Stamp Act crisis, Jefferson was not bothered by the author's reverence for the British constitution. He was impressed by Montesquieu's stress on the need for governments to adapt to time and place. Since the nature of laws was variable, laws should possess flexibility to change with climate, local conditions, and external circumstances.

He also made notations from Bolingbroke. Henry St. John, Viscount Bolingbroke, had a somewhat checkered career. An acquaintance with men of pleasure and fashion, and the reading of modern authors, had relieved him of moral and religious scruples, and, of brilliant personality, he enjoyed some early political success before he was condemned as a traitor, at thirty-eight, with the Old Pretender. In exile he wrote political essays which were much praised for their style, and Jefferson was typical of his literate contemporaries in admiring him. Although his essays were later regarded as shallow, those consistent with Jefferson's forming views held the point that the best government was that best suited to the spirit of the governed. Bolingbroke's ideas were spread in Alexander Pope's *Essay on Man*, published in 1733 — which also spread the doctrines of two of Jefferson's heroes, Locke and Bacon.

Along with political theory and the history of governments, Jefferson was deeply interested in moral conduct, and copied some quotations from Shaftesbury. Anthony Ashley Cooper, third Earl of Shaftesbury, rejected religious suppositions governing ethical theories in endowing man with a "moral sentiment." All through his impressionable years, Jefferson studied the Greeks and Romans for their insights into the nature of man, with their ideal of a republican form of liberty and political morality. The Roman world seemed familiar to him, not as history, but as a living part of his consciousness. He quoted most from Cicero, and wrote twelve quotations from Horace, including the familiar:

The snows have fled; already the grass is returning to the fields . . .
Pale death knocks equally at the door of the poor man's cabin and at
    the palaces of the rulers . . .
Enjoy today and put as little trust as possible in the morrow . . .
O country, when shall I see thee again?

He seemed to enjoy Shakespeare mostly for the moral insights in his plays. He read the poets popular in his day, such as James Thompson and David Mallet, and, along with his contemporaries, was taken in by James Macpherson's supposedly Celtic verses published as translations from Ossian. He was not much interested in the philosophical ideas of such writers as Voltaire and had little bent for purely abstract thinking. To the end of his life he could not abide Plato, and such was Jefferson's confidence in his own judgments, he made no apologies for dismissing Plato's writings as "vaporings."

From the range of his feelings and reflections, while studying law and assimilating the conversations of the older men in the evening gatherings in the Palace, it would be evident that the young Jefferson in 1765 was not politically motivated as directly as Henry and Lee. While events in the Colony would soon focus his broadly based theories into political action, nothing known about his days in the summer and early fall of 1765 indicates any interest in the approaching date, November 1, of the enforcement of the Stamp Act.

In October the General Assembly passed an act which legalized groups of private citizens to clear the James River at the Falls, the Chickahominy, "and the north branch of the James River" — the Rivanna. Jefferson inaugurated the project of clearing the obstructions from the Rivanna and, as he worked actively with the local group in Albemarle County, he was probably away from Williamsburg at the time when the citizens' anger mounted with the approach of the stamp tax collector.

3

Thomas Jefferson was a potential, or future, ally of the newly forming party when, during the months following the circulation of the Virginia Resolves, the people clearly showed a temper of resisting the new stamp tax. Since lawyers and printers, daily dealing with printed matter, would be the hardest hit by the tax, members of these literate professions were highly vocal in their protests and kept people talking about the stands they would take in all parts of Virginia. Near the end of summer in 1765 "the people" meant all classes and kinds of people. The determination not to "pay a farthing" had rapidly extended beyond the upcountry inhabitants encountered by the French traveler. Substantial planters of the Tidewater were as rebellious as Patrick Henry's constituents. In opposition to the use of stamps in court transactions, the justices in two counties had asked to be replaced.

A conservative's report was given by George Washington in a letter written in late September. "The Stamp Act imposed on the Colonies by the Parliament of Great Britain engrosses the conversation of the speculative part of the colonists, who look upon his unconstitutional method of taxation as a direful attack upon their liberties, and loudly proclaim against the violation; what may be the result of this and some other (I think I might add) ill-judged measures, I will not undertake to determine." But he predicted that the ministry would gain less than they planned, because the colonists, already aware that they could do without the luxuries they were importing from England, would find that many necessities were available in America. As for the actual collections of the tax, the people simply lacked the currency to buy the stamps.

Here the English government's earlier pressure for the retirement of paper money had, as Fauquier prophesied, created a crisis in currency, which now made the new stamp tax impossible to levy. Washington wrote that this absence of cash, for the purchase of stamps required in all legal transactions, would lead to a halt in "our judicial proceedings." As the courts were packed with cases of British creditors trying to collect debts, "I fancy the merchants of Great Britain trading to the colonies will not be among the last to wish for a repeal of it."

Washington's prediction, which proved to be as accurate as Fauquier's, was the judgment of a practical-minded planter in government. No more revolutionary than the Tidewater oligarchy, the master of Mount Vernon — from his excellent habit of attending to "the conversation of the speculative part of" the Colony — viewed the crisis as an intelligent, responsible citizen concerned less about his own immediate involvements than with the effect upon his country.

Because he was not among the political theorists of the era, and neither spoke with eloquence nor wrote with felicity, because the chief asset he brought to the colonies' revolutionary movement was an indomitable character with the intangible qualities of leadership, Washington could be seen as possessing slighter mental capacities than his more dazzling contemporaries. He had, in fact, a sound mind with a capacity to learn and grow continuously. While it was not a mind

capable of brilliant leaps, he was capable of developing the vision of
practical political programs. Whether or not he ever read Bolingbroke,
he comprehended the need for a government that was suited to the
spirit of the governed.

After the colonies had won their independence, while Henry and
Lee (with whom Washington broke in anger) were concerned with
Virginia, it was the man of action who envisioned the need for a
united republic and used his prestige to win the hard, bitter fight of
persuading Virginians to rally around a federal constitution. In his
great days as the first citizen in the new republic, brilliant younger
men around him, like Jefferson and Hamilton, were mentally quicker
and more fertile with political philosophy; but the gentleman of the
majestic presence made his own literally indispensable contribution by
the soundness of the practical political program which implemented
his steadfastly held vision.

George Washington, thirty-three years old during the Stamp Act
crisis, perhaps most typified those responsible members of Virginia's
General Assembly who, in contrast to Patrick Henry and Richard
Henry Lee, were termed conservatives in 1765. Leaving the promulga-
tion of the constitutional theories of their rights to Richard Bland and
Landon Carter, as he left the running of the House to the group
including Robinson, Peyton Randolph, Edmund Pendleton, Benjamin
Harrison, and George Wythe, Washington shared the attitudes of
these leaders. Believing that the tax introduced by Grenville's ministry was "ill-judged," but lacking the least desire then to bring
matters to a test of force, he believed — as he had believed about the
postwar proclamation of 1763 which forbade Virginians the western
lands they had won — that the practicalities involved would resolve
the issue pragmatically. The tax would not work.

This should not carry any implication that he was indifferent to
the principle of "taxation without consent," which ran into "taxation
without representation." As a businessman, however, Washington did
not expect the money-minded British merchants to let the issue come
to a test of principle. In his untheoretical thinking, if "taxation
without consent" ever came to issue over the principle, that would be
something else. As a soldier fought one battle at a time, he would cross
that bridge if and when he came to it.

In the September when he wrote that letter, Washington had his crops to think about. A drought had reduced his yield of wheat, less tobacco was grown on the Custis estate, and the London prices were, Washington said, "pitifully low." At the other end, his agent, Robert Cary & Company, charged him so exorbitantly for goods he ordered that he warned Cary he might have to change agents.

Washington's grand scale of living at Mount Vernon with Martha and her two children was not beyond his potential means, but when crops were short, prices low, and imports high, the systematic planter was kept in debt the same as the party-giving, fox-hunting planters who let managers do the work. This naturally did not endear to him the system in which the British ministry always acted for the good of the merchants and never for the planters.

Although he wrote only one letter about the approaching stamp tax, he probably discussed it in generalities with his neighbors from time to time as an added element in the problems they all shared. Five miles south of him at Gunston Hall, George Mason would have been likely to engage in thoughtful conversation about Virginia's whole relationship with Great Britain.

Mason, a Potomac River planter on the scale of the legends, could be likened to Landon Carter, without Carter's need of public life or popular recognition. Like the master of Sabine Hall, the fourth George Mason was an efficient and highly motivated administrator of his inherited estate, who enjoyed his leisure in the library. Along with his money crop of tobacco, he raised corn, general food products, and stock, and many of his slaves were highly trained artisans. Forty in 1765, he had been married for fifteen years to the former Ann Eilbeck of Maryland, and they were to have nine children who survived infancy. For the comfort of this family, Mason built Gunston Hall. Not one of the great manorial seats either in size or concept, it was designed by the self-sufficient Mason specifically to meet the needs of his family, and had the distinction of being the first house in America on which the architectural skill of William Buckland was employed. The future famous architect was a twenty-one-year-old "carpenter and joiner" when indentured by Mason to start work on Gunston Hall in 1755.

During his thirties, Mason became afflicted with a painful gout, which was to bother him — at times so severely as to put him on crutches — the rest of his life. Whether or not this affliction was related to his distaste for public life, after one dutiful session in the House of Burgesses (1759–60), he forswore politics. The endless debates in the House had bored him, and he found the exchanges of favors and influence to be irresponsible (an aspect of John Robinson's reign that also riled Landon Carter). Gout or no gout, essentially George Mason was a scholar, who liked to think out problems alone in his study. Although he was hospitable to thoughtful-minded visitors and a good neighbor, he was humorless and, when suffering seizures of pain, could be irritable and sarcastic. But he was high on the list of Washington's "speculative" friends, and many political leaders besides George Washington came to Gunston Hall to exchange ideas with his reflective mind.

For this nonpolitical, conservative planter was every bit as defiant as Patrick Henry or Richard Henry Lee in protesting England's disregard of colonial rights, and had written one of the most stinging of the letters to a British newspaper, which the English government ignored. Although in this letter Mason disassociated himself from "radicals," Washington's respected commentator on events was not behind any Virginian in libertarian principles.

4

Francis Fauquier tried to conceal his anxiety while daily expecting the arrival of Colonel George Mercer, the tax collector, for, he reported, "rumors were industriously thrown out that at the time of the General Court parties would come down from most parts of the country to seize and destroy all stamped papers." By chance the General Court, composed of the Councilors and the Governor, met on November 1, "when persons engaged in business of any kind constantly attend as well as those who have suits pending before the court; it being the time when all attempts of transactions of moment are settled, payments made and bills of exchange on Great Britain are drawn; so there is always a vast concourse of people then in town." During the last week in October the crowds gathered, when "this town was the fullest of strangers," and still no Colonel Mercer.

George Mercer ranked high among the Virginians who held the respect of the Colony. He had served in the French and Indian Wars as an aide of George Washington, whose friend he became, and advanced on merit to the rank of lieutenant colonel. After the war ended in 1763, he went to England with the highest possible recommendations to seek a remunerative colonial post. Governor Fauquier and the Council wrote a testimonial for the "brave and gallant officer" to the Virginia agent Edward Montagu: "That he has often been employed by the government in many important services, and ever discharged the trust imposed in him with the greatest expedition, exactness and fidelity. . . ." The Committee of Correspondence was more practical in its letter to Montagu, which was given weight by the personal signatures of most members of the Tidewater oligarchy. "This gentleman goes home to endeavor to be in some manner rewarded for his faithful service, and you are desired to introduce him properly, and at the same time to use all your interest and influence in his favor."

Montagu did his part, but Grenville's ministry showed little inclination to reward the faithful colonial. Colonel Mercer languished two years in England and Ireland before he was appointed in August, 1765, to the post of stamp collector for Virginia. To make the enforcement of the tax more palatable in the colonies, the ministry appointed only natives as collectors, and Mercer — whose salary would be £300 a year — was to select in Virginia twenty-five assistants.

This was not exactly the plum Colonel Mercer had sought. "From the beginning," he said, "I was convinced it would be an unpopular office, and took the liberty to mention it to Mr. Grenville." In talking with tough-minded Grenville, Mercer allowed himself to be convinced that the idea of the colonists' "union in any particular point" was an "absurdity," and that "the act would enforce itself." However, when Mercer read the Virginia Resolves (all seven of them), "I was alarmed and still more convinced of the difficulties I must encounter on my arrival in Virginia." By then it was too late for another tax collector to be appointed, and, "having accepted, too, when all was calm and quiet, I thought I could not be justified in quitting the charge when there were appearances of a storm."

He left London on the *Leeds* on September 12 and, with good winds, arrived in the York River on Wednesday, October 30. He left on the ship the stamps to be used in Maryland and North Carolina as well as Virginia and, apparently alone, rode to Williamsburg. Entering the crowded town unobtrusively, he went to a private residence where he was to be put up. Fauquier recorded that Mercer was "at his father's lodgings," which meant that the elder Mercer had earlier put up in the residence.

Despite Mercer's quiet entry into Williamsburg, word of his arrival reached the Governor. He immediately went to a place on the open Exchange in back of the Capitol often used as a rendezvous by persons of consequence. Usually referred to as "the Coffee House," this famous establishment, then operated by Mrs. Jane Vobe (later by Mrs. Christiana Campbell), was noted for its fine cuisine and for the sporty gentlemen among the grandees, such as William Byrd III, who stayed there during Public Times and turned the rooms into gambling halls. Fauquier joined John Robinson and several Councilors who were seated on the porch of the Coffee House, from where they viewed the Exchange.

"My particular reason for going," Fauquier wrote, "was that I might be an eyewitness myself of what did really pass, and not receive it by relation from others." The Governor turned out to be the only eyewitness who reported what happened, and he showed himself to be an excellent reporter.

"The mercantile people were assembled as usual," he wrote, in the Exchange, and the first alarming word the Governor heard was "One and all." As if this were a signal, the whole crowd surged toward the house where they had learned Mercer was staying. "This concourse of people I should call a mob, did I not know that it was chiefly if not altogether composed of gentlemen of property in the Colony, some of them at the head of their respective counties." Unknown to the crowd, Colonel Mercer had started at the same time for the Capitol, evidently to report his arrival officially. Right outside the red brick building he encountered the crowd, who blocked his path.

The men began to shout at him, demanding "of him an answer whether he would resign or act in this office as distributor of the stamps."

The confrontation by the crowd could not have been unexpected to Mercer. He kept his poise. "He said it was an affair of great moment to him, he must consult his friends, and promised to give them an answer by ten o'clock on Friday morning." That would be November 1, the day the tax was to go into effect. Then he started past them toward the Coffee House and his friends on the porch.

The crowd followed him, some of them mumbling that Friday would be too late. As Mercer and his followers approached the Coffee House porch, Speaker Robinson and the Councilors moved to post themselves between the crowd and the Governor. Fauquier and these dignitaries received Mercer "with the greatest marks of welcome, with which," judging by their countenances, the men in the crowd "were not well pleased." They paused uncertainly, most of them silent.

Then leaders among them sent up messages to Colonel Mercer, asking for an answer. He steadily replied that he had already given an answer.

Suddenly someone yelled, "Let us rush in." Immediately there was a surge toward the steps. On the porch, the Governor and his friends moved forward to the top step as if to meet the attack. "See the Governor," somebody shouted — "take care of him."

The meaning of that warning, in those days, was literally "take care that no harm befalls him." Immediately those already pushing up the steps fell back and a space was left between the front of the milling crowd and the small group on the porch. In his report Fauquier wrote, "If your Lordships will not accuse me of vanity, I would say that I believe this to be partly owing to the respect they bore my character and partly to the love they bore my person." With or without vanity, Fauquier had written the literal truth.

Seeing that the meeting had reached the danger point, where it could get out of hand at any moment, several of Mercer's friends urged him to promise an answer the next day. The ex-soldier was, as his recommenders had said, a brave man, and it was against his inclination to change his answer under threats. But, as too many other people were then involved in potential violence, he allowed himself to be persuaded to promise to give an answer the next day at the Capitol at five o'clock. Even then the crowd would not disperse.

As dusk began to deepen, Fauquier thought it would not be safe for Mercer when darkness fell. He advanced to the head of the steps and said aloud that he believed "no man there would do me any hurt." Then, turning to Mercer, Fauquier suggested that if he would walk beside him through the crowd, they could probably reach his house in safety. The two gentlemen walked side by side through the thickest of the crowd. Way was made for them, although, as the Governor reported, "there were some little murmurs." It was probable that there was nothing more than murmurs because of the character of the substantial citizens in the gathering, men who both reverenced the person of their courteous Governor and respected the calm courage of the two gentlemen.

Safely inside the Governor's intimate room in the Palace, with flames in the fireplace gleaming on the wood-paneled walls, Colonel Mercer showed the uncertainty into which the ordeal had thrown him. His father and brother had both urged him to resign and the two lawyers attending the court were "frightened out of their senses for him." He asked the Governor's advice as to what he should do. This presented a ticklish problem to the representative of the Crown, and Fauquier avoided a direct answer.

If Mercer were, understandably, afraid for his life, that was "too tender a point" for the Governor to advise him on. If both his honor and his self-interest demanded that he hold the office, then he must disregard the "reasonings of his father and brother" and the two frightened lawyers. The Governor had only articulated Mercer's inner conflict, and they talked on into the night without Mercer's coming to any resolution.

The next afternoon Colonel Mercer appeared at the Capitol, according to his promise, and faced a crowd swollen since the day before. He held in his hands a prepared statement, which he had presumably spent the day drafting. It was a finished draft ready for the printer, and he later gave it to the *Gazette,* which published it in a supplement. Reading from the prepared statement, Mercer caught the crowd's sympathy at once by referring to Virginia as his country.

"Gentlemen, I have now met you agreeable to yesterday's promise to give my country some assurance, which I would have been glad to do . . . with any propriety, sooner.

"I flatter myself no judicious man could blame me for accepting an office under an authority that was never disputed by anyone (by) whom I could have been advised of the propriety or right of the objections.

"I do acknowledge that, some little time before, I heard of and saw some resolves which were said to be made by the House of Burgesses of Virginia, but as the authority of them was disputed, they never appearing but in private hands, and so often and differently reported to me, I determined to know the real sentiments of my countrymen from themselves. And I am compelled to say that those sentiments were so suddenly and unexpectedly communicated to me that I was altogether unable to give an immediate answer upon so important a point.

"In however an unpopular light I may lately have been viewed, and notwithstanding the many insults I have from this day's conversation been informed have been offered me in effigy in many parts of this Colony, yet I still flatter myself that time will justify me and that my conduct may not be condemned after having been coolly inquired into.

"This commission so very disagreeable to my countrymen was obtained by the genteel recommendation of their representatives in the General Assembly, *unasked for*. And, though this is contrary to public report, which I am told charges me with assisting in the passage of the Stamp Act upon the promise of a commission in this colony, yet I hope it will meet with credit when I assure you that I was so far from assisting it or having any previous promise from the Ministry that *I did not know of my appointment until some time after my return from Ireland, where I was at the commencement of the session of Parliament and for a long time after the act had been passed.*

"Thus, gentlemen, I am circumstanced.

"I should be glad to act now in such a manner as would justify me to my friends and countrymen here and the authority which appointed me. But the time you have allotted me is so very short that I have not yet been able to discover that happy medium and therefore must entreat you to be referred to my future conduct with this assurance in the meantime, that *I will not, directly or indirectly, by my deputies or myself, proceed further with the Act until I receive further orders from England, and not then without the assent of the General Assembly of this Colony* (whom) *no man can more ardently or sincerely wish the prosperity of than myself* . . . *your sincere friend and humble servant. . . .*"

Mercer held the crowd in motionless attention during his measured reading. When he came to the end, where his signature would be inserted for the published version, Mercer's voice trailed off, and he made a movement as if he intended to leave. Instantly the crowd closed in on him in a surge of elated approbation. From the villain of the day before, his resignation transformed him into the people's hero, and he was boisterously hoisted up on men's shoulders. Like a conqueror, he was borne to the Coffee House, on whose porch the Governor had saved him from attack twenty-four hours before. When the crowd staged an impromptu feast for Colonel Mercer, forcing on him food and drink, Governor Fauquier could take comfort in having escaped violence in his dominion.

Although his relief must have been considerable, the Governor's worries were just beginning. The next day was November 1, when the General Court opened under the Crown's orders to use the stamps on all legal documents. The stamps were still on a ship in the York River and, without instructions to the contrary, the responsibility of the feted Colonel Mercer.

5

The next morning Fauquier was driven to the Capitol and, berobed, entered the General Court. The handsome room, of paneled walls and fluted columns, was curved at one end, where three deeply recessed circular windows were cut above the seats for the Councilors. Peyton Randolph, the King's Attorney General, sat at his table within the bar. But no lawyer appeared and not a single litigant.

The Governor had the proclamation to open court repeated, "once in the cryer's place and once at the door." Nobody stirred. Fauquier reported, "I called for Colonel Mercer and asked him in open court whether he could supply the court with proper stamps that the business might be carried on, according to law. He replied that he could not. . . . I then asked the clerk whether he could carry on the business without them. He said he could not, without subjecting himself to such penalties as he would not expose himself to."

Manifestly, the November session of the General Court was not going to meet. The Governor, through the personal loyalty he had won by his amiability and courtesy and fairness, had averted violence in his dominion. But here he confronted a passive revolt that had nothing to do with the Virginians' feelings for him. This was Patrick Henry's civil disobedience directed against Great Britain.

As on the day before, Fauquier kept his head. Avoiding all the issues involved, and holding only to the business at hand, he asked the

Councilors whether they might not legally adjourn to April 10, since "there was no business before us." One of them asked the Governor if he had received any particular instructions for such an occasion. The Governor replied that he had not. "Then," Fauquier reported, "the court was unanimous that we might adjourn to the next court in course, which was accordingly done."

As Fauquier turned to leave the chamber, Colonel Mercer stepped forward and offered to resign his commission to the Governor. This, as Fauquier said, took him by surprise. As the people in the court were listening, he thought himself "obliged to give some answer." He told Mercer that he was not authorized to accept the resignation, and he thought that all commissions should be resigned "into the hands of those from whom they were received." That was the first reason that came to his mind which he thought fit to give to the listening crowd.

What he could not well speak aloud was the consideration that if he accepted Mercer's resignation, he would be forced to appoint a successor. As, in the prevailing mood in Virginia, he did not believe he could find anyone who would accept, the office of tax collector could become cheap.

In his report, written two days later, Fauquier added another consideration which may have represented hope rather than conviction. He wrote that with Mercer still officially holding the commission, he would always be ready to distribute the stamps "whenever people's eyes should be opened and they should come to their senses, so as to receive them."

For the present, he approved of Mercer's proposals to the commanders of his Majesty's ships of war to take the stamps aboard for safekeeping, for, Fauquier wrote, "I am convinced . . . that it would be extremely dangerous to attempt to land them during the present fermented state of the Colony." Captain Sterling accordingly took the stamps aboard the *Rainbow*.

In the summation of his report to the Board of Trade, Fauquier wrote, "The first and most obvious consequences of all this must be the shutting up of all the ports, and stopping all proceedings in the courts of justice. A most melancholy prospect at first view; for what ideas can be formed of a more miserable condition than a state of general outlawry."

It was not only at first view. The county courts, the arteries of life in the Colony, became as emptied of their legal business as had the General Court on the first day. Not even the hounding Scottish merchants brought any debtors to the bar. Even before this complete standstill, however, the Governor had not injected any optimism into his summation to the Board. "What other consequences may follow from these are so buried in obscurity that it requires a sagacity and judgment much superior to my own, even to guess at them. . . . But it seems to me that disorder, misery and confusion are before us, unless this poor unhappy deluded people in the colonies in general should change their plan."

Fauquier could not have hoped that the "people in the colonies in general" would change their plan. Posts from the North brought news of the refusal to use the stamps in other colonies. In the seaport city of Boston mobs rioted and the governor of Massachusetts, who had not won the love of the populace, had to flee for his life. When Virginia shippers came to Fauquier "for registers for their shipping" without the stamps, he tried to point out to them the absurdity of their positions, in which they were making it impossible for themselves to recover large debts owing to them. "But the flame has spread so universally through the colonies, and every man was so heated thereby, that no reasons could gain admittance."

The Colony's naval officers, in charge of all shipping and the collection of fees, also came to the Governor to ask his advice on the release of those ships ready to sail with their cargoes, but without stamps on the ships' manifests and the bills of lading. He could only tell them that "an act passed in the last session of the Parliament of Great Britain, directing what stamps are to be used in your offices in carrying on the business thereof," must be obeyed.

Ships floated idly at the wharves from Chesapeake Bay to the heads of the tidewater on the big rivers. Even though ruin seemed to be the prospect if the revolt continued, no native Virginian seemed to think — at least not publicly — of giving in. With no cargoes going out, planters gave no orders for either luxuries or necessities from England. In unknown numbers artisans on the plantations began weaving homespun clothes.

At the end of November, Landon Carter addressed himself to the subject in a "letter" which he never sent. That is, what started as a letter to a gentleman in Britain extended to twenty-two long handwritten pages, more than six thousand words, without even coming to an end or making whatever was the single point Carter had in mind when he started writing in answer to an article published in England by a Mr. William Pym. Yet in the rambling pages, in which ideas crowded one another out, ran a refrain that, transcending the Stamp Act dispute, was to be basic in all the thinking that followed in Virginia and in the other colonies.

In the beginning he wrote of the "irremediable unhappiness" resulting from disputes "in which no umpire can be admitted as an indifferent judge to determine the cause of Rights; for inclination guided by different interests, however fixed the rules of Right and Wrong may be, will militate against every such rule. . . . Superiority in power . . ." will prevail: "This no doubt gave rise to the common observation, that Might overcomes Right." After developing this point with illustrations, he came to Mr. Pym's "warm disposition . . . against the colonies, especially the Assembly of Virginia, which he represents as *impetuous* and in *a prodigious ferment* . . . because they have dared in some resolutions to assert their claim to the Englishman's Rights. . . . A writer that could treat any legislative body of Englishmen, his fellow subjects, in such a disrespectful manner, for endeavouring to preserve, and continue their claim of right, down to posterity," was "centered in his mighty Fort of Terror," and impossible to deal with.

Referring again to "The rights of exercising (abstracted from the power of effecting) such measures," Landon Carter used the word "slavery" as it was to become increasingly used in the colonies for the state resulting from encroachment on their liberties. "Nothing can be pictured terrible enough to make an Englishman relish *slavery,* and give up his liberties on this side of the Atlantic, any more than it does or can on the other side."

Then he came to the point which could be said to summarize the position and the hopes of the responsible older members of the ruling class in the hardening dispute with the mother country. Referring to "some governors" who "had forbid with great influence the publishing of the complaints of the people, against the violation of their Rights," he wrote, "I am only in hopes that Englishmen (though situated in North America) may meet with some readers that are real *fellow-subjects* amongst you; not intoxicated with the deliciousness of extensive authority, but such who from the sacredness and immutability of Right, will feel the Justice due their fellow Britons; and at least shake their heads at every endeavor to inslave; though they might not be invested with an immediate power to prevent it.''

There was no question that Virginia's leaders hoped to appeal to a sense of justice in making their unified stand specifically against the Stamp Act. However, the Stamp Act itself so symbolized the general principles on which the stand was made that the year ended and January of 1766 passed without Governor Fauquier's being able to report a single break in the resistance to using the stamped papers.

6

In February one nonnative Virginia merchant decided he had had enough of the nonexportation movement. Archibald Ritchie was a shipowner as well as a merchant at Hobbs Hole (later Tappahannock) on the bank of the Rappahannock River across from Landon Carter's Sabine Hall in Richmond County. Ritchie declared in Richmond County court that he intended to clear his ships with their cargoes of wheat by using the stamps, and he knew where he could get them.

In nearby Westmoreland County, philosophical Richard Henry Lee had become transformed into a radical activist over the stamp tax. Adopting the name given originally by Berré in Parliament, he became a leader of the Sons of Liberty, with the determination to stir things up in his own county. Shortly before Mercer's arrival in Williamsburg the previous October, for want of more direct action, Lee had staged an elaborate ceremony in which Colonel Mercer was hung in effigy.

He went to considerable trouble and expense to dress some of his Negroes in the red coats, cocked hats, and high shining boots associated with John Wilkes. This reformist editor, a raffish and controversial figure in England, whose supporters chanted ''Wilkes and liberty'' had become identified with American liberties. The Negroes in ''John Wilkes'' costumes solemnly drew a hangman's cart in which were seated the effigies of Grenville and Mercer. To make sure that no one in the large crowd could mistake the identities, Lee had placards placed across the chests of the effigies: ''I am G—— G———, the infamous projector of American slavery," and "I am G——e M——r, C–l——r of St—— for Virginia." The parade included men dressed as sheriffs, bailiffs, jailers, and hangmen, and, as himself, the tall, stately Richard Henry Lee.

In the playacting, Lee was to pretend to hear the last words of the condemned Mercer and repeat these dying words to the crowd. Lee intoned, with his famous oratorical style, "With parricidal hands, I have endeavored to fasten chains of slavery on this, my native country, though, like the tenderest and best of mothers, she has long fostered and powerfully influenced me. But it was the inordinate love of gold which led me astray from honor, virtue and patriotism. As I am about to suffer the punishment which so great an offender deserves I hope my fate will instruct tyranny and avarice that Virginia determines to be free. . . ."

The performance was widely acclaimed and had contributed to the hostility which greeted George Mercer. With this success behind him, Lee was all ready to carry matters farther with the merchant Ritchie. He was one of the leaders who called for a quick assembly of planters at Leedstown, a river port on the other side of the Rappahannock and upriver from Hobbs Hole. More than a hundred citizens adopted the articles of resolution whose phraseology sounded similar to the impassioned lines that had become characteristic of Lee. The signers of the lengthy articles, which became generally known as the Westmoreland Resolutions, were called either Sons of Liberty or the Westmoreland Associators.

With only a little bombast, the opening articles restated the arguments about "fundamental rights" in general. Then, in the third article, the Associators got down to what they had in mind specifically about the merchant Ritchie, without referring to him by name. "We do determine at every hazard, and paying no attention to danger or death, we will exert every faculty to prevent the execution of the said Stamp Act in any instance whatsoever within this Colony. And every abandoned wretch, who shall be so lost to virtue and to public good, as wickedly to contribute to the introduction or fixture of the Stamp Act in this Colony, by using stamp paper, or by any other means, we will, with the utmost expedition, convince all such profligates that immediate danger and disgrace shall attend that prostitute purposes."

One of the men who signed this vigilante resolution was Spence

Monroe, a hardworking planter of modest estate. When he had hurried from his plain frame dwelling, Monroe left at home his eight-year-old son, James. The solemn boy was then attending Parson Campbell's school, a distance of several miles through primeval woods from his home. James Monroe carried his books under one arm and a rifle under the other, not only for protection but to shoot game. By the time he was ready to enter William and Mary, James Monroe was an expert shot.

He had also been impressed at an early age with direct action taken against laws imposed by the home government. For on the day following the Westmoreland Resolutions, the men crossed the river where, joined by even larger numbers from Ritchie's county, they descended on his home. There were more than four hundred of them when the merchant came to his door, and he saw at a glance they meant business. But Ritchie had the sizable amount of £2,700 tied up in wheat cargoes and he tried to parley with the leaders. They shook their heads grimly. They had a paper for him to sign. If he did not sign it, he would be seized and stripped to the waist, tied to the tail of a cart and drawn to the public pillory, where he would be fixed for one hour. If he did not comply after that treatment, the Sons of Liberty would determine his further punishment.

He signed the statement: "Sensible now to the high insult I offered this county by my declaration in the Richmond Court lately of my determination to make use of stamped paper for clearing out my vessels; and having been convinced any such proceedings will establish a precedent by which this hateful Stamp Act might be introduced into this Colony to the utter destruction of the public liberty, I do most submissively in the presence of the public sign the paper meaning to show my remorse for having formed so execrable a declaration, and I do hereby solemnly promise and swear on the Holy Evangelist that no vessel of mine shall clear on stamped paper; that I never will on any pretense make use of stamped paper unless that use be authorized by the General Assembly of this Colony."

Some of these phrases smacked of the "dying words" speech which Richard Henry Lee had taken from the mouth of Mercer's effigy. The imperious-looking scholar was beginning to rival Patrick Henry as a fiery patriot.

But for Lee personally, his activism in the stamp tax conflict had an undesirable aftermath. George Mercer, unhappy over his experience, had returned to England, leaving with his father and brother proof of Richard Henry Lee's application for the tax collector's post that had gone to their son and brother. This the embittered men caused to be published in the *Gazette,* claiming that Lee's acts in arousing hostility against Colonel Mercer were caused by sour grapes.

Lee replied to the charges, also in the *Gazette.* Unable to deny that he had sought the post, he gave the explanation that he had soon recognized his mistake and had done all in his power to prevent the passage of the Stamp Act. It was an unconvincing rebuttal, weak for a man of Lee's gifts in prose and debate, and did not explain his vindictiveness toward Colonel George Mercer. The Mercers returned to the attack in the *Gazette,* growing verbose in their hatred, and failed to score any points beyond the damning fact itself.

This revelation, however, made a smaller impact than it might have at other times, because when it came, in July, it was overshadowed by large events of great significance to the Colony. Although the stain remained on Lee's record, it did no significant harm to his political career. He was not the only unabashed office-seeker in Virginia and no one questioned his patriotism. Lee, of course, gave no evidence that his own sense of self-righteousness was in the least affected. But chiefly the airing of Lee's questionable motives were forgotten in the topic of conversation that dominated all others — the repeal of the Stamp Act.

7

The debates in Parliament about the Stamp Act repeal were not the important thing to the people in Virginia or in the other colonies. What was important was that the hated act was repealed. But those debates revealed much of the British attitude toward the colonies, just as the various memorials, protests, and pamphlets revealed the attitude in the colonies toward Great Britain.

It was true, as George Washington had predicted, that the British merchants, hurt in pocket, dismissed the principle of taxation in urging repeal. It was also true that it was evident to the most obtuse lord that the stamp tax could never be collected except by the use of force. However, a considerable number of members of Parliament were willing to use that force, and if George Grenville had still headed the ministry there was scarcely any doubt that Patrick Henry and Richard Henry Lee would have had their showdown right then. The collision was postponed by the entirely coincidental act of George III, who dissolved Grenville's ministry in July, 1765.

Grenville's removal from power as chief minister had nothing whatsoever to do with the Stamp Act. The young King, then fully recovered, simply could not endure domination by Grenville any longer. The Marquis of Rockingham, the leader of a small group of Whigs whom George III had politically exiled, was called to form a ministry. Its attention was turned to the American situation in January, 1766.

Rockingham had not been associated with the passage of the Stamp Act and seemed to have no strong feelings about it one way or another. When the reports of disorders and disobedience came from America, and petitions for repeal came from merchants all over England, his natural inclination was toward conciliation. An assertion of royal authority by force in the colonies would be a costly expedient, and even if the principle could be established by arms, the very acts of force would arouse a hostility to Great Britain with unpredictable consequences. Also, repeal of the act would serve the political purpose of discrediting Grenville's preceding ministry.

Grenville was still a power in Parliament and he led the members who predicted that the colonials' assertion, unless checked right then, would lead the colonies to independence from Great Britain. With his cold skill in marshaling statistical arguments, Grenville stood a good chance of gaining a majority to oppose repeal on the grounds that the colonials were getting out of hand.

Rockingham apparently started out with the idea of making conciliatory amendments in the act which would lessen the hardships the Americans complained of, rather than with the idea of outright repeal. As he drifted toward repeal, however, a political compromise was suggested to placate those members of the opposition who were determined that the colonies must be taught a lesson. This was a Declaratory Bill which asserted the rights of Parliament over the colonies. The resolution read that the British legislature "had, hath, and of right ought to have full power and authority to make laws and statutes of sufficient force and validity to bind the colonies and all the people of America, subjects of the Crown of Great Britain, in all cases whatsoever.''

The wording of this bill was a masterpiece of guile by the Rockingham ministry. Nowhere did it mention ''taxation.'' To the American demanders of ''no taxation without consent,'' the bill could be read as a general declaration of Parliamentary authority which the colonies had long accepted. To the opponents of repeal, those who wanted the colonies put in their place, the bill implied the right of taxation — implicit in those rights held by Parliament ''to make laws and statutes . . . in all cases whatsoever.''

William Pitt helped the Rockingham forces with a couple of fiery speeches, which indirectly did their part to cloud the issue. After speaking passionately of America's justified if not always prudently expressed sentiments of freedom, he came to the point of taxation. ''The Commons of America, represented in their several assemblies, have ever been in possession of the exercise of this, their constitutional right, of giving and granting their own money. They would have been slaves if they had not enjoyed it. At the same time, this kingdom, as the supreme governing and legislative power, has always bound the colonies by her laws, by her regulations and restrictions in trade, in navigation, in manufactures — in everything except that of taking their money out of their pockets without their consent. Here I would draw the line.''

Pitt did not make any distinction between internal and external taxation: he was opposed to all taxation. At the same time, his affirmation of the restrictions in trade included the collection of *revenues* from the colonies, such as the high duties on tobacco, as well as controlling trade for the primary interest of Great Britain. While the Declaratory Bill held implications of powers of taxation in which Pitt disbelieved, the Rockingham ministry was able to avoid hairsplitting entanglements in guiding the bill through Parliament. Every member could read into the bill — which passed as the Declaratory Act — what he wanted to.

By thus assuaging the imperialists on their principle of taxation, the Rockingham ministry focused attention on the commercial aspects of the Stamp Act (buttressed by the merchants' petitions) and gained repeal against bitter opposition. In the House the resolutions for repeal passed by 275 to 167 votes on March 5, and in the Lords a majority of 34 was won on March 18 only after a hard struggle. The King, who said privately that he favored modification of the Stamp Act, assented to repeal in a desire to avoid deepening conflict between Great Britain and the American colonies.

Actually, then, a political maneuver by a ministry headed by a conciliatory compromiser allowed the people of the colonies to feel that their civil disobedience had caused the government of Great Britain to repeal an act to which they objected. Whatever the more thoughtful Virginians may have made of the Declaratory Act — and, as in Parliament, each man could read into it what he wanted to — the general reaction was relief at the passing of the crisis. For, with all the opposition to the principle it represented, the Stamp Act would have been a money burden on the people, and the overwhelming feeling in the relief was the escape from more taxes.

When the people tended to give credit for their salvation, it naturally went to the Patrick Henrys, who bearded the English King, and not to the serpentine maneuvers of a British marquis who gained the repeal with the coating of an ambiguously worded bill.

The Declaratory Act had, in point of fact, defined the long-rumbling issues between the colonies and Great Britain with a clarity and a firmness which had never existed in the essentially pragmatic relationships by which each colony, according to its needs and character, had accommodated itself to the restrictions imposed by the home government. In Parliament it was hardly a question of taxation any more: it was a question of who was to govern the colonies — Parliament or their own legislative bodies.

In the colonies this tacitly drawn issue was not immediately recognized. Along with relief at the passing of the Stamp Act crisis, the people in each of the colonies had practical matters to turn their minds to — such as ships to clear and backlogs of cases for courts to dispose of.

In Virginia the leaders in the General Assembly were diverted by crises at home from any possibility of pondering or discussing the meaning of the Declaratory Act. Eight days after the news of the repeal reached Williamsburg on May 3, 1766, Speaker John Robinson died. With his death, the accounts of his Treasurer's office were at last investigated by unfriendly hands — Henry and Lee — and the money scandal was even greater than had been suspected when the ''loan office'' proposal was made the year before.

With repeal of the Stamp Act inevitably associated with Henry's Virginia Resolves, and with the new party of young westerners feeling confidence, this crack in the Tidewater oligarchy was all that Henry's party needed to establish itself as a force in the House of Burgesses. Political parties as such were frowned upon by nearly everyone as promoters of narrowly self-interested factionalism, but, with House control partly shared by the new powers, Robinson's death marked the end of the era when one will exercised absolute authority in the Burgesses — and, hence, in Virginia.

8

After the handsome eulogies to John Robinson appeared in the May 16 *Gazette,* 1766, and before the investigation of the Treasurer's office revealed the peculations, the late Speaker's father-in-law, John Chiswell, provided the Colony with the first big scandal in the ruling class.

In 1759, Robinson had taken as his third wife Susan Chiswell, whose family had long been conspicuous in the high social life of the wealthier planters. Robinson had been a friend of his wife's father, a contemporary, and they engaged in property transactions. Three weeks after the death of his son-in-law, on June 3 John Chiswell for some reason appeared in a tavern at Cumberland County Court House. Chiswell had had too much to drink and he fell into a quarrel with a Scottish trader, Robert Routlidge, who had been drinking wine. Suddenly Routlidge cursed the older gentleman and threw the contents of his wineglass in Chiswell's face. The enraged Chiswell called to his servant for his sword and ran the Scotsman through.

With all of Chiswell's eminence, the Cumberland sheriff had no choice except to put him in jail, preparatory to transporting him to Williamsburg. Capital crimes had to be tried in the General Court and, however it might be explained, Chiswell had committed murder. Had he regarded the trader as his equal, Chiswell would have challenged him to a duel. But, as gentlemen did not meet inferiors on the field of honor, the drunken Chiswell lost his head in reprimanding the trader for the insult of throwing wine in his face. In a few days, the thoroughly sobered gentleman started the ride with the sheriff for the capital.

News of the murder had run ahead, and Chiswell and the sheriff were met in the road by three Councilors, judges of the General Court — William Byrd III, John Blair, and Presley Thornton. They took their friend Chiswell into custody and in Williamsburg freed him on bail. Chiswell lay low in his house on Francis Street, a broad, leafy street mostly of residences, parallel to the Duke of Gloucester Street one block to the south.

There Chiswell and all his friends were astonished at the letters of protest pouring into the *Gazette,* the public forum. All letters charged that leniency had been extended the murderer because of his connections. No person in recent times had been so violently attacked *because* of his connections. The public protests showed that a new wind was blowing in Tidewater Virginia.

Shortly before his trial, Chiswell committed suicide in his Francis Street home. People were still talking about "how are the mighty fallen" when, on June 13, a notice appeared in the *Virginia Gazette* over the name of Edmund Pendleton, administrator of John Robinson's estate, announcing that all the estate's debtors "must make immediate payment." After referring to Robinson's "goodness of heart and benevolent disposition" which "could not resist the importunities of the distressed, but advanced large sums of money to assist and relieve his friends," the notice expressed the hope "that all those who have received favors from him will, in honor and gratitude to the memory of so kind a friend and benefactor, pay immediately what they owe . . ." and not "suffer the estate of their friend to be distressed for the payment of their debts."

This notice confirmed the suspicions that had been growing since Robinson's death about irregularities in the Treasurer's accounts. The irregularities had first become known to Robert Carter Nicholas, who succeeded to the Treasurer's post on May 21. The posts of Speaker and Treasurer were separated after Robinson died, and Peyton Randolph won out over Richard Bland in the election for Speaker of the House. As Treasurer Nicholas was circumspect to the point of secretiveness about the confusion he discovered in Robinson's accounts, but he quickly took into his confidence Edmund Pendleton, the late Speaker's protégé as well as administrator of his estate.

Nicholas had discovered that Robinson, in his capacity as Treasurer, had lent £100,000 to ''distressed'' friends out of the currency which had been retired from circulation and was to be burned in 1769 when the last of Virginia's paper money would be redeemed. Evidently Robinson had expected his friends to repay the loans before 1769. It was clear to all of Robinson's friends that he had dipped into public funds, as Nicholas said, ''more owing to a mistaken kind of humanity and compassion for persons in distress than any view to his own private emolument.'' This conviction was borne out by the further revelation that Robinson had lent friends £30,000 out of his own estate. The worst of the £100,000 shortage in currency was that all these loans were charged against the Robinson estate. To Pendleton fell the thankless task of trying to collect £130,000 from families who, in many cases, had needed money desperately enough to involve the public trust of the man of whom Fauquier said, ''Such was the sensibility of his too benevolent heart.''

The enemies of the shaken Tidewater oligarchy were of course unmoved by Robinson's motivations. But the oligarchy was not so shaken that it could not take care of its own. The names that came to light among Robinson's debtors cut through the heart of the ruling class, and there was legitimate reason to fear that demanding immediate payment — as well as publicizing the names — could have disastrous results in Virginia far beyond any effect on the oligarchy's power. Then, not one of the men most closely associated with Robinson politically and personally — Richard Bland, Peyton Randolph, George Wythe, Benjamin Harrison — was among the debtors.

The secret of the debtors' names was carefully guarded, and few were aware of their identities. Spendthrift William Byrd III topped the list with £10,000. Among the larger debtors were three of King Carter's grandsons (all cousins of Robert Carter Nicholas) — Carter Braxton, Lewis Burwell, and Charles Carter, Jr. Other large debtors were Archibald Cary, Bowler Cocke, Jr., Benjamin Grymes and Ralph Wormeley, kin by marriage to Landon Carter. The Lees of Northern Neck were among the debtors, and the Mercers and the Moores, and Henry Fitzhugh, whose ancestor had been one of the earliest of the large fortune-founders.

Since immediate payment would have meant anything from acute financial embarrassment to possible ruin to some of the debtors, the harassed Pendleton proceeded slowly to collect the money owed the Robinson estate, so slowly that some never paid fully and some not at all. While the ruling class as a whole was protected, Robinson's estate was the one to suffer, and the name of John Robinson bore the stigma for all the friends who had profited from his generous heart.

The new party of Patrick Henry and Richard Henry Lee could scarcely have hoped for such a political windfall. There was not much they could do with the opportunity immediately because, with no issue active between the Colony and the British government, the General Assembly turned to routine local concerns. The scars from the recent conflicts had not yet healed, and the tensions from the climactic Stamp Act crisis had not yet entirely eased, but there was hope that the quiet following the reconciliation might lead to a return to harmony. If the current relationship seemed unlikely to recapture the idyllic era of a "life in thrall," certainly the people in general — and particularly the families in the ruling class — anticipated a continuity in looking after their personal affairs without disruptiveness from the mother country.

However, before Virginians could really settle down into a sense of security in their relations with the home government, a new figure arose in the British ministry to keep Patrick Henry from becoming a revolutionary without an issue.

From the King's signing of the Declaratory Act in March of 1766, it was just a matter of time before some member of Parliament would decide to enforce the act's implied right of taxing the colonies. Charles Townshend was the cabinet member who did, and in June, 1767, just about one year after Governor Fauquier had enjoyed the satisfaction of officially announcing the repeal of the Stamp Act, King George III signed a new tax act.

Chapter Nine

TO THE PRECIPICE

To Virginians, and to their fellow colonials, the name of Charles Townshend became synonymous with villainy, and yet the American colonies owed to this fascinating neurotic the impetus for their revolution. After a checkered and dazzling career in British government since the age of twenty-two, Townshend rose sinuously in the ministry which, in July of 1766, replaced the briefly lived Rockingham ministry.

To form a new ministry, George III, having removed William Pitt from power when the great orator was at the height of his powers, now brought the lean, hawk-faced old Pitt out of semiretirement. Now Earl of Chatham, the former Commoner was ill and suffering from melancholia, and, never a party man, lacked probably even the will to deal with the factionalism in Parliament.

In the new ministry, Charles Townshend, just past forty as Chancellor of the Exchequer, maneuvered himself into a position of influence in the effective cabinet. Brilliant, witty, and charming, with an extravagant sense of satire which he used to ridicule anyone of importance, Charles Townshend was unstable, politically undependable, and consistent only in his inconstancy. He suffered at intervals from convulsive disorders: as Horace Walpole described one of the seizures, "he drops down dead in a fit." These weakening attacks were, long after his death, medically diagnosed as epileptic, though references in Townshend's lifetime never seemed to define the nature of "his old complaint."

His absolute lack of any loyalties or conscience, his outsize ego, and his irresponsible need to flaunt his disrespect of others made him a dangerous, though amusing, companion of the Parliamentary powers, but hardly well cast in the role of manipulator of events in affairs so consequential as the relationship between Great Britain and her American colonies.

Yet, among all the incongruities in the character of this warped and gifted man, in all the twists and turns of his life, there was one line to which he had held with unobtrusive consistency : this was a policy for the American colonies. When only twenty-four, back in the halcyon days of 1749, he had been appointed to the Board of Trade, on which he served for the next five years. While on the Board of Trade, Townshend drafted instructions for the governor of New York the purpose of which was to make the royal executive financially independent of the colony's legislature. Finding the New York Assembly guilty of trampling upon royal authority and prerogatives by assuming "to themselves the disposal of public money," Townshend wanted to remodel colonial government along lines which would, in effect, have removed from all assemblies their fundamental right of disposing of their own money.

When war with the French and Indians became imminent in 1754, Townshend had risen to the Board of Admiralty. There he regarded as both impractical and undesirable a proposed plan for concerted action among the American colonies. He was right in claiming that the colonies would not reach any agreement on their contributions. But he was opposed to the idea of their attempting it because, if successful, concerted action on contributions would confirm them in drawing to themselves the prerogatives of the Crown. Townshend had a plan, which was never introduced, for Parliament to impose a tax which "all the Provinces will, I am certain, approve and cheerfully pay."

That Parliament had the right to and should tax the colonies, and that the colonies should be not only subservient but grateful, was Townshend's view when he was twenty-nine. He never changed it when all the agitation from the colonies showed the incorrectness of his belief that they would ''cheerfully pay'' a tax imposed uniformly by Parliament. Townshend's feelings about the subservience of the colonies could well have been a reflection of his own life.

He had been totally dependent on his father, the third Viscount Townshend, until at thirty he had married the rich Lady Dalkeith. During the years of his dependency Charles Townshend had been forced to coddle a father whom he did not love. The third Viscount Townshend, lacking his son's brilliance, was an intelligent and formidable man in the world of affairs, and could play the heavy father with a son both as unusual and as guilefully vicious as ''Champagne Charlie.'' Thus, re-enacting his own life with himself as the parent in relation to the colonies, in a speech supporting Grenville's stamp tax bill in 1765, Townshend said, ''And now will these Americans, children planted by our care, nourished by our indulgence until they are grown to a degree of strength and opulence, and protected by our arms, will they grudge to contribute their mite to relieve us from the weight of that burden we lie under?''

This piteous appeal from the parent to an ungrateful child was another face of the stern parent of twelve years before who felt that the assemblies' disposing of their own money constituted a trampling on royal prerogative. In the 1760's his ''plan'' for America was recognized as dangerous by members of Parliament, at least two of whom felt that he would be an embarrassment to the Grenville ministry when it was forming.

Since his days on the Board of Admiralty, Townshend had served as Secretary of War (not then a cabinet post) and briefly as president of the Board of Trade, and from 1763 to 1765, the period of the Grenville ministry, he had been out of office. In 1765 he succeeded Henry Fox in the Paymaster's office where, in addition to the £700 salary, a fortune could be made on the side. From there he moved to the post of Chancellor of the Exchequer in the Chatham ministry, when the problems with America were quiet.

Townshend soon took care of that. Insulated from realities by the enormity of his ego, he learned nothing from England's experiences with the colonies and immediately sought to introduce his fourteen-year-old plan for ''improvement of government in the colonies.'' This began with the proposal to pay the salaries of royal governors and judges out of the fund accumulated by duties, and thus make civil authorities independent of their assemblies. Of immediate concern to the colonies was a tax, levied by Parliament, imposing new import duties on glass, lead, paints, paper, and tea. Townshend cynically said that since duties could be defined as an "external" tax, the colonies could not object. The funds derived from the duties would be used, along with defraying the expenses of garrisons in the colonies, for "defraying the charge of the administration of justice and support of civil government" in the colonies.

When the Townshend Acts received the royal assent on June 29, 1767, to become effective November 20, a man distrusted by his fellow members of Parliament, and kept out of Grenville's imperialistic ministry, had been allowed to put through a pet scheme of his own. As Charles Garth, South Carolina's agent and a member of Parliament, wrote of that House of Commons, "the friends of America are too few to have any share in a struggle with a Chancellor of the Exchequer."

Slightly more than two months after the Townshend Acts became law, on September 4 the author died at the age of forty-two. "Our comet is set," Horace Walpole wrote. "All those parts and fire are extinguished; those volatile salts are evaporated; that first eloquence of the world is dumb!" The comet did not die forgotten. In the American colonies, where neither his eloquence nor his deviousness had made any impression, he entered deeply into history by the act which bore his name — a not unfitting immortality.

2

The Townshend Acts did not arouse in Virginia the general response of the Stamp Act. While the tax on tea struck at the merchants and smugglers in the North, the other items on which duties were placed did not work any significant hardship on planters. Then, Townshend's cynicism in placing a duty as an acceptable "external" tax avoided a fresh collision over principles. Townshend's own deviousness failed to assert the point, which he actually believed, of Parliament's right of taxation, and the new duties need not be interpreted as an implementation of the Declaratory Act.

Along with the amalgam of all these factors, the planters in government were not looking just then for a new issue with the mother country. A relaxation had come with the passing of the Stamp Act crisis, and men of all classes were absorbed in their personal affairs — their debts and taxes, their crops and their children's education, and pleasures according to their station and means.

Thomas Jefferson, his preparations for life completed, left Williamsburg the year of the Townshend Acts and, with Shadwell as his base, began the practice of law. He did well, without being a dazzling success. He never earned appreciably more than £500 a year in fees and he was lucky if he collected more than half of that. Like Patrick Henry, he handled many small cases of obscure clients in the county courthouses. He was also retained by persons of consequence — not only his kinspeople the Randolphs and his friends the Pages, but Carters and Harrisons and Lees, and he noted with some pride that he was generally retained by Colonel William Byrd III. Not being the trial lawyer that Henry was, Jefferson was at his best in the General Court, where cases were more likely to be decided on points of law.

Jefferson began to return regularly to Williamsburg in the spring of 1769, when he was elected to represent his county in the House of Burgesses. During the two years that he had mostly been away, practicing law and looking after his planting operations, one major change had occurred. Francis Fauquier had died in the spring of 1768. His death came during a lull in the conflict in the relationship between Virginia and Great Britain, when the ruling class could almost recapture the illusion that the golden age would continue forever.

As if to confirm the Virginians in the era of good feeling, England had sent as Fauquier's replacement a full governor who was a nobleman. The Right Honorable Norborne Berkeley had only four years earlier ascended into the peerage as the Baron de Botetourt (pronounced Bot'-ti-tot), but Virginians regarded it as a compliment from the Crown to have a lord sent to be resident Governor General. That financial difficulties lay behind the fifty-year-old Botetourt's acceptance of the appointment was a minor point compared with the happy face the new Governor showed everybody upon his arrival in October, 1768. Botetourt was an experienced courtier, Lord of the Bedchamber, and he had the courtier's gift of a pleasing personality. He became immediately popular and won the love of all the people.

The amiable lord did not have long in Williamsburg; he died in

1770. During his felicitous administration, Landon Carter, who had grown bitter about the "dirty tyrannic ministry," noted in his diary that Botetourt "became the instrument of a dawning happiness. . . . Through his active and exemplary virtue, order everywhere revived out of that confusion that our dissipative indolence had thrown us into."

Thomas Jefferson believed that Botetourt's popularity, his flattering tactfulness in conciliating, was harmful to the revolutionary spirit in Virginia. Botetourt, much at home with those conservative Virginians of his generation who wanted to maintain harmonious relations with the mother country, never gave the young revolutionaries any issues to get their teeth in, as the problems caused by the Townshend duties were chiefly in New England. It was Jefferson's correct opinion that the senior statesmen — Peyton Randolph, Richard Bland, Benjamin Harrison, and Edmund Pendleton — needed to be prodded to take stronger united stands against England.

The men who only fifteen years before had been the vanguard had insensibly become the Old Guard. Richard Bland was then approaching sixty, and although Edmund Pendleton was in his late forties and Benjamin Harrison forty-four, both men had politically grown up in the heart of the Tidewater oligarchy and had been thoroughly formed before the changes brought by and with the French and Indian Wars. Leaders in defining and protecting Virginia's liberties, who essentially wanted the status quo with their liberties preserved, the Old Guardsmen were set in the habit of presenting protests based on finely reasoned constitutionalities, largely evolved from principles enunciated by their constitutionalist Richard Bland.

In 1766, before the repeal of the Stamp Act, Richard Bland had written the last of his important pamphlets, *An Inquiry into the Rights of the British Colonies,* which in 1769 was being studied in Virginia and read in England. Richard Bland had reached the age when a contemporary described him as "a very old experienced veteran at the Senate or the bar — staunch and tough as whitleather — has something of the look of the musty old parchments which he handleth and studieth much." In his *Inquiry,* Richard Bland went as far as could be expected for a man of his generation — "to the precipice," as Jefferson described it.

In his most finely reasoned examination of the relations between

Norborne Berkeley, Baron de Botetourt
(Reproduced through the courtesy of the Virginia Historical Society)

the Colony and Parliament, he briefly traced English history through the then popular Saxon tradition, touched upon the history of ancient colonization, and traced with exactness the developments in Virginia. He concluded this summation with the statement: "As then we receive no light from the laws of the Kingdom, or from ancient history, to direct us in our inquiry, we must have recourse to the law of nature, and those rights of mankind which flow from it." In the light of those rights of mankind, Bland disposed of the theory advanced during the Grenville ministry that the colonies enjoyed "virtual" representation in Parliament. He presented proof of Parliament's recognition of the colonies as a "distinct people." Then he came to the point of Parliamentary authority, which had not then — before the Declaratory Act — come squarely into the open.

"The colonies are subordinate to the authority of Parliament," he wrote, but, "subordinate I mean in degree, but not absolutely so: For if by a vote of the *British* Senate the colonists were to be delivered up to the rule of a *French* or *Turkish* tyranny, they may refuse obedience to such a vote, and may oppose the execution of it by force. Great is the power of Parliament, but, great as it is, it cannot, constitutionally, deprive the people of their *natural* rights; nor, in virtue of the same principle, can it deprive them of their *civil* rights. . . . If they are deprived of their civil rights, if great and manifest oppressions are imposed upon them by the state on which they are dependent, their remedy is to lay their complaints at the foot of the throne, and to suffer patiently rather than to disturb public peace, which nothing but a denial of justice can excuse them in breaking. But if this justice should be denied, if the most humble and dutiful representations should be rejected, nay, not even deigned to be received, what is to be done?"

The *what is to be done* question bothered the younger Burgesses, who were becoming ready to take up where Bland left off. In April, 1769, the *Gazette* published a London letter, describing the British lack of reaction to Bland's pamphlet and to John Dickinson's *Letters from a Farmer in Pennsylvania,* which had been widely circulated in the colonies. "I assure you that no arguments or pains have been omitted by the agents for the colonies; they have taken their instruction from the best writers: If the Parliament will not hear BLAND and DICKENSON, neither will they be persuaded if one rose from the dead."

With this sort of evidence, younger Burgesses, and by no means only the revolutionaries, felt that the time was past for statements of their position. Thirty-seven-year-old George Washington wrote to his reflective friend George Mason of the "inefficacy" of "addresses to the throne and remonstrances to Parliament."

Washington, with his unpleasant experiences with British officers during the war, with the problems caused by the 1763 proclamation to his land speculations in the west and his endless struggle to break even at Mount Vernon under the existing mercantile system, had begun to feel strongly about the reaction the Townshend duties aroused in New England. As advanced as any revolutionary in thinking in continental perspectives, Washington saw what was happening — by chance, right then — to the northward as an indication that "our lordly masters in Great Britain will be satisfied with nothing less than the depreciation of American freedom."

In a letter to George Mason in April, just before the 1769 spring session of the General Assembly, he wrote, "It seems highly necessary that something should be done to . . . maintain the freedom which we have derived from our ancestors; but the manner of doing it . . . is the point in question." Then the ex-soldier revealed how far even a conservative planter had been driven in his thinking: "That no man should scruple, or hesitate a moment to use a [r]ms in defence of so valuable a blessing . . . is clearly my opinion." Arms he regarded as "the last resource," but something had to be done more than send Great Britain memorials of protest.

It was Botetourt's job to avoid doing anything to encourage common cause between Virginia and New England and develop the spirit of union feared by Townshend and already regarded by Grenville as the imminence of rebellion. The last thing needed was the earnest forthrightness of a Dinwiddie, his double chins quivering with indignation at some affront to "his Majesty's prerogatives." Botetourt personally was as much a King's man as Dinwiddie (and probably more so than Fauquier), but he suggested the majesty of monarchy in more appealing and colorful ways.

His Lordship drove from the Palace to the Capitol in the most magnificent coach of state ever seen in the Colony, a present from the Duke of Cumberland and bearing the Virginia arms. Six white Hanoverian horses drew the grand vehicle up the Duke of Gloucester

Street, for all to see and admire, and when he alighted the Governor warmed everyone with his smile. When, in his scarlet robes, he addressed the Burgesses, his mellow voice dripped with words of good feeling. Even when he was forced to dissolve the Assembly, he did this as a reluctant "duty," between friends.

3

On the occasion of dissolving the Burgesses, Botetourt had been acting under instructions from home. The Massachusetts House of Representatives had sent out a circular urging the assemblies of the other colonies to a common front against the Townshend duties, and all colonial governors were instructed to dissolve any assembly which approved the circular.

This May session, 1769, was the first time that Thomas Jefferson, so often a visitor at the Capitol, entered it as a member of the House of Burgesses. It was also the first time since Jefferson had been a student at William and Mary that Landon Carter was not present. Richmond County had not returned the master of Sabine Hall to his seat in the 1768 elections, and the only reason Carter could think of was that he had lost close touch with his constituents.

Landon Carter had certainly not failed of re-election because of overly conservative views. In 1765, after he had urged the Burgesses to send protesting resolves on the threatened Stamp Act, such a revolutionary as Richard Henry Lee had called him "one of the best friends, as well as one of the most able of the community." Since the Stamp Act, Landon Carter had been profoundly shaken in his respect for and admiration of British principles as demonstrated by recent ministries. While denying the charge of Grenville's followers that the colonies had any intention of seeking independence, in September of 1768 he did concede that the "desire of independency" could possibly develop, as it had historically, out of an "impatience in suffering." (It could appear that George Grenville, the first person publicly to talk of the independence of the colonies, actually should be credited with giving birth to the concept.)

Most likely the complex Carter, suffering his inner conflicts with their manifestations of eccentric irascibility, had simply become too difficult a person for his neighbors. His scorn of courting popularity and his insistence upon a people's representative being governed by his own "reason and conscience" could appear as haughty superiority, rather than as the high-minded convictions which they were.

In contrast, Carter's nephew, Benjamin Harrison, also was governed by his own reasoning rather than by constituents' opinions. Later, when the more informed Burgesses felt that affairs with Great Britain were reaching a climax which called for a continental congress, big Harrison was waited upon by a group of his neighbors. Their spokesman said (as Harrison recounted it), "You assert that there is a fixed intention to invade our rights and privileges; we own that we do not see this clearly, but since you assure us that this is so, we believe you. We are about to take a very dangerous step, but we have confidence in you and will do anything you think proper." Harrison, a jovial and gregarious man, was a plantation master with whom the people could identify, and part of their trust in him was a liking for him as a person.

The tormented Carter, with his insatiably high self-demands, needed praise and flattery — needed "to be tickled," as Francis Lightfoot Lee had said — and by his fifty-eighth year, in the 1768 election, could not tolerate even the slightest disagreement or criticism. He felt surrounded by monsters of "ingratitude." The most ungrateful of them all was his oldest son, whom he regarded as no more than "a man of pleasure," an irresponsible, unlettered wastrel. When the son, Robert Wormeley Carter, replaced him in the House of Burgesses in the next election, the father said he "kissed the arses of the people and very servilely accommodated himself to them." Later, when the people failed to re-elect the younger Carter, the father wrote that they ungratefully threw him out in "a kind of April fool election," and commented that such "was the nature of popularity."

Away from his services in Williamsburg, Landon Carter had more time to brood over the disparity between the responsible services he had rendered his community and the little recognition that came to him. "Truly," he wrote in his diary, "a prophet is not without honor save in his own country." In passing years, as his fears for the colonies' liberties caused a deeper hostility toward Great Britain — and he became more revolutionary-minded than some members of the younger generation, such as his son-in-law Robert Beverley — the aging man nursed his sense of neglect. He was particularly embittered by the acclaim given Patrick Henry as "the first who opened the breath of liberty to America." Carter had attacked the threatened Stamp Act in 1764 when he was instrumental in getting the House to send those protests to the King, the Lords, and the Commons, well before Henry had ever paraphrased their arguments in the Virginia Resolves. Carter took what bleak satisfaction he could in writing in his diary that, at least, he had never "courted public applause" like Henry.

In the House, while Landon Carter had been a hard and dependable worker with Robinson's old oligarchy on important legislation, he had always remained an independent. His position as an independent of consequence would be filled to some extent by George Washington, whom Carter had befriended during his youthful struggles on the frontier and with whom he was still a close friend. Colonel Washington had come to that May session of the General Assembly with resolutions drafted by his scholarly friend George Mason, and he was prepared for the first time during his ten years in the Burgesses to stand up and speak before a deliberative body.

Before Washington's turn came, there were procedural matters in the House to be disposed of. First, as was customary, a committee was formed to draft an address in reply to Governor Botetourt's opening speech. With that sure instinct of Virginia's General Assembly for using the precise talents of its members, Edmund Pendleton gave newcomer Thomas Jefferson the honor of drafting a resolution along the lines on which the address would be written. As Peyton Randolph was employed at presiding at meetings, Benjamin Harrison at committee work, Richard Bland at drafting bills and developing constitutional points, Jefferson became "the Pen," as Henry was "the Voice" and Washington became "the Sword."

Jefferson's draft of resolutions was acceptable and, again at Pendleton's suggestion, he was assigned to write the address, subject to the approval of the old-liners on the committee. Of the old-liners, Treasurer Robert Carter Nicholas objected to Jefferson's lean, clear-lined prose. Saying that young Jefferson had done little more than follow the sparse language of the resolutions, Nicholas rewrote the address to make it more elaborate, with, as Jefferson said, more "amplification."

So sensitive was Jefferson to criticism that nearly fifty years later he remembered Nicholas's revision of his writing. He wrote in a letter when he was seventy-two that "Being a young man as well as a young member, it made upon me an impression proportioned to the sensibilities of that time of life." Unlike Landon Carter, however, Jefferson did not regard Treasurer Nicholas as a personal enemy who had set out to treat him with disrespect. He went about his duties and his life keeping his bruised pride to himself and, though he never forgot the cut, he drew no baleful conclusions about mankind from it.

After the address to the Governor, on May 16 a less routine matter had to be confronted. This was the circular letter from the Massachusetts House of Representatives, along with a new British ruling (actually the unearthing of a Henry VIII statute) which threatened to bring to England for trial persons accused of treason in the colonies. This Parliamentary threat was aimed specifically at Massachusetts, but it could just as well apply to Virginia, whose Patrick Henry had been reckless in making treasonable utterances.

On May 16, the House in committee of the whole adopted three resolutions. The first affirmed the principle that only the House of Burgesses could tax the inhabitants of Virginia, and the second, referring to the Massachusetts circular, affirmed the right of petition. "It is lawful and expedient to procure the concurrence of his Majesty's other colonies, in dutiful addresses, praying the royal interposition in favor of the violated rights of America." The third affirmed the right of trial in Virginia for any person accused of a crime in the Colony, stressing the point that sending any resident of the Colony suspected of crime "to places beyond the sea, to be tried, is highly derogatory to the rights of British subjects." Because of these resolutions, copies of which were sent to the King and to the presiding officers in the other colonies, Governor Botetourt was forced to dissolve the Assembly.

Most of the Burgesses regathered in the large Apollo Room of the Raleigh Tavern and, after electing Peyton Randolph as moderator, held an informal session. There the imposing Washington arose and spoke from the paper which George Mason had prepared at Washington's suggestion. The burden of the talk was the need to protect their liberties by joining the nonimportation associations which had sprung up in the North soon after the Townshend duties were imposed. In the

Boston area the nonimportation agreement had not been wholly successful, because a couple of mercantile houses had refused to go along, but throughout the North the boycott on tea was very successful.

In the unofficial session in the tavern nearly all the Burgesses present agreed with the principle of joining the Northern colonies in forming a nonimportation association. As well as showing the unity of resentment at Great Britain's encroachments, the Burgesses hoped to get at the British authorities indirectly through the merchants. Washington personally believed that boycotting certain items, especially luxuries, would check the spendthrift tendencies of those debtors who felt obliged to maintain a scale of living beyond their means. The trouble for Virginia, however, was in deciding upon the items to boycott, since the Colony lacked the manufacturing of New England, New York, and Pennsylvania.

Washington was appointed to a committee to decide on the proscribed articles, and it substantially followed the list drawn up by Mason. After September 1, and until the tax was lifted, the association agreed not to import any of the taxed articles — tea, pigment, paint, and paper — and an almost impossible list of untaxed luxuries and articles of British manufacture. Then ninety-four of the hundred and sixteen Burgesses signed for the association.

Not all of the twenty-two who failed to sign were in disagreement. There were always absentees. Edmund Pendleton had left Williamsburg before the May 16 resolutions, and George Wythe, as successor to John Randolph as Clerk, did not have a seat in the House. But some of the members were opposed, notably John Randolph, who had succeeded his brother as Attorney General.

The nonimportation association was not to be successful, but it represented an *action* of protest in concert with the continental colonial system. It was the step beyond words, beyond reasoned petitions: it was a gauntlet thrown down.

4

At the October session of the General Assembly, Governor Botetourt met the members as if nothing had happened. The smiling courtier, Botetourt told his friends that he had been assured by Lord

Hillsborough, Secretary of State for the Colonies, "that his Majesty's present administration have at no time entertained a design to propose to Parliament to lay any further taxes upon America for the purpose of raising a revenue, and that it is their intention to propose in the next session of Parliament to take off the duties upon glass, paper, and colors, upon consideration of such duties having been laid contrary to the true principles of commerce."

Attributing the reason to commerce, Botetourt of course avoided any reference to the principle of Parliament's right to tax. Then with honeyed words — as soothing to his listeners as Henry's passionate words had been provocative — the Governor gave his personal opinion that this policy would "never be departed from." He promised that he would "to the last hour of my life, at all times, in all places, and upon all occasions exert every power with which I either am or ever shall be legally invested, in order to obtain and maintain for the continent of America that satisfaction which I have been authorized to promise this day, by the confidential servants of our gracious Sovereign."

In his personal conciliation, Botetourt had summarized the attitude of those members of Parliament who believed it unwise to force the issue of the rights of Parliament. Believing in the English axiom "Least said, soonest mended," Botetourt was sincere in personally representing a position of retirement to the pragmatic practices in which Virginia's Old Guard had grown up. In those days of give-and-take compromises, in typically British political fashion, what worked was more important than the theory of how things should work.

Now it had become apparent that not only the commercial interests of Great Britain and the colonies were adversely affected by all the contention over the principles of rights, but that the bases of harmonious intergovernmental relationships were seriously undermined. As part of the tea boycott in the North, merchants in New York and Philadelphia opened regular trade with Holland in defiance of the Navigation Acts. There was nothing, except force of arms, to prevent any colony from defying trade restrictions which had been accepted for a century. The point was that always before all restrictions *had* been accepted, with the small pragmatic evasions overlooked by the governors according to the needs of the individual colonies. But the present evasions constituted openly illegal trade in large-scale civil disobedience.

Botetourt, a King's man on the scene, obviously was speaking for the moderates in London in making a promise which he could only hope he could keep — essentially, to let things alone. The problem for any stability of policy (like Walpole's during the idyllic era) was the continual changes of ministry. After nine years of George III's reign, with five hundred changes of office, the fifth ministry was about to be dissolved. When Chatham proved to be too old and ill for the post of chief minister, the King had formed a new ministry around the Duke of Grafton in 1768. Genial and friendly, devoted to fox-hunting and amours, Grafton was not really a leader, and was unhappy as prime minister.

However, before Grafton left office the following year, the Townshend duties were, as Botetourt had predicted, removed from articles except tea. In permitting this compromise, Lord Hillsborough was not as friendly to the colonies as the Governor had implied. If the colonial Secretary of State had had his way, the charter of Massachusetts would have been amended as a punitive measure. George III himself, then thirty-one, took one of his stands on colonial policy and opposed meddling with charters, on the grounds that such action would only exacerbate the present "unhappy feuds."

On the question of principle — which Botetourt thought wise to leave alone — George III said, "I am clear there must always be one tax to keep up the right, and as such I approve the tea duty." On this ground of the right to tax he would not yield, and later he said, "All men seem now to feel that the fatal compliance of 1766 [repeal of the Stamp Act] has encouraged the Americans annually to increase in their pretensions to that thorough independence which one state has in another, but which is quite subversive of the obedience which a colony owes to its mother country."

Thus, while Botetourt spoke honestly for himself and one attitude in Parliament, the King spoke for what was becoming the dominant sentiment in British government. As Chatham passed from the scene, and his supporters with friendly attitudes to the American colonies lost influence, the majority came to repudiate Botetourt's conciliatory approach based upon an avoidance of a clash over principles. Since the Declaratory Act established Parliament's sovereignty "in all cases whatsoever," this majority came to insist upon avoiding any compromise. The authority of Parliament must be recognized by the colonies, who by this recognition would accept their own subservience.

Beyond taxation without representation, beyond taxation altogether, the long-gathering dispute became focused on the issue of Parliament's power to legislate. With this, the British government began to make it impossible for Virginia's Old Guard to maintain the Colony's position within the British Empire with its liberties preserved: these men who earnestly desired the continuance of an equitable connection with the mother country were to have all alternatives removed. Once this was done, it became simpler for the young revolutionaries to prod the conservative leaders toward positions advanced beyond their most personal inclinations.

As always, Henry's party received timely help from England. When the beloved Botetourt died in 1770, the British government sent another nobleman whose only resemblance to his predecessor was in being a peer. John Murray, Earl of Dunmore, Viscount Fincastle, Baron of Blair, of Moulin, and of Tillymont — in brief, Lord Dunmore — was a Scotsman who came to Virginia by way of a tour as governor of New York. While he could make himself socially charming, Dunmore could also be haughty and arrogant, and he came to personify everything the Virginians found objectionable in British power. Actually preferring to govern without the General Assembly, this throwback to the Stuarts continually prorogued it.

During the administration of Dunmore, Virginia's last colonial governor, although Virginians were profoundly aggrieved by actions of the Crown in regard to their western territory and tight money became an acute problem, provocative incidents did not occur until Dunmore had been Governor two years, and then in the Northern colonies. Chiefly in the Boston area, the incidents were basically over the tea trade and repressive British countermeasures in reaction to mob action. Whatever the provocation of civilian violence in the North, the young revolutionaries in Virginia used the British reactions to prod their seniors to advanced positions on the stand of continental unity against concepts of "oppression" and threats of "slavery" conjured out of British authoritarianism.

After all the grievances, large or small, that had been aired, and that had been either settled or resolved in some working compromise, after all the assertions of their rights by the colonial assemblies and all the changes in the British attitudes from the Stuart kings to the Grafton ministry, after the century of accommodation between the interests of the colonial people and the national interests of British trade, by some headless momentum of its own the issue of Parliament's authority had become central to all else. It was fundamentally on this point that Virginia's so-called conservatives hung back.

But the issues were not so cut and dried, so black and white, to the senior members of the ruling class as could be viewed in perspective. The older generation may well have been like Botetourt and the opposition in Parliament in the conviction that a test over authority was neither necessary nor desirable. Seen according to their age in life and their backgrounds, these gentlemen responsible for Virginia's government were not the inert forces of conservatism which after-the-event judgments have sometimes pictured them in glorification of the younger men who, like Patrick Henry, were more advanced in their willingness to force issues.

5

Richard Bland, who articulated the basic viewpoint of the senior leaders, had taken his position on Parliament's authority in his 1766 *Inquiry,* published before the Declaratory Act laid the basis for the development of the argument. Then, before there was any test issue, Bland had written, "The colonies are subordinate to the authority of Parliament; subordinate I mean in degree, but not absolutely so." Jefferson, writing years later about Bland's reasoning, said, "He would set out on sound principles, pursue them logically till he found them leading to the precipice he had to leap, start back alarmed, then resume his ground, go over it in another direction, be led again by the correctness of his reasoning to the same place, and again back about, and try other processes to reconcile right and wrong, but finally left his reader and himself bewildered between the steady index of the compass in their hand, and the phantasm to which it seemed to point. Still there was more sound matter than in the celebrated Farmer's [Dickinson's] letters, which were really but an *ignis fatuus,* misleading us from true principles."

John Murray, Earl of Dunmore
Portrait by Sir Joshua Reynolds
(By courtesy of Mrs. Charles Murray)

Like many another reviewer after the fact, Jefferson (writing about Bland in 1815) looked back through the refraction of taken-for-granted conditions which had not existed, nor even been dreamed of, when Richard Bland approached "to the precipice he had to leap." Bland published his last pamphlet when all Virginians, including Jefferson, were loyal subjects of the King and, if shaken in the nature of their connection with England, did not (as Jefferson himself said) conceive of existing as an entity outside Great Britain. What was the precipice that Bland, in his writings, could not leap?

In 1752, only a few years after Gooch's benign administration, Bland had first been outraged into writing by Dinwiddie's pistole fee. This had been an entirely local affair, between Virginia and her Governor. Twelve years later, when he reached the peak of his powers in *The Colonel Dismounted,* his satirical attack on Camm, Bland had been writing about another local affair, the Two Penny Act. Although that 1764 pamphlet contained the most advanced arguments of the time in the colonies on the autonomy of colonial government, *The Colonel Dismounted* had still been essentially about Virginia. Bland first began to write about "the colonies" in the *Inquiry,* 1766, when the Stamp Act gave common cause to the separate colonies which only since 1763 had — as a result of England's single-continent policy — begun to share common interests and some singleness of identity.

At Bland's age, and with his privileged background in an established order, this common cause with the other colonies represented a unity of protest against a home government rather than anything approaching a political unity with an existence of its own. All of his pamphlets, from *A Fragment of the Pistole Fee* to the *Inquiry,* were written with the single intent of making appeals of reason to the British government which would cause the mother country to avoid legislation that abridged the colonists' rights and produced political alienation.

Jefferson himself, writing eight years after the *Inquiry,* in the drastically changed atmosphere of 1774 when the First Continental Congress was to assemble, followed the same line up to a point: "We are willing, on our part, to sacrifice everything which reason can ask to the restoration of that tranquillity for which all must wish." By then, however, the relationship had deteriorated to the stage where Jefferson was expressing a preference for a return of harmonious relations to separation: "It is neither our wish nor our interest to separate from [Great Britain]."

By then, things had moved so fast that James Madison, only seven years younger than Jefferson, never in his life referred to himself as a loyal British subject; Jefferson, in his first paper written in the 1769 session, had had no hesitation in humbly addressing himself to "his Majesty's sacred person and government." By 1774, Madison assumed the denial of Parliament's authority as the "orthodox" position.

The precipice from which Bland drew back was the implications of denying the authority of Parliament. A veteran constitutionalist, Bland would have perceived that the denial of *any* authority of Parliament threatened the breakdown of what he called in the *Inquiry,* "the compact" between Great Britain and the colonies. Without this compact, his legalistic mind could view beyond the precipice only chaos. That was as of 1766, when his position had advanced from the Colony's rights in a controversy over a governor's fees to the concept of the colonies' liberties under the threat of Parliament-imposed taxation. But in 1766, before the Declaratory Act, Parliament's authority had not then become the test in all the issues between the colonies and Great Britain.

In writing before the Stamp Act was repealed and the Declaratory Act passed, Bland had taken an extremely advanced position in subjecting to examination the *degree* of Parliament's authority. In writing that Parliament's power, or rights, could not be absolute, he anticipated the Declaratory Act's assertion of its authority which some of its members thought to be unwise. Once having asserted this authority, Parliament, with the support of the King, actually made the test where none need have existed. Thus, the Crown, in its meaning of the total British government, would no longer allow Richard Bland to continue to draw back from the precipice.

At his age, conditioned by his formative environment and his basic attachment to Great Britain, Bland, along with his contemporaries, ultimately drew back from the precipice of *change.* Having experienced the most golden years of the golden age, he could not conceive of a better order, a better world, than the society he had known. Not second to Henry or Lee or Jefferson in his commitment to the liberties of this society, Bland represented those who had to be convinced by George III that change was coming to his society in one way or another.

6

George III himself was in many ways the victim of the consequences of his character disorders on the British ministry system. The heedlessness which permitted the issue of Parliamentary authority to gain momentum was caused in part by George's delusion of being a "ruler." With this delusion, the King had the manic-depressive's typical compulsiveness, which kept him worrying at details not only to the confusion of his ministers but at the cost of any broad comprehension of the realities beneath the surface events. Then, once the equally uncomprehending leaders in Parliament had narrowed the issue to "obedience" from the colonies, George III, proud of his obstinacy, declared "the colonies must either submit or triumph." While his self-image of the beloved "Patriot King" was disturbed by the disobedience of his distant subjects, the men in the ministry — with their majority in Parliament — seemed as blind as he to the fundamental shift which was taking place.

Among the many factors involved in the shift in balance between the colonies and the mother country was the growth in the population of the thirteen colonies. Along with this physical growth there was considerable wealth, and a physical spread — as in Virginia's western lands — of individual self-sufficiency almost totally unrelated to Great Britain. Groups in Parliament were apprehensive, or even alarmed, at the rapid population growth in the vast physical expanse claimed by the colonies since 1763, and at bottom feared the continued capacity of the parent country to control the sprawling offspring. Behind all the rationalizations about Parliament's supremacy was the rarely spoken urge to maintain the growing offspring in a position of "obedience."

When obedience had been given freely it was given by a dependent, as by a child to loving parents, in respect and affection. When a child, growing into adulthood, develops interests outside his home environment and a self-sufficiency beyond his home, his obedience will still be given in respect and affection, but his parent is no longer in a position to demand obedience. The British government was *demand-*

ing obedience from the no longer dependent offspring, and accompany-
ing the demand with actions which lost the respect of those who
wanted to continue the affections. This came in a period of growth and
change when large segments of the colonial population — as in the
Virginia areas west of Tidewater — had already lost the affection.
Yet, for the British Parliament to have perceived that it was trying by
legislation to halt organic change would be asking a lot of any group
of politicians.

The shift in the balance of relative strength, inherent with the
colonials' growing sense of their capacity to maintain themselves on
their own, limited the future of the existing relationship between the
new people on the American continent and the nation on the little
island. In the inevitable drift to change, neither Great Britain nor the
colonies could draw back from Bland's precipice. For his concession to
the supremacy of Parliament ''in degree,'' but ''not absolute,'' could
not have been established as a permanent solution. Either Parliament
was supreme or it was not. But with a comprehension of the inevi-
tableness of change in the nature of the compact, the governing body
of the presumably mature parent country could have found a solution
in the shifting balance of the relationship without forcing the issue
over authority in that atmosphere of tension on both sides of the
Atlantic.

However, Grafton's successor as chief minister in 1770, Lord
North, was required to maintain the commitment to Parliamentary
supremacy as exercised through its right of taxation. Within this by
now established government policy, North wanted to be conciliatory to
the colonies and, as Botetourt had promised, had no intention of
adding any taxation to the tax on tea. This tax was all that remained
after the repeal of the other Townshend duties, which North had
regarded as ''ridiculous'' and ''uncommercial.''

Thirty-eight years old in 1770, and a boyhood friend of the
King's, Lord North was amiable and held a sound, if not brilliant,
record in financial offices. Without a personal fortune, North, while
permitting friends to make money from their offices, seemed content to
subsist off government posts, with debts which at intervals the King
paid off. His policy toward the colonies, expressive of the man, was
more tactical than strategic. Without examining the fundamentals
involved or ultimate objectives, North tried to avoid any action that

would deepen the solidarity between the colonies and sought means of breaking their present united front. Drawing back from the precipice as sharply as the Blands, he was really playing for time — for tempers to cool and issues to subside, and for practical considerations to weaken the patriotism among the more rampant colonials.

In this limited objective, North succeeded well for two years. In Virginia, and everywhere except what had become the danger spot of Boston, a lull quieted tensions until 1772. Then came an "incident" over which North had no control.

7

In Rhode Island, their profitable smuggling had operated so openly that the natives felt affronted when a British naval officer, Lieutenant Dudingston, began using his ship the *Gaspee* to run down smugglers. One night in March, 1772, the *Gaspee* ran aground after one of its chases, and while Dudingston was waiting for high tide at midnight to put his ship afloat, a party from Providence boarded the helpless vessel. Dudingston was shot and turned loose in an open boat, and the *Gaspee* was burned.

This was civil disobedience on a scale of outlawry. The North ministry, which for two years had been diligently turning the attention of Parliament to any subject except the American colonies, could not ignore it. The home government sent a commission of inquiry to Rhode Island to investigate the "atrocious offense." With a blind disregard for its effect on the other twelve colonies, the government empowered the commission to hold suspects for trial in England. This was the precise point on which a circular letter from the Massachusetts House of Representatives had gained strong support from the other colonies in 1769, and one of the three items in those resolves of the House of Burgesses which had forced Botetourt to dissolve the General Assembly.

In the March following the burning of the *Gaspee,* while the Court of Inquiry was sitting in Rhode Island, Virginia's House of Burgesses made a profoundly significant change of strategy. No committees were formed to address petitions to England or to the Crown's representative in the Colony on the subject of accused persons to be transported "to places beyond the seas to be tried." When the House was resolved into a committee of the whole, Dabney Carr, Jefferson's brother-in-law and friend, proposed the formation of a Committee of Correspondence, to be made up of eleven Burgesses, to open "communication with our sister colonies."

Beginning specifically with an investigation of the Rhode Island Court of Inquiry, the Committee of Correspondence had as its full objective an exchange of intelligence on all acts in the British Parliament which related to the colonies and an exchange of the sentiments in the separate colonies. For its passage in the House, the ground had been carefully laid by night meetings of the young revolutionaries in Raleigh Tavern. Thomas Jefferson and his former classmate Dabney Carr, Patrick Henry, Richard Henry Lee and Francis Lightfoot Lee were the nucleus of the group who drafted the resolution for the Committee of Correspondence, as a step toward unity of action among the colonies. Jefferson had been asked to introduce the resolution in the House but, disliking public speaking, he gave the honor to his sister's husband as a means for Dabney Carr to make his public debut in the General Assembly.

Although Jefferson and his political allies felt that their seniors might need some prodding to move from a unity of protest to a unity of intercolony action, the proposals were quickly accepted in the House acting as committee of the whole and then unanimously adopted. As temperamentally resistant to change as were Richard Bland and his fellow conservatives, they had also grown convinced of the futility of further protests. If the initiative had then passed to the younger men, the seniors showed willingness to make common cause in the protection of their liberties by whatever methods seemed necessary.

The support of the Committee of Correspondence introduced a solidarity of action in the thirteen colonies of exactly the nature which Lord North had sought to prevent. However, he still misread the deadly seriousness of the unity reflected in the Committee of Correspondence and believed the newly formed solidarity could be broken. Partly from this motive and partly to save the East India Company — which was taking enormous losses due to the boycott on taxed tea and the open smuggling — Lord North came up with one of those expedients which showed a kind of genius in missing the heart of the matter.

North's double-purposed plan of 1773 was to make it possible for the East India Company to unload its warehouses of accumulated tea and at the same time undermine the patriotism of a people to whom tea was a necessity in their diet and in their daily rituals. The East India Company was given a large loan and concessions by which, eliminating the middleman, it could sell its tea directly into the colonies at a price so low, including the tax of threepence per pound, as to undersell the smugglers. British merchants trading to the colonies, especially in the North, guaranteed safe delivery of the tea.

The double-purposed plan caused a double-barreled reaction. Unrelated to taxes or the principles of taxation, the proposed price of tea threatened with ruin the smuggling industry flourishing out of New York, Philadelphia, and Rhode Island, as well as threatening the profits of American merchants engaged in tea-selling. Then, as the tax did continue, the radicals seized upon that as the principle on which Lord North proposed to deprive them of their liberties. Both radicals and merchants predicted that the monopoly given the East India Company on tea was the first wedge in a monopolistic system designed to ruin American enterprises.

In a climate in which the radicals either believed this or induced others to believe, only an incident was required. Incidents were avoided in the chief smuggling centers because of the lack of British forces to protect either the consignees of the tea or the ships with their cargoes of tea. The ships' captains wisely avoided encounters, and the consignees made themselves as scarce as had the tax collectors during the Stamp Act crisis. In Boston, the consignees and the customs officials took refuge among the British soldiers in Castle William and the three tea-laden ships rocked under the guns of British men-of-war in the harbor. On the night of December 16, 1773, Bostonians, disguised as Indians, met no opposition when they boarded the ships and dumped the cases into the sea.

While this act of mob violence was not widely applauded in the other colonies, the destruction of property formally under the protection of British men-of-war struck the members of Parliament as no words from America ever had. The conciliators from Chatham's days had nothing to say in defense, and even Chatham, now in retirement, admitted that the act was "criminal." Lord North was dumbfounded by "fanatics" to whom he had been offering "relief instead of oppression.'' His ministry could no longer avoid the issue of authority. That issue was suddenly beyond the realm of theory. The British government either accepted rebellion or asserted its authority by force. Since the act occurred in riotous Boston, a hated trouble spot to the English, North never had any choice except to assert the government's authority by force.

He introduced into Parliament the Boston Port Bill, which closed the port city to all shipping until the East India Company had been compensated for the tea destroyed and the citizens of Boston showed an inclination to mend their ways. The bill sailed through Parliament with little opposition, and on May 11, 1774, Boston received the news that it was to be placed under economic blockade. Once again North had miscalculated the capacity for united action in the colonies.

North was right in assuming that the rioting habits of Boston were not regarded entirely with favor in other American cities, particularly Philadelphia; Benjamin Franklin, among other Philadelphians, thought Boston should pay for the tea and take its medicine. In Virginia even such strong libertarians as George Washington and Edmund Pendleton had disapproved of the Tea Party. But threatening an entire city with starvation for the action of a small mob presented a threat which went beyond Boston. Despite the apathy in some colonies toward ''mobbish'' Boston, there was a swing during the summer toward not leaving Boston, as Samuel Adams wrote in a plea for help, ''to struggle alone.''

In declaring that their plight represented a common cause, a group in Boston had proposed that the citizens of the other colonies join in an agreement neither to purchase goods from nor export commodities to Great Britain. This proposal had not been received with any enthusiasm by the colonial merchants. New York countered with a proposal for a continental congress in Philadelphia, where the whole situation could be discussed dispassionately. While the conservatives and the revolutionaries in all the colonies outside Massachusetts were maneuvering for advantage over exactly what action to take about Boston and the Port Bill, Lord North — exemplifying the home government's perverse gift in timing — passed the Coercive Acts, designed to change the government of Massachusetts.

With that, the fat was in the fire. There could be no turning back.

8

The House of Burgesses had been dissolved by Lord Dunmore when in late June its members, many of whom were still in Williamsburg, learned of the Coercive Acts directed at Massachusetts. An informal convention of the Burgesses had been scheduled for August 1, and during the summer the Committee of Correspondence became active in exchanging reactions and plans with other colonies. At home, Burgesses felt out the sentiments of their constituents. Perhaps the clearest statement of the Virginians' position was made in the resolutions of Hanover County, Patrick Henry's home county, which he then represented in the Assembly.

"Whether the people there [Boston] were warranted by justice when they destroyed the tea we know not; but this we know, that the Parliament, by their proceedings have made us and all North America parties in the dispute . . . insomuch that, if our sister colony of Massachusetts Bay is enslaved, we cannot long remain free."

When the Burgesses met on August 1, they encompassed the two general proposals for action into one: they voted to send delegates to a continental congress in Philadelphia, with instructions to propose resolutions for the end of British importations on November 1 and the end of exporting on August 10, 1775. Beyond that they suggested that this continental congress be only the first of annual meetings. The Richard Blands, who had tried to control events with measures that would fend off fundamental changes in their order, did not wince in voting to cease exporting their money crop, tobacco, on the following year.

The seven delegates chosen to go to Philadelphia just about showed the balance in the General Assembly: Peyton Randolph, Richard Bland, Benjamin Harrison, and Edmund Pendleton represented the older men, who could be considered comparatively conservative; Patrick Henry and Richard Henry Lee represented the younger revolutionaries; George Washington was the independent.

Before the meeting adjourned, a group of its members met in Peyton Randolph's broad, sprawling frame house. Since the days of the "life in thrall" era when Colonel William Byrd took tea in the small upstairs sitting room with Peyton Randolph's mother, the house had been expanded across its front, and the convention delegates gathered in an enormous oblong room on the ground floor of the new extension. Among them as a guest was Randolph's twenty-one-year-old nephew Edmund Randolph, the grandson of Byrd's hostess at tea and Sir John Randolph. Although his own father, Attorney General John Randolph, became a Tory and renounced Virginia, Edmund would serve as an aide to General George Washington and later as Attorney General of the United States.

While young Randolph was a guest at the meeting in his uncle's house, a paper of resolutions written by an absent Burgess was read to the group. Thomas Jefferson, his sense of grievances brought to a climax by the Coercive Acts, had written the pages of the resolutions to be presented to the convention in a burst of accumulated outrage. On his way to Williamsburg he had been taken ill with dysentery and had sent the unpolished draft on to Peyton Randolph.

Jefferson's resolutions, a distillation of the advanced political thought in Virginia for the preceding twenty years, bore down heavily on the recent incidents and, in intemperate and unconciliatory language, took that precipice from which his cousin Richard Bland had drawn back. He declared the legislative bodies in Virginia to be independent of Parliament.

Surprisingly for the bold and rash nature of the resolutions, "most of them," Edmund Randolph recollected, were received with "applause." "The approbation was not equal" for all the resolutions, as the Virginians were indoctrinated with the theory of external and internal taxation. From John Dickinson's *Letters of a Pennsylvania Farmer,* Randolph recalled, "we had been instructed to bow to external taxation, as resulting from our migration." Jefferson's resolutions "shook this conceded principle," and went to the source of American rights. "The young ascended with Mr. Jefferson to the source of those rights; the old required time for consideration before they could tread this lofty ground, which, if it had not been abandoned, at least had not been fully occupied, throughout America."

Jefferson himself, looking back on the paper from his mid-sixties, wrote, "If it had any merit, it was that of first taking our true ground, and that which was afterwards assumed and maintained."

Neither modest nor vainglorious, this was an accurate appraisal of the place of his resolutions in the events culminating in the Revolution. Out of all the bombast and grievances and inappropriate advice offered George III in the twenty-three pages, the ground Jefferson took was clear and simple: "The true ground on which we declare these acts [of the British home government] void is that *the British Parliament has no right to exercise its authority over us.*" (Not his italics.)

There it was out in the open: the head-on clash of the test issue over the authority of Parliament. But Jefferson did not stop with merely a declaration of independence of Parliament: he proposed the existence of the colonies and of Great Britain as separate entities, "having the same executive chief but no other necessary political connection." With the King, then, as the "mediatory power between the several states of the British Empire," Jefferson proposed in effect what eventually emerged as the British Commonwealth of Nations.

With this bold concept, Jefferson made the ultimate *logical* extension of the denial of Parliamentary authority in a continuing compact between the colonies and the mother country. Since this would require the parent country's acceptance of its offspring as a coequal, and since this was manifestly unthinkable in the British climate of 1774, Jefferson actually presented an impossible ultimatum.

There was no chance that his resolutions for the Virginia delegates would be adopted, not anywhere in the American colonies in August of 1774. However, admirers of the paper, without Jefferson's knowledge, had it published by Clement Rind of Williamsburg under the title *A Summary View of the Rights of British America. Set Forth in Some Resolutions Intended for the Inspection of the Present Delegates of the People of Virginia Now in Convention.* In the published version, which appeared also in London, the points at which the listeners might have applauded stood out clearly.

In pushing to the ultimate logical extension the doctrines of Richard Bland, Jefferson followed and expanded his cousin's use of the popular misconceptions about the libertarian history of their Saxon ancestors, and followed in vehement language his outline of the relationship between Virginians and British authority from the time of the first settlers. As was then acceptable practice in presenting their side of the argument, Jefferson somewhat glorified the self-sufficiency of the early colonists and, except for the admission that the destroyers of tea in Boston might have acted impetuously, presented the residents of all thirteen colonies as a people possessed solely of virtues. Coming up from the reigns of past kings to the reign of George III, Jefferson wrote of the ''rapid and bold succession of injuries which is likely to distinguish the present from all other periods of the American story'' when ''a series of oppressions, begun at a distinguished period, and pursued unalterably through every change of ministers, too plainly prove a deliberate, systematical plan of reducing us to slavery.''

Except for the violence of the tone and the intemperate language, especially in denouncing the Boston Port Bill and the Coercive Acts, Jefferson's general narrative of the historic grievances was familiar enough. But in his general narrative he brought to the surface the long-smoldering resentments of such exercises of the King's power as the suspending clause on all laws passed by the General Assembly. By the instructions laid upon the Governor, ''however immediate may be the call for legislative interposition, the law cannot be executed until it has twice crossed the Atlantic, by which time the evil may have spent its full force.''

The decade before, Richard Bland and Landon Carter had written of the need for emergency exceptions to the suspending clause (in the Two Penny Act), and Patrick Henry had skyrocketed into fame by denouncing the King for disallowing the emergency exception. Now Jefferson charged the King with ''inattention to the necessities of the people here'' by the whole practice of the suspending clause, in which ''his Majesty permitted our laws to lie neglected in England for years, neither affirming them by his assent, nor annulling them by his negative.''

The most fundamental of the dissatisfactions which Jefferson brought into the open was that with the commercial system itself — that which restricted American trade to Great Britain. In contrast to his hyperbolical writing in other sections, Jefferson demanded free trade in the most casual manner, as if offhandedly referring to an inevitability. Addressing himself to the King, and referring to the King's advisers, Jefferson wrote, ''But let them not think to exclude us from going to other markets, to dispose of those commodities which they cannot use, to supply those wants which they cannot supply.''

In these two points alone — the resented exercise of the King's will in their legislation and the rejection of the trade restrictions imposed by the home government — Jefferson was closer to the exacerbating fundamentals of the conflict between the loose union of colonies and the mother country than in all the points of argument about taxation.

Taxation imposed by agencies other than their own assemblies (going back to Dinwiddie's pistole fee) had gradually become the point of issue in the assertiveness against authority imposed from without, assertiveness going to such extremes in the principle of the thing that the colonists chose to pay more for tea brought in by smugglers than to submit to a tax. This was not only in Boston: by less riotous methods, the tea of the East India Company was kept off the market in ports from New York to Charleston.

Then, as successive ministries (with a variety of motives, none of which was to "enslave" the colonists) and the King accepted the principle of "the right" to tax, the quarrel over the details of the principle (as Townshend's "ridiculous" duties) obscured the basic shift in the balance between the offspring, surging with its self-sufficiency, and the parent country determined to hold the offspring in subservient dependence. George III spoke for the majority government in 1774 when he said, about Boston specifically and by implication all the colonies, "We must master them or totally leave them to themselves and treat them as aliens."

This talk of "mastering" the colonials, cutting beneath all the superficialities of the argument over the principles of taxation, represented the fundamental attitude of the British majority, just as Jefferson's resolutions went to the underlying fundamentals of the Americans' conflict with British authority. Since the failure of communications began after the French and Indian Wars, with these two irreconcilable attitudes the lack of communication had become complete. Regardless of what arguments were at issue at any moment, the point had been reached when the basic issue could not be rationally discussed.

Jefferson's seminal document, *A Summary View,* had carried the doctrines of Bland and Carter to their logical extension in demanding, in effect, that the two political bodies on either side of the Atlantic exist as coequals under the same Crown; in doing this, he still maintained his elders' purpose of retaining their connection with Great Britain. But the British ministry and the King could not accept any shift that changed the nature of the relationship from colonial dependence to partnership.

Such enlightened members of Parliament as Edmund Burke, perceiving the shift to be inevitable, strongly urged the government to consider the advantages of healthy commercial intercourse, in mutual self-interest, between the colonies and Great Britain as opposed to what advantages might accrue from an assertion of authority. The question was, Burke said, "not whether you have the right to render your people miserable; but whether it is not to your interest to make them happy." His eloquent words on the benefits of the natural affection "from kindred blood, from similar privileges, and equal protection," could not sway a majority who had come to feel that Great Britain's prestige and prosperity would be fatally damaged if the government did not use force to check the rebelliousness of a dissident minority. For to the end the North ministry could not rid itself of the delusion that a rebellious minority could be isolated and unity of colonial action could be kept to minimal effectiveness.

Of course, to give some support to the ministry's convictions, there were Tories in the colonies, especially among prosperous and influential merchants in the Northern colonies. In all the colonies, as in Virginia, there were also among the most ardent defenders of American liberties those older men, temperamentally conservative, who needed to be convinced that the status quo was gone, or going fast.

The Tory and conservative elements, however, could not muster any effective restraint, because the younger men of the revolutionary minority carried the weight of the natural shift in the balance in the relationship. They were part of the momentum of a change in the nature of the compact, whatever the nature of the change. Jefferson's *A Summary View* was implicit in the acceptance of, as well as a demand for, a change in the basic nature of the compact.

It was usual at that time to charge Parliament and the "corrupt ministries" with their grievances rather than, as Patrick Henry had done, to single out the King for blame. Jefferson laid his charges upon all three sources of grievance, and ended his paper with a most irreverent address directly to George III.

"Open your breast, Sire, to liberal and expanded thought. Let not the name of George the Third be a blot in the page of history. You are surrounded by British counselors, but remember that they are parties. You have no ministers for American affairs, because you have taken none from among us. . . . The whole art of government consists in the art of being honest. Only aim to do your duty, and mankind will give you credit where you fail. No longer persevere in sacrificing the rights of one part of the empire to the inordinate desires of another: but deal out to all equal and impartial right. Let no act be passed by one legislature which may infringe on the rights and liberties of another. This is the important post in which fortune has placed you, holding the balance of a great, if a well-poised empire. This, Sire, is the advice of your great American council, on the observation of which may perhaps depend your felicity and future fame, and the preservation of that harmony which alone can continue both to Great Britain and America the reciprocal advantages of their connection."

This was the sentiment echoed by Edmund Burke a year later.

Then, writing that the colonies had no wish to separate from the mother country, but were willing to "sacrifice everything which reason can ask to the restoration of" tranquillity, Jefferson stated that the English government must be ready to "establish union on a generous plan." This included free trade and, of course, no taxation "regulated by any power on earth but our own. The god who gave us life, gave us liberty at the same time: the hand of force may destroy, but cannot disjoin them."

His summation to the King was contained in the last "determined resolution: and that you will be pleased to interpose with that efficacy which your greatest endeavors may insure to procure redress of these our great grievances, to quiet the minds of your subjects in British America against any apprehensions of future encroachment, to establish fraternal love and harmony through the whole empire, and that that may continue to the latest ages of time, is the fervent prayer of all British America."

It would seem that the thirty-one-year-old, newly married Burgess was writing for those "ages of time" rather than for George III. He had stated to the older delegates in the Virginia convention the conditions which, he believed, were necessary for a continuation of the connection between Virginia and the mother country. He could scarcely have hoped the older gentlemen would adopt his resolutions as part of their program in the continental congress in Philadelphia. As the young Edmund Randolph wrote, "the old required time for consideration before they would tread this lofty ground." However, the impressions of Jefferson's words had been made.

9

Before the seven delegates left for Philadelphia at the end of the month, they had the opportunity to read and discuss the published version of *A Summary View*. By late August, when they were ready to climb into their carriages for the long trip by road, a revolution was already taking place in their minds — as a revolution had been gathering in the minds of men throughout the colonies. In varying degrees, the seven Virginians were being led to the acceptance of political independence, with implications that were different for each man — just as the implications were different in each colony.

Beyond the repudiation of monarchy there was the abyss from which Richard Bland drew back. For the union of protest, as symbolized by the First Continental Congress, must develop eventually into a union of constructiveness. Certainly thirteen colonies, widely differentiated in geography and economics and culture, could scarcely maintain a sound, or even safe, existence between the ocean and the wilderness merely by severing their connections with Great Britain. Emancipation from colonial status could only be a beginning. In this foreshadowed change, expectations were in the atmosphere, caused by all the writings and the talk under Locke's influence on the rights of man and natural rights. Only two years later, Thomas Jefferson would epitomize these expectations as "the pursuit of happiness."

Jefferson, continually changing in the continual development of his democratic, humanistic concepts, would in time conceive of the destruction of the class structure which produced him. The conservatives, staring into the abyss of change, were not likely to have feared a threat to their society from one of themselves; but Richard Bland was too learned in history not to have felt the presence of an unknown threat as inherent in the nature of change.

In the Northern colonies the leading spirits among the revolutionaries seemed largely to be merchants and city radicals. In Virginia the leading spirits were aristocrats. There were no city radicals, no city elements at all, and most of the large merchants (since the passing of the shipping centers of the great merchant-planters) were English and Scottish, usually representing home firms. Although there were small native merchants, some middling and a few (like the Yorktown Nelsons) of large operations, these either subscribed to or were subordinate to the planter class. The internal revolution was occurring entirely in the minds of the planters. With all their learning and mental sophistication, plantation masters were, like the English country squires, essentially rural, with the innate personal conservatism of land-rooted agricultural people. Their control of the colony-wide protests, beginning with the Stamp Act, accounted for the urbanity of the prerevolutionary movements in Virginia; it also explained in part the relative slowness of the class's leaders in the General Assembly to exchange the known for the unknown.

Not one of the leaders could hope to improve his aristocratic condition in a new order. As responsible members of the ruling class, these older men were concerned with the economic well-being of their society in the changes that had already taken place. Since the issues of paper money during the war (1755–1763) and the scarcity of currency since the Currency Act of 1764, all classes had suffered from the ill effects of inflation. Thomas Adams, of Williamsburg, wrote of "the distress of numbers of worthy people which don't know which way to turn themselves for want of money to pay their just debts."

The planters who maintained their scales of living on credit were seriously threatened by credit inflation. At the one house of Norton, the debts of Virginians on his books rose from £11,000 in 1760 to £40,000 in 1773. Jefferson estimated, during the War for Independence, that by 1775 planters owed English merchants as much as £2,000,000 sterling.

In the financial crisis concurrent with the crisis with Great Britain, the bottom fell out of the old standby of land. Since there was little money available for purchasers, the landowners could not bail themselves out by selling off tracts except at a great sacrifice. Jefferson's friend John Page, at baronial Rosewell, needed to sell land for cash, but, he wrote, "I should not expect to get near the value of it." Somehow, imperceptibly, the problems of the Virginia society since the war had become associated with the problems created by the mother country, and solutions were complex for those men long habituated to responsibility.

At the center of the known problems was the widely spread, generalized problem of the decline of the tobacco market. The source of the country's wealth since the early days at Jamestown and the foundation of the first fortunes on which the ruling class was built, tobacco was failing the planters at so great a rate that a decade later Jefferson would note, ''It is a culture productive of infinite wretchedness.'' After years of fluctuating prices — mostly down, with some recovery, and then down again — prices fell so low in 1773 that a serious depression was upon Virginia when attention became concentrated on the coming Continental Congress.

It is possible that the conservative leaders, still hoping for reconciliation, believed the tangled economic problems of the Colony could better be solved by a continuing connection with the home government. In an atmosphere of harmony, where the home government's self-interest became sufficiently enlightened to encompass the interest of the planters, many adjustments would have been possible to make a gradual shift from the manifestly unhealthy dependence on the outworn money crop of tobacco. However, instead of showing the enlightened self-interest which would have considered the very fundamental problems in Virginia's economy, the distant legislative body seemed concerned only with imposing its will. Confronted with this attitude, the leaders in the ruling class, whatever their personal inclinations, were left with no choice.

Richard Bland, as their constitutionalist, had exhausted the resources of his mind and taxed his eyes (his sight was failing) in efforts to restrain the mother country from making this intolerable imposition of will on the planters. By August, 1774, there must have been a sense of hopelessness in his purpose of protecting his familiar society *with* guarantees from the mother country of recognizing the adult status of the colonial world. Yet he had reached the ground on which, regardless of the risks, he would take no backward step that might encourage Great Britain to try to force them to yield on what had become a test of wills.

In his determination not to yield, Bland was representative of all the seven delegates who went to Philadelphia. John Adams wrote, ''These gentlemen from Virginia appear to be the most spirited and consistent of any. Harrison said he would have come on foot rather than not come. Bland said he would have gone, upon this occasion, if it had been to Jericho.''

On the way to Philadelphia, Edmund Pendleton and Patrick Henry broke the journey with a night visit at Mount Vernon, to which Washington had made a second addition the year before. The blondly handsome Pendleton and the sallow Patrick Henry, representing the conservative and the firebrand forces in the revolutionary movement — which caused them often to clash in debate — both were momentarily freed from personal problems by their northern trip. For Pendleton it was a breather from the oppressive chore of disentangling the John Robinson estate, and for Henry a respite from the grief caused by the madness of his wife, incarcerated in a basement room of the manor house which, with his success, he had acquired from the Robinson estate.

During the evening the two lawyers spent at Mount Vernon they were joined by George Mason, and the talk turned only to the stand they would make in Philadelphia. The next morning as Washington and his two guests were leaving the house, Martha Washington accompanied the gentlemen to the door. She turned earnestly to them and said, ''God be with you, gentlemen. I hope you stand firm. I know George will.''

Epilogue

Epilogue

THE PRODUCTS OF THE GOLDEN AGE

MEN WHO WERE products of Virginia's golden age began, in 1774, to assume on the continental stage the responsible roles in government for which the General Assembly had so long been a training ground. For the next half-century (exactly fifty years) these products of the golden age served as leaders successively in the War for Independence, in the formation of a new nation based on the new principles of the inalienable rights of man, and in governing the republic during its formative years. After George Washington had served two terms as President and John Adams one term, the "Virginia Dynasty" — Jefferson, Madison, and Monroe in the White House, and John Marshall as Chief Justice — governed the nation the first twenty-four years of the nineteenth century.

Jefferson, the single individual continuity from 1774 to 1824, had been born the year before the death of Colonel William Byrd II and died (in 1826) two years before the advent of Jacksonian Democracy in Washington. His life spanned the social changes from the idyllic era of life in thrall, when Virginia was the largest colony, to the state's declining position in a nation expanding westward from the original coastal colonies. The lines of a sectional schism were already drawn in the Missouri Compromise (1820), which allied the oldest colony with the numerically inferior new region where Jefferson's outlook of enlightened liberalism would be replaced with the defensive thinking associated with protecting an archaic institution.

Virginia would produce other Presidents: Benjamin Harrison's son, William Henry Harrison, born at Berkeley, although elected from Ohio; John Tyler, born near Berkeley in Charles City County, who succeeded to the Presidency on Harrison's death; and Zachary Taylor, born in Orange County, adjoining Jefferson's Albemarle and near the home of James Madison, although he was elected as a military hero rather than as a Virginian. None of these three Presidents, while born in Virginia, could be remotely associated with the golden age which produced the generation that died with the Virginia Dynasty.

While that half-century, which began with the First Continental Congress in 1774, was an era of glory for the Virginians who were the *products* of the golden age, the age itself — of an aristocratic ruling class advancing those best qualified to govern through Virginia's General Assembly — in one sense had been gradually passing for twenty years before 1774. In one sense, the golden age had begun its wane when the external involvements brought on by the French and Indian Wars exposed the weaknesses inherent in a system that permitted Inheritors to live on the false assumption that their class could exist in perpetuity without the adaptiveness with which their ancestors had built the estates.

The fortunes had been founded by money-minded, broadly based, resourceful entrepreneurs who did far more than plant and ship tobacco. Inheritors who depended chiefly on tobacco shipments to meet expenses, in a system where prices were determined by the buyers and the prices of imported commodities were determined by the sellers, needed large amounts of rich land for tobacco and a combination of advanced agricultural methods and businesslike trading such as Landon Carter constantly employed. The market had to be good for even the most practical-minded, systematic planters to hold their own when they got the short end both in selling their product and in buying their necessities. The majority of the conspicuous consumers made the temporary solution of going into debt, mostly without a John Robinson estate to pull them through their crises. This way was, of course, limited in time.

In bad years, as in 1774, the very big planters could ship less tobacco and grow more wheat. A shift from tobacco to wheat would have offered some solution to planters of all sizes, but they were usually magnetized by tobacco. Other crops did not have the aura of quick riches which were still associated with tobacco; they were more mundane, less of a gamble. Then, the planters with large slaveholdings were committed to the use of this labor force in the money crop of tobacco.

Landon Carter's nephew, Robert Carter of Nomini Hall, was a special case in that he had heavily invested in the Baltimore Iron Works. However, his course following the 1773 depression illustrated the whole problem of changing the system based on the money crop of tobacco. When the market made it unprofitable to ship tobacco, Robert Carter could afford to curtail his production and derive his income from industry rather than planting. Once he stopped growing tobacco in volume, he found the presence of five hundred slaves an embarrassment. To avoid the disruption to them and to the farming community of turning loose five hundred freed Negroes in the county, he started an emancipation plan of releasing thirty a year and trying to set some of those up on land either owned or rented.

As it worked out, the plan seemed to disrupt some of the freed Negroes anyway. They in turn made neighborhood slaves restless and rebellious, and the white families began to protest bitterly against freed Negroes being released in the neighborhood. Since these families could not afford to free their own Negroes, as could King Carter's grandson, and this was some years before new plantations in the Deep South created a market for Virginia slaves, Robert Carter's eighteenth-century experiment in emancipation came to an end which made more insoluble the complexities besetting the plantations built upon a fading one-money-crop operation.

As of 1774 the eastern sections of the Colony were approaching something of the plight of a mining community whose ore was petering out. When the Revolution totally ruined the tobacco trade, planters were forced to turn to the less glamorous wheat. Though new great fortunes were not made, some establishments were maintained by selling wheat to the flour manufacturing industry that began to flourish with no mother country to forbid manufacturing. This meant the end of the great plantations, the disbursement of the large labor forces and, in brief, the collapse of the structure which had supported the ruling class in the golden age. Tobacco was still grown, but mostly south of the James River and mostly by "farmers" or planters modest in comparison to the grandees of the mid-eighteenth century.

To whatever extent the conservatives might have feared the economic effect of the break with England, the severance under war conditions — with British men-of-war preventing Virginia from shipping — brought to a dramatic end the tobacco-based culture out of which the golden age had flowered. Limited in time and space (as the Tidewater lands became exhausted by tobacco), the society built upon the tobacco-growing plantations would have passed gradually even without the Revolution. In either case, as a hereditary aristocracy capable of continuously producing "those best qualified to govern," the golden age had been on the wane for twenty years.

What the Revolution did in bringing the age to a sudden end, without twilight, was to provide the opportunity for the finest products of the age to flourish for another half a century in another climate, of new and changed conditions. However, for all the glory of those Virginians in the new nation, they and their climate were as remote from the golden age as was Jacksonian Democracy, which followed Jefferson, from the practices of government which produced Jefferson.

It would be idle to speculate upon the changes in the system that might have been introduced under harmonious relations with Great Britain, with its government actuated (as the Virginia conservatives had so devoutly prayed) by an enlightened self-interest which included the interest of Virginians. The fact was that concurrent with the fiscal problems brought by the French and Indian Wars, the attention of the educated, responsible members of the ruling class was diverted to struggles with the mother country over areas of self-rule; and in those struggles many of the weaknesses in their economic system became entangled with and obscured by political issues. The result was that concentration on the political crises of the present prevented any objective study of the economic future of their society.

Landon Carter was an unheeded Cassandra in lamenting the irresponsible and frivolous acceptance of privilege in the younger generations. The thoughtless were too conditioned to the appearance of stability in the plantation world which would last forever, and the thoughtful men were too absorbed in the climactic conflict with Great

Britain. Thus, while the unthinking Inheritors brought to the top of the society a splendor and style and a fox-hunting, party-giving pattern of pleasure that duplicated the English country-gentry during the decline of the golden age, the responsible leaders neglected the future of their society to bring to the united colonial effort their genius for politics — the real fruit of the golden age, of which the social gallantries were the trappings.

In time, the elegance and the magnificence of the few who briefly played the peacock while their age was waning would give color to the era. And, although their assumption of hereditary wealth was an illusion, and their descendants were forced to find means of earning money, some quality of the aristocratic attitude did persist across time and the mutations of fortune, and was diffused in the character of the society with many sociological effects. Yet, in 1774, the hardworking and hard-pressed farmers who constituted the vast majority of the Colony's population looked to the leadership of the men who were bringing to Virginia and the colonies the true genius of the civilization which characterized the golden age.

2

Virginia's representation in the First Continental Congress of 1774 marked the beginning of the end of the Colony's government as it had existed since 1619. In Virginia the Convention, composed of former members of the General Assembly, met at intervals and gradually assumed the legislative functions of government. Lord Dunmore, totally estranged from the people, went his own way in the Palace until the spring of 1775. Then, during the night of April 20, he seized the gunpowder stored in the Powder Magazine and had it placed on a schooner in the James River. Sending his family to safety on a British man-of-war, the Governor barricaded himself in the Palace.

In the previous month, during a meeting of the Convention in St. John's Church in Richmond, Patrick Henry had delivered his famous "Give me liberty or give me death" speech on the subject of arming for defense. Nobody in the Convention had taken any stand against "liberty," and discussion on the issue of arming for defense was —

like the debate on the Stamp Act resolutions — simply a difference over tactics. Whether Henry's impassioned eloquence or the size of his popular following, or both, won the vote, the Convention decided to expand the militia and change its status to that of volunteer regular companies.

Dunmore's seizure of Virginia's main supply of gunpowder presented a real problem to the arming of troops in a Colony without facilities for making gunpowder. As with other threatening actions of the British government, the serious loss of their gunpowder infuriated rather than alarmed the Virginians. Patrick Henry, whose ambitions had suddenly veered toward military glory, led a Hanover County company to Williamsburg. Dunmore sent out some money as compensation for the Colony's powder and bloodshed was averted then. But, if there was a point from which there was no turning back in Virginia, the estranged governor precipitated it here. His seizure of the gunpowder followed by one day the armed clashes at Lexington and Concord, and by the time the news of those skirmishes reached Virginia, Dunmore joined his family on the British warship.

To provide subsistence for the crew, Dunmore started pillaging plantations on the south bank of the James in the Norfolk area, and sent out warnings that unless the Virginia troops ceased gathering at Williamsburg he would free the Negroes. He also warned the magistrates and others supposedly loyal to the Crown that unless they came to his assistance, ''I shall consider the whole country in an actual state of rebellion, and myself at liberty to annoy it by every possible means, and that I shall not hesitate at reducing their houses to ashes, and spreading devastation wherever I can reach.''

On board the warship on which Dunmore took refuge was Captain Thomas Taylor Byrd, son of Colonel William Byrd III. Captain Byrd remained in the British Army throughout the Revolution, although he never fought against Americans, and after the war he returned to Virginia and took up residence in the Shenandoah Valley. His brother, Otway Byrd, served in the Continental Army on the staff of General Charles Lee. So strong were the English loyalties of Colonel Byrd that he disinherited Otway. Then, disillusioned by Dunmore and bewildered by independence, in combination with despairing of his debts, the third William Byrd shot himself in the temple with a dueling pistol on New Year's Day, 1777.

(Byrd's widow lived on in Westover until 1814, when the beautiful house was sold and the money distributed among the children — except the disinherited Otway. He followed the course of his Harrison neighbor and settled in Ohio, on a 6,000-acre government grant.)

With Virginia's fugitive Governor actually an enemy of his supposed subjects, the Convention struggled futilely at reaching any decisive action until August. Then the members were joined by the delegates returning from the Second Continental Congress at Philadelphia. Then the Convention decided to elect an eleven-man Committee of Safety to act as the governing body of Virginia.

On this Committee went two of the conservatives who had gone to Philadelphia among the original seven delegates — Richard Bland and Edmund Pendleton. Bland, after serving two sessions with the Continental Congress, felt that he had grown too old for the stresses of service away from home. Stooped and bent and nearly blind, the revered Bland was still valuable for advisory work in the slower-paced familiar surroundings that made fewer physical demands on him. Edmund Pendleton was in ill health on returning to Virginia, and also begged off from serving in Philadelphia. However, in accepting the heavy work of chairman of the governing Committee of Safety, this self-contained man, with his fine intelligence and pleasing appearance, emerged as the new leader of the conservative revolutionary forces in Virginia.

Patrick Henry, with new ambitions for glory in the field, also stayed in Virginia, and his followers secured his election (over that of men qualified for military leadership) to command of the two regiments forming at Williamsburg. By this choice, Henry was not on the Committee of Safety.

Thomas Jefferson, who had then become a delegate at Philadelphia, was also eliminated from service, along with George Wythe, another replacement. Benjamin Harrison and Richard Henry Lee returned to Philadelphia, where Peyton Randolph dropped dead of apoplexy in October. George Washington was away in Boston commanding troops. Yet, despite the absence of these conservative stalwarts and revolutionary leaders, such was the quality of leadership produced in the General Assembly that the Committee of Safety performed without a lapse in assurance and aristocratic control the functions of governing the Colony during the upheavals when Lord

Dunmore brought war to Virginia before the colonies declared their independence.

The Committee was essentially conservative, although Richard Bland, wearing an eyeshade to keep the light out of his ruined eyes, was the only old man, at sixty-five. Edmund Pendleton was in the fullness of his powers at fifty-four and, except for fifty-year-old George Mason, the others were in their forties or thirties. The youngest, thirty-two, was Jefferson's friend John Page of Rosewell, who was rising steadily into prominence in Virginia politics. Three of the members were Councilors: Page, Thomas Ludwell Lee, and Dudley Digges, whose father had also been a Councilor. Carter Braxton was the son and grandson of former Council presidents George Braxton and King Carter; he would resign to serve in the Continental Congress and become a signer of the Declaration of Independence. All the men on the Committee were persons of substance, several of immense wealth, and they were as restrained as they were responsible in exercising greater power than had ever been wielded by a governor.

The Committee's immediate problem in the fall of 1775 was to meet what amounted to Dunmore's war on Virginia. His pillagings and threats reached a climax with a proclamation of martial law on November 7. Every person capable of bearing arms was ordered "to report to his Majesty's standard" or be branded a traitor, liable to such penalties as "forfeiture of life, confiscation of lands, etc." Freedom was promised to all slaves who would join "his Majesty's troops" in "reducing this Colony to a proper sense of duty to his Majesty's crown and dignity."

When several hundred Negroes fled from the plantations to join Dunmore's force of British regulars, the citizens began leaving Norfolk and the surrounding areas in droves. Most of the prominent citizens who remained in the city were Tory merchants, loyal to Dunmore. The military purpose of the Committee was simple: to force Dunmore to evacuate the base of the port city. The execution required some political courage.

Patrick Henry, in titular command of the Virginia forces, was in actual command of the First Virginia Regiment. Colonel William Woodford, a man of military experience and demonstrated leadership in the field, commanded the Second Virginia Regiment. Edmund Pendleton, as chairman of the Committee of Safety, ordered Woodford with his regiment to the Norfolk area, and ordered Henry to remain with his regiment at Williamsburg. Pendleton also ordered Colonel Woodford to communicate directly with him. Henry was enraged at being passed over for the post of honor, and his followers, then and for years afterward, accused Pendleton of playing politics to deprive a rival of his chance at glory.

The decision had, in point of fact, been made by the whole Committee, whose opinion of Henry's unfitness for field command was shared by George Washington. Woodford soundly vindicated their choice of him. At Great Bridge, an approach to Norfolk from the south, his companies of native-born volunteers defeated the British regulars and their Negro allies in open battle. Forced to evacuate Norfolk, Dunmore abandoned his Negro recruits, left the Tories to the mercies of the patriots, and fired shells from a warship into the city until the buildings caught fire. From then on, the last occupant of the Governor's Palace was no more than a peripheral nuisance.

Woodford's vindication of the Committee's choice, of course, did not mollify Henry's followers, who might have forgiven Pendleton if Woodford had been defeated. As it was, this split in Virginia politics presaged the end of the golden age's aristocratic order when a ruling class, by comprehending the implications of power, consistently advanced those best qualified to govern. Whether or not Patrick Henry had become a demagogue, as some called him, he exerted a new kind of popular appeal, and he had used this appeal to advance himself to a position of military power for which even his grandson said he was not qualified.

3

On May 6, 1776, delegates from all the Virginia counties assembled, in a Williamsburg abandoned by all British authority, to discuss the critical question of the Colony's independence from Great Britain. Old Richard Bland placed in nomination for the presidency of the Convention the name of Edmund Pendleton, now the leader among the successors of the oligarchy whose leader in its heyday had been John Robinson. The mellow Pendleton was elected and, under his hand, the meetings proceeded smoothly.

With the moment at last at hand, the slower-moving conservatives revealed that they had caught up with the revolutionaries and it was obvious that the humor of the Convention was to pass a motion for independence. Patrick Henry, sobered by responsibilities, was not the headlong firebrand of other gatherings. During the weeks immediately preceding the Convention, Henry had turned cautious about a break before foreign allies were secured. Richard Henry Lee had written him prodding letters from Philadelphia in which he argued that a declaration of independence was necessary before French assistance could be obtained. When, during the first days of the meeting, Henry committed himself to independence, he said he felt it would be inappropriate to stir people with his "eloquence." The fact was that there was no need for anybody's impassioned oratory.

Within a week, three resolutions had been prepared for presentation to the Convention on May 14. Colonel Meriwether ("Fiddlehead") Smith proposed the dissolution of the present ties with the Crown, the appointment of a committee to prepare a Declaration of Rights, and a plan of government to "secure substantial and equal liberty to the people." It was not a very bold proposition, considering the temper of Virginians after Dunmore's marauding "war," and perhaps it was intended to leave the future open to negotiations. Colonel Smith lived in Essex County, across from Landon Carter's holdings on the broad Rappahannock, which could serve as an inland highway to British warships, and his resolution doubtless represented a trace of caution in some of the families (not Landon Carter) living in the exposed Tidewater areas.

Edmund Pendleton's resolution held more finality in declaring the former union "totally dissolved" and discharging Virginians from any allegiance to the Crown. His resolution differed from Smith's mainly in the shadings in which Pendleton did not leave the door open for future negotiations.

Patrick Henry's resolution went beyond those two in proposing "a full Declaration of Independency" for "the united colonies." Not limiting his resolution to Virginia's independence, he proposed that their delegates in the Congress at Philadelphia "be enjoined . . . to exert their ability in procuring an immediate, clear, and full declaration of Independency."

The Convention's debate on the three resolutions was neither long nor heated. Except for the highly regarded Robert Carter Nicholas, who still clung to reservations about independence at all, the drift of the Convention went rapidly toward sending some sort of instructions to their delegates to declare for independence of the united colonies. This was a manifestly practical course, in that Virginia would not stand alone as an independent colony.

The bland Pendleton experienced no difficulty in drafting a compromise resolution which, winning over the last-ditch Nicholas, pleased everyone and was unanimously adopted. Pendleton's compromise was to instruct their delegates in Philadelphia "to propose" to the Congress "to declare the United Colonies free and independent states, absolved from all allegiance to, or dependence upon, the crown or parliament of Great Britain."

By this instruction, May 15, 1776, to its delegates *to propose* a declaration of independence, Pendleton went as far as the conservatives would accept and, at the same time, by placing the burden of decision on the Continental Congress, assured Virginians of being part of a united movement.

However, long before Virginia's delegates made that proposal in Congress on June 7 and before Jefferson started writing the Declaration on June 11, the Virginians considered themselves freed from Great Britain. The British flag was hauled down in Williamsburg, where the House of Burgesses had passed out of existence on May 6. By May 27 George Mason presented the Declaration of Rights, which was adopted June 12 as the epochal Virginia Bill of Rights. "All power is vested in, and consequently derived from, the people," and "government is, or ought to be, instituted for the common benefit, protection and security of the people." By June 29 the written constitution of the independent Commonwealth of Virginia was adopted, and the next day Patrick Henry was elected governor.

Thus it was not the revolutionaries, later so often praised at the expense of the "conservatives," who alone led England's first colony to be the first to declare for independence and, while the Continental Congress was debating the Declaration, to become the first independent commonwealth on the North American continent. Nor were the famed revolutionaries the leaders when Virginia became the first to embrace those universal principles in Mason's Bill of Rights, which were adopted in Jefferson's Declaration of Independence.

George Mason himself, Washington's political adviser, so hated public life that he refused to serve in Philadelphia, served only irregularly even on the Committee, and was the most politically detached of all the Virginians who contributed to the development of broadly applicable principles. From his draft of the nonimportation resolutions which Washington presented to the Burgesses to his membership on the Federal Constitutional Convention in 1787 (after which he refused to sign the Constitution because, with other items he disliked, it failed to prohibit the importation of slaves after a given date), Mason continuously gave of his knowledge of libertarian governmental theory; but when chosen as Virginia's first United States Senator, he refused to serve. Yet Mason's authorship of the Virginia Bill of Rights won him recognition in the galaxy of the revolutionaries, although he was never politically allied with them.

Richard Bland and Landon Carter, who had begun the examination into the nature of the compact when they entered the first protests against threats to their rights more than twenty years before these examinations and protests culminated in the Declaration, had become old men from another age by the time Virginia became an independent commonwealth.

James Madison, who made his first political appearance in the convention which established Virginia as a free commonwealth, had been one year old when Richard Bland was aroused by Dinwiddie's pistole fee, and John Marshall, one of the minutemen who fought against Dunmore, had not been born.

Considering the lags in communications, the leaders in the ruling class had changed very rapidly. Richard Bland and Landon Carter had grown up in the high noon of the golden age and each was past forty before Dinwiddie cast the first small shadow on the era of life in thrall epitomized by William Byrd. An old man at sixty-six, Bland had supported the Convention's move toward a declaration of independence along with Patrick Henry.

"Moderate," the term Henry used denigratively of Edmund Pendleton, would be more apt for the Peyton Randolph–Richard Bland group of senior leaders than would "conservative," with its implications of inertia, of immovability. They moved continuously, but with moderation. Perhaps they never moved as fast as Jefferson desired, but having prepared the ground on which Jefferson took his position — having created the atmosphere in which he flourished — they moved as a group more rapidly than any group from any other colony. And, unlike the groups of many colonies, all of them were men of position and estate, which they risked by their actions.

Most of all, what they lost for a certainty was the political structure of the golden age. If the controversies with Dinwiddie during the preliminary actions which led into the French and Indian Wars marked the beginning of the decline of the golden age, its end could be said to have come on May 6, 1776, when the House of Burgesses quietly ceased its hundred and sixty-seven years of legislation.

During the latter half of its existence, the Burgesses became the political body which expressed the will of the ruling class. As a political body it was not entirely noble: much time was wasted on petty local concerns and in profitless wrangling, favoritism was practiced, and the individual members were inclined to look after their own kind. But in the larger issues the House was characterized by responsible and usually enlightened legislation, and unquestionably — in meeting the definition of an aristocracy — it advanced those best qualified to govern. In doing this, Virginia's General Assembly produced those rarities in government, men of ideas as men of action. From the pistole fee controversy to the proposal for independence, ideas came before action, and action implemented *matured* ideas.

Every delegate to the Continental Congress went to Philadelphia with ideas formed in the House of Burgesses and, except for a few Councilors, former Burgesses were the leaders in the Committee of Safety which sagely governed Virginia in its dislocations and nebulous status during Dunmore's "war."

Then, suddenly, the political world that had been centered in the House of Burgesses was gone, the aristocratic rule belonging abruptly in the past.

In the constitution of the new Commonwealth of Virginia, the Governor's base of political power was in the House of Delegates, composed of two representatives from each county. With Henry as Governor, popular representation gave him a following from which he built an organization that replaced the defunct oligarchy.

Of the late John Robinson's core of powers, a year after Peyton Randolph's death in Philadelphia, Richard Bland collapsed on a Williamsburg street in October, 1776. Taken into the house of a friend, he died two hours later. Already a figure of another age, Bland's immeasurable services in preparing the way for a new age — which he had never really wanted — were then obscured by the personalities who dominated the great events of the day.

Of the two comparatively younger survivors of the old oligarchy, both fifty-one, Benjamin Harrison was in Philadelphia and Edmund Pendleton had turned to the judiciary: he became the senior judge ("first judge") of the High Court of Chancery and, after the formation of the republic, the presiding judge of the Virginia Court of Appeals. Harrison, a signer of the Declaration of Independence, later became the Governor of Virginia and drifted toward the sentiment of Patrick Henry in opposing Virginia's ratification of the Constitution. George Wythe, who had represented Fauquier's views in the House during the era when the age still seemed golden, after signing the Declaration of Independence joined Pendleton on the High Court of Chancery.

As Patrick Henry had demonstrated when he promoted himself for military command, in the popular following he enjoyed at the head of his political organization there was little left of the aristocratic principle of advancing those best qualified to govern. This was not so much because Henry's followers usurped political power as because of the decline of political power in the ruling class.

The prophecies of Landon Carter about the frivolous-minded spendthrifts among the Inheritors were being borne out. Compared to the society that had existed for the seventy-five years of the golden age, there were fewer men in the aristocracy who could be considered those best qualified to govern. Many, softened by luxury and addicted to pleasure, lacked both the necessary sense of community responsibility and the ambition for political power. Then, the rapid decline of the system of the great plantations removed from many the bases of wealth which had permitted successive generations during the golden age to divert the main currents of their energy and mental interests into government.

Benjamin Harrison V, though a conscientious manager of his inherited estate, had devoted so much of his time to the House of Burgesses, particularly to political crises, during the bad tobacco markets, that by 1770 he was forced to borrow small sums of cash from his nephew, Robert Carter of Nomini Hall. (Carter's industrial interests permitted him to lend cash to other men in government, such as Peyton Randolph and William Byrd III.) With his resources already strained, when simultaneously with his long absences in Philadelphia the bottom dropped out of the tobacco market, Harrison's estate declined to the extent that he could not provide for his younger sons.

The best Benjamin Harrison could do for William Henry was to solicit from his friend George Washington a modest military appointment in the wilds of Ohio: there the scion of Tidewater grandees, in tune with the Jacksonian Democracy of his maturity, invented the log-cabin birthplace as a sentimental appeal for a Presidential candidate. Nothing could illustrate more clearly the passing of the aristocratic order than the moment when the son of a stalwart of the old oligarchy that had dominated the golden age was elected President on the myth of humble birth.

William Henry Harrison came back to write his inaugural address in the room that had been his mother's bedroom. The adopted Westerner probably was untroubled by the ghosts of the elegant ladies and gentlemen who had strolled the terraces sloping, below his window, to the tidal river. Having been born in 1773, Harrison knew as his earliest memories the plantation with his father absent in Philadelphia under the stringencies of a war which halted shipping at its wharves and tobacco-growing in its fields, and then the flight when British soldiers under Benedict Arnold occupied the grounds and practiced target-shooting on the Berkeley cattle. Thus, although born in the mansion built by his grandfather, King Carter's son-in-law, Benjamin Harrison's son would have no memories of the golden age in which his father was a powerful figure. Through William Henry Harrison, the President-elect of the United States, could be seen the completeness with which the age had ended.

An afterglow colored Virginians' minds for generations to come, during which the legends of the plantations grew and became part of the national heritage — as legends. The real achievements of the plantation society, however, would never fit too comfortably into the traditions of American democracy, because its aristocratic principle — which cultivated for governing the best qualified citizens the civilization could produce — was based most solidly on inequality.

On the premise that some men were superior to others, the Virginia ruling class, by principle and by practice, devoted itself to advancing its superior men to positions of responsibility. And one of the supreme products of this principle and practice, Thomas Jefferson, demonstrated his superiority with a mind which, formed in Virginia's golden age, grew in its vision to belong to the seminal ages of mankind. But his opportunities to develop his mind and use its developments in responsible politics were provided by the plantation society, which was so much more and so much less than the legends.

Virginia's white population, during the age when it was producing this startling array of leaders, did not exceed two hundred thousand, the size of a small city. Ultimately, its golden age should be measured by the fruit of its civilization: it produced more great men in government than any other society in a comparable period and a comparable space.

Acknowledgments, Bibliography
and Index

Acknowledgments

In the research on this book, I am particularly grateful to Mr. Francis L. Berkeley, archivist of the University of Virginia Library and currently executive assistant to the president of the university. Beyond generously making available to me the Carter letters which he had personally collected and deposited in the Library, Mr. Berkeley continuously offered collaborative details from his own background in the period. He thoughtfully mailed photocopies of various items, and provided encouragement and guidance in the practical aspects of gathering and collating research material. I am also indebted, for supportive guidance and very real help in the practical aspects of the work itself, to Dr. Edgar F. Shannon, president of the University of Virginia; to the Honorable Colgate W. Darden, Jr.; to Congressman David E. Satterfield III; to Dr. George Modlin, president of the University of Richmond; to Mr. John M. Jennings, director of the Virginia Historical Society; and to the late Colonel W. H. K. Fitzroy, director of the Virginia Area University Center. I wish gratefully to acknowledge the financial assistance provided by a Senior Fellowship awarded by the National Foundation of the Arts and Humanities.

In working at the Alderman Library, I cannot sufficiently thank Mr. Edmund Berkeley, Jr., for his continually thoughtful cooperativeness in making available to me photocopies of documents. For this kindness I also wish to thank Mr. Stocking and members of the staff.

For work at the Virginia Historical Society, I am grateful to Mr. William M. E. Rachal, and to Mr. Howson Cole, curator of manuscripts, who deserves incomparably more than an acknowledgment for his untiring patience in producing documents from the Society's illimitable storehouse and recommending documents out of his encyclopedic knowledge of the material available. I am also grateful to Mr. John M. Jennings, the director, for his unfailing supportiveness on this book and many before; to Mr. James A. Fleming, curator of printed books; and to Mr. Virginius Cornick Hall, curator of rare books. For work at and through the Virginia State Library, I owe the deepest gratitude to Mr. Milton Russell, who through many years, and especially on this book, gave unstintingly of his time and background in guidance on research material, and who generously performed innumerable acts of thoughtfulness in getting material into my hands. I am also grateful, for continually courteous cooperativeness, to members of the staff: Miss Eudora Elizabeth Thomas, Mrs. Margaret N. Causby, Mrs. William A. Jarrell, Mrs. Lois J. Fields, Mrs. Francis B. Richmond, and Miss Carolyn De Camps.

I am warmly grateful to Mr. McDonald Wellford, of Richmond, for his sustained encouragement, for the sharing of his family lore, and for his practical help, including a research trip to Sabine Hall, the home of Landon Carter, Mr. Wellford's ancestor, and now owned by Mr. Wellford's kinsmen. Mr. Carter Wellford generously gave me copies of unpublished Landon Carter letters. I wish to thank Miss Margaret Cook, curator of manuscripts at the Earl Gregg Swemm Library of the College of William and Mary; Dr. Edward Riley, head of the Research Department of Colonial Williamsburg; and Mr. Duncan Cocke and Mr. J. Randolph Ruffin, of Colonial Williamsburg, for their friendly assistance in facilitating research work in Williamsburg. I wish to thank Mr. Malcolm Jamieson, of Berkeley plantation, for his kindness in continuously making available to me material on the Harrisons and their seat at Berkeley, and for his generous hospitality across the years. I wish to thank Dr. Robert M. Calhoun, of the University of North Carolina at Greensboro, for guidance on background reading on Thomas Jefferson.

I would like to express a personal acknowledgment of gratitude to Mr. Robert Rawls, of Richmond; Dr. Edward Peple, dean of the University of Richmond Graduate School; and Mr. Joseph Heistand, rector of St. Paul's Episcopal Church.

I am deeply grateful to Miss Carolyn De Camps, formerly with the Virginia State Library, for her tireless assistance in research for the book (with particular helpfulness in making available the physical materials of research), and for her steadfast work on the manuscript.

C.D.

Selected Bibliography

Two main sources, the *Virginia Magazine of History and Biography* and the *William and Mary Quarterly,* are listed here as *VMHB* and *WMQ.*

Principal Unpublished Sources

Carter, Robert. Letterbooks. University of Virginia Library.
Gooch, William. Letters. Virginia Historical Society.
Matthews, John Carter. Richard Henry Lee and the American Revolution. Ph.D. dissertation, University of Virginia, 1939.

Primary Sources in Print

Flournoy, H. W., William P. Palmer, S. McRae, and R. Colson, eds. *Calendar of Virginia State Papers and Other Manuscripts Preserved in the Capitol in Richmond.* Richmond, 1875–1893. 11 vols.
Hening, William Waller. *The Statutes at Large, Being a Collection of All the Laws of Virginia.* Richmond, 1819–1823. 13 vols.
McIlwaine, Henry R., ed. *Executive Journals of the Council of Colonial Virginia.* Richmond, 1925–1930. 4 vols.
———, ed. *Legislative Journals of the Council of Colonial Virginia.* Richmond, 1918–1919. 3 vols.
——— and John P. Kennedy, eds. *Journals of the House of Burgesses of Virginia, 1691–1776.* Richmond, 1905–1915. 13 vols.

Principal Published Sources

Abernathy, Thomas Perkins. *Western Lands and the American Revolution.* New York, 1937.
Alvord, Clarence P. "Virginia and the West: An Interpretation." *Mississippi Valley Historical Review.* III (June 1916), pp. 19–38.
Anburey, Thomas. *Travels Through the Interior Parts of America; in a Series of Letters, by an Officer.* New ed. London, 1791. 2 vols.
Andrews, Matthew Page. *Virginia, the Old Dominion.* Richmond, 1949.

Bailey, Kenneth P. *The Ohio Company of Virginia and the Westward Movement, 1748–1792.* Glendale, Calif., 1939.

Bailyn, Bernard. "Political Experience and Enlightenment Ideas in Eighteenth-Century America." *American Historical Review,* LXVII (January, 1962), pp. 339–351.

———. "Politics and Social Structure in Virginia." In James Morton Smith, ed. *Seventeenth-Century America: Essays in Colonial History.* Chapel Hill, N.C., 1959, pp. 90–115.

Bassett, John Spencer. "The Relation Between the Virginia Planter and the London Merchant." *American Historical Association Annual Report.* I (1901), pp. 553–575.

Beloff, Max, ed. *Debate on the American Revolution, 1761–1783: A Sourcebook.* New York, 1960.

Berkeley, Francis L. "The War of Jenkins' Ear." In Darrett Bruce Rutman, ed. *The Old Dominion.* Charlottesville, 1964, pp. 41–61.

Blair, John L. "The Rise of the Burwells." *VMHB.* LXXII (July, 1963), pp. 304–329.

Bland, Richard. "Bland's Constitutional Argument in 'The Colonel Dismounted,' 1763." *WMQ.* Ser. 11, XIX (July, 1910), pp. 31–41.

———. *A Fragment on the Pistole Fee, Claimed by the Governor of Virginia, 1753.* Ed. Worthington Chauncey Ford. Brooklyn, 1891.

———. *An Inquiry into the Rights of the British Colonies.* New ed. Ed. Earl Gregg Swem. Richmond, 1922.

———. *A Letter to the Clergy of Virginia.* Williamsburg, 1760.

———. "Letter to Thomas Adams, Virginia, August 1, 1771." *VMHB.* VI (October, 1898), pp. 127–134.

Bland, Theodorick. *The Bland Papers: being a selection from the manuscripts of Colonel Theodorick Bland.* Ed. Charles Campbell. Petersburg, Va., 1840–1843. 2 vols. in one.

Bradley, Harold W. "The Political Thinking of George Washington." *Journal of Southern History.* XI (November, 1945), pp. 469–486.

Brant, Irving. "An Introduction to Patrick Henry." In his *James Madison.* Indianapolis, 1941, vol. I, pp. 177–189.

Bridenbaugh, Carl. *Myths and Realities: Societies of the Colonial South.* Baton Rouge, 1952.

———. *Seat of Empire: The Political Role of Eighteenth-Century Williamsburg.* Charlottesville, 1958.

Brown, Robert Eldon and B. Katherine Brown. *Virginia 1705–1786: Democracy or Aristocracy?* East Lansing, Mich., 1964.

Brown, Stuart Ellett. *Virginia Baron: The Story of Thomas, 6th Lord Fairfax.* Berryville, Va., 1965.

Brydon, George MacLaren. *Virginia's Mother Church and the Political Conditions under Which It Grew.* Richmond, 1947. 2 vols.

Buranelli, Vincent. "Colonial Philosophy." *WMQ.* Ser. 3, XVI (April, 1959), pp. 343–362.

Burk, John Daly. *The History of Virginia from Its First Settlement to the Commencement of the Revolution.* Petersburg, Va., 1822. 3 vols.

Burke, Edmund. *Thoughts on the Cause of the Present Discontents.* London, 1770.

Burnaby, Andrew. *Travels Through the Middle Settlements in North America, in the Years 1759 and 1760. With Observations upon the State of the Colonies.* London, 1775.

Byrd, William. *Another Secret Diary of William Byrd of Westover, 1737–1740. With Letters and Literary Exercises 1696–1726.* Ed. Maude H. Woodfin. Tr. and collated by Marion Tinling. Richmond, 1942.

———. *The London Diary, 1717–1721, and Other Writings.* Ed. Louis B. Wright and Marion Tinling. New York, 1958.

———. *The Secret Diary of William Byrd of Westover, 1709–1712.* Ed. Louis B. Wright and Marion Tinling. Richmond, 1941.

———. *The Writings of "Colonel William Byrd of Westover in Virginia Esqr."* Ed. John Spencer Bassett. New York, 1901.

Carson, Jane. *Colonial Virginians at Play.* Williamsburg, 1965.

Carter, Landon. *The Diary of Colonel Landon Carter of Sabine Hall, 1752–1778.* Ed. with an introduction by Jack P. Greene. Charlottesville, 1965. 2 vols.

———. "Not to Be Governed or Taxed, but by . . . Our Representatives." Four essays in opposition to the Stamp Act. Ed. Jack P. Greene. *VMHB.* LXXVI (July, 1968), pp. 259–300.

Chastellus, François Jean, Marquis de. *Travels in North America in the Years 1780, 1781 and 1782.* Revised translation with introduction and notes by Howard C. Rice. Chapel Hill, N.C., 1963, 2 vols.

Chinard, Gilbert. "Thomas Jefferson as a Classical Scholar." *American Scholar.* I (March, 1932), pp. 133–143.

Christie, Ian Ralph. *Crisis of Empire: Great Britain and the American Colonies, 1754–1783.* New York, 1966.

Colbourn, Harold Trevor. *The Lamp of Experience: Whig History and the Intellectual Origins of the American Revolution.* Chapel Hill, N.C., 1965.

Colonial Williamsburg. *Cross and Gown.* Colonial Williamsburg Report, 1965.

———. *Serenity and Growth.* Colonial Williamsburg Report, 1966.

Craven, Avery Odelle. *Soil Exhaustion as a Factor in the Agricultural History of Virginia and Maryland, 1606–1860.* Urbana, Ill., 1926.

Cunliffe, Marcus. *George Washington, Man and Monument.* Boston, 1958.

Curti, Merle Eugene. *The Growth of American Thought.* New York, 1943.

Davis, Curtis Carroll. "A Long Line of Cupbearers: The Earliest Littlepages in America." *VMHB.* LXXII (October, 1964), pp. 434–453.

Eckenrode, Hamilton James. *The Revolution in Virginia.* Hamden, Conn., 1964.

Ernst, Joseph Albert. "The Robinson Scandal Redivivus: Money, Debts and Politics in Revolutionary Virginia." *VMHB.* LXXVII (April, 1969), pp. 146–173.

Evans, Emory G. "Planter Indebtedness and the Coming of the Revolution in Virginia." *WMQ.* Ser. 3, XIX (October, 1962), pp. 511–533.

———. "The Rise and Decline of the Virginia Aristocracy in the Eighteenth Century: The Nelsons." In Darrett Bruce Rutman, ed. *The Old Dominion.* Charlottesville, 1964, pp. 62–78.

"The F.F.V's of Virginia." *WMQ.* Ser. 1, XXIII (April, 1915), p. 277.

Fithian, Philip Vickers. *Journal and Letters of Philip Vickers Fithian, 1773–1774.* Ed. with an introduction by Hunter Dickinson Farish. New ed. Williamsburg, 1957.

Fitzpatrick, John Clement. *George Washington Himself: A Commonsense Biography Written from His Manuscripts.* Indianapolis, 1933.

Flexner, James Thomas. *George Washington: The Forge of Experience, 1732–1775.* Boston, 1965.

Flippin, Percy Scott. *The Royal Government in Virginia, 1624–1775.* New York, 1919.

———. "William Gooch: Successful Royal Governor of Virginia." *WMQ.* Ser. 2, V (October, 1925), pp. 225–258; VI (January, 1926), pp. 1–38.

Freeman, Douglas Southall. *George Washington: A Biography.* New York, 1948. 3 vols.

Ganter, Herbert L. "William Small, Jefferson's Beloved Teacher." *WMQ.* Ser. 3, IV (October, 1947), pp. 505–511.

Gipson, Lawrence Henry. *The British Empire Before the American Revolution,* vol. II, *The British Isles and the American Colonies: The Southern Plantations, 1748–1754.* New York, 1960.

———. *The Coming of the Revolution, 1763–1775.* New York, 1954.

———. "Virginia Planter Debts Before the American Revolution." *VMHB.* LXIX (July, 1961), pp. 259–277.

Goodwin, Rutherford. *A Brief and True Report for the Traveler Concerning Williamsburg in Virginia.* 2d ed. Richmond, 1936.

Greene, Jack P. "The Case of the Pistole Fee." *VMHB.* LXVI (October, 1958), pp. 399–422.

——— and Richard M. Jellison. "The Currency Act of 1764 in Imperial-Colonial Relations, 1764–1776." *WQM.* Ser. 3, XVIII (October, 1961), pp. 485–518.

———. "Foundations of Political Power in the Virginia House of Burgesses, 1720–1776." *WMQ.* Ser. 3, XVI (October, 1959), pp. 485–506.

———. *Landon Carter: An Inquiry into the Personal Values and Social Imperatives of the Eighteenth-Century Virginia Gentry.* Charlottesville, 1967.

———. "Landon Carter and the Pistole Fee Dispute." *WMQ.* Ser. 3, XIV (January, 1957), pp. 66–69 .

Griffith, Lucille Blanche. *Virginia House of Burgesses, 1750–1774.* North Port, Ala., 1963.

Harper, Laurence A. "Mercantilism and the American Revolution." In Carl N. Degler, ed. *Pivotal Interpretations of American History.* New York, 1966, vol. I, pp. 73–90.

Harrison, Fairfax. The Equine FFV's: A Study of the Evidence for the English Horses Imported into Virginia Before the Revolution." *VMHB.* XXXV (October, 1927), pp. 329–370.

———. "A Portrait of Governor Fauquier." *Fauquier Historical Society Bulletin.* IV (July, 1924), pp. 343–350.

———. *The Virginia Carys: An Essay in Genealogy.* New York, 1919.

Henderson, Archibald. *Dr. Thomas Walker and the Loyal Company of Virginia.* Worcester, Mass., 1931.

Hendrick, Burton Jesse. *The Lees of Virginia: Biography of a Family.* Boston, 1935.

Herndon, Melvin. *Tobacco in Colonial Virginia: "The Sovereign Remedy."* Williamsburg, 1957.

Howell, Wilbur Samuel. "The Declaration of Independence and Eighteenth-Century Logic." *WMQ.* Ser. 3, XVIII (October, 1961), pp. 463–484.

Hughes, Rupert. *George Washington: The Rebel and the Patriot, 1762–1777.* New York, 1927.

Jefferson, Thomas. *The Commonplace Book of Thomas Jefferson: A Repertory of His Ideas on Government.* With an introduction and notes by Gilbert Chinard. Baltimore, 1926.

————. *The Literary Bible of Thomas Jefferson: His Commonplace Book of Philosophers and Poets.* With an introduction by Gilbert Chinard. Baltimore, 1928.

————. *Notes on the State of Virginia.* Edited with an introduction by William Peden. Chapel Hill, N.C., 1955.

————. *Papers.* Vol. I, *1760–1776.* Ed. Julian P. Boyd. Princeton, N.J. 1950.

Johnson, Allen S. "The Passage of the Sugar Act." *WMQ.* Ser. 3, XVI (October, 1959), pp. 507–514.

"Journal of a French Traveler in the American Colonies, 1765." *American Historical Review.* XXVI (July, 1921), pp. 726–747; XXVII (October, 1921), pp. 70–89.

Knollenburg, Bernhard. *Origin of the American Revolution, 1759–1776.* New York, 1960.

La Rouchefoucauld-Liancourt, François Alexandre Frédéric, duc de. *Travels Through the United States of North America . . . in the Years 1795, 1796, and 1797.* 2d ed. London, 1800.

"The Leadership of Virginia in the War of the Revolution." *WMQ.* Ser. 1, XVIII (January, 1910), pp. 145–164; XIX (July, 1910), pp. 10–27.

Lecky, William Edward Hartpole. "America 1763–1776." In his *A History of England in the Eighteenth Century.* New York, 1882, vol. 3, pp. 290–499.

Lee, Richard Henry. *The Letters of Richard Henry Lee.* Collected and edited by James Curtis Ballagh. New York, 1911–1914. 2 vols.

Long, John Cuthbert. *George III: The Story of a Complex Man.* Boston, 1960.

"The Ludwell Family." *WMQ.* Ser. 1, XIX (January, 1911), pp. 199–214.

Macaulay, Thomas Babington. "The Earl of Chatham." In his *Critical, Historical and Miscellaneous Essays and Poems.* Chicago and New York, 1885, vol. 3, pp. 162–239.

Malone, Dumas. *Jefferson and His Time.* Boston, 1948.

Mapp, Alf Johnson. *The Virginia Experiment: The Old Dominion's Role in the Making of America, 1607–1781.* Richmond, 1957.

Maury, James Duprey. "A Dissertation on Education in the Form of a Letter from James Maury to Robert Jackson, July 17, 1762." Edited with an introduction by Helen D. Bullock. *Albemarle Historical Society Papers.* II (1942), pp. 36–60.

Mayo, Bernard. "The Enigma of Patrick Henry." *Virginia Quarterly Review.* XXXV (Spring, 1959), pp. 176–195.

Mays, David John. *Edmund Pendleton, 1721–1803.* Cambridge, 1952. 2 vols.

McGill, John. *The Beverley Family of Virginia.* Columbia, S.C., 1956.

Meade, Robert Douthat. "Judge Edmund Winston's Memoir of Patrick Henry." *VMHB.* LXIX (January, 1961), pp. 28–41.

————. *Patrick Henry.* Philadelphia, 1957/1969. 2 vols.

Miller, E. I. "The Virginia Committee of Correspondence, 1759–1770." *WMQ.* Ser. 1, XXII (July, 1913), pp. 1–19.

Miller, John Chester. *Origins of the American Revolution.* Stanford, 1959.

Morgan, Edmund Sears. "Colonial Ideas of Parliamentary Power, 1764–1766." In Carl N. Degler, ed. *Pivotal Interpretations of American History.* New York, 1966, vol. 1, pp. 40–72.

―――. *Virginians at Home: Family Life in the Eighteenth Century.* Williamsburg, 1952.

Morison, Samuel Eliot. *The Oxford History of the American People.* New York, 1965.

Morris, Richard Brandon. *The American Revolution Reconsidered.* New York, 1967.

―――. "Class Struggle and the American Revolution." *WMQ.* Ser. 3, XIX (January, 1962), pp. 3–29.

Morton, Louis. *Robert Carter of Nomini Hall: A Virginia Tobacco Planter of the Eighteenth Century.* Charlottesville, 1945.

―――. "Robert Wormely Carter of Sabine Hall: Notes on the Life of a Virginia Planter." *Journal of Southern History.* XII (August, 1946), pp. 345–365.

Morton, Richard Lee. *Colonial Virginia.* Chapel Hill, N.C., 1960. 2 vols.

Mumford, Robert. "The Candidates." Ed. Jay B. Hubbell and Douglass Adair. *WMQ.* Ser. 3, V (April, 1948), pp. 217–257.

Namier, Lewis Bernstein. *Crossroads of Power: Essays on Eighteenth-Century England.* New York, 1962.

―――. *England in the Age of the American Revolution.* 2d ed. New York, 1961.

Norton, John & Sons. *John Norton and Sons, Merchants of London and Virginia: Being the Papers from their Counting House for the Years 1750 to 1795.* Ed. Frances Norton Mason. Richmond, 1937.

Padover, Saul K. "George Washington: Portrait of a True Conservative." *Social Research.* XXII (Summer, 1955), pp. 199–222.

Page, Richard Channing Moore. *Genealogy of the Page Family in Virginia.* 2d ed. New York, 1893.

Pargellis, Stanley M. "The Procedure of the Virginia House of Burgesses." *WMQ.* Ser. 2, VII (April, 1927), pp. 73–86; (July, 1927), pp. 143–157.

Parker, Alton B. "The Foundations in Virginia." *WMQ.* Ser. 2, I (January, 1921), pp. 1–15.

Pate, James E. "Richard Bland's Inquiry into the Rights of the British Colonies." *WMQ.* Ser. 2, XI (January, 1931), pp. 20–28.

Peterson, Merrill Daniel, ed. *Thomas Jefferson: A Profile.* New York, 1967.

Pole, J. R. "Historians and the Problem of Early American Democracy." *American Historical Review.* LXVII (April, 1962), pp. 626–646.

Price, Jacob M. "The Rise of Glasgow in the Chesapeake Tobacco Trade, 1707–1775." *WMQ.* Ser. 3, XI (April, 1954), pp. 179–199.

―――. "Who Was John Norton?" *WMQ.* Ser. 3, XIX (July, 1962), pp. 400–407.

Randolph, Edmund. "Edmund Randolph's Essay on the Revolutionary History of Virginia, 1774–1782." *VMHB.* XLIII (July, 1935), pp. 209–232.

Riley, Edward M. "William Prentis & Co.: Business Success in Eighteenth-Century Williamsburg." *Financial Executive* (April, 1968), pp. 35–41.

Rosenblatt, Samuel Michael. *The House of John Norton and Sons: A Study of the Consignment Method of Marketing Tobacco from Virginia to England.* Ann Arbor, Mich., 1960.

———. "Merchant-Planter Relations in the Tobacco Consignment Trade: John Norton and Robert Carter Nicholas." *VMHB.* LXXII (October, 1964), pp. 454–470.

———. "The Significance of Credit in the Tobacco Consignment Trade: A Study of John Norton & Sons, 1768–1775." *WMQ.* Ser. 3, XIX (July 1962), pp. 383–399.

Rossiter, Clinton. "Richard Bland: The Whig in America." *WMQ.* Ser. 3, X (January, 1953), pp. 33–79.

Rusk, Dean. *Mason and Jefferson Revisited: An Address on the Occasion of the Celebration of the Prelude to Independence at the Eighteenth-Century Capitol Williamsburg, Virginia, May 28, 1966.* Williamsburg, 1966.

"Sketch of John Camm." *WMQ.* Ser. 1, XXIX (July, 1910), pp. 28–30.

Slaughter, Philip. *Memoir of Colonel Joshua Fry.* Richmond, 1880.

Smith, Glenn Curtis. "The Affair of the Pistole Fee, Virginia 1752–55." *VMHB.* XLVIII (July, 1940), pp. 209–221.

Smith, Preserved. *A History of Modern Culture,* vol. II, *The Enlightenment, 1687–1776.* New York, 1934.

Smyth, John Ferdinand Dalziel. *A Tour in the United States of America.* London, 1784. 2 vols.

Soltow, James Harold. *The Economic Role of Williamsburg.* Williamsburg, 1965.

———. "Scottish Traders in Virginia, 1750–1775." *Economic History Review.* Ser. 2, XII (August, 1959), pp. 83–98.

Sydnor, Charles Sackett. *Gentlemen Freeholders: Political Practices in Washington's Virginia.* Chapel Hill, N.C. 1952.

Tate, Thaddeus Wilbur. "The Coming of the Revolution in Virginia: Britain's Challenge to Virginia's Ruling Class, 1763–1776." *WMQ.* Ser. 3, XIX (July, 1962), pp. 323–343.

Taylor, William Robert. "William Wirt and the Legend of the Old South." *WMQ.* Ser. 3, XIV (October, 1957), pp. 477–493.

Thomson, Robert Polk. "The Tobacco Export of the Upper James River Naval District, 1773–75." *WMQ.* Ser. 3, XVIII (July, 1961), pp. 393–407.

Trevelyan, George Otto. *The American Revolution.* Ed. with an introduction and notes by Richard B. Morris. New York, 1964.

Tyler, J. E. "Colonel George Mercer's Papers." *VMHB.* LX (July, 1952), pp. 405–420.

Virginia Committee of Correspondence. "Proceedings of the Virginia Committee of Correspondence, 1759–1767." *VMHB.* XII (July, 1904), pp. 1–14.

Washington, George. *Washington's Rules of Civility and Decent Behavior in Company and Conversation.* Ed. with notes by J. M. Toner. Washington, 1888.

Wertenbaker, Thomas Jefferson. *The Planters of Colonial Virginia.* Princeton, 1922.

Wineman, Walter Ray. *The Landon Carter Papers in the University of Virginia Library.* Charlottesville, 1962.

Index

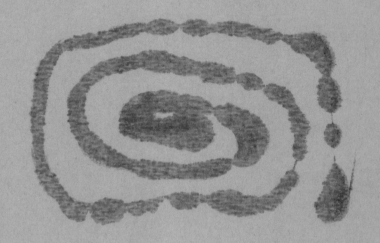

DATE DUE

DEMCO 38-297